INTRODUCTION TO EDUCATION

Teaching in a Diverse Society

William E. Segall
Oklahoma State University

Anna V. Wilson
North Carolina State University

Merrill,
an imprint of Prentice Hall
Upper Saddle River, New Jersey   Columbus, Ohio

Library of Congress Cataloging-in-Publication Data

Segall, William E. (William Edwin)
    Introduction to education : teaching in a diverse society / William E. Segall, Anna V. Wilson.
        p.   cm.
    Includes bibliographical references (p.   ) and indexes.
    ISBN 0-02-408711-4 (pbk.)
    1. Teachers—Training of—United States.
    2. Education—Study and teaching—United States.
    3. Multicultural education—United States.
    4. School management and organization—United States.   5. Effective teaching—United States.
    I. Wilson, Anna Victoria.   II. Title.
    LB1715.S414   1998   97-39532
    370'.71073--DC21   CIP

© 1998 by Prentice-Hall, Inc.
Simon & Schuster/A Viacom Company
Upper Saddle River, New Jersey 07458

Printed in the United States of America

10 9 8 7 6 5 4 3 2 1

ISBN: 0-02-408711-4

Prentice-Hall International (UK) Limited, *London*
Prentice-Hall of Australia Pty. Limited, *Sydney*
Prentice-Hall of Canada, Inc., *Toronto*
Prentice-Hall Hispanoamericana, S. A., *Mexico*
Prentice-Hall of India Private Limited, *New Delhi*
Prentice-Hall of Japan, Inc., *Tokyo*
Simon & Schuster Asia Pte. Ltd., *Singapore*
Editora Prentice-Hall do Brasil, Ltda., *Rio de Janeiro*

Editor: Debra A. Stollenwerk
Production Editor: Mary Harlan
Copy Editor: Peg Gluntz
Design Coordinator: Karrie M. Converse
Text Designer: John Edeen
Cover Designer: Russ Maselli
Cover photo: Terry Vine/Vine Stone Images
Photo Coordinators: Dawn Garrott and Nancy Harre Ritz
Production Manager: Patricia A. Tonneman
Illustrations: The Clarinda Company
Director of Marketing: Kevin Flanagan
Marketing Manager: Suzanne Stanton
Advertising/Marketing Coordinator: Julie Shough

This book was set in Garamond by The Clarinda Company and was printed and bound by R. R. Donnelley & Sons Company. The cover was printed by Phoenix Color Corp.

Photo credits: Photos copyrighted by the companies or individuals listed. Corbis-Bettmann: pp. 45, 50, 57, 72, 77, 78, 85; Scott Cunningham/Merrill/PH: pp. 118, 127, 128, 158, 261, 324; The Design Council/British Information Services: p. 106; El Paso Public Library: p. 79; Mimi Forsythe/Monkmeyer Press Photo Service: pp. 160, 190, 253; Images by Tina Manley: pp. 112, 255, 262, 265, 278; Anthony Magnacca/Merrill/PH: pp. 161, 187, 229, 231, 234; Lynn Maslowski/Westerville City Schools: p. 171; Jeanne M. Rasmussen/Monkmeyer Press Photo Service: p. 251; Barbara Schwartz/Merrill/PH: p. 320; Skjold Photographs: p. 284; UPI/Corbis-Bettmann: pp. 86, 90, 123; Anne Vega/Merrill/PH: pp. 1, 31, 247, 279, 298, 304; Bernard Wolf/Monkmeyer Press Photo Service: p. 88: Todd Yarrington/Merrill/PH: pp. 219, 254; George Zimbel/Monkmeyer Press Photo Service: p. 272.

This book is dedicated to
my father
—Bill

and

O. L. Davis, Jr., friend and professor
—Anna

Preface

Introduction to Education: Teaching in a Diverse Society is written for students who want to become teachers. The focus of the text is to help prospective teachers grasp the essence of the classroom. The text characterizes children as representatives of a society that is increasingly more diverse. Because teachers are continuing to represent middle-class America, many of our prospective teachers will experience a clash of cultures in the classroom in their beginning years.

Introduction to Education: Teaching in a Diverse Society presents our philosophy that teacher education students want to learn as much as possible about teaching, students, classrooms, and schools in their introductory course. Therefore, this textbook stresses a critical approach to learning. It is intended to challenge teacher education majors to look at what teachers do as more than a continuation of what students do. It helps students recognize that teachers are part of a pluralistic society whose students bring to school differing cultural histories. The text presents educational issues within a socially diverse or multicultural context. It challenges students to critically examine these issues from differing perspectives.

The combined experience of the authors is a half-century of classroom instruction. We have taught at all classroom levels, from elementary school to advanced doctoral students. Our professional experiences include teaching criminal justice courses to prison workers and law enforcement officials. One of us even was a principal of a Japanese *juku,* or cram school. We have also drawn on teaching experiences in a multiracial college and a historically African-American university. As education professors, we recognize that the single most important experience prospective teachers will have in their teacher preparation program is an introduction to education course. It is in this course students will decide if they truly want to become teachers.

Organization of the Text

Introduction to Education: Teaching in a Diverse Society is divided into 6 sections. Each section begins with an overview that explains the connections between the chapters.

Part One Chapters 1 (Becoming a Teacher) and 2 (Teaching as a Profession) are practical. They discuss why adults are motivated to become teachers and explain the hallmarks of the teaching profession.

Part Two   Chapter 3 (The Framework of Our Multicultural Nation), Chapter 4 (Coming of Age: Education in the Twentieth Century), and Chapter 5 (Schools in the Global Community) discuss the historic role of schools and their importance in a diverse society. Chapter 5 also discusses schools in England, Japan, and Mexico, to help students understand international aspects of education.

Part Three   Chapter 6 (Putting Philosophy to Work in Culturally Diverse Classrooms) and Chapter 7 (Learning and Teaching in the Classroom) explore classical European, Asian, African-American, and Native American philosophies that affect classrooms. These chapters also explain how these philosophies influence the curriculum and teachers' instructional approaches.

Part Four   Chapters 8 (The Organization of Schools and How They Are Governed), Chapter 9 (Teachers and Students as Citizens: Rights and Responsibilities) and Chapter 10 (Educating Children Takes Money: Financing Education) focus on schools' operation, legal aspects, and funding.

Part Five   Chapter 11 (The Child's World Beyond the Classroom) and Chapter 12 (The Child's World of the Classroom) describe the lives of some of the children who live in a complex society and their influence on teachers. This section sensitizes teacher-education students to children who have different cultural histories than they do.

Part Six   Chapter 13 (Educational Reform and Effective Classrooms) and Chapter 14 (Joining the Profession) trace the recent reform movements and what they mean to the beginning teacher. The section is designed to help students recognize some of the important issues found in schools today. Finally, it tells students how to become employed as classroom teachers.

Special Features

Introduction to Education: Teaching in a Diverse Society is written with the student in mind. The book easily engages students and allows them to interact with the information and activities in the chapters, their fellow students, and the instructor. Each chapter includes:

- **What You Will Learn.** At the beginning of each chapter is a list of the major concepts students will learn in that chapter.
- **Becoming a Teacher.** A vignette based on professional experiences of classroom teachers and others helps students reflect on the major concepts presented in the chapter. The following question challenges students to get involved in learning by reflecting on what they would do.
- **What You Have Learned.** This checklist at the end of each chapter summarizes the main concepts for easy student review.

- **Key Terms** Terms that are important to understand or which students will use in further study are boldfaced in the chapter and defined in the Glossary.
- **Applying What You Have Learned.** Questions at the end of each chapter help students test their understanding.
- **Interactive Learning.** Students are presented with situations or activities that encourage them to learn what the chapter has introduced. Students are expected to explore or test their leadership abilities in searching out answers.
- **Expanding Your Knowledge.** This annotated list of books at the end of each chapter encourages students to read more about topics they studied in the chapter. It helps motivated students go a step beyond the course requirements.

Supplements

Supplementary teaching and learning tools have been developed to accompany this text. Please contact your Prentice Hall representative for details.

- **Instructor's Manual.** This valuable resource presents and describes different instructional approaches for each chapter and suggests answers to the activities and text questions.
- **Test Bank.** A bank of approximately fifty objective and essay questions for each chapter is available on disk in both Mac and PC formats as well as in hard copy.
- **Transparencies.** These transparencies of text figures and tables help reinforce student learning.

Acknowledgments

We gratefully acknowledge the valuable comments and suggestions from those who reviewed a portion or all of the manuscript in its various stages: Robert H. Baldwin, Clarion University of Pennsylvania; Carlton E. Beck, University of Wisconsin, Milwaukee; John Bertalan, Hillsborough Community College; Mary Lou Brotherson, St. Thomas University; Grace M. Burton, University of North Carolina, Wilmington; Wade Carpenter, Berry College; Donna Cole, Wright State University; Stephen Garger, Trinity College; Samuel Hinton, Eastern Kentucky University; Michael Jacobs, University of Northern Colorado; Robert W. Kinderman, Kutztown University; James C. Lawlor, Towson State University; Suzanne MacDonald, University of Akron; Albert H. Miller, University of Houston; Louis F. Miron, University of New Orleans; Robert L. Mulder, Pacific Lutheran University; Emmanuel C. Nwagwu, Texas Southern University; Trevor J. Phillips, Bowling Green University; Augustina Reyes, Texas A&M University; John A. Stirton, San Joaquin Delta College; Janice Streitmatter, University of Arizona; and James Towers, St. Mary's College of Minnesota.

We would not be finished if we did not recognize those who took special interest in our work. Dean Ann Candler Lotven, School Heads Drs. Martin Burlingame and David England, and Interim Head Bruce Petty, all of the College of Education at Oklahoma State University, continually asked questions about the text and encouraged its completion. Their special and friendly concern is appreciated. At the University of Texas at Austin, College of Education, we would like to thank Dean Manual Justiz, Drs. Mary Black, Ann Brooks, Don E. Carlton, O. L. Davis, Jr., Douglas Foley, John Martin Rich, Diane Schallert, and James Scheurich. Their input was valuable and appreciated. We want to mention Rita Moreno, without whom little would happen. Above all, we wish to thank the late Dr. JoAnn Cutler Sweeney, who, prior to her death, continually encouraged us and saw the worth of the text. At North Carolina State University we would like to recognize Dean Joan Michael, Dr. Cathy Crossland, Department Head, and colleagues in the College of Education and Psychology, who became aware of the text's importance and supported its conclusion. We also want to thank our families and friends. Without their forbearance, our work would have been much more difficult. Lastly, we have enjoyed the challenge of working as co-authors. Each of us has appreciated the depth of knowledge and professionalism of the other in contributing to the completion of the text.

Brief Contents

Contents

Teaching as a Career

In Part One you will learn about teaching and the classroom. When you decided you wanted to become a teacher, what were your thoughts? Did you want to become a teacher because you were interested in a high-paying position? Or did you want to be involved with children? Perhaps others in your family are teachers, and you wanted to continue the tradition. In Chapter 1 you will learn some of the things that motivate people to become teachers, and you can compare your motives with others. After you have studied the chapter, ask yourself, How did the people profiled differ from you? How were they the same?

This first part of the book is practical. It discusses many questions you thought about when you considered teaching as a career. For example, how much money do teachers earn? How difficult is it to get a teaching position? Will your teacher preparation program prepare you to become an effective classroom teacher?

These are the types of questions Laurie Ferriri, whom you will meet in Chapter 1, was concerned about when she began teaching at Carson Junior High. She wanted to be a teacher, and had the jitters on the first morning of her teaching career. You may want to remember Laurie Ferriri. We will meet her again in Chapter 14, so you can see how her first day as a classroom teacher ended.

Ester Gonzales, who you will meet in Chapter 2, became a teacher while living in Sonora, Mexico. Although her life was filled with difficulties—including leaving her home to live in another country—Ester recognized that teaching was an integral part of her life. When she became a teacher in the United States, Ester discovered children are anxious to learn regardless of culture.

Laurie and Ester became classroom teachers for different reasons, yet both believed teaching was a profession. In Chapter 2 you will learn about the characteristics of professions. You will learn that teaching is different from other professions, such as medicine and law. As you read Chapter 2, keep in mind what you think a profession is. After you have studied Chapter 2, compare your present thoughts with the beliefs you held before starting this book. Are your ideas different? Why?

Chapter 1

Becoming a Teacher

In this chapter you will learn about classroom teaching and teachers. You are joining millions of others who consider classroom teaching the highest priority in their professional lives. Teaching is challenging, exciting, and fun. Teaching is rewarding: you have a profound influence on children's lives. Remember the teachers who have challenged you throughout your education.

On the surface, teaching seems easy. We typically see only a part of what teaching is all about. A major objective of this textbook is to introduce you to classroom teaching as a teacher, not as a student. Being a teacher is different than being a student. Teaching requires special personal and professional characteristics.

Have you thought why you want to become a teacher? What made you choose teaching as a career? Teaching attracts all kinds of people, but in general, teachers are less interested in salaries and other extrinsic rewards. They are more interested in the personal rewards their profession offers.

Becoming a teacher is complicated. If you understand your teacher preparation program, you will see there is a logic to it. After studying this book, we hope you will see why teachers are called professionals.

What you will learn

- Teaching is a complex profession involving both intrinsic and extrinsic rewards. Teachers sometimes suffer from stress and burnout.
- Demand for new classroom teachers is continuing to expand because of the maturity of those in the profession and increasing numbers of students.
- Although there are many different types of teacher preparation programs in this country, all programs are concerned with academic, professional, and practical preparation.
- Effective teachers are those who are able to incorporate their personal and professional characteristics into the classroom.

The first day of teaching

When Laurie Ferriri walked into Carson Junior High, she was more nervous than she had ever been in her life. She couldn't believe it! This was her first day in a new career as a junior high teacher. She was nervous, but she felt she was equal to the challenge.

Laurie enjoyed her teacher preparation program in college. It forced her to think about what classroom teaching would be like. Her student teaching experience helped her realize she wanted to make classroom teaching a career. Laurie believes she was born to be a teacher. She especially appreciates Mr. Markham, her principal. She knows he wants her to succeed and would help her if she got into difficulty.

As Laurie walks to her classroom, it seems that Carson Junior High has changed. Whenever she had been at staff development seminars and meetings, the building had been quiet. Now, it is abuzz with students talking, joking, pushing, and shoving. She feels self-conscious. Some students are looking at her as if she doesn't belong.

"Hey!! You a teacher?" The voice belongs to a huge boy in a coat and a strange hairstyle. "You goin' be the new math teacher?"

Several students look at her carefully. They seem to Laurie to be almost her age. "Hope you're better than the last one," one student says.

The buzzer sounds and the huge boy with the strange hairstyle comes into the classroom with twenty or so others. In her methods classes, Laurie had been taught to take control of the class at the start.

"All right, class," Laurie says in a calm voice, "please take your seats. My name is Ms. Ferriri, and I am your new math teacher. Today, I would like us to get to know each other."

After Laurie and the class introduce themselves, she gives them a brief assignment. She wants to know how much algebra the students remember from last year. The class murmurs about having an assignment on the first day of school, but it is obvious they are enjoying the structure of the classroom after summer vacation. The huge boy with the strange hairstyle, whom Laurie had first noticed in the hall, bends over his desk. He seems to enjoy math.

As Laurie is wiping the chalkboard, Mr. Markham walks in the room. As usual, he smiles. "Don't forget all the teachers are guests at a dinner in the cafeteria this evening. The students' parents will be our hosts."

Laurie watches Mr. Markham. He has been looking at the classroom and the activity of the students. "I know he is interested in how things work out for me," Laurie thinks. "I know I am doing the right thing."

??? *Picture yourself in Laurie's place on the first day of your teaching career. Describe the rest of Laurie's first day of teaching. Talk with some new teachers at your local school. Have them describe their first day of teaching. If you would like to find out how Laurie's first day ended, read "Becoming a Teacher" in Chapter 14.*

Who Becomes a Teacher?

Have you ever asked yourself why you want to be a teacher? This is one of the most important questions you can ask yourself as a college student. Obviously, there is not a single right answer. There are as many motives for becoming a teacher as there are teachers. People develop their motives at different stages of their lives. For example, some classroom teachers say they always knew they wanted to teach. Perhaps a special elementary teacher influenced them early in their life, or their mother or father was a teacher. For these people, the decision to make classroom teaching a career was easy. There are also people who initially planned to become an engineer, accountant, or some other kind of professional, but who felt personally incomplete and changed their major to education. Others believe they simply fell into teaching by accident.

Motivations for Teaching

People are motivated to become classroom teachers at different stages in their lives. Sometimes we stereotype beginning teachers as young college students. While many beginning teachers are, in fact, young, others are not. Some beginning teachers are nontraditional students who have been in the workplace for several years. Some beginning teachers are mothers or fathers who worked and waited for their children to finish their education before focusing on their own personal goals. Other beginning teachers have retired from one career, such as the military, and are pursuing a second career in teaching.

In a study of 156 teachers, Huberman, Grounauer & Marti (1993) looked at the motivations of **entry-level teachers,** or teachers in the first several years of their career. On the average, each teacher mentioned three reasons for choosing classroom teaching as a career. The largest percentage of teachers were like Laurie Ferriri in the vignette: they were interested in working with children or they wanted to share their love of subject matter or knowledge. Their primary motivation was to help others. Their success in substitute teaching was also critical for choosing teaching as a career.

Some people enjoy classroom teaching because it reinforces their experiences as students or as substitute teachers. Others become teachers for very narrow, personal motives; for example, they want to control others. Still others choose teaching because they feel that, as children, they were not taught very well.

Teaching as a Career

Do you remember the reactions of your friends or family when you told them you were planning to make classroom teaching your career? Perhaps the general reaction you received was something like, "That's great! It's fun to work with kids, and just think: you'll have your summers free. Salaries are getting better and there *is* job security."

This reaction does, in fact, reflect reality. Teaching as a career has several types of rewards. Huberman, Grounauer & Marti (1993) asked a sample of classroom teachers if they would choose to become teachers again if they had their lives to live over. They discovered that, in general, classroom teachers enjoyed their career because they received two rewards. The first reward was intrinsic: teachers expressed their personal satisfaction with what they accomplished in the classroom. The second reward was extrinsic: teaching careers enhanced teachers' lives outside the classroom.

Notice that the rewards for teaching are very similar to the motives for choosing teaching as a career. Let's find out what happens when career rewards do not meet expectations or motivations.

Intrinsic Rewards.   Intrinsic rewards focus on a teacher's desire to work with young people. Teaching allows you to share your students' excitement as they learn more about their world. It is impossible for many classroom teachers to imagine doing something other than teaching. Most teachers classified "being born to teach" as an intrinsic reward. Others described "doing something worthwhile" as primarily important for teaching (Huberman, Grounauer & Marti, 1993).

There are other intrinsic rewards as well. In one national study (Haselkorn and Calkins, 1993), teachers said what they liked best about the classroom was that the quality of their schools continued to improve. Working conditions were slowly improving. The amount of classroom supplies and equipment was increasing. Classes had fewer students. As a result, teachers had more opportunities to enjoy their personal interactions with students. In fact, these teachers described their personal relations with students as either excellent or good. The most important intrinsic reward for these classroom teachers was that parents and students appreciated their work.

Extrinsic Rewards.   The teaching profession offers extrinsic rewards as well. For example, salaries and fringe benefits continue to improve. Tenure allows teachers to enjoy job security not found in business or industry. A teaching career fits in well with family time: holidays, summers, and weekends are free.

Another extrinsic reward for teaching is that teachers can express their creativity in their work. They are not bound by a large number of constraints (Huberman, Grounauer, Marti, 1993). In fact, many teachers think of themselves as independent managers. As a teacher, you will exercise creative autonomy in the classroom. You will make a multitude of decisions in just one hour in your classroom, ranging from curricular and teaching decisions to deciding how to cope with behavioral problems.

Stress and Burnout.   In spite of the intrinsic and extrinsic rewards we've just discussed, many teachers leave the profession every year. A study of classroom teachers' personal and professional lives found that 42 percent will either leave or want to leave the profession within the first ten years of teaching. Almost half—48 percent—of all classroom teachers will leave or consider leaving teaching between their seventh and fifteenth year (Boyer, 1983; Goodlad, 1984; Huberman, Grounauer & Marti, 1993; Sizer, 1984).

What types of teachers are more apt to leave the teaching profession? Huberman, Grounauer & Marti (1993) discovered classroom teachers in such areas as language arts and social studies expressed more dissatisfaction with teaching than music or physical education instructors. They note, however, that there is no difference between the number of men and women who wish to leave the classroom.

What are the reasons teachers leave the profession? For many, stress within the classroom or complications in their personal lives precipitate leaving. Personal interruptions, such as divorce or illness within the family, may cause some teachers to refocus their lives. Other teachers leave the profession because teaching simply does not give them the intrinsic or extrinsic rewards that originally motivated them. For some, the personal investment of the classroom becomes overpowering, in that it squelches other creative interests.

Perhaps the most dramatic reason classroom teachers leave the profession is burnout. A crisis or personal conflict with other teachers, the principal, or students may prompt some teachers to simply decide it is not worth the effort. Some teachers feel they are not contributing to society and believe that what they are doing is not important. Other teachers quit because they are frustrated with routine paperwork or endless meetings and are not encouraged to do their best. They feel overworked. But whatever the immediate reason for resigning, teachers quit because they can no longer participate in the rewards teaching promised them in the first place.

What Is Teaching?

Teaching is a profession in which you interact daily with children, their parents, and society. Teaching is more than delivering a **curriculum,** or the subject matter. Teaching includes the personal histories each of us brings into our classes. Teaching is not a job in which you are expected to punch a clock and accomplish certain tasks by the end of the day.

Classroom teachers have described what they do in a multitude of ways. Some think of teaching as a set of skills; others as an art form. Which description best suits you?

Teaching as a Skill.   Some classroom teachers think teaching is a structured activity that follows certain prescribed steps and results in children learning. These teachers compare the classroom to a laboratory in which children's learning is managed. "Skill teachers" organize the curriculum and decide how students should learn. They expect students to behave in a prescribed manner. They inform students what level of success they must achieve in order to succeed.

VIGNETTE 1.1   *A conversation between Karl and Mrs. Moffet*

> Karl: *Mrs. Moffet, I've finished the reading assignment you gave us. May I start tomorrow's assignment?*
>
> Mrs. Moffet: *No. I want you to review your reading assignment. I want all the students to stay together in learning this material. I want you to learn the next assignment along with the rest of the class tomorrow.*

Skill teachers, like Mrs. Moffet, want to control the classroom, the students, and the expected accomplishments. These teachers dominate the classroom.

Teaching as an Art Form.   The opposite of a skill teacher is an "art form teacher." These teachers appear to be disorganized in comparison to skill teachers. Art form teachers are more willing to extemporize in the classroom. They are willing to experiment using different teaching methods, depending on the subject matter and the students. Art form teachers teach students by allowing them to share responsibility for their learning. Because art form teachers recognize that students learn differently, their classrooms are less structured and more noisy than skill teachers' classrooms.

VIGNETTE 1.2   *A conversation between Fran and Mrs. Newcomb*

> Fran: *Mrs. Newcomb, I am having trouble answering some of the math questions. Can Terry help me?*
>
> Mrs. Newcomb: *That's fine with me if Terry has time to help you. If you still don't understand, ask me after class and I'll work with you.*

In this case, Mrs. Newcomb feels Fran can take charge of her own learning and should be able to ask for help. Did you notice Fran asked another student for help and not Mrs. Newcomb?

Integrating Art Form and Skill Teaching.   Many professional teachers combine both art and skill in their teaching methods. These teachers use both art form and skill methods, depending on the curriculum, learning styles of students, and the personal histories they bring into the classroom. They have clear objectives for students but may improvise tactics for reaching the objectives. Their learning activities are based on students' needs, interests, and abilities. These teachers are willing to modify a teaching strategy if students seem to be having difficulty.

The Need for Teachers

In the United States, the need for classroom teachers is continually growing. You will be joining the nation's largest profession, with 2.9 million public and non-public teachers. What will your colleagues be like? Teachers are a diverse group of men and women. The average age of a classroom teacher today is 40. Approximately three-fourths of all teachers are female. As shown in Figure 1.1, 87 percent of teachers are white, 7 percent are African-American, 4 percent are Hispanic, 1 percent are Asian/Pacific Island, and 1 percent are Native American. Teachers are employed in 200,000 school districts throughout our country. Teachers are part of a cadre of approximately 4.5 million educational employees, approximately half of whom are administrators, counselors, librarians, instructional technicians, and other support personnel (National Center for Education Statistics, 1995).

Figure 1.2 demonstrates that the demand for classroom teachers is increasing. The demand for classroom teachers is expected to continue to increase until 2006. In 1996, 3 million K–12 teachers were needed in U.S. classrooms. It is projected that by 2006 our nation will need 3.4 million teachers (National Center for Education Statistics, 1996, p. 9).

Increasing Number of Students

One reason teacher demand is expected to increase is an anticipated 6 percent increase in the number of students attending our nation's classrooms between 1996 and 2006. As Figure 1.3 illustrates, classroom teachers will teach approximately 54.6 million children in the year 2006 (National Center for Education Statistics, 1996, p. 9). The greatest increase is expected to occur between 1996 and 2000.

Today's Teachers

The characteristics and descriptions of America's teaching force continue to change. Our teaching force is maturing. Eighteen percent of our classroom teach-

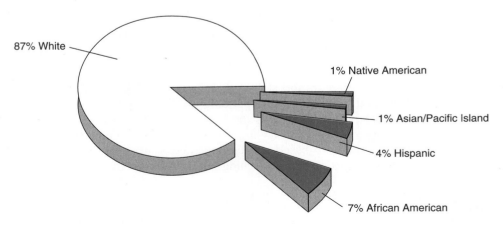

Figure 1.1   Race/Ethnicity of Teachers in Public and Private Schools: 1993–1994

Source: Data from *Digest of Education Statistics, 1995* (p. 7) by the National Center for Education Statistics, 1995, Washington, DC: U.S. Government Printing Office.

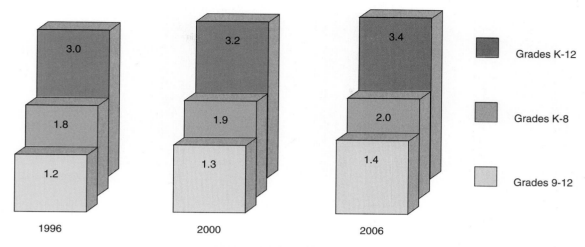

Figure 1.2 Teacher Demand (in millions): 1996–2006

Source: Data from *Projections of Educational Statistics to 2006* (p. 9) by W. J. Hussar and D. E. Gerald, 1996, Washington, DC: U.S. Government Printing Office.

ers are over the age of 50 and will soon retire. Classroom teachers presently in their 40s will also be eligible for retirement during the next two decades. With only 14.5 percent of our classroom teachers presently under the age of 30, school districts anticipate needing a steady supply of classroom teachers simply to replace retirees. At the same time, school districts will need to hire new classroom teachers to meet increasing student enrollments.

In 1970, more than 12 percent of teachers were **people of color,** but that number appers to be on the decline; some estimate that by the year 2000, only 5 percent of our teachers will be African Americans, Native Americans, Hispanic Americans or Asian/Pacific Islanders. As you can see in Figure 1.4, although people of color make up about 34 percent of the school-age population, they account for about 13 percent of current teachers and only 10 percent of teachers in training.

There are several reasons for the growing shortage of teachers of color. First, people of color can today pursue a wider variety of professional opportunities than in the past. Second, fewer people of color are enrolled in college. Although people of color comprise 25 percent of the college-age population, only 23.4 percent are actually enrolled in college. Third, many states and school districts increasingly rely on teacher licensing tests to measure projected teacher effectiveness. Critics argue that these tests have built-in cultural biases that systematically disadvantage people of color. Finally, the dissatisfaction that led to steep declines in the overall number of people entering the teaching profession has had the same impact on people of color.

To counteract these trends, a wide range of programs have been developed to ensure continued diversity in the teaching profession. For example, Florida Inter-

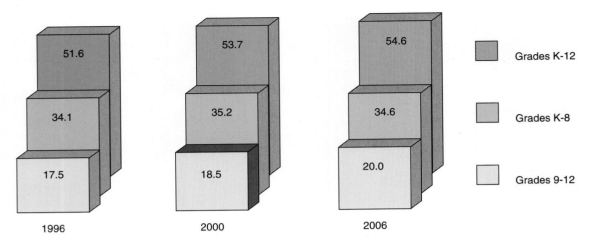

Figure 1.3   Student Enrollment (in millions) in the Nation's Schools: 1996–2006

Source: Data from *Projections of Educational Statistics to 2006* (p. 9) by W. J. Hussar and D. E. Gerald, 1996, Washington, DC: U.S. Government Printing Office.

national University has established a program, FOCUS, that recruits and trains teachers of color for Dade County inner-city schools. Other universities actively seek Hispanic students. St. Edward's University (Austin, Texas), The University of Texas at Austin, Texas A & M, Stanford, and Harvard were rated among the top 25 colleges for Hispanics (Top 25 listed, 1997). These universities were selected if a minimum of 10 percent of their students were Hispanic and they "demonstrate overall excellence . . . or succeed in making Hispanics welcome by offering programs, recruitment outreach, student organizations and/or fields of study designed to appeal to Hispanic students" (Top 25 colleges for Hispanics, 1997).

Figure 1.4
Percentage of People of Color in Education

Source: Data from *Projections of Educational Statistics to 2006* (pp. 9, 73) by W. J. Hussar and D. E. Gerald, 1996, Washington, DC: U.S. Government Printing Office.

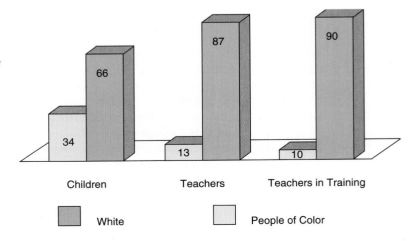

Surpluses and Shortages

The supply and demand for teachers are not equal throughout the United States, or in every specialty. For example, California, Texas, Florida, and New York have a greater need for bilingual classroom teachers than other states.

Teaching fields that have experienced shortages have been special education, mathematics, and science. Other teachings fields, such as home economics, English, social studies, physical education, and some elementary areas are encountering surpluses. Demands for a specific teaching field can quickly change. When you begin applying for teaching positions, be sure your college or university placement office gives you the latest information.

Salary Trends

In recent years, the salaries of classroom teachers have seen a slow but continual increase. As you might expect, when demand for teachers outstrips supply, salaries usually increase. One reason for this is the public's understanding of the importance of teachers.

Table 1.1 shows that average starting salaries for graduates in education are below salaries for graduates in computer science and engineering. However, starting salaries for education graduates are very similar to the starting salaries of graduates in the humanities and social and behavioral sciences.

As you might surmise, teacher's salaries differ by state. Table 1.2 lists the average annual salaries of classroom teachers by state for the years 1980–81 and 1994–95 and the percentage of salary change for classroom teachers between 1981 and 1995.

Table 1.1
Average Starting Salaries of College Graduates, 1993

Major field of study	Average starting salary
Education	$ 19,450
Humanities	20,413
Social and behavioral sciences	20,903
Natural sciences	21,248
Computer sciences and engineering	31,187
Business and management	25,347
Other professional or technical	23,731

Source: Data from *Condition of Education, 1996* (Indicator 35, Chart 2), by the National Center for Education Statistics, Washington, DC: U.S. Government Printing Office.

Table 1.2
Average Annual Salaries (in 1995 constant dollars) of All Teachers for School Years Ending 1981 and 1995

Region and state	All teachers 1980–81	All teachers 1994–95	Percentage change 1981–1995
50 states and D.C.	$31,102	$37,436	20.4
New England	28,299	42,685	50.8
Connecticut	*30,679	50,808	65.6
Maine	24,668	32,459	31.6
Massachusetts	*32,969	42,817	29.9
New Hampshire	23,642	35,249	49.1
Rhode Island	34,908	41,305	18.5
Vermont	22,927	*36,864	60.8
Mideast	34,534	46,365	34.3
Delaware	32,091	39,671	23.6
District of Columbia	40,336	43,614	8.1
Maryland	33,489	41,255	23.2
New Jersey	32,162	46,789	45.5
New York	37,593	48,338	28.6
Pennsylvania	31,536	45,188	43.3
Southeast	26,510	31,754	19.8
Alabama	26,803	31,619	18.0
Arkansas	23,397	28,842	23.3
Florida	27,157	33,085	21.8
Georgia	27,226	32,689	20.1
Kentucky	27,764	32,749	18.0
Louisiana	29,186	26,971	−7.6
Mississippi	22,946	27,227	18.7
North Carolina	27,954	31,262	11.8
South Carolina	25,301	30,579	20.9
Tennessee	26,650	32,972	23.7
Virginia	27,385	34,267	25.1
West Virginia	26,350	32,431	23.1
Great Lakes	32,577	40,866	25.4
Illinois	34,242	41,666	21.7

Salaries vary widely from state to state for many reasons. One reason is that the cost of living differs throughout the country. Classroom teachers in high cost-of-living states must have higher salaries so they can enjoy the same living standards as their colleagues who live in low cost-of-living states. A second reason classroom teacher salaries differ has to do with the strength of each state's economy. For example, Los Angeles classroom teachers experienced a 10 percent pay cut in 1993 because of the slowdown of California's economy.

Table 1.2
Average Annual Salaries (in 1995 constant dollars) of All Teachers
for School Years Ending 1981 and 1995 (continued)

Region and state	All teachers 1980–81	All teachers 1994–95	Percentage change 1981–1995
Indiana	*30,417	37,360	22.8
Michigan	*37,394	*48,134	28.7
Ohio	29,798	37,349	25.3
Wisconsin	31,037	38,321	23.5
Plains	*26,945*	*32,934*	*22.2*
Iowa	28,435	31,991	12.5
Kansas	26,882	35,180	30.9
Minnesota	31,337	36,496	16.5
Missouri	27,184	31,661	16.5
Nebraska	26,234	31,393	19.7
North Dakota	24,439	26,728	9.4
South Dakota	24,104	26,390	9.5
Southwest	*28,307*	*31,286*	*10.5*
Arizona	30,321	32,665	7.7
New Mexico	29,636	29,305	−1.1
Oklahoma	25,546	28,397	11.2
Texas	27,725	31,699	14.3
Rocky Mountain	*29,813*	*31,985*	*7.3*
Colorado	31,584	35,098	11.1
Idaho	26,634	30,237	13.5
Montana	28,123	29,224	3.9
Utah	29,727	29,360	−1.2
Wyoming	32,996	31,762	−3.7
Far West	*37,588*	*40,337*	*7.3*
Alaska	*51,205	48,682	−4.9
California	*36,540	*41,287	13.0
Hawaii	37,277	39,105	4.9
Nevada	31,201	35,367	13.4
Oregon	*31,813	39,462	24.0
Washington	37,491	36,711	−2.1

*Estimated by National Education Association (NEA)

Source: National Education Association, *Estimates of School Statistics* (Copyright © 1995 by NEA). Reprinted by permission of National Education Association.

Individual states' rules governing tenure and salary are also important. For example, in some states in the northeast, teachers receive high salaries after teaching six or seven years in the same school district. In some southern and southwestern states, classroom teachers are required to remain in the school district for twenty or more years before they are paid the highest salaries.

Teacher Preparation Programs

There are 1,280 state-approved teacher preparation programs in the United States. (Haselkorn and Calkins, 1993, p. 57). Teacher preparation programs are found in all types of colleges and universities, from community colleges to the nation's largest research universities. These programs lead to licensure or certification. **Licensure** is the legal recognition by the state that allows an individual to teach in a classroom. **Certification** may mean the same thing, but it is usually defined as special recognition given to classroom teachers by private or nongovernmental agencies, such as the National Board for Professional Teaching Standards.

Regardless of what college or university you are attending, your teacher preparation program shares three components with all other programs. These components include academic programs, professional courses, and clinical field experiences. Each component is essential for classroom instruction and each interrelates with the others. Each is important for your success as a classroom teacher.

Preparing to Be a Teacher

Colleges and universities usually divide their academic programs into two divisions. The lower division comprises core or general education courses intended to give each student a broad education. Core or general education courses act as academic support for your major field of study. General education courses are particularly important because classroom teachers are expected to have a well-rounded general education.

Academic Courses.

Of course, you will be required to chose a major within your program. This is the academic discipline, or curriculum, you plan to teach. If you are planning on teaching in secondary schools, you probably have been informed by your advisor of the need to have one or several majors depending on your state's certification or licensure requirements. For example, if you want to teach senior high school social studies, your counselor probably has informed you of your state's academic requirements concerning courses in history as well as approved courses in related areas such as sociology, geography, and economics. In many states even elementary teachers are required to have a major, such as foreign language or mathematics.

Professional Courses.

Most colleges and universities officially admit students to education programs in the beginning of their third year of college. Most professional courses in methods, foundations, child or adolescent psychology, and others are taken in the last two years of college. These courses are called *professional* because they focus on teaching, students, and issues important to a successful career in education. While the majority of teacher preparation programs are at the undergraduate level, there is a trend toward 5-year programs. The Teacher Education Program at the University of Maryland/College Park, the Stanford

Teacher Education Program at Stanford University, and the Harvard Graduate School of Education Program are well-known five-year programs.

Undergraduate Education Experiences.

Traditionally, student teaching has been the capstone experience in teacher preparation programs. Today, many colleges and universities involve education students in the practical aspects of teaching as early in the program as possible. You may visit a variety of schools and classrooms, share the first several days of the school year with a classroom teacher, or participate in a tutorial program to help students. These field experiences are designed to provide students opportunities to experience firsthand various aspects of teaching. Two of the most common field experiences are classroom observations and classroom internships.

Classroom Observations.   Many students find that observing a classroom in session helps them reach a final decision to choose teaching as a career. Other students decide, after their classroom observations, that teaching is not for them. In either case, the observation experience is beneficial.

Structured observations are more productive than unstructured observations. You may focus on students, the teacher, interaction between students and the teacher, the structure of a lesson, or the actual setting—whatever aspect of teaching most intrigues you.

Classroom Internships.   Serving an internship in the classroom is another way of gaining valuable experience prior to student teaching. Some internship programs have students assist a teacher in preparing class schedules and keeping records. In other programs, education majors get the chance to teach a single-concept lesson to a small group of students while practicing a specific teaching skill. Some programs include tutoring in the classroom as part of the internship. For example, St. Edward's University in Austin, Texas, sponsors a program where college students from migrant families tutor migrant children in local elementary schools.

Student Teaching.   Obviously, the culmination of your teacher preparation program is student teaching. During **student teaching,** teacher preparation students teach in classrooms under the direction of master teachers and university professors. Every classroom teacher remembers the student teaching experience. Many mention that it was during their student teaching experience that they knew for certain they had made the right career choice. During student teaching you are allowed to demonstrate your teaching ability with real students. You will work on a day-by-day basis with a master teacher, planning and developing teaching materials and instructional units. You and your master teacher will develop a close professional relationship in which you will be allowed to focus on your teaching techniques and all the other information you learned in your academic and professional course work.

How long should you student teach? Typically, states require student teachers to be in a classroom setting from ten to fifteen weeks. Many classroom teachers believe this period should be lengthened, so that student teachers can have many different types of classroom experiences before they are licensed or certified. In some states, such as Oklahoma, teacher preparation students are required to teach one year after graduation before they are certified or licensed. There, entry-level teachers get experience teaching under the direction of a master classroom teacher, an administrator, and a professor.

Preparation Beyond the Classroom

A good classroom teacher (or teacher preparation student) develops skills that transfer easily to other positions within the school. A practical understanding of management, goal setting, and leadership qualities will serve you well in the classroom and beyond. Many students discover their teacher preparation program has prepared them for careers as principals, superintendents, or educational specialists.

School Administration.
Many teachers discover, after a few years in the classroom, that they would like to continue their interaction with students in another capacity. Some continue their professional growth by becoming principals or superintendents. If you decide, in several years, that you would like to become an administrator, you will probably be required to have several years of successful classroom teaching experience and a degree from an administration preparation program. Because administrators are educational leaders, they study such topics as curriculum, law, finance, and school organization.

Educational Specialists.
There are many experts in the school other than classroom teachers and administrators. Counselors, psychologists, technologist-librarians and other specialists generally are required to have classroom teaching experience and many are required to have advanced degrees. For example, superintendents traditionally hold Ed.D. or Ph.D. degrees in educational administration. Guidance counselors and school psychologists hold master's degrees in their specific fields.

Teaching Abroad.
It is the dream of many classroom teachers to teach in another country. Many teachers find it exciting and professionally rewarding to briefly live and work in another country and culture. Beyond the wealth of personal experiences teaching abroad gives, it helps classroom teachers develop cultural understanding. When they return to the United States, they are more sensitive to the complexities and issues children of different cultures bring to the classroom. Obviously, what you learn in your teacher preparation program is transferable to schools in other lands!

If you are interested in teaching abroad, when and how should you apply? A teaching certificate or license and several years of successful classroom teaching experience is usually required by most national departments or ministries of education. However, some third world or developing nations are willing to interview those who are in the process of being certified.

Most overseas teaching contracts are for two or three years. You are expected to be physically and emotionally healthy and certified or licensed to teach a variety of subjects. You may also want to learn a foreign language. If you are interested in teaching abroad, see Figure 1.5.

Who Is an Effective Teacher?

The question uppermost in your mind now probably is, "Will I be a good teacher?" To help you answer the question, let's study some of the characteristics effective classroom teachers demonstrate. As you would expect, there are many—but not all classroom teachers exhibit every characteristic. Let's look at some of the personal and professional characteristics classroom teachers may have.

Personal Characteristics

What are the personal characteristics of an effective classroom teacher? As shown in Figure 1.6, the effective teacher is usually an extrovert, a person who is able to openly express a warm and caring attitude about others. As you might expect, most classroom teachers enjoy working with and relating to students, administrators, and other teachers. Teachers are accessible to those who need them, and, at the same time, are leaders. Classroom teachers are flexible in their relationships and the way in which they solve problems. Teachers are willing to change their approach to solving problems or to explore new techniques to improve their teaching strategies. Teachers enjoy learning. Many teachers develop a strong belief

Figure 1.5   Teaching in Other Countries

Department of Defense dependents schools.   Write to: Overseas Employment for Educators, U.S. Department of Defense, Office of Dependents Schools, Room 152, Hoffman Building #1, 2461 Eisenhower Avenue, Alexandria, VA 22331.

The Peace Corps.   Write to: Peace Corps Recruiting Office, 1990 K Street NW, Washington, DC 20526.

Church-affiliated schools.   Write to: United Church Board for World Ministries, 475 Riverside Drive, New York, NY 10015.

Company schools.   Write to: ISS Directory of Overseas Schools, International Schools Service, P. O. Box 5910, Princeton, NJ 08540.

Private schools affiliated with the U.S. Department of State.   Write to: Office of Overseas Schools, Room 234, SA-6, U.S. Department of State, Washington, DC 20520.

International placement services.   Write to: Overseas Academic Opportunities, 949 East 29th Street, 2nd Floor, Brooklyn, NY 11210.

Figure 1.6   Characteristics of Effective Teachers

- Tend to be good managers
- Have high expectations of their students and themselves
- Believe in their own effectiveness
- Vary teaching strategies
- Handle discipline through prevention
- Are usually warm and caring
- Are democratic in their approach
- Are task-oriented
- Are concerned with perceptual meanings rather than facts and events

- Are comfortable interacting with students
- Have a strong grasp of subject matter
- Are readily accessible to students outside of class
- Tailor their teaching to student needs
- Are reflective practitioners, open to new learning theories and classroom techniques
- Are highly flexible, enthusiastic, and imaginative

Source: W. Deman-Burger, *Effective Teaching: Observations from Research* (1986). Excerpted with permission from the American Association of School Administrators; 1801 N. Moore St., Arlington, VA, 22209-9988; (703) 528-0700. Home Page: http://www.aasa.org.

in themselves and their abilities in the classroom. Most teachers like to finish a job once it's begun. Many classroom teachers think on several levels at the same time. While they are interested in facts, they are also interested how they relate to their students.

Professional Characteristics

What professional characteristics do effective classroom teachers usually display? Because of the diversity of students, teachers must be good managers. Regardless of the complexity of the task, teaching requires inordinate amounts of planning, organization, and understanding. Just as effective classroom teachers have high expectations of themselves, they also have high expectations of their students. As a teacher you want your students to succeed. Meeting a former student as an adult, seeing that student as a successful professional, gives a teacher a great feeling of personal accomplishment.

Good teachers are flexible. They readily change their teaching methods to help students learn. An experienced high school teacher recounted the first teaching year,

> At first it was a mess; even if there wasn't any catastrophic situation, even if I never had them walking all over me. . . . It's a tone I had set, a "way of being" in the classroom that I had to learn in order to feel confident. As soon as I knew why I was there, that I had something to offer, the rest fell into place. (Huberman, Grounauer, & Marti, 1993, p. 221)

Effective classroom teachers have strong backgrounds in their subject matter, and they recognize the importance of continually improving themselves professionally. Many teachers trade their summer vacations for student desks at local colleges and universities as they pursue advanced degrees.

How does an effective classroom teacher combine the best of his or her personal and professional characteristics? Vignette 1.3 is an English teacher's weekly journal about Jeremy, a high school student whose history of failure made him feel he was a social outcast. As you read, place yourself in the role of the classroom teacher.

 VIGNETTE 1.3 *Jeremy's purple hair*

Monday: Jeremy came to my first period junior English class today wearing his newly dyed hair in a spike. I was a bit startled when I saw him, but this wasn't the first unusual hairstyle he has sported. I asked him, "How did you get it to stand straight up?" "What did you use to create that shade of purple?" "May I touch it?" He seemed surprised I was interested. The bell rang and my students resumed the reading of *A Raisin In The Sun.*

Near the end of class, an intercom announcement interrupted the dramatic presentation. "Will you please send Jeremy to Mr. McClain's office?" Jeremy collected his belongings and quietly said, as he left, that he probably wouldn't be back for the rest of the day. Another student volunteered to read Jeremy's part. I wondered if he would be dismissed for the day by the assistant principal.

Tuesday: Jeremy came to class with his hair showing only a hint of purple and combed in his usual style. I asked him about his meeting with Mr. McClain. He said Mr. McClain didn't like his purple hair and was surprised I had. He sent Jeremy to his second period class with the caution his hair should return to normal today. Jeremy told me he would recreate his spiked look on the last day of school. And I promised him I would bring my camera to take his picture.

Friday: Today is the last day of school. Even though Jeremy's class didn't meet, he came to my room at his usual time. His hair was spiked and the purple was even more vibrant than on Monday. He reminded me he had promised to show me his hairstyle. I took my camera from my desk and asked him to pose. He seemed a little embarrassed but willing to humor me. Jeremy laughed when I told him I would send him his pictures over the summer break.

Epilogue: I have thought a lot about Jeremy and his end-of-the-year statement. Although he is academically capable of performing well, Jeremy prefers not to. I know his personal history in English for the past three years has included failure and summer school make-up.

When the school year began, he became my challenge. During the year his unwillingness to complete assignments lessened. He learned to respond to others without being cynical. He tried to participate in class discussions. He shared his feelings with me about his English classes in general—but he qualified that it wasn't personal. Jeremy's purple, spiked hair wasn't a distraction for me. It was his way of saying, "Look at me. I'm special." That's what I had wanted him to recognize all along.

???   *How would you describe Jeremy's teacher? What did he or she do that might have made a difference for Jeremy? What concerns might the assistant principal have had?*

Have you noticed that the personal and professional characteristics of effective classroom teachers interrelate? This is because teaching is a profession requiring people to interact with each other on a personal level. This is especially true as our society becomes more multicultural.

As you will learn in this textbook, our classrooms are becoming more diverse. More children representing different cultures, ethnicities, and races are enrolling in our schools. They experience **culture shock** when they enter our classrooms, because they speak different languages, express different values, adhere to different religions and family styles. Effective classroom teachers must use their personal *and* professional characteristics to help *all* children learn.

Effective classroom teachers are aware of their attitudes and feelings about children who represent cultures other than their own. By being sensitive to the needs and personal histories of others, effective teachers create classroom environments in which *all* children can learn. Effective teachers allow children to learn according to their own personal and cultural styles. Figure 1.7 identifies the attributes of masterful teachers. Review these attributes and compare them with the characteristics of effective teachers described in Figure 1.6.

Public Evaluation of Effective Teachers

We've studied the characteristics of effective teachers, but how does the public evaluate classroom teacher effectiveness? Do all parents and taxpayers evaluate classroom teacher effectiveness in the same way? It is obvious that classroom teachers have gained public recognition and respect during the last several years. In a recent study (Elam, Rose, & Gallup, 1995), more than two-thirds of all parents thought they would like their children to become classroom teachers. In the same poll, 90 percent of all Americans said they would be willing to increase their taxes if it meant the education of their children would be improved. In fact, 81 percent of all citizens were willing to spend more tax money on the education of inner-city children. Sixty-eight percent stated they were willing to help finance educational improvements in the poorer states. And 70 percent of all Americans thought it was possible to have a national consensus on what values classroom teachers should teach children.

But the public has difficulty understanding the difference between classroom teacher effectiveness and school effectiveness. If teachers are seen as effective, schools are described as effective. For the past 27 years, Phi Delta Kappa and Gallup have conducted a poll of the public's attitude toward public schools. Let's

Figure 1.7 Attributes of Masterful Teachers

- They tend to be nonjudgmental.
- They are not moralistic. They do not believe that preaching is teaching.
- They are not easily shocked, even by horrific events.
- They not only listen, they hear. They not only hear, they seek to understand. They regard listening to children, parents, or anyone involved in the school community as a potential source of useful information.
- They recognize they have feelings of hate, prejudice, and bias and strive to overcome them.
- They do not see themselves as saviors who have come to save their schools.
- They do not see themselves as being alone. They network.
- They see themselves as "winning" even though they know their total influence on their students is much less than that of the total society, neighborhood, and gang.
- They enjoy their interactions with children and youth so much they are willing to put up with irrational demands of the school system.
- They think their primary impact on their students is that they've made them more humane and less frustrated, or raised their self-esteem.
- They derive all types of satisfactions and meet all kinds of needs by teaching children or youth in poverty. The one exception is power. They meet no power needs whatever by functioning as teachers.

Source: M. Haberman, *Star Teachers of Children in Poverty* (1995). Reprinted by permission of Kappa Delta Pi, an International Honor Society in Education.

discuss some of the findings from the lastest poll, including how the public "grades" public schools on both a national and a local level. The survey asks people to "grade" the public schools using A, B, C, D, or Fail. First, the public is asked to grade their local public schools and then to grade the public schools on a national level. As you can see from Figure 1.8, local schools are graded much higher than public schools nationally.

VIGNETTE 1.4   *Talking with the authors*

Bill: *Well, Anna, now that the students have read this chapter, what do you think we should tell them so they know what classroom teaching is really like?*

Anna: *Actually, reading about something you have never experienced makes it difficult to understand what it all means. Therefore, I think pre-service teacher students should have as much practical classroom experience as early as possible. These experiences will help students make up their minds about becoming a classroom teacher.*

Bill: *I understand what you mean. I remember how little I knew about my classroom when I first taught. I really felt unprepared.*

Anna: *Do you think classroom teachers are better prepared now?*

Bill: *Yes. But, classroom teaching is also changing. Teachers have made great strides in the last few years. That's the reason the next chapter on professionalism is important. Many classroom teachers don't seem to understand what it means to be a professional.*

Anna: *Well, classroom teaching is certainly different than when we started. Much of that change has come about because students are more diverse today. Our society is rapidly changing.*

Bill: *That's right. One reason for that change is we have a large number of people immigrating from other nations to the United States. We are a multicultural nation.*

Anna: *But isn't that what we have always been, Bill? Remember, there were many people living here before the Europeans came. We are a diverse country—and that's good. Just think how much ability and talent kids from different cultures and ethnicities are bringing us!*

Bill: *Let's close the chapter for the students who are reading this. What would you like them to understand about classroom teaching?*

Anna: *I want them to know teaching is a wonderful, rewarding, career in which classroom teachers make a difference in the lives of students.*

Bill: *Thanks. I agree. Also, I want to say teaching is easy to love. Here is your chance to decide what you want to do with the rest of your professional life. Good luck!*

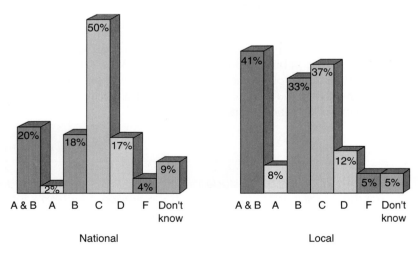

Figure 1.8   Grade Cards of Public Schools

Source: Data from S. M. Elam, L. C. Rose, & A. M. Gallup (1995). "The 27th Annual Phi Delta Kappa/Gallup Poll of the Public's Attitudes Toward the Public Schools." *Phi Delta Kappan, 77* (1) pp. 41–56.

What You Have Learned

✔ There are many motivations for becoming a teacher. They range from enjoying children to trying to correct an educational defect. The desire to become a teacher may come early in a person's life or much later at the end of another career.

✔ A controversy among teachers is whether teaching is a skill or an art form. Master teachers are able to use both methodologies.

✔ The demand for teachers is increasing in the United States. Increasing student populations and the maturation of the nation's teaching force are the primary reasons.

✔ Classroom teacher salaries are increasing, but they are still low in comparison to other professions. Salaries differ throughout the nation because of local economic factors.

✔ The design of teacher preparation programs differ throughout the nation, but all include academic, professional, and student teaching experiences. As a consequence, teacher preparation programs help prepare classroom teachers for many different roles in schools.

✔ Effective teachers are those who use their personal and professional characteristics in the classroom to help children learn.

Key Terms

entry-level teachers   certification
curriculum   student teaching
people of color   culture shock
licensure

Applying What You Have Learned

1. In *Becoming a Teacher,* Laurie Ferriri felt self-conscious with her students. What techniques did she use to control her class?

2. Laurie Ferriri demonstrates some of the differences between teaching as a skill and as an art form. Can you identify them?

3. Talk with other students in your class. Why do they want to be classroom teachers? How do their motives differ from yours?

4. Teacher salaries are influenced by different factors. List several factors that influence salaries in your state.

5. Become familiar with your teacher preparation program. List the curriculum of the three main components. How will they help you become a better teacher?

Interactive Learning

1. Interview several teachers. Do they classify their rewards for teaching as intrinsic or extrinsic? Which rewards do they mention as lacking?

2. The demographics of the teaching profession indicate that a large percentage of teachers will retire during the next decade. Interview several of your friends who are planning nonteaching careers to find out what rewards would entice them to become classroom teachers.

3. As you become more familiar with the classroom, you will notice many types of people involved in the educational process. Interview several individuals, such as administrators or educational specialists. What were their reasons for choosing to leave the classroom for their present assignment? How were their reasons similar and how were they dissimilar?

4. List your motivations for teaching. Do you think your motives will help you become a better teacher? Discuss this question in a small group and compare the ideas you discussed.

Expanding Your Knowledge

Haselkorn, David and Andrew Calkins. *Careers In Teaching Handbook*. Belmont, Massachusetts: Recruiting New Teachers, Inc., 1993. (A small book that gives updated information about schools, teaching, how to find a job, and all the other things teacher preparation students want to know about classroom teaching.)

Huberman, Michael. *The Lives of Teachers*. New York: Teachers College Press, 1993. (This is an excellent book about the personal lives, characteristics, and experiences of classroom teachers in several countries. The quotes are true to life. The research is excellent.)

Johnson, Lou Anne. *The Girls in the Back of the Class*. New York: St. Martin's Press, 1995. (This delightful book is about a young, idealistic classroom teacher beset by all types of student problems. She tries to find ways to help her students stay in school. If you like this book, you will enjoy *My Posse Don't Do Homework* by the same author. This book was made into a movie, *Dangerous Minds*.)

MacLeod, Jay. *Ain't No Makin' It*. Boulder: Westview Press, 1995. (The author describes what it means to teach children from low-income homes. Sometimes, the author says, children succeed or fail because of who they are, not what they can do.)

Ryan, Kevin. *The Roller Coaster Year: Stories of First-Year Teachers*. New York: Harper-Collins, 1991. (If you want to know what the first year of teaching can be like, this book will tell you, in the words of a dozen new teachers.)

Silverman, Rita, William Welty and Sally Lyon. *Case Studies For Teacher Problem Solving*. New York, McGraw-Hill, Inc., 1992. (This small book describes a series of classroom problems. You are challenged to use your analytical skills in finding solutions. It gives teacher preparation students an idea about the real life of the classroom.)

Chapter 2

Teaching as a Profession

It used to be that teachers were not expected to be very smart, because teaching children was thought to be simple. The assumption was that teacher education students only studied the basics in college, while smarter students—who were becoming lawyers and doctors—studied higher-level mathematics and science. Many people—including college counselors—believed that if you were not "smart enough" to become a "real professional," you could always teach. Teachers were viewed as as quasi-parents, more interested in nurturing or "mothering" children than in guiding them to learn.

Teaching has come a long way in a very short period of time. Today, most everyone—students, business executives, politicians and parents—acknowledges that teaching is a sophisticated and complicated professional activity, requiring extensive academic and professional preparation. A teacher requires a vast array of knowledge in many different academic areas. Let's look at the professionalism of teaching.

What you will learn

- All professions have specific hallmarks that define their organization and purposes for their members and the public.
- A goal of teacher organizations such as the National Educational Association and the American Federation of Teachers is to help teachers become professionals.
- As society becomes more complex, the problems teachers encounter in the classroom are reflected in teacher organizations.

BECOMING A TEACHER

I am a teacher

My name is Ester Gonzales and I am 53 years old. I was born on a small farm in Sonora, Mexico. Life was difficult then. I remember both my parents and four older brothers working the land in the hills outside the village of San Bernardino. Because the land was poor, we knew crops would never yield enough for all of us to eat well. As I grew older and my brothers married, we wondered how all of us would be able to live together as a family.

As I look back now, I realize two important events changed my life. The first event was a series of sad departures. My brothers—first Ernesto, then Eduardo, and finally Augusto—left the farm with their families and moved north to El Paso, Texas. When they visited my parents and me on the farm they would tell us about the richness of the United States. We marveled at the pictures of the home they had. They had running water and electricity!

The second event was a decision I made. I wanted to stay in Mexico and realized if I could not make a success of my life working with my hands, it would have to be with my head. Therefore, I went to school. I found learning easy. I enjoyed being a student. It wasn't long before I realized the more I learned about others the more I learned about myself. In fact, it was this realization that helped me want to be a teacher. I wanted others to have the same experiences and joys I had in the classroom.

When my parents died, Ernesto and his family invited me to live with them in El Paso. While I didn't want to leave Mexico, I realized it was best for me to go. I wanted to continue my teaching career in El Paso, but I quickly learned that in the United States teachers must be citizens. Yet it was important for me to bring money into our household. I tried many jobs. Because my Spanish and English were excellent, it was easy for me to get a job. First, I was a waitress in a cafe close to the border. I liked my employers, but I decided to quit when I learned they were paying me less than minimum wage. Then I became a domestic. I liked the family I was with. I arrived at their home at 6 A.M., helped the children get ready for school, fixed breakfast, cleaned the house, and prepared lunch for the lady of the house. After putting the dishes in the washer, my employer gave me a bus ticket and I returned home to eat, cook, and clean while Ernesto and his wife were at work.

Although life was good to me, I was unhappy. When I was 45, I went to school to learn how to become a citizen. American citizenship was important to me because I wanted a better life. Although my brothers couldn't understand what I was talking about, I knew in my heart that the joy of my life was teaching children.

Today, I am a teacher in a small country school outside El Paso. It is much like the school I taught in during my years in Mexico. So many things are the same: the greatest pleasure is watching the children come to school eager to learn. Their parents are like those of the children in Sonora. They know the value of an education. I love the classroom because I know the more children learn about others, the more they will learn about themselves.

??? *Why do you think Ester continues to teach? Can you identify with her experiences? In what way?*

 ## Defining a Profession

When you decided to become a teacher, did you think about whether you were joining a profession or developing vocational skills? You may not have given this topic much thought, other than to recognize your reaction to both descriptions.

Identifying *professionals* and defining a *profession* is complicated. While there are many definitions of professional, we want you to have a clear idea what this term means to teaching and teacher organizations.

Hallmarks of a Professional

A **professional** is an individual who performs a unique task that sets him or her apart from society. This unique task is so important to society, each individual agrees to follow a special code of ethics. The code of ethics, administered by a professional organization, guarantees that those with certain knowledge and skills meet high standards. Thus, the three hallmarks of a profession (Segall, 1967) are:

- unique knowledge and skills to offer society,
- a code of ethics agreed upon by all members of the profession,
- professional organizations

Unique Knowledge.   Unique knowledge consists of an organized set of skills and information that individuals obtain through advanced education in an accredited institution or university. These skills and information are so important to society that those who have learned them are recognized as being special. Persons who possess unique knowledge are often identified through special titles, such as *Doctor, Professor,* or *Counselor.*

Code of Ethics.   Another hallmark of a profession is that members agree they will act in a certain fashion. Each member agrees to follow a specific code of ethics. A **code of ethics** is a set of guidelines used by an organization to monitor its members, so they will maintain high standards of integrity and quality of service.

Organization.   The third hallmark of a profession is professional organizations. **Professional organizations** are associations of individuals with similar skills who agree on a specific code of ethics. Members of organizations believe they are able to maintain high standards if they voluntarily join together. Members may be disciplined if they fail to follow the profession's codes of ethics. For example, in the legal profession, applicants to the state bar association must hold a Bachelor of Law degree (LL.B) or a Doctor of Jurisprudence degree (J.D.) from an accredited law school. Members of the bar also pass an entrance examination. Members can be removed from the state bar association if they violate the code of ethics.

The Professionalism of Teachers

As you read the previous section about professional hallmarks, you were probably asking yourself whether teaching qualifies as a profession in the same sense as law or medicine.

You may have asked yourself whether the courses you are taking in your teacher education program can be defined as unique knowledge, or whether teachers have developed a code of ethics that all members of the profession adhere to. While it is true that some teacher organizations have codes of ethics which their members follow, teachers cannot be disciplined by their professional organizations in the same way as lawyers or doctors can be. Finally, you may have also wondered whether there is a professional teacher organization you must join in order to be recognized as a professional.

The answers to these three questions demonstrate that teaching has yet to become a full-fledged profession. It is still in the process of becoming a profession in the fullest sense of the term.

Ensuring the Quality of Teachers

Perhaps the major reason teaching is not looked upon as a profession is because teachers have difficulty transferring the unique knowledge learned in their teacher preparation program to their classrooms. The theoretical nature of teacher education programs is difficult for many classroom teachers to apply to the practical problems they face, many of which require immediate solutions. Another reason appears to be that many schools do not have sophisticated mentoring programs to help beginning teachers understand the practical problems of the classroom in relation to unique knowledge. It is for these reasons, we believe, that teaching remains a semi-profession.

Certification/Licensure of Teachers.   Some believe state legislatures recognize teachers as professionals through certification. **Teacher certification** legally endorses those who we call teachers to teach children. Like a driver's license, teacher certification is a privilege. State legislatures notify state departments of education of the types of curriculum teacher preparation students must possess in order to be certified in the state. The state departments of education inform universities and colleges of education.

Certification has undergone major changes recently. State legislatures have become more interested in teacher certification and, as a result, more involved in the process. Not surprisingly, teacher certification procedures vary greatly from state to state.

Presently, the terms *certification* and *license* are used interchangeably. However, there are subtle but important differences. For example, in some states a license is the final document an individual receives from the state department of education that allows her or him to teach in a classroom. In other states, such as Oklahoma, a license allows you to be employed after graduation by a local school district for a specified period of time, usually one or two years. During this period you are expected to continue to learn about teaching in a real-life classroom setting. When you successfully complete the **entry-year program**, you are awarded state certification. It is important to understand the terminology in your state.

Alternative Certification Programs.   **Alternative certification** allows college graduates to teach in classrooms even though they do not have teaching certificates. Local school districts have found alternative certification programs useful because they allow individuals who have critical skills that are needed in the classroom to be employed.

Schools are for students.

For example, as local school districts discover teaching shortages in specific curriculum areas, teachers who are certified in other academic fields sometimes are assigned to fill in either temporarily or permanently. For example, teachers with a minor in mathematics and a major in history may find themselves teaching mathematics along with their regular history assignments. Some school districts, especially in rural and inner-city areas, have discovered they may not have a certified classroom teacher available to teach students in specific academic areas. Appendix A includes a list of state offices of teacher licensure and certification and identifies the states offering alternative programs.

Professional Standards Boards

Because of the recent reform movement (which you will learn about in Chapter 13), 48 state legislatures have developed professional standards boards. (Maine and South Dakota do not have professional standard boards.) These boards have attempted to professionalize teaching by establishing a **minimum competency:** what teachers are supposed to know at a basic level. Some boards also have the power to reprimand or remove a teaching certificate from an individual found to be incompetent. The National Education Association has endorsed the professional standards board concept because it enables the NEA to monitor professional teacher standards. However, the NEA is extremely critical of the poor representation by teachers on state professional boards. In fact, only six states that have a professional standards board (Nevada, Michigan, Montana, West Virginia, Minnesota, and Oregon) have a majority of teachers on their professional state board.

National Board for Professional Teaching Standards.   While the NEA is generally critical of the lack of teacher representation on professional standards boards, it has joined the American Federation of Teachers in endorsing one: the National Board for Professional Teaching Standards (NBPTS). The majority of members of the NBPTS are teachers. The purpose of the NBPTS is to provide strong classroom leadership in explaining to states what should be the criteria for the certification of teachers. The Board also develops ideas about what the role of the teacher should be in the classroom, school, and community. The NBPTS is taking leadership both in the assessment of teacher competency and the increasing delegation of decision-making responsibility to teachers.

 ## Professional Teacher Organizations

Professional organizations are important to teachers. They have, on the whole, improved the public's perception of teachers and their importance to society. Through research, lobbying, and strikes, teacher organizations and unions have improved the quality of education children receive in our schools. They have also improved the quality of education teachers receive in teacher education programs and have helped teachers improve salaries and working conditions. While salaries are still less than what many consider a livable wage, they are more than the "pin money" teachers received not long ago. These advances have allowed teaching to be looked upon by society as a semi-profession.

Teachers have not always felt the need to organize into professional associations. It was only at the beginning of the twentieth century that teachers in the United States began to see the need to join together. Until that time, most teachers thought of themselves simply as workers who were employed by a local school board. Salaries, working conditions, and the teaching methods they were supposed to use were issues over which they had no control. Teachers felt they had little or no right to ask questions about these topics. They did not expect local boards of education or superintendents to ask them for their advice, nor were they asked. As teachers became more aware of their importance to the local community and society in general, they began to desire professional recognition, and teacher organizations began to appear. Today, teacher organizations differ according to membership, goals, and purposes. But all strive to give teachers a greater voice in their own affairs while increasing teachers' prestige and salaries. In short, the goal of teacher professional organizations is to help teachers become full professionals.

Teacher Specialty Associations.   Teacher specialty associations serve the needs of classroom teachers who specialize in a certain curriculum or in the type of children they teach. These associations can focus on the specialty area in a way not possible in a more general teacher organization. Teachers join these organizations because they give members opportunities to network with others in the same teaching field. Figure 2.1 is a partial list of national organizations concerned with specific types of curriculums and teachers.

Figure 2.1   A Partial List of Content-Specific Teaching Organizations

- American Association of Physics Teachers
- American Council on the Teaching of Foreign Languages
- American Industrial Arts Association
- American Mathematical Society
- Council for Exceptional Children
- International Reading Association
- Modern Language Association
- Music Teachers National Association
- National Association of Biology Teachers
- National Business Education Association
- National Council of Social Studies
- National Council of Teachers of English
- National Council of Teachers of Mathematics
- National Science Teachers Association

State and Local Affiliates.   Another form of teacher organization is state and local affiliates of national organizations, such as the National Education Association and the American Federation of Teachers. These organizations are important because they address the specific local problems members consider important. In essence, they are lobby groups interested in improving working conditions and salaries of teachers or changing or improving the curriculum.

Nonpublic Associations.   If you are interested in teaching in a private school, you will want to know what teacher organizations address the unique problems and interests of nonpublic school teachers. These organizations are usually financed or controlled by whatever group it is that sponsors the school. The goal of nonpublic teacher organizations, like the others we have discussed, is to improve the quality of education students receive. Organizations for parochial teachers include the National Catholic Educational Association, the Council for Jewish Education, the National Association of Episcopal Schools, and the Religious Education Association.

University Associations.   Associations that influence the professionalism of classroom teachers are also found at the university level. They attempt to influence how prospective teachers like yourself are prepared at the college level.

The Holmes Group.   One of the most influential professional organizations in education is scarcely known beyond the ranks of professors of education. Membership in the **Holmes Group** is restricted to deans of colleges of education in the United States. While this organization is very small (89 members), its influence is far-reaching. Its goals are many, but perhaps the most important is the belief that teaching can only become a profession when college teacher preparation programs improve their standards. The Holmes Group wants teacher education programs to become more rigorous and intellectually stimulating. For instance, it believes the time it takes to prepare teachers at the college level is much too short.

The Holmes Group encourages universities to develop five-year teacher preparation programs. It advances the notion that those who wish to teach should have a basic college education before they are admitted into teacher education programs. And the Holmes Group wants prospective teachers to pass a test to become a professional classroom teacher, just as the American Bar Association requires prospective lawyers to pass a test.

While you may feel the Holmes Group is primarily interested in making your life more complicated, it is extremely interested in helping teachers in their day-to-day teaching. The Holmes Group has continually called for better working conditions in our schools. This organization is extremely aware that poor physical environments are not conducive to teaching or learning. Therefore, another goal of the Holmes Group is to make schools good environments for teachers and students alike.

The National Council for Accreditation of Teacher Education.   Another organization that influences teachers is the **National Council for Accreditation of Teacher Education (NCATE).** This organization **accredits,** or evaluates the quality of, teacher education programs throughout much of the country. While the evaluation process is extremely complicated—and at the moment controversial— some evaluation criteria include the quality of the teacher education faculty, types of curricula taught to prospective teachers, amounts of money spent on teacher education by the university, and extensiveness of the physical facilities.

Every five years, NCATE sends out accrediting teams, composed of teacher education professors and administrators, to evaluate teacher education programs. If the accrediting team concludes that the teacher education program falls short of the standards set by NCATE, it can place the teacher education program on probation or remove the teacher education program from its accreditation list altogether.

Education Honor Societies.   There are three education honor societies we encourage you to consider joining: Kappa Delta Pi, Phi Delta Kappa, and Kappa Delta Gamma. These organizations are honor societies. As a student, you will be invited to join if you have maintained a GPA of 3.0 or higher (depending on the honor society). These organizations are active in educational issues at local, national, and international levels. Each organization publishes a newsletter and a journal addressing current topics in education. In addition, each sponsors several scholarships for undergraduate and graduate students. If you are not a member, contact the representative in your education department.

National Education Association (NEA)

The **National Education Association** is the largest and oldest teacher organization in the United States. Founded in 1857 as the National Teachers' Society, it changed its name to the National Education Association in 1870. While the words written in 1857 may appear old-fashioned, the NEA has never forgotten its mission:

> To elevate the character and advance the interests of the profession of teaching and to promote the cause of popular education the United States. (Myers, 1967, 387–389)

With an estimated 1995 membership of 2.3 million educators, the National Education Association has been able to establish itself as a tremendous power-house in national and state government affairs. The NEA's impact on schools and teachers is felt in every area of the country, and it is the nation's second-largest government lobby group.

What types of people belong to the NEA? As you might expect, they vary a great deal, but approximately 80 percent of all members are classroom teachers. Other members are college students, retired teachers, college professors, adminis-trators, and other types of support personnel. The NEA generally has its greatest support and most of its membership in suburban and rural America.

National Education Association Structure.

The NEA's structure is compli-cated because of affiliated organizations in every state as well as Puerto Rico. There is also an Overseas Educational Division, which represents American teach-ers in the military and large international businesses.

The NEA's national administration in Washington, D.C., consists of a board of directors responsible for carrying out the goals of the Association. This process is conducted through a series of annual summer conventions, at which more than 8,000 members gather, debate, discuss, and vote on what the NEA should do. Del-egates come from the local and state affiliates. This is known as the Representa-tive Assembly. However, the day-to-day business of the NEA is conducted by the board of directors and an executive committee headed by an executive director, president, vice-president, and secretary–treasurer. Two of the organization's most famous presidents have been Charles Eliot, president of Harvard, and William T. Harris, U.S. Commissioner of Education.

Standing committees operate throughout the year to advance the goals of the NEA. Some address the constitution, bylaws and rules of the Association. Oth-ers are concerned with the agenda of the summer convention and identifying the delegates who will attend the conference. Still other standing committees focus on such significant issues as Legislation, Women's Concerns, Student Members, and Civil Rights. These committees underscore the social and welfare problems class-room teachers experience in their daily lives.

The NEA, like other organizations, is committed to remaining in continual con-tact with its members through its publications, such as *Today's Education* magazine.

Code of Ethics.

The National Education Association Code of Ethics (Appendix B) is the official statement of the types of professional conduct the Association considers important.

The preamble of the NEA code of ethics addresses two major issues:

- The need for teachers to maintain the highest ethical standards.
- NEA's desire to provide standards by which to judge the professional conduct of teachers.

The NEA Code of Ethics outlines professional behavior towards students and other teachers, as well as the principles of fairness in the classroom. In other words, the

NEA wants teachers to understand that it favors a code of ethics to police the professional behavior of its members. The code of ethics describes how the NEA wants *you* to act as a professional.

American Federation of Teachers (AFT)

The **American Federation of Teachers** (AFT) began as a union in Chicago in 1916, with the eminent educational philosopher John Dewey as one of its first members. Many teachers at the time were leery of the AFT. Some thought it was a duplication of the National Education Association. Others were convinced professionalism and unionism were not compatible. For much of its history, the American Federation of Teachers was simply "playing catch-up" with the NEA.

It is much different now. The AFT's strength is felt throughout the nation's schools. It's aggressive efforts to represent and help teachers have, on more than one occasion, caused boards of education and school administrators to change their attitudes about teachers being submissive. At present it is affiliated with the Congress of Industrial Organizations (CIO) and the American Federation of Labor (AFL). It has approximately 780,000 members, most of whom are found in medium-sized cities and large urban areas. Led by its president, Sandra Feldman, half its membership comprises classroom teachers. The other half comprises service personnel such as cafeteria workers, bus drivers, and paraprofessionals. College professors are also active.

American Federation of Teachers' Structure.

The AFT national structure is supported by its state and local affiliates. From the very beginning, the AFT has insisted its members belong to these affiliates because they are designed to be the frontline of the union's defense to protect teachers. The AFT uses its affiliates to safeguard teachers and aggressively seek higher salaries and better fringe benefits for its members. Through its affiliates, the AFT is able to identify strong teacher leadership.

The Executive Council comprises a secretary–treasurer, president, and 38 vice-presidents. Each of the vice-presidents is in charge of specific activities the AFT considers important. Like the NEA, the American Federation of Teachers has standing committees that are specifically interested in such topics as Colleges and Universities, Special Education, Women's Rights, Retired Teachers, State Employees, and others. Its council committees are concerned with Human Rights, Legislation, Educational Research, and the organization's Constitution.

Code of Ethics.

The AFT does not have a code of ethics in the same sense as the NEA. Rather, it has a Bill of Rights and Responsibilities for Learning: Standards of Conduct, Standards for Achievement (see Appendix C). The Bill of Rights is equally concerned about teachers and students. As you read it, notice the positive manner in which the Bill of Rights affirms the concepts of student and teacher conduct and achievement.

Local and State NEA and AFT Affiliates

The American Federation of Teachers and the National Educational Association consider their affiliate organizations at the state and local levels to be the most important part of their organizations. Both organizations believe the democratic process works best at the local level, when classroom teachers come together and discuss local school problems. As we mentioned earlier, the affiliates also are proving grounds for teachers to develop their leadership skills.

Of course, topics such as **teacher welfare** (salaries and fringe benefits), educational reform, and other issues critical to teachers throughout the country are traditionally brought before the national organizations. Through this process, both organizations are able to keep in contact with classroom teachers throughout the nation.

Both the AFT and the NEA want their members to join the local and state affiliates when they join the national organization. It is through the affiliates that classroom teachers have a greater opportunity to become involved at the local, state, and national level.

Comparison of the NEA and the AFT

Prior to the 1960s, competition for members between the AFT and the NEA was not significant. Teachers' loyalty was somewhat divided between the organizations, but most teachers felt they could not be a professional and belong to the AFT—a union—at the same time. Although the AFT was aggressive in its attempts to improve teacher welfare, many teachers felt it was not professional to strike or walk a picket line. Teachers in those days, like today, wanted the public to think of them as professionals, and give them the same respect given lawyers and doctors. It was difficult for teachers to think of a union giving them that social status. Another reason teachers did not have a high regard for unionism was that some well-known union organizers, such as Jimmy Hoffa, were convicted criminals. Hoffa was seen nightly on T.V. news programs defending himself in federal courts or before Congressional anti-crime subcommittees. Teachers found it difficult to explain to their students (and themselves) how they could associate with such individuals.

Thus, the NEA and AFT attracted different types of members. The NEA appealed primarily to suburban classroom teachers, while AFT members represented urban areas. The NEA attracted administrators, while the AFT attracted cafeteria workers and school bus drivers. So, while both groups wanted to increase teachers' professional standing, each seemed to draw its strength from different groups. The question of whether teachers could belong to a union and be professionals at the same time came to a head in 1961. In what is now a famous election, New York City classroom teachers voted to have the American Federation of Teachers represent them as their sole bargaining agent in negotiations with the school board. A **sole bargaining agent** is the organization authorized to represent members and nonmembers alike when negotiating contracts with an employer. After that, the American Federation of Teachers and the National Education Association stopped publicly airing their real or imagined differences concerning union-ization and professionalism. Each got to the serious business of competing for members. Each tried to demonstrate to classroom teachers its ability to improve teacher salaries and working conditions.

In the long run, the organizations have discovered that many of their goals are similar. Shortly after the New York election, the NEA became more militant. By the 1990s both organizations were accepted by the public as teacher unions. Many are beginning to wonder whether the NEA and the AFT will join together into one large association–union: they have discussed a merger on occasion.

Problems Facing Teaching Organizations

Public Perceptions

Today's teachers are in a dilemma: As the public becomes more convinced of the need for schooling, it is becoming more divided about what type of education chil-dren should receive. When you become a teacher, you will notice parents actively supporting your role in the classroom. Yet what parents want their children to learn may be exactly opposite of what you consider important. Although parents expect schools to teach their children how to read, they are less clear about what books their children should read. They do not always trust the school to make the right choices for their children. Parents want teachers to give their children an edu-cation which can be used on a daily basis; they distrust an education that cannot be used. The noted historian Henry Steele Commager (1962) believed Americans want schools to teach children how to use knowledge, rather than to know some-thing for its own value. No wonder some teachers consider teaching stressful.

Education Goals and Expense

Closely connected to the public perception of schools is the question of how the public wants to fund schools. During the last several decades it has become clear that the United States must compete with industries in other countries around the world. International business competition engenders the public perception that schools must produce better prepared workers so American goods will be more competitive on the international market.

At present, it is estimated that 5 percent of the **gross national product** (the total cost of all goods and services sold in the United States) is allocated to schools and education. Taxpayers are looking for new and different ways to decrease edu-cation costs, and they are requiring more from teachers than before.

Improving Working Conditions

Teachers have long talked about their poor working conditions. Teachers in gen-eral lack privacy in schools. They are often restricted in their use of telephones, copy machines, faxes, and other forms of communication at the school. In some schools, teachers do not even have essential instructional supplies. Many teachers complain that the schools they teach in are dirty and unsafe. Clifford and Guthrie found:

> Polls of both current and former teachers repeatedly reveal the distressing effect of poor working conditions upon their morale and professional outlook. Arguably, teachers have the least comfortable environmental surroundings of any professional group, save possibly journalists. (1988, 27)

Teachers know their salaries are constructed differently than those of other professional groups. Teacher salaries are influenced by experience (the number of years a teacher has taught in a school district) and education (the number of academic degrees they have). Teachers also understand that their salaries are closely related to how many children are going to school. Clifford and Guthrie (1988) found that teacher salaries increase as the number of children in school increases, and decrease as the school-age population decreases. As the numbers of school-age children decreased during the mid-1980s, the beginning teacher's salary declined to approximately half that of a beginning electrical engineer (Clifford & Guthrie, 1988, 29–30).

Teacher organizations are very concerned about the nontraditional methods of paying teachers now being developed by school boards and state legislatures. One such experiment, **merit pay** or differential pay, involves increased salaries for teachers who have reputations for teaching excellence or who teach in critical areas. While many taxpayers and teachers have hailed merit pay as a good idea, few know how it should work. For example, teachers want to know what criteria will be used to differentiate a good teacher from a bad teacher. Some legislators and taxpayers suggest student test scores on state and national exams would be a good method of identifying a good teacher. Others suggest that principals and superintendents should have the responsibility for judging which teachers are good and which are not. Of course, teachers are concerned about the quality of the principals and superintendents. Who, they ask, will evaluate them? Obviously, the problem is more complicated than many wish to admit. Good teaching is difficult to describe.

Presently, schools and teaching are at a crossroads. As our society becomes more diverse, teachers will be asked to become involved in more and different types of educational activities. This requires teachers to guarantee high standards of personal and professional conduct for themselves and their fellow teachers as they interact with their clients (children).

Many teachers feel that professionalism will only come when they are included in the decision-making process of their schools. In surveys, teachers have reported that they feel left out of the decision-making process. They wish to contribute their abilities to improving the system. For example, in a study conducted by the Carnegie Foundation for the Advancement of Teaching (1987), only 20 percent of teachers believed they had contributed to decisions about how schools spent their money. Only 47 percent felt they had any say about what discipline standards should be set for students, and only 43 percent felt they had contributed to structuring staff development programs.

These issues are a reflection of how teachers are striving to become professionals in the fullest sense. Professional organizations assist in this transformation.

Our History: The Road to Professionalism

We hope as you've read this chapter your thoughts about teaching as a profession have become clearer. Next we will discuss what early teachers faced in our country and discuss the need for teachers of color in our schools today.

In the late 1800s and early 1900s, teachers thought of themselves as workers who independently contracted to teach with a local school board. Teachers seldom negotiated their salaries or their duties in those days. In fact, it was rare that teachers were even offered fringe benefits. They simply took what the local school board offered.

Teacher contracts reflected the public attitude of the day. While the public considered teaching to be very noble, they did not believe it was a profession. Most thought of teaching as a good job for a young, single woman interested in making a little money before she married. In fact, many teacher contracts specifically mentioned that when a woman married, she was expected to resign or she would be fired. School boards, usually composed of men, were only reaffirming the general public's social values when they insisted that it was unbecoming for married women to work outside the home. Among the things typically stipulated in teachers' contracts at that time were:

- Teachers may be escorted by a gentleman only in the accompaniment of a brother or father.
- Teachers who are caught smoking or drinking in public will be fired.
- Teachers will dress in colors such as gray, black, blue, or other colors befitting a lady. A teacher will not color her hair.
- School board permission is required for teachers to date a gentleman. She will be fired if her date escorts her to a movie theater or similar location.
- Teachers will attend church and teach Sunday School at the church of their choice.
- Teachers will assume the position of janitor, cleaning floors, water fountains, chalk boards, and furniture. These duties will be performed before and after school hours.

Early teacher contracts reflected the public's attitude that teachers were role models for children, not professionals. Teachers were expected to represent what "good" adults were supposed to be like. They were to reflect in their lives the noble characteristics parents wanted their children to have as adults. Sadly, while parents thought of teachers as role models, school boards usually treated teachers as children.

Since teaching in the late 1800s and early 1900s was generally considered a woman's occupation, and because social values discouraged married women from working, most teachers taught for only a few years. Only men were allowed to make teaching a career, and they were usually promoted quickly to positions as principals or superintendents. If a man insisted on remaining in the classroom, he was usually expected to teach in high school. Female teachers were traditionally relegated to the elementary classroom. They were seldom chosen by their boards of education to become administrators.

During the early years of this century, few teachers had a college education, and most people did not think of them as possessing a unique professional knowledge. Another reason why teachers were not considered professionals was that values in the late nineteenth and early twentieth centuries did not accept the idea of women as professionals. Doctors, accountants, and lawyers were considered to be professionals because they made decisions impacting adults' lives. Teachers, on the other hand, affected the lives of children. Teachers, like nurses and secretaries, were thought to be helpers. Just as the nurse helped the doctor and the secretary helped the lawyer, teachers helped parents educate their children. Female teachers received a minimum salary compared to male professionals.

 ## Our Future: Giving Hope

Our country has always been a diverse society, but we will be even more diverse in the future. However, as our school children are becoming more multicultural and multiethnic, our teachers are remaining Euro-American and middle class. Teachers of color are urgently needed to serve as role models and to bring the full diversity of American life into the classroom for *all* children, regardless of race or ethnicity or social class.

Margaret Brown is an African-American teacher who believes she has a unique opportunity to lead by example and help her students learn that people of all colors can play a role in making this world a better one. Read Vignette 2.1 to see what she has to say about teaching.

      VIGNETTE 2.1   *Giving hope: Margaret Brown*

Margaret Brown teaches at an alternative school for pregnant high school girls, J. B. Harville School Away From School in Shreveport, Louisiana.

> I had a student who, when she first came into our program, was very unconventional. She did not knock on the door. She kicked the door in. We kept her for three years. When she came to us, she could not read or write. Three years ago, she graduated from us.
>
> She came to me one day and said, "Thank you, dear lady. You have given me hope . . . I'm going to make it just because you have faith in me."
>
> And that was the moment I knew I was going to continue to do this as long as I can. She kicked the door in when she walked in, but she walked out like a lady.

Source: David Marshall Marquis and Robin Sachs, *I Am a Teacher: A Tribute to America's Teachers,* 1990.

???   *What is the ratio of people of color to Euro-Americans in your school district and in your community. What is Margaret Brown saying to you and other education students?*

A society that reflects the full participation of all its citizens will be difficult to accomplish if only one in twenty teachers is a member of a minority group. At this rate, the average child will have only two minority teachers—out of about forty—during her K–12 school years (Haselkorn & Calkins, 1993, 7).

Ever-increasing numbers of minority children are attending **resegregated schools;** schools are becoming less and less integrated (Kunen, 1996). In 1994, 35 percent of African-American students in Hillsborough County, Florida, attended predominantly minority schools; in Dallas, the average Hispanic child attends schools that are only 24.1% white; and in San Francisco, the average African-American student attends schools that are only 12.2% white (Usdansky, 1994). Yet the vast majority of our teachers continue to represent white middle-class America.

Increasing the numbers of teachers who represent the various cultures and ethnicities of the United States is an important part of the teaching profession's quest for professionalism. Just as it is important for women to become principals and superintendents so they can be decision-maker role models for girls and boys, just as it is important for male teachers to enter the elementary and preschools so they can act as models for children who have few experiences with men or father figures, so it is crucial for us to increase the numbers of minority teachers. Only in that way will teaching become a true profession, whose members can identify with *all* students.

What You Have Learned

✔ The definition of *profession* centers around the key concepts of unique knowledge, professional organizations, and codes of ethics.

✔ Teaching is a semi-profession, because it has yet to meet all the hallmarks of professionalism. For example, while classroom teachers are prepared with unique knowledge in their teacher preparation programs, they have yet to develop codes of ethics that bind them together.

✔ Teacher certification is a process in which state legislatures acknowledge that teachers must have a certain knowledge to teach in the classroom. However, teacher supply and demand allows legislatures to develop other forms of certification to allow others to teach in the classroom.

✔ There are many different types of teacher organizations. Some of them are concerned with specific academic or interest areas that help teachers in the classroom.

✔ The National Education Association is the country's oldest and largest teacher organization. It traditionally has maintained that teachers cannot be both professionals and union members. On the other hand, the American Federation of Teachers, a teacher union, has improved the working conditions, welfare, and salaries of teachers throughout the country. Presently, the NEA and the AFT have discovered that, while they may compete against each other for members, the public generally considers them both to be unions.

✔ The structure of the National Education Association and the American Federation of Teachers is similar: each has local and state affiliates. These national organizations have annual conventions or meetings at which members vote on what the association or union should accomplish each year.

✔ The American Federation of Teachers Bill of Rights and the National Education Association Code of Ethics are intended to be used by members as guides to professional behavior.

✔ The struggle for professionalism is ongoing. While today's teaching conditions are much improved, teacher organizations believe that there are problems in public perception and teacher working conditions which must be overcome before classroom teachers can be called professional in the fullest sense of the word.

✔ Just as American society is changing, so are America's teachers. Professional organizations are becoming increasingly aware of the need to encourage more people of color to become classroom teachers.

Key Terms

professional
code of ethics
professional
  organization
teacher certification
entry-year program
alternative
  certification
minimum
  competency
Holmes Group
National Council for
  Accreditation of
  Teacher Education
  (NCATE)

accredit
National Education
  Association
American Federation
  of Teachers
standing committees
teacher welfare
unity memberships
sole bargaining agent
gross national
  product
merit pay
resegregated schools

Applying What You Have Learned

1. The three hallmarks of a profession are: unique knowledge, code of ethics, and a professional organization. Explain why each is important.

2. What are the courses you are expected to take to be certified in your teacher education program? As a pre-service teacher, do you think it should be the role of your state department of education to certify you? Support your answers.

3. The American Federation of Teachers and the National Education Association are presently competing for members. Which organization do you think you will join? Why?

4. How do you think teachers should be paid? Some people believe teachers should be paid according to how well their students score on national and state exams. If you knew your instructor's merit pay increase was based on your final exam grade, how would that influence what you were expected to learn?

5. There are many problems that must still be overcome before classroom teachers are considered professionals. Which is the most important for you? Why?

Interactive Learning

1. Canvass the professors in your teacher education program about what organizations they joined and why.

2. Do you know fellow students in your teacher preparation program who represent other cultures, ethnicities or races? Interview several to discover why they want to become teachers.

3. It is expected that only one in 20 teachers in the United States will be a member of a minority group. That means the average student will have only two minority

teachers during her or his school experience. Ask several classroom teachers to react to this statement. What new thoughts did they introduce to you?

4. Find out if your state has an entry-year program as described in this chapter. If it does, describe the program. If not, does your state have a comparable program?

5. Should teacher education programs become more rigorous by offering more course work on campus or by giving students greater opportunities to be involved in real-life teaching situations prior to student teaching? Form a small group in your class and debate the pros and cons.

Expanding Your Knowledge

Clifford, Geraldine J. and James W. Guthrie. *Ed School: A Brief for Professional Education*. Chicago: The University of Chicago Press, 1988. (*Ed School* is for people who are interested in teacher preparation and how colleges of education relate to other academic departments on college campuses. It is an excellent text because it discusses teacher professionalism in relation to other fields, such as law. It talks about undergraduate and graduate programs and describes problems teacher education faces. It's a book you should read if you are interested in why we teach teachers the way we do.)

Fuller, Wayne E. *The Old Country School: The Story of Rural Education in the Middle West*. Chicago: University of Chicago Press, 1982. (A history professor, Fuller has written a delightful book explaining what it was like to teach in middle America during that period when schools had one room, teachers taught as many grades as necessary, and parents felt education was fine as long as it didn't get in the way of real life. This is a charming book about what teachers were like before they *wanted* to become professionals.)

Holmes Group. *Tomorrow's Teachers*. East Lansing: Holmes Group, 1986. (This report is an important contribution to teacher professionalization. While some of its recommendations may appear to be dated, it gives the reader an excellent point of reference from which to evaluate the education of teachers.)

Kidder, Tracy. *Among Schoolchildren*. Boston: Houghton Mifflin Company, 1989. (This book is based on observations in real life classrooms. Many times talk about professionalism drives educators to dissect teaching. Kidder puts warmth and love back into "professionalism.")

Weber, Sandra and Claudia Mitchell. *That's Funny, You Don't Look Like a Teacher*. Washington, D.C.: The Falmer Press, 1995. (This is a book about the images of teachers and teaching that infiltrate the everyday lives of children and adults, shaping in important but unrecognized ways their personal notions of who teachers are and what they do. It provides critical insight into the relationships between schooling, gender, teacher identity, and popular culture. Illustrated with color reproductions and telling excerpts from interviews and journals, this book asks provocative questions and offers insightful perspectives to teachers and students.)

Wynne, Edward A. and Kevin Ryan. *Reclaiming Our Schools: Teaching Character, Academics, and Discipline* (2nd ed.). Upper Saddle River, NJ: Merrill/Prentice Hall, 1997. (This paperback [which has a forward by James S. Coleman] states that teaching others is a moral act. Therefore, teachers teach values whether they realize it or not. A major challenge for the professional teacher, therefore, is to understand the consequences of the complicated task of teaching children.)

Part Two

Schools in America and Other Societies

In Part Two, you will learn about the historical and comparative foundations of education. In Chapter 3 you will meet several students in Mr. McCartney's sophomore American History class who are having a disagreement. Gina cannot understand why Tomas, a Native American student, and Rodney, an African American, dislike American history. Both feel their family histories have been marginalized. Gina feels Tomas and Rodney are making a big deal out of a small problem. She believes everyone should give up their past to become an American.

Gina, Tomas, and Rodney are important people for teachers to understand today. As a classroom teacher you will have day-to-day experiences with the ways schools are becoming more diverse. Chapter 3 traces the history of many of the diverse groups represented in our classrooms, highlighting events that shaped our educational system and what we want our students to learn.

In Chapter 4 you will learn about some of the more recent events that are changing our schools and classrooms. How are schools and classroom teachers expected to react to these forces? In Chapter 4 teachers Roxanne James and Aaron Black are shocked when their colleague, Kumar Singh, reacts strongly to their criticism of textbooks teaching students about other cultures. Take a few minutes to think about the people you know who represent different ethnicities, races, and cultures. What would you like to know about each individual's heritage?

Just as the United States is a multicultural society, it exists in a multicultural world. Chapter 5 discusses why students in other countries learn differently than we do. For example, students in Japan study a different curriculum than children in Mexico, England, or the United States. Teachers use different teaching methods, schools are administered differently than ours, and people view the role of schools differently. The purpose of Chapter 5 is to highlight why world schools differ and help you recognize what we can learn from them.

The Framework of Our Multicultural Nation

In Chapter 3, you will learn about our nation's history, beginning with the native people of North America. This history begins prior to the arrival of Columbus in 1492 and takes us up to the twentieth century. The history you will read in this chapter is perhaps different from the traditional histories you have read in school, because it integrates the educational histories of many people. It is essential to have a common understanding of our diverse heritage in order to appreciate the history of our educational system.

Until very recently our nation's history was Eurocentric in focus: it excluded Native Americans, African Americans, Asian Americans, and Hispanic peoples (Takaki, 1993). As a teacher, you will want to represent history within an *inclusive* context rather than an *exclusive* one. A Eurocentric focus disenfranchises *all* of us by depriving us of an awareness of the rich tapestry of our nation's heritage. In considering the history of our educational system, think about how our education system has influenced our country, what the history of education in the United States means for you as a teacher, and what it has meant for those whose history was misrepresented or was not discussed. We hope the culturally diverse history presented in this book will give you a greater understanding and appreciation of various cultures, and how each has made significant contributions to our nation as a whole.

What you will learn

- Our educational history is culturally diverse.
- Significant events and movements in our educational history shaped schools in the United States.
- Cultural and historical trends influence the purposes and objectives of education.
- You can develop a framework for understanding educational and cultural traditions and use it as a guide for making future judgments.

BECOMING A TEACHER   *Whose history?*

Mr. McCartney's sophomore American history class has just completed studying the late 1800s. Several students seem confused, but when Mr. McCartney asks for questions, the students do not raise their hands. He thinks maybe they are just tired from trying to learn the dates and has them break up into small discussion groups.

"I am really confused," says Rodney. "We haven't studied anything about my ancestors, except that they were slaves. My parents told me that African Americans fought in the Civil War and that some were involved in education and other important things."

"I understand what you're saying," replies Tomas. "This class has made my ancestors look like savages who only wanted to kill 'the white man.' My grandparents often tell of the great leaders in my tribe and in other tribes."

"Well, I sure don't understand why you guys are so upset. Everyone is an American, and we're learning American history," retorts Gina. "My ancestors aren't identified by their nationality. What's the big deal anyway? Either you're an American or you're not. Why should your ancestors get more attention than mine?"

"Boy, you just don't get it, do you?" answer both Rodney and Tomas. "All we talk about are your ancestors, because they all came from Europe and they are white. You don't think it's a big deal, because *you* are included. How would you feel if you weren't part of the story like us? Bet you wouldn't like that one bit!"

Maria joins in the discussion. "I really understand what you're saying, Rodney and Tomas. My ancestors lived in Texas long before 'Americans,' but suddenly we found ourselves outsiders in our own land when the United States decided to take over that part of Mexico. I resent only hearing one side of my history."

Mr. McCartney overhears this discussion and thinks about how most textbooks present only one side of American history. He realizes that many of his students are excluded in the traditional perspective of American history. He decides to discuss this situation with other teachers in the department to see if they have encountered similar discussions and to learn what they have done to resolve the issues.

???   *Reflect on this conversation. What is the major theme of the discussion between Rodney, Tomas, Gina, and Maria? What happens to a culture, race, ethnicity, or gender that is not included in the history of our country?*

Historical Roots of Education

Two important European reform movements (the Renaissance and the Reformation) had significant and long-lasting effects on education both in Europe and America.

The Renaissance

The **Renaissance** (or rebirth) began in the 1200s and lasted until the start of the Reformation in the 1500s. During the Renaissance, religious points of view were replaced with secular ones. This approach, sometimes called **humanism,** made man, not God, the focal point of art, literature, and the government. The Renaissance movement revived an interest in Greek and Roman civilization.

In about 1445, Johann Gutenberg invented a printing press that enabled the production of manuscripts (including the Bible) at a reasonable cost. Prior to this, priests transcribed manuscripts by hand, and few common people had access to them. Thus, common people were able to read and think about the Bible for themselves, instead of relying on scholars to interpret information for them.

A leading writer of this period, Erasmus (1466–1536), developed a humanistic theory of education, which he outlined in two major texts, *Colloquia Familiaria* and the *Gargantua*. Erasmus, and other humanists of this period, believed people should be educated. At this time, the Catholic church had almost absolute control over Western Europe, and many clergymen opposed the education of the masses. Indeed, the Renaissance was the first time large numbers of people questioned the authority of the church. But it was not to be the last.

The Reformation

A religious reform crusade known as the **Reformation** began in the mid-1500s. In 1517, a German monk named Martin Luther posted his Ninety-five Theses attacking certain practices of the Catholic Church. One fundamental difference between the religious reformers and the Catholic Church concerned education. The Church held that the priest should act as an intermediary between God and the average person. Martin Luther argued that the average person was saved directly by faith; thus an intermediary (the priest) became an impediment. Because Luther felt people needed direct access to the Bible, he believed the average person needed to be able to read. Luther translated the Bible from Latin into German so more people would have access to the scriptures.

Martin Luther and other reformers soon came to stress the need for universal education. (At the time, "universal" education included only men. Women were expected to rely on their fathers or husbands to interpret the Bible for them.) Protestant groups in Germany and throughout Europe established educational programs for rich and poor children alike. Do you see the influence the Reformation had on education not only in Europe, but also in America?

The Americas during the Renaissance and Reformation

During the Renaissance and Reformation in Europe, the Americas were populated by **indigenous** (or native) peoples numbering 15 to 25 million. About 5 million people lived in the area now called the United States (Lyons & Mohawk, 1992;

Takaki, 1993; Weatherford, 1988; Zinn, 1980). Prior to the arrival of northern Europeans in the 1600s, many Native American nations had stable social structures, healthy populations, political and economic independence, and a structured educational system (Lyons & Mohawk, 1992).

We often hear America described as a "virgin land," meaning it was unpopulated and untouched by people (Josephy, 1992). This description completely excludes the indigenous (native) peoples of North America and perpetuates the myth of Euro-American superiority. As you can see in Table 3.1, the indigenous peoples of the "New World" made numerous contributions.

The indigenous peoples of the Americas influenced our modern democratic society in ways which have only recently been discovered and acknowledged. For example, the League of the Iroquois was founded between 1000 and 1450 A.D., under a constitution called the *Great Law of Peace*. This constitution served as one

Humboldt fragment XVI: Aztec hieroglyphics.

Table 3.1

Examples of Indigenous Peoples' Contributions Prior to 1492

Indigenous peoples' nations	Contributions
Incas	Engineering, architecture, cultivation of various plants for food and medicine
Mayans	Astronomical observatories, solar calendars
Anasazi/Hopi	Developed agricultural methods for desert southwest
Inuits	Developed survival methods for the Arctic
Lakotas	Developed significant political confederations
Haudenosaunee	Laid foundation of principles of democracy and freedom
Iroquois	Laid foundation for U.S. Constitution

Source: Data from "American Indians in the Past" by Oren Lyons from *Exiled in the Land of the Free: Democracy, Indian Nations and the U.S. Constitution,* O. Lyons and J. Mohawk, eds., 1992, Santa Fe: Clear Light Publishers. Copyright © 1992 Five Rings Corporation. Reprinted by permission of Five Rings Corporation.

of the models for the U.S. Constitution (Lyons & Mohawk, 1992; Weatherford, 1988). For example, the United States Congress allows only one person to speak at a time—an Iroquois political custom. Another important political institution borrowed from the Iroquois is the caucus. Although many believe the word *caucus* is Latin in origin, it is actually derived from the Algonquian language and means to meet informally to discuss a problem without needing to vote *yes* or *no* on the issue (Weatherford, 1988). Iroquois women had the right to vote and played a major role in their nation's political structure.

The indigenous peoples were faced with the same basic questions we are:

- How and where should they live?
- How would they feed and protect themselves?
- How and who should govern?
- What should their children be taught?
- How should they transmit ideas, traditions, values, skills and knowledge to the next generation?

Native Americans depended primarily on oral traditions to express their deepest beliefs, thoughts, and values. Ceremonies formed the basis for social order and

The Great Tree of Peace, planted by the Iroquois prophet Deganawidah to foster peace among the five founding nations of the Iroquois Confederacy, or Haudenosaunee—the Mohawk, Oneida, Cayuga, Seneca, and Onondaga.

Source: Painting by Chief Oren Lyons from *White Roots of Peace: The Iroquois Book of Life*, ISBN 0-940666-30-8, Santa Fe: Clear Light Publishers.

individual integration into the order. This was similar to the use of ceremonies by many European nations.

Vignette 3.1 is an example of a story that is hundreds of years old and that has been passed from one generation to another through the art of storytelling.

VIGNETTE 3.1   *The arrow maker*

If an arrow is well made, it will have tooth marks upon it. That is how you know. The Kiowas made fine arrows and straightened them in their teeth. Then they drew them to the bow to see that they were straight.

Once there was a man and his wife. They were alone at night in their tipi. By the light of a fire the man was making arrows. After a while he caught sight of something. There was a small opening in the tipi where two hides were sewn together. Someone was there on the outside, looking in.

The man went on with his work, but he said to his wife, "Someone is standing outside. Do not be afraid. Let us talk easily, as of ordinary things." He took up an arrow and straightened it in his teeth; then, as it was right for him to do, he drew it to the bow and took aim, first in this direction and then in that. And all the while he was talking, as if to his wife. But this is how he spoke: "I know that you are there on the outside, for I can feel your eyes upon me. If you are a Kiowa, you will understand what I am saying, and you will speak your name." But there was no answer, and the man went on in the same way, pointing the arrow all around. At last his aim fell upon the place where his enemy stood, and he let go of the string. The arrow went straight to the enemy's heart.

Source: "The Becoming of the Native: Man in America before Columbus" by N. Scott Momaday from *America in 1492: The World of the Indian Peoples Before the Arrival of Columbus,* A. M. Josephy, Jr., ed. 1991, NY: Alfred A. Knopf, Inc. Copyright © 1991 by The Newberry Library.

???   *As you read this story, think about its meaning. What do the arrows symbolize? Does the arrow maker vanquish his enemy through the use of arrows or language? How might Mr. McCartney, the teacher in the U.S. History class at the beginning of this chapter, use this story in his teaching?*

First Colonial Schools

Most historians believe numerous peoples discovered the Americas prior to 1492, but it was not until the arrival of the Spanish that the New World became the object of European curiosity and a popular land for exploration. Beginning with Columbus's landing in the New World, and followed by Cortez's and Pizarro's defeat of the Aztec and Incan empires, and the Conquistadors' Mexican settlements, much of the vast territory now known as the United States was swiftly explored in search of precious metals, gold, and silver. During the process of exploration, the Spanish brought both their culture and their schools to the New World.

Schools That Preceded the English Model

Like other European nations during the sixteenth century, Spain believed it was obliged to help Native Americans appreciate the European or "civilized" world. Priests who came with the Spanish conquerors believed they had a mission to convert Native Americans to Catholicism. As the priests established missions (often to protect the Indians from the ravages of the Conquistadors), they included schools to educate the Indians in both agricultural and vocational skills.

However, **ethnocentrism,** the practice of evaluating another race and/or culture using the criteria of one's own culture, prevented the Spanish colonists from understanding and appreciating the potential contributions of the indigenous peoples. Lyons and Mohawk (1992) believe that this ethnocentrism blinded the Spanish to the legitimacy of the Native Americans and their contributions. In other words, the colonists' ethnocentrism caused them to see Native Americans as different from themselves. They were unable to see the wealth of knowledge Native Americans could have shared with the colonists.

Colonial Schools Modeled After Those in England

The east coast of America was settled primarily by the English in the Southern and New England colonies. A number of different nations, such as Belgium, France, Italy, and others, settled the Middle Atlantic colonies. Because of these diverse influences, each colony's approach to education was different. As we discuss the factors that were involved in developing each colony's primary educational philosophy, think how the influence of that educational approach may be felt today.

Southern Colonies.   Settlers arrived in Jamestown, Virginia, in 1607. These settlers wanted to replicate the institutions of England as closely as possible. These were people who had left England for economic, not religious, reasons, and they saw no need to change the English system, which favored the landed gentry or aristocrats. The gentry devoted themselves to business and the growing of crops on their plantations.

In the beginning, the settlers expected Native Americans would work on their plantations plowing, planting, and harvesting crops. When the Native Americans refused, the settlers brought the first African slaves to Virginia in 1619. There is some question as to whether these Africans were indentured servants or slaves. In either case, the colonists soon entered the slave trade, and the colony's slave population grew from about 2,000 in 1670 to about 150,000 a hundred years later (Elson, 1993). As we will discuss later, slavery had serious consequences for our educational system.

The South, comprising such colonies as Virginia, Maryland and the Carolinas, was a mirror of conservative England. Like their English counterparts, the Southern planters knew well their sons' need for education in order to run government and business affairs of the South. (Girls were not educated for fear they would take on masculine characteristics.) During the 1600s, Southern society was dependent on England for the education of its youth. Young graduates of Oxford and Cambridge were hired as tutors for children of the aristocracy. Just as if they lived in England, boys were drilled in the elements of Latin, reading, writing, and other subjects. Many of these young men went on to attend the best universities in England, returning to the colonies ready to take on the cares and duties of leadership. Some free schools, financed by wealthy plantation owners or merchants, were established in the southern colonies, but, in the majority of the southern colonies, formal education was nonexistent for the lower class.

By the late 1600s, the landed gentry no longer wanted to send its sons to England for completion of their education. So in 1692, the College of William and Mary was founded in Williamsburg, with a typical English curriculum. It soon developed a curriculum more in tune with the needs of its gentlemen students. By introducing new courses in the arts and sciences and experimenting with new teaching methods, William and Mary quickly gained a reputation for excellence.

The college originally invited male children of prominent Native American chiefs to attend a preparatory school which had been established for their education. Assuming the Native American families would value the same type of education as the colonists, college administrators were shocked to discover these parents were displeased with their children's education. Especially, the parents were horrified to discover that professors were responsible for hosting all night drinking sessions at local "pothouses" or taverns (Meyer, 1967, p. 81). Thus the College of William and Mary had the distinction of being the first American school at which the parents questioned the value of their children's classroom experiences!

Unlike the New England and Middle Atlantic colonies, the Southern colonies did not develop consistent educational practices. The landed gentry believed that all private citizens were responsible for the education of their own children. There were some exceptions to this, including the regulation of apprenticeship programs and the efforts of philanthropic or religious societies on behalf of the poor. Table 3.2 offers a comparison of educational patterns in the colonies. As you can see, some practices were uniform throughout the colonies, while others were unique to a specific area.

Middle Atlantic Colonies.   Unlike the Southern and New England colonies, the Middle Atlantic colonies were noted for their extraordinary diversity. The first people to settle this area, now known as New York, New Jersey, and Pennsylvania, were from Belgium, quickly followed by the Dutch, English, Irish, Scandinavians, French, Italians, Portuguese, and Spanish. Within this gathering of various cultures, the Dutch outnumbered the others. Although the Dutch Reformed Church was the major theological establishment in the Middle Atlantic colonies, others soon appeared, including the Huguenots, Baptists, Quakers, Lutherans, Catholics, and Presbyterians. Even small numbers of Jews and Puritans were represented. In other words, the Middle Atlantic colonies were ethnically, linguistically, culturally, and religiously diverse. This diversity was in direct contrast to the religious and cultural homogeneity of both the New England and Southern colonies. Schools in the Middle Atlantic colonies reflected the multicultural heritage of the original settlers. The diversity of languages, cultures, and religions engendered an intellectual freedom and tolerance of different perspectives.

Because of the diversity of the population, many different types of schools were established in the Middle Atlantic colonies. Intellectual freedom was greater there than in any other region of the New World. The Middle Atlantic colonies did not have a rigid class structure (like the Southern colonies) or a dominant and controlling religious structure (like the New England colonies). As a result, many types of schools were established. Some schools were supported by churches. Others schools were developed by individuals who responded to social demands that children learn a trade.

Table 3.2
A Comparison of Educational Practices Among the Colonies

Colonies	Type of school	Characteristics
Southern	Tutorial Schools	Primarily for landed gentry. Curriculum for boys: Classics (including Latin and Greek), surveying, and mathematics. For girls: French, music, dancing, "Polite Manners."
Southern	Old Field School	Local elementary school maintained through private support (usually in an unused field house; hence the name). Operated only a few months out of the year. Curriculum: reading, writing, and arithmetic.
Southern Middle Atlantic New England	Dame School	Beginning classes held in a woman's home. Operated only a few months out of the year. Curriculum: Basics of the alphabet, some reading, and prayers.
Middle Atlantic	Quaker Schools	Apprenticeship training for teachers. First school for freed slaves. Curriculum: Reading, writing, arithmetic, some bookkeeping. Students included the poor, females, and African Americans, as well as males.
Middle Atlantic New England	Latin Grammar	Secondary schools preparatory for college. Curriculum: Focused on classics. Upper-class white males were primary students.
	Common Schools	Available to working class. Curriculum: Writing, arithmetic, reading, navigation, surveying, and mathematics.
Middle Atlantic New England	Academies	Vocational in nature. Curriculum: Navigation, merchandising, trade, business, as well as reading, writing, and arithmetic.
New England	Reading/Writing	Small schools. Curriculum: Rudiments of reading, writing, and religion.
	Charity Schools	Run by missionaries for poor children. Curriculum: reading, writing, arithmetic, and religion.

New England Colonies.   The South mirrored much of traditional English society; New England did not. These colonists had left England to escape religious persecution and to establish communities which they believed would be better than those they had left in England.

The New England colonists probably had the most profound impact upon our educational system. The Puritans believed that people were basically evil, and that a person's nature had to be controlled. Because of this belief in "man's depravity," Puritans believed specific efforts were needed to bring people to salvation. They established elementary schools for the express purpose of overcoming idleness and showing people the way to salvation. The Puritan ethic stressed education as a means of ensuring that children would grow up to be literate, God-fearing, hard-working, frugal, industrious, and law-abiding adults. The school was the method by which the Puritans guaranteed their children were brought up properly.

Unlike the Middle Atlantic colonies, the New England colonies were homogeneous in language, religion, and culture. In these colonies the church and state governed jointly through the use of public disapproval, whipping, banishment, and fines. Conformity in behavior and belief was expected of all people, including children. Puritans advocated this close relationship between church, state, and schools because they believed education was critical for salvation. This belief was derived from Martin Luther, who had advocated education because each person was responsible for his or her own salvation. Every Puritan was expected to be able to read and understand the Bible. Of equal importance to education was the Puritan idea of the child. The Puritans believed that children were born in sin and that their behavior needed to be molded through the use of corporal punishment (Fleming, 1933).

The typical New England school offered the basic curriculum of reading, writing, arithmetic, and religion. Children learned to read by memorization, first learning the alphabet, then words, and finally sentences. Since there were no chalkboards,

The *New England Primer* reflected the grim Puritan outlook and focus on religion as the point of education. Other early American textbooks reflected the importance of moral character and national pride.

A In *Adam's* Fall
We Sinned all.

B Thy Life to Mend
This *Book* Attend.

C The *Cat* doth play
And after flay.

D A *Dog* will bite
A Thief at night.

E An *Eagles* flight
Is out of fight.

F The Idle *Fool*
Is whipt at School.

students used a horn book or slate, and instead of a pencil, they used a stylus. The curriculum was narrow, limited, and moralistic. Children of various ages were grouped together in one classroom, and a whipping post was standard equipment. Puritan philosophy called for literally "beating the devil" out of the child. Equal emphasis was given to the Four R's—reading, religion, writing, and arithmetic—and to the shortness of life, the torments of hell, and the damnation of the soul. A widely used schoolbook first published in 1690, *The New England Primer,* was often called New England's Little Bible because it illustrated the close relationship between education and religion in the Puritan settlements.

The Puritans believed both in parliamentary rule and in the Christian duty of educating children. They enacted laws requiring children to be educated, but left the details of education up to the local community. This influence is felt even today: our education system is still characterized by school districts that have local autonomy.

Two legislative acts in the Massachusetts Bay General Court became the model for public education from that time forward. The first was the **Massachusetts Act of 1642,** which made the education of children a responsibility of the state. This law mandated that parents assume responsibility for educating their children. Prior to this, parents could choose whether they wanted their children to be educated at home or in school. But church and civic leaders believed many children were receiving an inadequate education at home, and both groups understood that organized schools would strengthen and preserve Puritan religious beliefs. The Massachusetts Act of 1642 was the first educational law in this country, and a landmark decision.

The Puritans found this act was not being enforced, and in 1647 the General Court passed the second major legislation to impact education, the **Massachusetts Act of 1647,** also known as "the Old Deluder Satan Act." This piece of social legislation stated that education was required so children would not fall into the clutches of Satan. This legislation is significant in our educational history because it gave communities control of their schools through financing teacher salaries, purchasing educational supplies and materials, and setting up the curriculum. The legislation provided that:

- Townships of fewer than 50 householders were required to financially support the school in the nearest township.
- Townships of more than 50 householders were required to appoint someone to teach reading and writing to all the children who wanted to learn.
- Townships of more than 100 households were required to have a Latin Grammar School, to prepare young men for entering a university.

Another major influence of the New England colonies on modern education was the requirement that public schools be supported by taxes. In 1648, the first property tax to support education was levied in Dedham, Massachusetts. By 1693 New Hampshire required towns to support elementary schools through taxes. The taxes were used to pay teacher salaries and construct school buildings. Other monies came from tuition fees, which were universal in the New England colonies.

The New England colonies greatly influenced our present educational systems by legislating that all children attend school and leaving educational administration up to local communities. They created compulsory education, local autonomy, district schools, taxation, and separate educational levels (Pulliam and Van Patten, 1995). These factors are still evident in our approach to education.

The Revolutionary Period

By 1750, just 150 years after the first colonists landed in the New World, the 13 independent colonies were searching for common ground. The population had grown to more than 2.5 million, of which one-fifth were slaves or indentured servants.

The Native American population, unlike the European and African populations, was decreasing. This decrease was due to several factors. First, the colonists brought diseases from Europe, like measles and smallpox, that decimated whole Native American tribes. Second, the colonists' ethnocentrism prevented them from seeing the valuable contributions Native Americans could make. The settlers wanted land that belonged to the Native Americans, and they took this land by force. Those Native Americans who were not killed by disease or war were forced to move farther west. Native Americans discovered early on that the settlers did not want to share the land with them (Lyons & Mohawk, 1992; Takaki, 1993; Zinn, 1980).

By the 1780s, the frontier was expanding. People were moving westward. Colonists moved down the Ohio River and through the Cumberland Gap into Kentucky and Tennessee. Land was abundant and, best of all, it was free. Many felt the thrill of being independent from the governmental authority of the colonies.

In the late 1700s, a dual system of education was prevalent in the colonies: members of the upper class enjoyed a good education while the poor received little or none. Because of the need to educate people in practical matters, Latin Grammar Schools began to decline while vocational academies, such as Franklin's Academy, became more popular. The educational institutions moved from focusing on the elite to educating the majority in the fledgling country.

Legislation Affecting Education

Although our early leaders believed education was important, they did not specifically mention it in the Constitution. That omission explains why control of education has remained with the states ever since.

Laws Affecting Education at the National Level.   Before the U.S. Constitution was ratified, the Continental Congress, under the Articles of Confederation, enacted the Land Ordinance of 1785 and the Northwest Ordinance of 1787. These acts advocated education as "necessary to good government and the happiness of

mankind" and detailed a division of land to provide monetary support for schools (Gutek, 1992).

Land Ordinance of 1785.   The **Land Ordinance of 1785** detailed how the land west of the Alleghenies, north of the Ohio River, and east of the Mississippi was to be regulated. The land was to be laid out in townships made up of 36 sections, each section being 1 square mile. The 16th section of each township was reserved for the support of schools in each township. This legislation would set the stage for the public school movement in the next century.

Northwest Ordinance of 1787.   The **Northwest Ordinance of 1787** mandated that the 29th section of each township be reserved for the support of education. The significance of the Ordinance is that it recognized education at all levels as important to the maintenance of democracy. Therefore, two years later, as the framers of the United States Constitution were debating federal involvement in education, a tradition had been established in which that government would indicate a commitment to helping citizens learn. Such was the spirit in which the Morrill Act (1862), the Smith-Hughes Act (1917), and the G.I. Bill of Rights (1945) were written.

Educational Laws at the State Level.

As our nation grew, many states mentioned education in their constitutions. For example, North Carolina, Pennsylvania, and Vermont established schools in each county with some financial support from the state. Pennsylvania required the state to pay teacher's salaries. Massachusetts codified its tradition of the local district system and chose to admit girls. New York made public lands and other funds available to free schools.

Leaders in Education

Many of the men who were involved in the birth of the United States believed that only an educated populace could support a democracy. But views about how the populace was to be educated illustrated the divergence among the young nation's leaders. Table 3.3 lists the major influences on education up to the twentieth century.

George Washington.

George Washington believed gentlemen should have the kind of classical education offered at Oxford or Cambridge in England, or Harvard or William and Mary in America. He did not find the Constitution binding on African Americans, Native Americans, or women.

Thomas Jefferson.

Jefferson believed that his greatest achievement was in the field of education. As a student at William and Mary, he saw the need for well-educated citizens. His **Virginia Plan,** although never adopted, was the first attempt to achieve mass education for a colony. The plan also advocated decentralized control and localized financial responsibility. Although Virginia did not

Table 3.3

Historical Events and Leaders of Importance to Education 1500s–1895

Year	Event
1520s	Spanish settlements in North America
1607	Jamestown established
1619	African slaves brought to Virginia
1620	Plymouth Colony established
1636	Harvard College was the first college in North America
1642	Massachusetts Compulsory School Law
1647	Old Deluder Satan Act
1690	*New England Primer*
1692	College of William and Mary established in Virginia
1701	Yale established
1746	Princeton established
1751	Franklin's Academy in Philadelphia—an alternative for schooling for the middle class
1754	Columbia established
1755	College of Philadelphia established
1764	Brown established
1766	Rutgers established
1769	Dartmouth established
1776	Declaration of Independence
	Thomas Paine's *Common Sense*
1780	English Sunday School founded by Robert Raikes
1783	Revolutionary War ended
1785	Northwest Ordinance
1787	Constitutional Convention
1789	Constitution accepted without mentioning education
1791	Bill of Rights ratified
	Philadelphia Sunday School Society
1798	Joseph Lancaster and Andrew Bell start monitorial schools
1819	Emma Willard pushes for educational opportunities for women in New York
1821	First public high school opened in Boston
1825	Noah Webster's *The American Dictionary* is published
1836	*McGuffey Readers* published
	Oberlin College established in Ohio, first coeducational college
1837–1848	Horace Mann calls for sweeping reforms based on principles of universal free education
1839	First normal school established in Lexington, Massachusetts
1852	Massachusetts enacts first compulsory school attendance law
1854	Lincoln University, first college for free African Americans, established in Pennsylvania
1860	Elizabeth Peabody opens first English-speaking kindergarten in Boston
1861–1865	The Civil War
1862	Emancipation Proclamation
	Morrill Land-Grant College Act passed
1874	Kalamazoo Case established the use of local taxes for funding of high schools
1892	Committee of Ten

adopt his plan, it became the model for other states' educational plans. Jefferson later single-handedly established the University of Virginia, which was chartered in 1825.

Noah Webster.   Many believed that a new and unique language needed to be developed for America. A primary force in this development was Noah Webster, who maintained that the development of a unique American language was the means by which Americans could achieve cultural identity and unity. To facilitate the development of this unique language, Webster wrote *The American Spelling Book* and the *American Dictionary.*

Women and Minorities.   We have already said that formal education, beyond rudimentary reading and writing, was limited mainly to white, upper-class males. For example, parents were required to teach reading and writing to their sons, but only reading to their daughters. Beyond reading, a formal education was not generally available to women, slaves, or Native Americans. Not long after the Revolutionary War, many states began to codify prohibitions against the education of slaves and Native Americans (Cremin, 1980).

 ## Immigration, Citizenship, and the Role of Education

Immigration was modest at the beginning of the nineteenth century. Only about 4,000 people, excluding slaves, entered the United States annually (Elson, 1993). Remember, the African population was increasing at a higher rate than the Euro-American population. In 1790, a federal law was passed that limited naturalized citizenship to white persons only. This prohibited freed slaves or Black indentured servants from becoming citizens of the United States. This legislation also prevented other minorities, such as Native Americans, Hispanics, and Asians, from applying for citizenship, until it was repealed in the twentieth century (Takaki, 1992). But it wasn't until the 1820s and 1830s that immigrants began flooding into the United States, bringing with them cultures and languages quite different from those who were native born.

Schools were seen as the appropriate means by which to "Americanize" the new immigrants. Schooling was the way in which the majority of people could achieve full benefits of a democratic society. The principles of freedom and equality outlined in our Constitution supported freedom of speech and a free press. These principles pointed out the need for *all* people, not just the wealthy, to receive an education. Through education, American culture and values could be transferred to the newcomers as well as succeeding generations.

The need to educate children who represented so many different cultures and traditions raised several significant social and economic issues. Communities used local taxation to start schools or to expand them. Influential citizens were elected to local school boards and these boards employed teachers (some of whom were women). New immigrant children came to the schools (most of which were one room) to study and learn with others. Using such texts as Noah Webster's *American Spelling Book,* teachers instructed their charges in the mysteries of new words (memorization was the teaching method), new ideas (America is the best place to live in the whole world) and new friends.

Bright young minds found learning a new language fascinating. Within two generations, American English was the spoken tongue of most Americans. Through education, immigrants were able to assimilate the same history and literature of the United States as their schoolmates whose families had come to these shores in colonial times. However, it was the process of deciding what children should learn (curriculum), who should teach children, and who should pay for education that became the focus for educators and taxpayers alike.

The Effect of Industrialization on Schools: Educating the Masses

In the early 1800s, it was clear the United States would become an industrial giant. The nation was moving from a rural-agricultural economy to an urban-industrial economy, and the need for workers seemed never-ending. While the South remained agrarian and the West continued to expand, it was the Northern states such as Massachusetts, New York, Pennsylvania, and Connecticut that grappled with the questions of mass education. These states—which had the greatest populations located in the largest cities—were first to address the need for mass education. It was in these major cities, such as New York, Philadelphia, and Boston, that workers demanded the development and advancement of public schools. These workers believed that schools would provide a ladder by which people could climb socially and economically.

Public Support.   During this period before the Civil War, the majority of citizens moved away from the belief that education was a private, rather than a state, function. People who still advocated a private approach believed that voluntary or philanthropic schools, such as the Public School Society of New York, were the best way to educate lower-class children. Voluntary schools tried to provide basic literacy and character education for poor children, but they were unable to meet the needs of the working-class people, who began to call for tax-supported schools.

Others wanted government to provide an education to their children. They believed every person should be taxed to support the education of all children. Out of this belief developed a general public policy that education should be free and supported by taxes, that curriculum should be the same for all students, and education should be practical.

There were several educational responses intended to educate the various cultural groups in America's early industrial years. Many of these attempts, discussed in Table 3.4, were modifications of European educational plans.

Table 3.4
Educational Responses to Mass Immigration

Type of school	Characteristics
Infant School	First developed in England by Robert Owen. Boston opened the first Infant School in 1816, for children ages 4 to 6. These schools were open year-round and employed mostly women. Curriculum: Moral, physical, and intellectual instruction.
Sunday Schools	Established by private charity organizations for working-class children and orphans who worked in the factories and mines during the week. Curriculum: Basics of reading, writing, religion, and character formation.
Monitorial System	Adapted from England in the early 1800s. Using a minimum teaching staff assisted by students, lessons based on memorization were provided to large groups of young children.

The population was growing at a fantastic rate—because of tremendous growth within the nation and vast numbers of immigrants. Factory workers demanded better educational opportunities for their children, but opportunities for education actually decreased. As factories grew, they often employed entire families. In many cases, children began working at age eight. For example, in New England in the 1830s, 40 percent of the work force was under sixteen.

Common School Movement

The challenge of educating a growing population was left to state and local governments. Historically, the development of public schools is referred to as the **common school movement.** The movement's goal was to build schools in every community that offered a basic curriculum of reading, writing, history, geography, arithmetic, physical health, penmanship, and grammar.

Many states set up permanent school funds for educational support. However, reliance on these funds impeded efforts to get strong tax support from the local community. Beginning in the 1830s, states passed legislation allowing local districts to use tax monies to support schools.

Primary schools were established to provide basic reading and writing skills to young children. These schools, based on the infant school model, were taught by women and eventually were combined with grammar schools. Combining the primary and grammar schools created the eight-year elementary school which is still common in the U.S. By 1850, 45 percent of our country's children attended school.

The High School.   The English Classical High School opened in Boston in 1821. It was renamed the English High School in 1824. Adopting a shorter name, the **high school** admitted qualified elementary students and provided them with a three-year (later four-year) educational experience that, when completed, met

college entrance requirements. Students were required to meet specific academic entrance standards and pass exit examinations. Since elementary schools educated children for the first eight years of their academic career, high schools referred to their first year as the "ninth grade" and the last year as the "twelfth."

Educational Leaders Who Led the School Reform

Such educational giants as James Carter and Horace Mann of Massachusetts and Henry Barnard of Connecticut led reform movements in state governments to develop educational agendas. They were advocates of the common school and believed the common school should emphasize basic skills as well as community values, fitness, observations, and contemplation. Carter, Mann, and Barnard showed educators how to build a strong state-wide system of schools based on local control and state support.

Reform leaders were not limited to men; certain women were leaders in the establishment of advanced education for females. However, the majority of women in the United States did not participate in schools beyond learning the rudiments of reading and writing. However, by the mid-1800s, a number of colleges opened their doors for women in the South and West. The first coeducational program was offered at Oberlin College in Ohio in 1838, followed by Antioch (1852) and Iowa (1856). By the 1860s, Vassar, Smith, Wellesley, and Bryn Mawr offered a college education to women equal to the best offered and available to men (Meyer, 1967; Pulliam and Van Patten, 1995; Solomon, 1985).

Formal education for Native Americans was practically nonexistent. Although missionaries had established schools for Native American children, they were unsuccessful because the teachers did not understand—and were not trained to teach—Native American culture.

Native Americans were provided *some* opportunities to learn Euro-American traditions; African Americans were not. Although a small number of freed African Americans were able to attend Quaker schools in the North, most states disapproved of slaves learning how to read or write. After Nat Turner's rebellion in 1831, most Southern states specifically prohibited the education of African Americans. In spite of these difficulties, several educators made it their goal to provide educational opportunities for African Americans during this period.

In spite of the many prohibitions against educating African Americans, several schools were established for the education of African-American children in the early 1800s. A school was opened in 1807 in the District of Columbia for African Americans, but it wasn't until 1824 that this school had its first African-American teacher, John Adams. Myrtilla Miner established an academy for African-American girls in 1851 in Washington, D.C. Although we think of the North as more liberal than the South, Indiana and Illinois required schools only for white children (Pulliam & Van Patten, 1995). Prudence Crandall encountered major problems when she allowed an African-American girl to enter her boarding school in Canterbury, Connecticut. When Euro-American parents removed their daughters, Crandall recruited more African-American children to keep her school open. In 1820,

Boston opened its first primary school for African-American children. During this period, a few African-American colleges were established, including Lincoln University in Pennsylvania (1854) and Wilberforce College in Ohio (1856).

Henry Barnard.   Henry Barnard (1811–1900) almost single-handedly developed a state department of education in Connecticut. In 1867, he organized what is now known as the United States Department of Education. Barnard was a leader in educating teachers, establishing fair compensation for teachers, and writing about educational issues. In fact, Barnard's greatest accomplishment lay in his ability to arouse public interest through the distribution of information about education. For these reasons, Barnard is often called the father of American school administration.

Catherine Beecher.   Catherine Beecher (1800–1878), the sister of Henry Ward Beecher and Harriet Beecher Stowe, advocated women's education. She lashed out at the idea that women were only good for housework, and strongly supported nursing and teaching as appropriate occupations for women. In 1828, she opened a Female Seminary at Hartford, where she attempted to promote her views. She spent her life working for the creation of more and better schools for young women.

James Carter.   James Carter (1795–1845) is known as the father of the Massachusetts school system and of **normal schools** (post-secondary schools that taught teacher education). He was primarily responsible for legislation that provided for public school education in Massachusetts. Carter also attempted to establish public normal schools to train teachers and helped set up the Massachusetts state board of education (1837). In these ways, he made a significant contribution to the belief in a democratic education for all people, regardless of wealth or social class.

John Chavis.   Chavis, born a free man in the late 1700s in North Carolina, served as a role model for other African Americans during a difficult and dangerous part of their history. Chavis was helped by sympathetic Euro-Americans to obtain an education and attended Princeton. Later, he became a successful teacher of the white upper class.

Frederick Douglass.   Douglass was born a slave in 1817 in Maryland. He later ran away and began talking to abolitionist groups about being a slave. He dedicated his life to improving African-American lives, especially through education.

Mary Lyon.   Mary Lyon (1797–1849) came from a working family; as a result, she focused on education for the working-class woman. She envisioned a college for women on the same academic level as colleges for men. In 1837 she established Mount Holyoke Female Seminary in Massachusetts. She was so successful with her original 80 students that she had to turn away 400 applicants the next year for lack of space.

Horace Mann.   Horace Mann (1796–1859) was the common school movement's strongest advocate. Along with James Carter, he persuaded Massachusetts to develop a state board of education, then served as Secretary of Education for the next twelve years. During Mann's tenure as Massachusetts Secretary of Education, he wrote twelve annual reports which detailed how schools could be improved. Mann was able to accomplish many things during his lifetime, including obtaining support for liberal taxation which provided better teacher's salaries and new school buildings. He also organized the first three normal schools in our country and established fifty new high schools. Mann believed schools could be used to improve social conditions and provide opportunities for members of the lower social class to better themselves.

Sequoya.   Sequoya (Se-kwo-ya) (1760?–1843) was born in eastern Tennessee, into a prestigious family that was highly regarded for its knowledge of Cherokee tribal traditions and religion. As a child, Sequoya learned the Cherokee oral tradition; then, as an adult, he was introduced to Euro-American culture. In his letters, Sequoya mentions how he became fascinated with the writing methods Euro-Americans used to communicate. Recognizing the possibilities writing had for his people, Sequoya invented a Cherokee alphabet in 1821. With this system of writing, Sequoya was able to record ancient tribal customs. More importantly, his alphabet helped the Cherokee nation develop a publishing industry, so newspapers and books could be printed. School-aged children were thus able to learn about Cherokee culture and traditions in their own language.

Sojourner Truth.   Sojourner Truth (1797?–1883) was born into slavery as Isabella Baumfree. In 1827, she was freed and became a leading abolitionist and a prominent advocate for the rights of all women. She worked extremely hard to increase educational opportunities for African Americans. She is widely known for her statement: "I have borne thirteen children and seen them most all sold off into slavery. . . . And ain't I a woman?" (from a speech in Akron, 1851).

Emma Hart Willard.   Emma Hart Willard (1787–1870) started a seminary for girls at Middlebury, Vermont, in 1807. However, she is best known for her establishment of the Troy Female Academy in 1821. She believed women should have the same privileges and opportunities as men, including the chance to study science, mathematics, geography, and metaphysics.

 # American Education: 1850–1900

The Civil War was America's largest and most destructive war. It raised social, political, and economic issues that are still with us today. The Civil War changed how Americans perceived themselves and their world. Although many expected the Emancipation Proclamation to fundamentally improve social and educational conditions for African Americans, they soon found it did not. For example, when

Congress granted former slaves the full rights of citizenship (Civil Rights Act of 1866), the South chose to ignore the legislation by denying its constitutionality. Two years later, the Fourteenth Amendment to the Constitution was passed, but the southern states refused to ratify it. It was then Congress enacted the Reconstruction Acts of 1867. In retaliation, states passed Jim Crow laws which were purposely designed to refuse African Americans the rights of citizenship. For example, Jim Crow laws prohibited African Americans from riding in the same railway cars or drinking from the same water fountain as whites. As recently as the 1950s, African-American men in some states were prohibited from having their hair cut by white barbers. African Americans were often deprived of an education or sent to inferior schools because it was assumed they could not learn.

The Civil War and Its Consequences for Education

The Civil War interfered with educational reform both in the North and the South. In the North, schools remained open in spite of a reduction in funds and teachers. However, southern schools were devastated by the war. The southern states were left in physical and economic ruin: farmlands destroyed, cities burned to the ground, industries wiped out, and the work force either dead or demoralized. The destruction of the South's agrarian economy effectively stopped the ability of the public there to fund schools.

The common school movement, so prevalent in the North, was rejected as a Yankee idea in the South. The major question for the South was whether African-American children were to be granted access to public schools on free and equal terms with Euro-American children or educated separately. Should African Americans study the same subjects as Euro-American children, or should they study something more practical like industrial arts or homemaking? Educational leaders disagreed on the answers to these questions.

Education of African Americans

Oddly enough, the most significant impact on Southern education came from two northern millionaires, George Peabody and John Slater. They established trust funds for the promotion and encouragement of intellectual, moral, and industrial education among the young and destitute of the southern and southwestern states (Meyer, 1967). It was this flow of money that offered African Americans an education and made it possible for many African Americans to become teachers.

Samuel Armstrong, a general during the Civil War, wanted African Americans to have a basic education. It was his intent to supply former slaves with practical and useful information so they could solve everyday problems. He opened the Hampton Institute for African Americans in 1868, with an emphasis on farming, manual arts and crafts, and, in some cases, the art and science of teaching. Much of Armstrong's work might have gone unnoticed except for a graduate of Hampton Institute, Booker T. Washington.

African-American Leaders in Education.   Many African-American leaders attempted to help African Americans receive an education. George Washington Carver, William Du Bois, and Booker T. Washington each had different ideas about the education of African Americans.

Booker T. Washington (1856–1915).   Washington influenced education for African Americans for years. He focused his ideas on basic or vocational training, not higher education. Washington believed African Americans did not need a liberal education, which included Latin and Greek. He advocated the teaching of "practical learning" so they could be more useful to themselves and society. He founded the Tuskegee Institute in Alabama in 1880 and presided there until 1915. Tuskegee Institute offered vocational education for about 30 different industries. It also had special classes in cookery, a night school, and a home for its teachers' children.

George Washington Carver (1864–1943).   Like Sojourner Truth, Carver was born a slave in Diamond, Missouri. In spite of having to work in the fields, Carver managed to complete high school by attending at night. After graduating from Simpson College in Iowa, the only job he was able to obtain was as a janitor at what is now Iowa State University. While working as a janitor, he earned a degree in agricultural science and then earned his master's degree from Iowa State, where he became a faculty member. He became Director of Agricultural Research at Tuskegee Institute, where he dedicated his life to bettering the position of African Americans through education and to improving the economy of the South through soil improvement and crop diversification.

William E. B. Du Bois (1868–1963).   William E. B. Du Bois, who held a Ph.D. from Harvard University, was a major critic of Washington's "practical learning." Du Bois argued that being subservient to Euro-Americans gained African Americans nothing. He also believed that without the right to vote, nothing would change for African Americans. After earning his Ph.D. from Harvard, Du Bois taught, first at Wilberforce College in Ohio and then at Atlanta University in Georgia. He later became director of research for the National Association for the Advancement of Colored People (NAACP) and editor of its magazine *Crisis*. Du Bois believed in the power of education to overcome inequality.

How Were Native Americans Affected by the Civil War?

After the Civil War, the majority of Native Americans were relocated by the federal government to reservations, which were designated by the federal government as Native American land. The Office of Indian Affairs, established in 1819, was responsible for the reservations and the people who lived there.

Native Americans continued to be viewed by Euro-Americans as savages to be conquered or destroyed. They were subjected to rigid reformatory discipline and required to learn vocational skills, farming, and the American language. It was thought that Native Americans needed to be "civilized," and they were required to denounce their heritage and embrace the Euro-American culture.

To better control Native Americans, boarding schools were established on the reservations. Parents were forced to send their children to these boarding schools, often far from home, to learn "the white man's ways and language." These boarding schools continued well into the twentieth century. However, some Native Americans attended the Hampton Institute, and in 1879, a Native American vocational school was established in Carlisle, Pennsylvania.

Growth of Public Schools

After the Civil War, Americans generally agreed that public schooling should be free and available to all peoples. Our nation adopted a **single ladder system** of education, under which any person could begin his or her education in the first grade and continue through college. In theory, a child could begin at the lowest level and proceed as quickly and as far as his or her abilities would allow. Common elementary schools became a reality for the majority of Americans.

Kindergartens.
Elizabeth Peabody established the first American kindergarten in Boston in 1860. **Kindergartens,** which were first developed by German educator Friedrich Froebel, were designed to nurture the growth of young children through activities such as play, songs, and stories. It wasn't until the late 1960s and early 1970s that kindergarten was incorporated into most public school systems.

Kalamazoo Case.
The 1874 **Kalamazoo case** established the first public secondary school supported by locally collected taxes. Three Kalamazoo, Michigan, taxpayers sued to stop the school board from collecting and using taxes to support the high school. The Michigan Supreme Court decided in favor of the school district and held that high schools were common schools—an essential connection between elementary schools and state universities. This case set the precedent for states to levy taxes to support public high schools.

Committee of Ten.
Differences regarding secondary school standards, curriculum issues, and educational philosophies caused the National Education Association to appoint a **Committee of Ten** in 1892. This committee tried to clarify the purposes of the high school and made the following recommendations:

- High school should consist of grades 7 through 12
- Courses should be arranged sequentially
- Students should be given very few electives in high school
- One unit, called a Carnegie unit, should be awarded for each separate course that a student takes each year. The course must meet four to five times each week for the year.

Growth of Higher Education

Colleges and universities expanded during the late 1800s. Prior to the Civil War, universities did not allow students a free selection of courses. In the late 1800s, most universities moved to requiring some courses, while allowing a greater selectivity among the rest of their classes. Graduate programs were established at many universities, and departments of education were instituted at several major universities.

The Morrill Acts.   In 1859, Senator Justin Smith Morrill presented legislation that would offer public lands to the states for colleges. These colleges would specialize in areas of agriculture and mechanical arts. The Land Ordinances of 1785 and 1787 had already established the use of federal lands for schools and colleges. Although there was widespread support for this legislation in Congress, President Buchanan vetoed it. Congress passed it again in 1862 and President Lincoln signed it into law. **The Morrill Act of 1862** gave 30,000 acres of public land to every state for each one of its senators and representatives. At least one college in each state was to specialize in agriculture and mechanical arts, hence the name, *A.&M. colleges*. In 1890, a second Morrill Act was passed, which increased funding for this process.

Segregation and Schools: The End of the Century

Communities with large African-American populations eventually developed two educational systems, one for Euro-American children and another for African-American children. These segregated schools, especially in the South, gave little encouragement to African-American children. It was not uncommon for these schools to have few or no textbooks, poorly educated teachers, and no supplies or facilities. Especially in the South, a rigid racial segregation system of separate schools and transportation facilities was instituted through state law. The segregation laws enacted by the states denied African Americans the legal rights of American citizens.

Plessy v. Ferguson.   In 1892, Homer Plessy, a 23-year-old African-American shoemaker in New Orleans purposely rode in a railroad car reserved for whites from New Orleans to Covington, Louisiana. He wanted to test the constitutionality of the Separate Car Act the Louisiana legislature had passed in 1890. He was arrested and appeared before Judge Ferguson, who ruled that Plessy was guilty and should pay a $25 fine. In 1896, the **Plessy v. Ferguson** case was heard by the United States Supreme Court. The primary issue in this case was whether Homer Plessy's rights, privileges, immunities, and equal protection under the Fourteenth Amendment had been abridged by the state of Louisiana. The Court ruled against Plessy, establishing a precedent of **de jure segregation,** or segregation through law. The *Plessy v. Ferguson* decision affected all aspects of the lives of African Americans. In this way, the United States Supreme Court established the precedent of "separate but equal" facilities. The Court ruled that separation by race—or segregation—was *not* discriminatory as long as racially separate facilities were equal.

African-American children attended segregated schools at the turn of the century, as shown in this 1883 woodcut.

This decision had profound consequences for the education of African-American children. It legitimized segregation by law *(de jure)* and by practice **(de facto segregation)**. African-American children were branded as inferior, while Euro-American children were valued as superior. Today it is clear that the practice of separation based upon race is destructive to *all* people regardless of race, ethnicity, culture, or gender. Sixty years were to pass before this U.S. Supreme Court decision was reversed. Our nation continues to suffer from the consequences of the 1896 *Plessy v. Ferguson* decision.

What You Have Learned

✔ Two important reform movements, the Renaissance and the Reformation, had significant, long-lasting effects on education.

✔ Native American societies were complex and diverse in their organizational struc-

tures before Europeans landed here. They utilized oral traditions of education, rather than the written word.

✔ The arrival of the Spanish in the Americas opened the continent for exploration by Europeans. The Spanish brought their culture and schools to America by the beginning of the 1600s, even before the English colonists.

✔ The southern colonists tried to replicate the English system of life as closely as possible. They established an agrarian economic base, began importing slaves to work the land, and promoted education for the sons of the landed gentry.

✔ The Middle Atlantic colonies were extraordinarily diverse, which led to the establishment of both private and parochial schools. The Middle Atlantic colonies established the first academy for the vocational education of students.

✔ The New England colonies were established by the Puritans. They passed the first legislation in the colonies mandating compulsory education with local control.

✔ Schools were not a priority on the frontier: the settlers needed to till the land first, in order to survive. Women and minorities were not educated, because society believed they had no use for education.

✔ Schools were viewed as the best way to "Americanize" new immigrants to the United States. Webster advocated a New American language as a way to bring everyone together.

✔ Education was viewed as important in the 1800s, but the approach to education varied by region. There were two major philosophical approaches prior to the Civil War: (1) education was a private rather than a state function, and (2) public schools were to provide a sound education to all.

✔ By the mid-1800s, several colleges were established for the education of women. This education was focused on traditional women's roles: nursing and teaching.

✔ Education for Native Americans and African Americans was practically nonexistent from the 1600s on. In many states, there were prohibitions against education of African Americans.

✔ After the Civil War, African Americans continued to be denied an education. Booker T. Washington and W. E. B. Du Bois advocated education for African Americans, but the 1896 *Plessy v. Ferguson* case established segregation through the law. This "separate but equal" argument allowed for and encouraged racial discrimination.

✔ During this period, Native Americans were being forced to give up their native lands and herded onto reservations. They were to be "Americanized" by the schools in rigid, even cruel, ways.

Key Terms

Renaissance	Virginia Plan
humanism	common school
Reformation	movement
indigenous	high school
ethnocentrism	normal school
Massachusetts Act	single ladder system
of 1642	kindergarten
Massachusetts Act	Kalamazoo Case
of 1647	Committee of Ten
Land Ordinance of	Morrill Act of 1862
1785	*Plessy v. Ferguson*
Northwest Ordinance	de jure segregation
of 1787	de facto segregation

Applying What You Have Learned

1. How has your original understanding of history changed since reading this chapter?

2. What is important for teachers in our culturally diverse society to understand about children of color? What do you think we can learn from each other's cultural history? How can we use this to enhance our teaching styles?

3. Compare and contrast the educational approaches in the New England, Middle Atlantic, and Southern colonies. What effect has each of these approaches had on cur-

rent educational systems? Have our educational needs changed?

Interactive Learning

1. Interview several teachers about how they value children's ideas, values, and personal priorities because of their cultural history. From your interviews, describe how you would approach this in your classroom.
2. In the past, girls were not educated for fear they would take on the masculine characteristics of their brothers. In a small group composed of both men and women, debate this issue. Begin with the statement, "At one time girls were not educated the same as boys, but today it is different."
3. Sometimes circumstances outside school impact education, such as the case of Louisiana's Separate Car Act mentioned in this chapter. Through role playing, develop a Supreme Court with nine judges, as well as attorneys for the prosecution and defense. After your "Supreme Court" rules on the case, discuss why it arrived at its decision. For example, did the decision agree or disagree with the 1896 *Plessy v. Ferguson* ruling?
4. Reread Washington's thoughts about who should be educated. Why do you think he felt gentlemen should be educated and others not? Write a letter to Washington explaining what your education would be like if his ideas were still considered appropriate today.

Expanding Your Knowledge

Bennett, Lerone, Jr. *Before the Mayflower: A History of Black America,* 6th edition. New York: Penguin Books, 1993. (An excellent account of the struggles and triumphs of African Americans. This book traces Black history from its origins in western African, through the transatlantic journey that ended in slavery, the Reconstruction period, the Jim Crow era, and the civil rights upheavals of the 1960s and the 1970s, culminating in an exploration of the complex realities of African-American life in the 1990s.)

Lyons, Oren & John C. Mohawk, eds. *Exiled in the Land of the Free: Democracy, Indian Nations, and the U.S. Constitution.* Santa Fe: Clear Light Publishers, 1992. (Lyons and Mohawk cogently chronicle the influence Native Americans have had on the development of democratic tradition in Western culture and the inspiration they provided for the writing of the United States Constitution and Bill of Rights. They present a view of history that sheds new light on old assumptions about American Indians and the beginnings of democracy.)

Morgan, Harry. *Historical Perspectives on the Education of Black Children.* Westport, CT: Praeger Publishers, 1995. (A superb description of historical perspectives related to the education of Black children, including their heritage, their family and community, and institutions of learning. Morgan discusses the complex interactions between Blacks and Whites, and the roles enacted by philosophers, theorists, and practitioners in this process.)

Pulliam, John D. & James Van Patten. *History of Education in America,* 6th edition. Upper Saddle River, NJ: Merrill/Prentice Hall, 1995. (An excellent overview of the history of American education, with a broad base of facts and excellent resource materials.)

Solomon, Barbara Miller. *In the Company of Educated Women.* New Haven: Yale University Press, 1985. (An excellent discussion of the history of women in education in the United States. Solomon explores the connection between education and choice in women's lives and how this influences change for women and for the country.)

Zinn, Howard. *A People's History of the United States.* New York: HarperRow Publishers, 1980. (A brilliant and moving history of the American people, from the point of view of those who have been exploited politically and economically and whose plight has been largely omitted from most history texts.)

Chapter 4

Coming of Age: Education in the Twentieth Century

Now that you have studied the roots of education in the United States we want to focus on how schools continue to struggle to reflect a pluralistic society and, at the same time, prepare children to live in an increasingly complex world. You may notice this contemporary history is different from others you have read.

Today's teachers face problems that are similar to those teachers faced in the seventeenth and eighteenth centuries. We all want to provide the best education for our children. In this chapter, we will learn how technology, international events, and immigration are changing our nation and how our schools reflect these changes.

What you will learn

- Technology is changing our culture, and that change is reflected in schools.
- International events have caused Americans to become more aware of their cultural diversity.
- Reforming schools is important to the education of our children.
- Schools must react to the conflicting demands placed on them by an increasingly multicultural society.

BECOMING A TEACHER   *We are all Americans*

It's lunchtime and several teachers are discussing problems they are having in their classrooms.

Roxanne James says, "I'm so frustrated. I'm supposed to be teaching sixth grade science, but many of my students have trouble understanding their assignments because they don't read or speak English very well."

Aaron Black agrees with Roxanne: "Not only do my students speak English poorly, when I've met with their parents, I find they don't speak English at all!" Jose adds, "I don't think my students or their parents want to be Americans—they cling to their old ways. I remember my parents telling me how they had to change so we would fit in."

Bill Neilson asks, "Have you seen the new textbooks we've been assigned to use next year? They're supposed to help us integrate a multicultural approach in all our classes, but I'm really upset by all the emphasis on multiculturalism. I thought

America was a melting pot. Our grandparents didn't want to be separate from the mainstream. They learned English and what the current customs were. They wanted to become Americans."

Roxanne adds, "Now Hispanics and Native Americans want us to include them in the history of America. Everyone knows this country was settled by the English and others from Northern and Western Europe. I'm just tired of all the fuss and furor over inclusion of minorities."

Kumar Singh walks into the room. "I'm confused," he says. "I thought diversity was appreciated in this country—that's why I came here. I find it exciting to learn all I can about my students' backgrounds. Besides, I thought the Native Americans were here first and everyone else came later."

Aaron listens intently, "Maybe you're right, Kumar. I guess I hadn't really thought about how diverse we all are. I certainly don't want to deny my heritage and neither do any of you."

???   *Reflect on your personal cultural heritage. What do you think makes an American? Is it important to recognize and validate the cultural diversity of students?*

Roxanne, Aaron, Bill, and Kumar are expressing their very personal feelings about being an American. Roxanne, Aaron, and Bill believe new immigrants should follow the same paths to citizenship that their parents or grandparents did when they first came to this country. That is, they want new citizens to reject their old culture so they and their children can fit into a Euro-centered American society. Yet when faced with Kumar's comments about diversity and what it means to him as a teacher and new American, Roxanne, Aaron, and Bill find it impossible to deny him his own personal heritage.

Becoming a Teacher describes the dilemma our society has about what classroom teachers should teach children about themselves, their community, their state, and their nation. Like all teachers, Roxanne, Aaron, Bill, and Kumar understand that education consists of more than children sitting in classrooms, patiently waiting to be taught. Rather, they recognize that teaching and learning are very personal experiences that enable adults and children to change.

 ## Into the Twentieth Century

As you read in the last chapter, the *Plessy v. Ferguson* decision (1896) found that state laws mandating "separate but equal" accommodations for African Americans were reasonable. In making this decision, the Supreme Court allowed public facilities, including schools, to be segregated. While all children had the right to an education, the U.S. Supreme Court interpreted that the Constitution did not require all children to attend the same school. The question of how to include children from different races, genders, and social classes has remained a dilemma for educators throughout this century.

Prior to World War I, Americans had very little need to travel. Most lived on farms or in small rural communities. In many ways, people's lives were centered around their families, farms, and communities.

World War I was an extraordinary cultural and social experience for our nation. It forced us to learn about ourselves and people in other countries. It changed the way we lived. Industrial growth created large numbers of jobs in cities across America, and thousands of agricultural workers left the land for better wages in fast-growing urban areas.

Urbanization and Migration

To better understand the consequences of industrial growth, let's look at some of the major changes in urban areas of the Midwest and Northeast during the early years of the twentieth century. For example, in Chicago, the population of African Americans more than doubled between 1910 and 1920. In 1910, 44,000 African Americans were living in Chicago, but by 1920 their population had increased to 109,000. Detroit's African-American community increased from 5,000 in 1910 to

African-American children picking cotton in the 1920s.

40,800 in 1920. During the same period, Cleveland's African-American population increased from 8,400 to 34,400, and New York's African-American population increased from 91,700 to 152,000 (Lemann, 1991).

African Americans moved from the South to Northern cities between 1910 and 1930 (Lemann, 1991; Takaki, 1993). Usually, these migrants were young men who had lived and worked on plantations or as sharecroppers. As they became settled in the North, their families would follow. Men were moving north to find any type of unskilled work in factories and women were finding jobs as domestics. African Americans moved to the cities because of economics. In the South, they lived in abject poverty, and they believed that, in the North, many opportunities existed to pursue a better way of live.

Immigration.   Cities were growing for other reasons as well. While African Americans were migrating within our nation's boundaries, increasing numbers of immigrants from Asia and Mexico were coming to American cities looking for work. By 1924, 380,000 Japanese had immigrated to Hawaii (then a territory) and the U.S. Mainland.

Immigration from Europe decreased because of the war. In 1914, the first year of the war, 1,200,000 Europeans came to these shores. In 1918, the last year of the war, only 110,000 immigrated to the United States (Takaki, 1993).

Immigrants from Europe arriving at Ellis Island, 1909.

Hispanic immigrants crossing into El Paso, Texas.

Hispanic Americans.   Like African Americans, Hispanics found work as miners, cowhands, railroad laborers, servants, seamstresses, and factory workers. Between 1910 and 1920, approximately 170,000 Hispanics arrived in the United States, mostly from Mexico. To give some perspective to that number, only 25,000 Mexican citizens moved to the United States during all of the previous decade (Takaki, 1993). In 1920, 95 percent of the Hispanic community living in El Paso held manual labor jobs. Seventy percent of the Hispanics living in Los Angeles were unskilled workers. The salary for a Hispanic seamstress in Los Angeles in 1918 was $3 a day, or approximately $936 a year. At the same factory, an Anglo seamstress earned $4 a day, or approximately $1,248 a year.

Impact of the War on Schools

As soldiers returned home from World War I, the demographic change began to accelerate. Just as African Americans, Hispanics, Asians, and others were moving to urban areas, so did the veterans. Students attending elementary and secondary schools represented all social classes and races, especially in major urban areas. Education was critical to the new city dwellers. Many jobs now required people to have an education beyond elementary school. Parents began to expect their children to continue their education into senior high school. By the 1920s, 30 of the 48 states required students to remain in school until the age of 16 (Krug, 1972).

Smith–Hughes Act.   The **Smith–Hughes Act** (1917) was passed at the end of the war to help educate secondary school students. Its purpose was direct and simple: the federal government would give grants to rural secondary schools to develop programs in agricultural education and to urban secondary schools to teach vocational skills. Since technology and urbanization was changing the way families lived, the Smith–Hughes Act also encouraged secondary schools to develop programs in home economics. The federal government had long assisted higher education (the Land Ordinance of 1785, the Northwest Ordinance, the Morrill Act), but this was the first time local secondary schools received direct aid.

Home economics students were usually girls, who were taught how to manage homes, develop a budget, cook, and sew. The vocational and agricultural education programs were primarily directed to boys, who were taught skills that would help them in the expanding automobile factories of Detroit, the railroad yards of Kansas City, the stockyards of Chicago, or on the family farm. Gender roles were clearly defined during this time: men were expected to have a job, and women were expected to stay at home and raise children.

The Smith–Hughes Act was a phenomenal success. For decades, federal monies have supported secondary programs in the fields of homemaking, agriculture, and vocational education. The federal government continues to help secondary students through such legislation as the **Perkins Vocational Education Act** (1984), which extends federal assistance to single parents, people with disabilities, and incarcerated citizens.

Cardinal Principles of Secondary Education.   In 1918, the National Education Association formed the Commission on the Reorganization of Secondary Education to answer the question, "What should secondary schools teach students so they can succeed in a society becoming more urban and industrial?"

The Commission's findings were published as seven principles, called the **Cardinal Principles of Secondary Education.** The Commission intended the seven Cardinal Principles to be ideals upon which learning could be based. The Commission was not asking schools to work towards specific goals, but to use the Cardinal Principles as axioms to evaluate what they were teaching in relation to the ideal of "complete living." The idea of **complete living** was that secondary education should give students sufficient skills and knowledge to lead a full life after graduation. In the past, secondary schools had focused on students who wanted to go to college. The recommendation of the NEA Commission on the Reorganization of Secondary Education changed that focus. Now, all students were to receive an education, whether they were planning to go to college or work in industry. The Commission believed secondary schools were important because every child—regardless of his or her place in society—had a right to succeed in a changing world. The NEA's seven Cardinal Principles of Secondary Education pertained to:

1. *Health*. Schools should collaborate with parents and the community in promoting healthy life-styles. Schools should teach students the fundamentals of being healthy and physically fit.

2. *Command of Fundamental Processes.* The basic skills taught in elementary school should be continued in secondary school. Urban life requires more knowledge and skills than can be taught in eight grades.
3. *Worthy Home Membership.* Students should be made aware of the qualities and responsibilities required to participate in and benefit from family life.
4. *Vocation.* Individuals must have employable skills and understand the importance of work if they are to have successful lives and be productive members of an industrial society.
5. *Civic Education.* Civic education should be taught so students can become productive citizens of their neighborhoods, communities, states, and nation. Students should also learn about international problems.
6. *Worthy Use of Leisure.* Education should not just be for work. People should also be encouraged to use their leisure hours productively. In order to live a complete life, students should be taught to appreciate life.
7. *Ethical Character.* While teachers cannot teach ethical character, they should model it—through proper selection of curriculum, teaching methods, and social contact with students.

School Reorganization

At the end of World War I, schools were typically divided into grade schools (now called elementary schools) and high schools (secondary schools). Students generally remained in grade schools for eight years, learning reading, writing, and arithmetic as well as art, music, and physical education. They then entered high schools, which were four years in length.

High School Programs.   While there were differences among the states, all students took basic courses in mathematics, sciences, history, and English. Then, in most states, students focused on one of four programs.

A college preparatory program, the most prestigious, gave students who were planning on attending college a strong academic background in English, history, mathematics, sciences, and foreign languages.

The second program, business education or commercial program, focused on training young women who wanted to enter the work force as secretaries or stenographers. Students learned a variety of practical office-related skills, such as bookkeeping, shorthand, typing, letter-writing, and filing.

The third program was vocational education (in urban areas) or agricultural education (in rural areas). This program was intended for boys who wanted to join the work force or manage the family farm. Vocational courses included woodworking, drafting, and mechanical repair. Agricultural education included courses in animal husbandry, land management, and agricultural economics.

A fourth program was offered in some secondary schools. This general studies program was for students who clearly knew their academic career would end after high school, had no interest in the other programs, but planned on working.

Home economics was taught to satisfy girls who were not interested in becoming secretaries.

Junior High School.   In Chapter 3 you learned that the Committee of Ten (1892) recommended the development of six-year secondary schools. The Committee found that senior high schools did not have sufficient time or expertise to help entering ninth graders make choices or help them adjust to an environment that was different socially and academically from elementary school.

To solve this problem, elementary schools were reorganized, to offer six, not eight, years of study. Secondary schools were also reorganized to last three years: Grades 10, 11, and 12. In junior high—Grades 7, 8, and 9—teachers were to help students become more aware of their talents and abilities.

The first junior high school opened in 1907 in Berkeley, California. In the beginning, the junior high schools appeared to meet both the academic and social needs of students. Yet they were not without problems. As will be discussed later in this chapter, the junior high school eventually gave way to the middle school during the last part of the century.

Educational Testing

Perhaps one of the most important educational influences of World War I was the intelligence test. The war had given psychologists an opportunity to test large numbers of individuals in a controlled setting. Army psychologists developed intelligence tests and administered them to young men as they were inducted into the military. For the first time, intelligence tests were administered on a large scale.

In 1895, a French lawyer, Alfred Binet, and his medical doctor colleague, Theodore Simon, developed a test they thought could identify a person's **intelligence quotient** or **I.Q.** Psychologists in this country were anxious to learn whether it was actually possible to measure a person's intelligence. Because the Binet test was concerned with French culture, a professor at Stanford University, Lewis Terman, published a revision intended to reflect American culture, the Stanford–Binet, in 1916.

The Stanford–Binet (and the other tests that soon followed) proved indispensable to schools as well as to psychologists. Intelligence testing was a routine part of the educational process by the 1940s. But as you will read later in this chapter, critics have voiced concern about the validity and reliability of these tests and their use in schools.

Compulsory Attendance

Secondary school was becoming a required academic experience by the 1920s. Junior and senior high schools were expanding, as more elementary students continued their education and immigrants increased urban populations. In 1920, 2.5 million students, or one-third of all 14- to 18-year-olds in the nation, were attending secondary schools. By 1930, all 48 states had **compulsory attendance laws** designed to keep students in schools. The length of the school year and compulsory attendance laws differed widely between states from a low of three months in Mississippi to a high of 172 days in Massachusetts. Not until the *Brown v. Board of Education* Supreme Court case (1954) was it illegal for states to require African Americans to attend separate schools, so it is difficult to know how long African-American children attended school.

It is easier to understand the importance of secondary schools to compulsory education when we study the 1940 census. The median education of those who attended school prior to 1940 was 8.4 years. In fact, 3.7 percent of all citizens had never attended school, and only 4.7 percent had graduated from college (Debo, 1949). The continuing proliferation of junior high schools allowed the senior high schools, secondary schools with Grades 10 through 12, to focus on the older adolescent. To encourage and keep students in school, secondary schools had to meet the needs of all students, regardless of their interest in going to college or entering the world of work. Of course, this did not include African Americans, Native Americans, or other non-white Americans.

Education Reform Movements

Comprehensive Education

The **Progressive Education Association** was founded by university professors in 1919. Public school teachers and administrators soon joined the association, which strived to advance the cause of comprehensive education. The idea of **comprehensive education** was that secondary schools should meet the needs of all students, whether they were preparing for college or the workplace.

These reformers, including John Dewey and William H. Kilpatrick, insisted that traditional schooling was much too regimented. They believed teachers were more interested in having students memorize facts than helping students understand what the facts meant. The Progressivists wanted schools to be child-centered. Dewey, Kilpatrick, and others believed the traditional method of teaching forced students to be passive participants in the learning process. Students were not allowed to ask questions or take charge of their education, because many teachers were dictatorial in the classroom. The teacher's total reliance on textbooks meant students seldom were able to express their own ideas. The reformers insisted that the reason children didn't like school was that it was so different from their lives and experiences, in which they were able to ask questions, solve problems, and use their imagination.

You can see that the Progressives understood the revolutionary impact World War I had on American society. They believed that if our nation was to remain a democracy, schools would have to help children learn freely. They felt if schools allowed children to learn naturally, children would naturally discover how exciting learning was. These ideas are expressed best in their 1944 statement of basic purposes, issued when the Association changed its name to the American Educational Fellowship.

The Association's basic purposes speak clearly about the importance of schools, curriculum, and children. For example, it believes all children should be given equal opportunity to learn, that all children should be allowed to advance as far as their abilities allowed them. The Association, now Fellowship, insisted schools were significant to American society and that quality teachers should be encouraged to continue in the classroom. The Association understood that the curriculum of the school was significant to both students and society. Therefore, students who have graduated from high school but elected not to attend college should be allowed to enter youth programs designed to help them become part of the adult community. School equipment should be used by the community after school hours. All of this was to help schools cooperate with all segments of the community, demonstrate social leadership, and participate in educational research and experimentation (Meyer, 1967).

Teacher Education

The steady increase in students attending schools had a direct impact on teacher education. Demand for teachers, especially in rural areas, was extremely high. State departments of education granted many beginning teachers, usually young girls, temporary or emergency certificates based on passing an examination after a year or two of college.

During the nineteenth century, many states had developed normal schools. These colleges taught the elements of teaching to young women who wanted to become teachers. Teacher education was limited to teaching students how to be authoritarian teachers in structured classrooms, favoring memorization and sarcasm as teaching techniques. As more students of varied abilities and cultures entered normal schools at the end of the nineteenth century, teaching became less autocratic.

Teacher education textbooks were also changing. Faxon's (1912) text, *Practical Selections,* attempted to give normal school students a more kindly introduction to education. Her text included examples of the best classroom teaching experiences of teachers who had contributed to the journals *Normal Instructor* and *Primary Plans* at the turn of the century.

> Teachers need to know that scarcely any credit attaches to teaching bright pupils. The teacher's great opportunity lies in awakening into life the latent germ of some slow soul. The teacher's attitude toward his pupil must be a perfectly frank, honest one that will beget confidence. It should be full of sympathy and should stimulate the child to do his best always. It should inspire respect for teachers and self-respect at the same time. Anything that might prevent these things should be avoided. Sarcasm is one of the instruments used by teachers that will prevent the existence of good relations. Sarcasm destroys any respect a pupil may have either for the teacher or for himself. It leaves a bitterness and a sting from which the pupil never recovers. (F.A. Cotton, State Superintendent of Indiana as quoted by Faxon, 1912, p. 11)

Women's Medical College of Pennsylvania anatomy class, composed entirely of women, dissecting cadavers, circa 1900.

Faxon mirrored the more progressive teacher education curriculum then coming into vogue. Teacher education students were taught "gateway courses," which usually included educational principles and values, educational philosophy, child study, school organization, and methods of teaching in elementary and secondary school (Meyer, 1967).

Like teacher education students today, normal school students were worried about how they would be able to relate to their students and discipline them as well. In a short article entitled "Control Yourself, Then Others," Faxon (1912) said that the better teachers understood themselves, the more confident they would be. She believed poor student discipline was the result of teachers who were not prepared emotionally or academically for the classroom.

During the 1920s, normal schools expanded their curricular offerings to include the liberal arts and general education, to reflect the growing sophistication of the profession. As states continued to raise certification requirements, teachers found it necessary to get a college degree in order to teach. In fact, of the 42 normal schools in the United States in 1920, all had matured into four-year universities or colleges by the 1930s (Pulliam & Van Patten, 1995). In fact, most universities had developed teacher education programs by that time, eliminating the need to find a college that specialized in teacher education.

African-American women in outdoor gymnastics class, Tuskegee Institute, early 1900s.

Federal Involvement in Education

The 1930s were devastating for this country. Much of the wealth that factory workers, farmers, and small businesses had accumulated in the 1920s was lost in the social and economic upheaval of the Great Depression. The impact on schools was startling. Public confidence in education eroded. Child-centered teaching, as proposed by Dewey and other reformers, was even blamed for the Depression.

The federal government actively campaigned to improve schools. Because of the poor economic situation, significantly fewer property taxes were collected, so schools had no money. School boards were forced to let teachers go even though there was no one to take their place. Lack of tax money forced many cities and rural community schools to close their doors, and many students were turned away.

One federal program that helped schools was the **Works Progress Administration (WPA).** This program, begun in 1935 by the Roosevelt administration, paid teachers to teach adult education classes in citizenship to newly arrived immigrants and to help with nursery schools. The WPA also employed local teachers to write histories of their communities. This not only helped the teachers, it kept alive the pride of the community.

In addition, the WPA provided low-interest loans so that communities could build new schools, libraries, and other public buildings. Artists were employed to paint murals in public areas to reflect the history and character of the vicinity. These beautiful works of art can still be seen throughout the United States.

The Eight-Year Study

It is hard, so many years after the Great Depression, to understand the emotional tension experienced by teachers and schools during that period. Education critics did not believe students who were enjoying school were learning anything. The child-centered curriculum and teaching methods espoused by Dewey, Kilpatrick, and others fell out of favor. Teachers were criticized for being poorly educated, not being able to control their classes, and, ultimately, being unable to teach.

Fortunately, the Carnegie Corporation and the General Education Board were concerned about the same issues in 1930. They commissioned the **Eight-Year Study** to compare the education of children who had received a progressive education with those who had received a traditional education. This national, comprehensive study included all types and sizes of schools: private and public, rural and urban. It even included several colleges and universities.

After eight years of study (1930–1938), the results were astounding. The study found that students who attended progressive schools knew more information than students who had attended traditional schools. In dealing with new and different types of social and academic situations, these students were more creative and more willing to take a chance. Further, they were well rounded. They enjoyed the arts and humanities as well as the sciences. In fact, university professors found them more teachable, because they asked more questions, tried different approaches, and won more scholarships and awards.

Other results of the Eight-Year Study are now taken for granted by students and teachers alike. Many examples of what the Eight-Year Study found to be good educational methodology are now incorporated into state and federal law. Today, most teachers would never dream of slapping or spanking children with their open hands, or hitting them with boards and rulers—in fact, such treatment is illegal. Yet you may know of cases in which teachers still humiliate children in front of their classmates.

State departments of education now require anyone who wants to be a teacher to take college classes in child or adolescent psychology, so they can understand how children mature and behave. Public school textbooks and curricula are continually evaluated for contemporary information, and schools are now served by the medical community, including nurses, sociologists, and psychologists. The progressive education measured by the Eight-Year Study has become part of our approach to education.

As you read about the Eight-Year Study, keep in mind that it focused on Euro-American students. Minority students were not included; schools were segregated. It is this exclusion of minorities that we now discuss.

Education of Minorities

Education of Native Americans.   By the end of the 1800s, Native Americans had been moved to reservations. There, Native Americans maintained citizenship within their particular tribal nation. It was not until 1901 that Native Americans

were granted U.S. citizenship by Congress. However, this act applied only to Native Americans living in Indian Territory. It was not until 1924 that Congress granted U.S. citizenship to all Native Americans.

The U.S. government set out to deliberately destroy the languages and cultures of the Native Americans by removing Native American children from their families and placing them in boarding schools. In these boarding schools, the use of native languages and customs was forbidden. The conditions in the boarding schools have been described as extraordinarily cruel. For example, children were given a dose of castor oil if they spoke their native languages. In most cases, those were the only languages children knew. It was not until 1933 that the Indian Service removed this policy as an approved practice in "civilizing" Native American students (Debo, 1949). Children in these institutions lived in horrific conditions, and even though these were supposedly schools, they often attended classes for only half a day. The rest of the time, the children were forced to work on the land, raising crops and tending animals.

In 1928, the Meriam Report concluded that the removal of Native American children from their families was destructive. It recommended that education worked best when it occurred in the natural settings of home and family life. The policy of boarding schools was discontinued, and federal policy began to stress community day schools and the support of native customs and languages. Native Americans are still working to overcome the legacy left by the boarding school approach, through the restructuring of the Bureau of Indian Affairs and leadership of such chiefs as Wilma Mankiller of the Cherokee.

A teacher and child in a reservation school.

Education of African Americans.   Mary McLeod Bethune (1875–1955) exerted influence beyond her years and paved the way for the Civil Rights movement (discussed in the next section). She was born a sharecropper's daughter in South Carolina. Through extraordinary ability, she attended the Scotia Seminary in North Carolina and the Moody Bible Institute. At 29, she founded Bethune-Cookman College in Daytona, Florida, to educate African Americans so they could free themselves from the chains of Jim Crow laws and sharecropping. The college taught vocational, academic, and religious courses. Perhaps her greatest success was as Director of the Negro Affairs Division of the National Youth Administration (NYA) in the Roosevelt administration. Firmly and publicly she criticised Nazi racism when others remained quiet. As a delegate to the United Nations in the Truman administration, she spoke against racism abroad and at home. Bethune's contributions shine as a beacon of hope in human and minority rights.

The Civil Rights Movement

U.S. involvement in World War II accelerated the movement of rural Americans to the city. Urban living styles, types of employment opportunities, and the war itself forced many traditional social barriers to crumble. For example, Native Americans from reservations were working in urban factories alongside former farmers. While 5 percent of Native Americans lived in cities in 1940, by 1950 20 percent lived in cities (Takaki, 1993). In short, World War II forced Americans to look at themselves differently.

As soldiers returned from Europe, many found they wanted to change their lives. Some wanted to find jobs in cities or start their own businesses. Many wanted to marry and build homes, while others wanted to continue their education. The Servicemen's Readjustment Act (1944) or, as it was better known, the **G.I. Bill of Rights,** was intended to help returning soldiers adjust to peacetime society. The legislation was a tremendous success: between 1945 and 1951, more than 7 million service personnel attended some type of post-secondary school.

Segregation and Education

Wartime hysteria caused thousands of Japanese Americans to lose their basic Constitutional rights. While more than 9,000 young Japanese-American soldiers died in defense of the nation, Japanese Americans at home lost their homes, businesses, and close family relationships when they were sent to internment camps. African-American soldiers, too, felt the extraordinary consequences of segregation. Fighting Nazi hatred of Jews in Europe, African Americans realized they were fighting to protect the very rights they and their families were denied at home. Jewish-American soldiers were constantly aware that some people at home had the same anti-Semitic feelings the Nazis did. Indeed, World War II was, in many ways, the breeding ground of the Civil Rights movement. As our nation defended democracy overseas, our citizens demanded racial justice at home. These demands became challenges to injustice and discrimination, forcing our political institutions, especially our courts, to acknowledge equal access for all persons regardless of their race or ethnicity.

Yet the nation retained the "separate but equal" principle of the 1896 *Plessy v. Ferguson* Supreme Court decision. Changes in this policy began when the Commission on Civil Rights (1947) recommended that federal legislation be enacted to outlaw segregation. The following year, President Truman integrated the military. Nevertheless, African Americans continued to be disenfranchised. In 1955, less than 1 percent of all graduate engineers in the United States were African Americans, only 200 African Americans graduated from medical school, and most professions (with the exception of teaching) were closed to them. To compound these problems, few non- or semi-skilled jobs were available for African Americans. You can imagine the frustration of young, bright African-American children. On one hand, they were barred from the high-paying professions and, on the other hand, were thwarted if they competed with better-educated whites for the decreasing number of low-paying manual or factory jobs.

Brown v. Board of Education.

In 1954, the Supreme Court reversed *Plessy v. Ferguson* (1896) with the **Brown v. Board of Education** decision. The Supreme Court concluded that the concept "separate but equal" retarded the educational, social, and mental development of children who were segregated. That is, segregation violated the equal protection clause of the Fourteenth Amendment. Chief Justice Warren, writing for the court, stated:

> To separate them from others of similar age and qualifications solely because of their race generates a feeling of inferiority as to their status in the community that may affect their hearts and minds in a way unlikely ever to be undone. (*Brown v. Board of Education*, 1954)

Separate but equal?

The *Brown v. Board of Education* decision was controversial. Many white parents found it unimaginable that their children would be forced to attend school with African Americans. They felt their children's education would suffer. Many school districts either refused to comply or purposely dragged their feet. Of the 2,909 segregated school districts in 1954, only 802 had desegregated by 1960. In Alabama, South Carolina, and Mississippi, state and local school officials simply refused to integrate. Local school districts probably would have continued to resist integration if it had not been for the violence televised from Little Rock, Arkansas, in 1957. The scenes of federal troops escorting African-American students to Central High School sparked public scorn for the segregation so common in the South and border states.

VIGNETTE 4.1   *Richard's story*

On September 4, 1963, a 15-year-old student walked up the steps of Ramsay High School in Birmingham, Alabama. He was accompanied by several attorneys for the NAACP and the SCLC and federal marshals. Richard Walker became the first Black student to desegregate Ramsay High School. Thirty-one years later, he described his experience:

> Governor George Wallace had called out the State Troopers to surround Ramsay to keep me from registering. After getting a second court-ordered injunction, the Birmingham School Board was forced to let me register and attend Ramsay High School. The State Troopers, by order of Governor George Wallace, continued to surround Ramsay High School with orders to support the civilians who were protesting my attending Ramsay. As I walked up the steps of Ramsay, whites were chanting: "Two, four, six, eight. We don't want to integrate." The State Troopers remained for the next two years, and I was escorted to and from Ramsay by the Federal Marshals the full time I was a student there.

After obtaining a second court-ordered injunction, Ramsay High School officials agreed to enroll Walker as a student. He remembers very vividly his first weeks there, and how the State Troopers were not there to protect him but, if possible, prevent his attendance.

> Especially in the beginning of integration at Ramsay, there would be lots of civilian crowds at the school. You would never know what the crowds would do. They would yell and vilify me as I entered school. On at least two occasions, they caught people trying to bomb the house where I lived. We had people in the neighborhood who actually stood guard for at least a couple of years to keep the bombers away. You have to understand the white people were ruthless. They did not want integration.

Richard Walker always sat in the same seat in each class, at the same table in the cafeteria, and always ate lunch alone. At one point during the two years he was at Ramsay, some white students came to his table and sat down and tried to talk to him. Subsequently, he learned that they had been suspended from school for talking with him.

This story illumines the commitment and courage of a young Black man willing to risk his life for the right to an education denied him and others solely on the basis of their skin color. For this contribution, Richard Walker's experiences must be acknowledged and not forgotten.

Source: "Stranger in a Strange Land: One Black Student's Experience of Desegregation of a Birmingham, Alabama High School" by A. V. Wilson, in *Journal of Midwest History of Education* (1996, 23): 117–123. Copyright © 1996 by *Journal of Midwest History of Education.*

The War on Poverty

The assassination of President Kennedy in 1963 shocked the nation. In the extraordinary spirit of the times, Congress passed a series of social legislation President Kennedy had felt important. The legislation, primarily enacted under President Johnson, came to be known as the **War on Poverty.** This term had first been used in 1960 by President Kennedy, when he was describing how Social Security was helping the aged. President Johnson used the term to describe his desire to remove poverty from the lives of all Americans.

Compensatory Education.   During the first year of the War on Poverty, $1 billion was spent on improved health care, social services, and schooling for economically disadvantaged children. In 1965, Congress passed the **Elementary and Secondary Education Act (ESEA).** This landmark legislation provided funds to public schools for compensatory education. **Compensatory education** consisted of a variety of enrichment programs aimed at helping children compensate for the problems created by poverty and poor social environments. Since then, federal funds have been earmarked to help students in a variety of programs throughout the nation. For example, in the Job Corps, secondary school dropouts who are destined to remain unemployed are taken out of the inner city, placed in special rural camps, and given intensive job training. Other compensatory education programs are listed in Figure 4.1.

Of all the compensatory programs, perhaps the best known is **Project Head Start.** Its purpose was to give economically disadvantaged children a head start in life. These children, unlike middle-class children, had few opportunities to travel, read, play, or even live in stable family environments. Head Start's goal was to help children rise above poverty by giving them the enriching experiences middle-class children received at home, allowing them to meet their own expectations.

Head Start programs were hugely successful. They were found everywhere in the country, from churches to schools. Most programs served lunch, and many served breakfast. In some cases, parents were invited to eat with their children as an attempt to improve their nutrition. Children received medical checkups as part of the program. Problems like sickle-cell anemia and hearing and visual problems were quickly discovered and treated. Head Start's success continues today.

Some teachers were shocked to discover the extent of poverty. Coming from the middle class, few teachers truly understood the impact of poverty on children.

Figure 4.1   Selected Compensatory Education Programs

- *Early Childhood Education.*   Programs like Project Head Start recognize that disadvantaged children can learn in school if they are given special opportunities before kindergarten to increase their readiness.
- *Personnel Training.*   These faculty development programs are intended to help teachers improve their instructional ability.
- *Reading, Language, and Mathematics Skill Programs.*   These programs are intended to improve the basic skills of disadvantaged children.
- *Dropout Prevention.*   These programs are aimed at encouraging secondary school students from dropping out of school through work–study programs and on-the-job training.
- *Bilingual Education.*   These programs are intended to help children learn English. Presently, bilingual education programs are taught to children who represent almost 70 different languages; Spanish is the most common.

For poverty is more than a lack of money: it is a degrading, grinding thrust downward that people feel when they are unable to meet their expectations.

Today it is difficult to evaluate the impact of the War on Poverty on American schools. Most people who lived through it have very personal feelings about its success or failure because of their own experiences. Many consider the War on Poverty a failure: ghettos are still with us, and they are the worst places in America to raise and educate children. The downward push of poverty on children and their families is still a stumbling block to learning in school. The resulting lack of education denies employment to millions of adolescents and young adults.

On the other hand, the War on Poverty expressed our nation's values and goals: that all citizens of the United States, regardless of race, creed, color, gender, or national origin, have fundamental rights which cannot be abridged. National attention was focused on the rights of the individual and the responsibility of the schools to accept all children in a pluralistic society.

 ## Our Changing Nation

During the final quarter of the twentieth century, schools faced a dilemma. International economic competition, factory layoffs, and businesses moving out of the country caused many politicians and citizens to feel that schools were not doing their job.

The Middle School

As we discussed earlier in this chapter, the junior high school was developed in the 1920s to accomplish several goals which could not be met by high schools. One goal was to help students meet the more rigorous academic and social demands placed on them when they attended senior high school. The second was to give senior high schools time and opportunities to prepare students for college or the world of work.

The junior high school's primary goal was to help young adolescents understand their role in society and experiment with new knowledge. This goal, while important, was seldom reached. The reasons differed depending on the school district. In some cases, the rationale of the junior high school was not understood by school administrators. In other instances, teachers were not properly educated or prepared to teach junior high school students. Many ended up teaching as if they were teaching elementary or senior high school students.

The middle school concept was developed to make education more accessible to adolescent children who are undergoing fundamental physical, emotional, and intellectual changes. Middle schools attempt to socialize children to a greater extent than either senior or junior high schools. This is especially important for children as they develop an awareness that their world is becoming more diverse and they must interact in a multicultural society. For example, middle school children are encouraged to participate in noncompetitive activities so they can develop self-esteem while enjoying physical activities. As you would expect, most sports programs are intramural. Most of the academic subjects are interdisciplinary, so students are able to understand relationships between concepts and ideas. Cooperative learning, creative writing, and theater give children the chance interact with each other while developing a sense of social and individual responsibility.

Some insist the middle school has yet to articulate a specific purpose. Whatever the case, it is clear middle school teacher education programs understand the importance of helping children socialize themselves in a complex, multicultural world.

Children with Special Needs

In no small measure, the history of education in the United States has been the struggle to include more and different types of children in the learning experience. In colonial days, only white boys were welcomed in schools. Only very gradually have children of different cultures, race/ethnicities, genders, and economic conditions been able to obtain an education. Most recently, schools have realized their obligation to encourage youth with disabilities.

Special educators struggle to find the right terms to refer to these forgotten children. Many terms, like *retarded,* only contribute to a stereotype. We are all different in one way or another. Derogatory terms have been applied to some of history's most extraordinary figures. Winston Churchill, Thomas Edison, Albert Einstein and many others were classified as dunces and fools as children. Our society needs to develop better terminology that will describe, rather than classify or label, all of us.

Remember when we discussed intelligence testing in the 1940s and that some educators were critical of schools' placing great credence in the results? Critics of these tests pointed out group intelligence tests could be culturally biased; that is, they can give misleading information about people who are not part of a specific culture. Many educators feared these tests would label some students as slow learners simply because they were not part of the dominant Euro-centered culture. It was not until the 1960s and 1970s—through the special education movement—that educators recognized these tests *did* mislead teachers and parents about children's abilities. In fact, test results did not even accurately reflect the intellectual abilities of economically disadvantaged children. Adolphe E. Meyer (1967) concluded

> . . . the fact that children from impoverished homes commonly do not fare so well in the scores they make has brought the group intelligence test under sharper fire than ever. In truth, largely because of the charge that such testing is unfair to such hapless youngsters, several cities, including New York, have ceased the practice of group intelligence testing. (p. 297)

The history of bringing children with special needs into schools began in the 1970s. Prior to that, children with disabilities were often hidden from view. It was not uncommon for parents to seclude their children in their homes or institutionalize them, feeling that their children's disabilities reflected their own worth. Even after these special children began to attend school, they were, for the most part, segregated from the rest of the student body. Underlying this practice was the assumption that these children would never be productive members of society. Children with hearing or visual impairments or mental or physical handicaps were kept out of mainstream classes—and the mainstream of life.

No one knows how many children were removed from regular classrooms and placed in special education classes because teachers found them to be troublemakers or just different. Many of these troublemakers or children who could not learn were, in fact, just poor or culturally different.

> General educators happily sent problem students to special classes, and special educators accepted a number of students who should not have been so placed. Toward the end of the era, contradictory and inconclusive efficacy studies as well as court cases suggested that special classes were used as dumping grounds, vehicles of segregation, and, in some geographic areas, convenient ways to do something with children who were culturally or linguistically different. (Gearhart, 1992, p. 10)

The major impetus in helping special children was the 1954 *Brown v. Board of Education* Supreme Court decision. While that decision specifically outlawed the segregation of African-American children, it helped parents of special children realize that their sons and daughters were being segregated, too. Since then, much of the history of special education has been forged in the courts. Chapter 9 will explore in detail the legal and legislative battles fought by parents and others that culminated in the Education for all Handicapped Children Act (1975), which mandates the inclusion of children with special needs in traditional schools.

Reform Measures

A series of reform measures took place in the 1980s, in which schools were challenged to become more academic, teachers were challenged to become more rigorous, and students were challenged to become more committed to learning. The purpose of the reform movement, begun during the presidency of Ronald Reagan, was to create schools that would supply better quality workers for American industry. Many business leaders felt schools were not preparing students to live in a high-tech world, in which American industry competed with other nations throughout the globe. Schools were encouraged to modify their curricula to include more courses in mathematics, science, geography, and foreign languages.

A plethora of reports described the ills of public schools, teachers, students, and curriculum and were presented to the American public with much media fanfare. The various reports forced state legislatures and governors to reevaluate their educational systems, appropriations, curriculum mandates, quality of teacher education programs, and student achievement. While states exhibited different problems, most everyone felt teacher preparation was too easy (*America's Competitive Challenge: Need for a Response,* 1983).

The 1980s reform movement was a reaction to several social changes in American society. Just one year after the Civil Rights Act, the 1965 Immigration Act was passed. The relationship of this legislation to schools is extremely important. For the first time since the original immigration act (1790), this country chose *not* to have racial or ethnic immigration quotas. Prior to 1965, if you were planning to become a U.S. citizen, you were sometimes required to wait your turn, because the number of new citizens from any country could not be larger than the percentage of Americans already represented by that culture or ethnic group. If you were Asian, your chances of citizenship were much less than if you were British— because of where you were from, rather than who you were. In 1965, the United States made a fundamental decision about what it wanted to look like. Its image of itself, which was once essentially European, became global.

Changes in the Classroom

As society changed, so did our schools. By the 1990s, more children than ever before spoke languages other than English. In fact, schools in New York City, Chicago, and Los Angeles presently have students who represent more than a hundred distinct languages. In Los Angeles, San Francisco, New York City, Houston, and Chicago, 7 to 21 percent of all schoolchildren are first-generation Americans. Three percent of all U.S. schoolchildren are foreign born. A 1993 Urban Institute study (Time, 1993) noted that school enrollments increased 4.2 percent between 1986 and 1991. At the same time, the number of non-English speaking children rose 50 percent. That is, students who do not speak English rose from 1.5 million to more than 2.3 million in just five years. In California, the most populous state, one of every six students was born outside of the United States, and one of every three children speaks a language other than English. States like Texas, California, Florida, and Illinois are widely recognized for diverse classrooms, but other parts of the nation are impacted as well. In Garden City, Kansas, during 1993, 19 percent of the elementary student population of 3,666 children—more than 700 students—were not able to speak English sufficiently to meet minimal classroom standards (*Time,* 1993).

As our culture continues to change, American schools and society are faced with extraordinary challenges. While some are concerned that society is changing for the worse, teachers are optimistic. Local school districts are becoming more aware of the need for new methods of teaching English to non-English-speaking children.

Two language methods are presently being used. One, **English as a Second Language (ESL)** immerses children in the study of English. After thorough training, students are then taught subjects in English. Because some teachers feel this method wastes children's time, the second method, **bilingual education,** is taught. With this method, students learn school subjects in their native language. Students are then expected to translate what they have learned into English. While bilingualism is more popular, both methods aim to help all children, regardless of their social history, live and succeed in American society.

Some social critics believe the nation's ability to compete internationally is jeopardized by the numbers of non-English-speaking children coming into our schools. Local school districts, they point out, can only provide so much before they go bankrupt. Yet state laws have historically required all children to attend school regardless of citizenship. Both sides agree the nation will be much weaker if not all children are educated.

The next century will be exciting for us and our children. Schools will continue to change as they reflect our increasingly pluralistic society. Teachers, like teachers before them, will have to rise to the challenges created by change.

What will schools be like when you become a teacher? As you have learned by now, schools reflect the community. Children bring the world, as they and their parents see it, to the classroom. Schools mirror communities as they cope with change caused by new technologies, different life-styles, new types of work and employment, continued immigration, and international conflicts. All this means teaching will continue to be an exciting adventure for those who welcome the friendly nudge of change.

What You Have Learned

✔ World War I changed the way we live, work, and learn. Schools became increasingly important as we became an industrial society.

✔ Progressives like Dewey wanted schools to teach the whole child, rather than just academic subjects.

✔ The Great Depression caused schools and teachers to become more accountable for their actions.

✔ World War II was a breeding ground for the Civil Rights Movement. Citizens from diverse backgrounds were able to see the racial significance of the war and began to envision full equality at home.

✔ The Civil Rights movement changed American schools by guaranteeing basic Constitutional rights to *all* citizens.

✔ While *Brown v. Board of Education* was considered a victory for African Americans, it was also a victory for children with special needs.

✔ The educational reform movement of the 1980s addressed the concern that American industry would not be able to compete in an international market if schools did not become more rigorous with regard to teaching academic subjects, such as mathematics and science.

✔ Schools today reflect a different America than they did a century ago. Then, African Americans were segregated into a second system, children with disabilities were hidden by their parents, and girls were assumed to need less schooling than boys. Present-day schools are faced with the challenges of teaching children in a multicultural, multiethnic society.

Key Terms

Smith–Hughes Act	Eight-Year Study
Perkins Vocational Education Act (1984)	G.I. Bill of Rights
	Brown v. Board of Education
Cardinal Principles of Secondary Education	War On Poverty
complete living	Elementary and Secondary Education Act (ESEA)
intelligence quotient (I.Q.)	
compulsory attendance laws	compensatory education
Progressive Education Association	Project Head Start
comprehensive education	English as a Second Language (ESL)
Works Progress Administration (WPA)	bilingual education

Applying What You Have Learned

1. In this chapter you have read about how technology has changed our culture. How is it changing your education?

2. World Wars I and II gave Americans opportunities to become aware of their roots when they fought in Europe and Asia. What types of experiences do you think your students might have to remind them of their cultural beginnings?

3. What reasons do people have for coming to this country? Are these reasons different today than they were a generation ago?

Interactive Learning

1. As our the nation becomes more multicultural, what types of problems do you believe teachers will have to solve so that students from many different cultures can receive an education? Interview several teachers about their perspectives.

2. Do you remember your first day in senior high school? In a small group discuss how your junior high school helped or hindered your transition from elementary school to senior high school. Did the group agree or disagree junior high schools helped students enter senior high schools? What were their reasons? Reread the section on the junior high school in this chapter to help you begin the discussion.

3. Many times teachers and parents do not want children to know their I.Q. scores. What do you think are the advantages or disadvantages of students knowing their I.Q. scores? Interview several teachers and discuss their views in a small group.

4. In 1930 the average school year was 172 days. But the average number of days in a present school year is 185. Interview several parents and school administrators and ask them if the number of school days should be increased. How were their views different or similar?

Expanding Your Knowledge

DeYoung Alan J. *Economics and American Education*. Boston: Longman, 1989. (DeYoung's thesis is that the history of American education is controlled by European economic philosophers such as Marx, Smith, and Mill. Therefore, he points out, the reform movement of the 1980s is inspired by economics, not concern for children. A must-read book.)

Faxon, Grace B., ed. *Practical Selections,* Dansville, NY: F. A. Owen Publishing Co., 1912. (This book may be difficult to find. It's reminiscent of education that gave solid advice to young teachers during the early part of this century.)

Giroux, Henry A. *Living Dangerously.* New York: Peter Lang Publishing, Inc., 1993. (This is an excellent text that asks questions about how to raise children in a democratic society that is becoming more diverse. Living dangerously is what Giroux believes our children are required to do in order to survive.)

Lemann, Nicholas. *The Promised Land: The Great Black Migration and How it Changed America.* New York: Alfred A. Knopf, 1991. (A very readable book about African Americans who moved from the Mississippi Delta to Chicago. The book also provides a wonderful history of President Johnson's War on Poverty. Lemann is not only exciting to read, he is accurate.)

Santoli, Al. *New Americans: An Oral History.* New York: Viking, 1988. (This history is a series of personal reflections of immigrants who came to this country during the twentieth century. This history demonstrates compassion and explores why new Americans value school.)

Schools in the Global Community

In Chapter 5, you will study comparative education. The study of **comparative education** focuses on learning how schools in other countries are organized and administered and how teachers in other countries teach. Because governments develop schools they believe best meet the needs of their nation, school systems differ from country to country. Comparative education helps us look at the global society and identify its contribution to America.

Demography refers to the study of people, including the cultural and ethnic composition of a population. Demography helps us explore how schools are influenced by the increasing diversity of our student population. Demography explains why schools in some nations may suffer from severe teacher shortages and overcrowded classrooms while others do not. The methods used to solve demographic problems such as these vary widely among countries. As we learn to appreciate and understand school systems in other nations, we will develop a more complete understanding of our own educational system. As we study the schools of England, Mexico, and Japan, compare them with what you know about the United States educational system. Ask yourself how you would feel if you were a teacher in these countries. That's what Mrs. Sugiyama, in *Becoming a Teacher,* is doing.

What you will learn

- Comparative education is important for teachers to study, so they can understand the impact of society on schools.
- English and Mexican schools are administered at the central government and local level, while Japanese schools are administered at the central government level.
- National economic and social priorities cause schools to change.
- In any country, the curricula children learn depend on their culture.

BECOMING A TEACHER   *Other nations' schools*

It's a beautiful Monday morning when Mrs. Sugiyama drives into the principal's parking space at Capitol Hill Elementary School. As usual, she is early to work. She feels the principal should be the first person to arrive at school in the morning. She enjoys meeting parents as they drop off their children for the day and greeting students as they bound off the buses. Having brief conversations with her staff and faculty is a private delight for her, because she knows the principal's presence gives them a feeling of stability. Also, she enjoys the silence before the many sounds of people working, learning, and living together begin.

It bothers her to see how many children are already playing in the schoolyard. Even though school does not start for another ninety minutes, many parents work and need to bring their children to school early. The Carpenters, parent volunteers, are supervising the children, but it bothers Mrs. Sugiyama that so little can be done to help the children.

As Mrs. Sugiyama walks into her office, she reflects on the conversation she had with Ito, her husband, at breakfast this morning. For their anniversary he had proposed they take a trip to Japan during the summer. It's been years since they've been in Osaka, and their parents are growing older. "I wonder if elementary principals in Japan have the same types of problems with children of working parents that I do," she muses. "I wonder if schools in other countries have the same types of problems we have in the United States—I wish I had time to find out." She thinks, "Tonight we'll talk about going to Japan, and how I could visit some Japanese schools. I would love to talk with principals and teachers about their schools. What a wonderful experience that would be." With her mind made up, she goes out to greet the buses filled with children. It's going to be a wonderful day, she knows.

???   *If you had an opportunity to visit another country's school system, where would you like to go and what would you like to learn?*

Schools in Other Countries

In this chapter we will study the school systems in England, Mexico, and Japan. Each school system is important for a different reason. We will discuss English schools first because of the dominant influence that culture has had on the United States.

Many of our ideas about schools originally came from England. Because British and American societies have continually changed since then, it is difficult today to see their common roots. England today is a conservative, class-oriented society that is quickly becoming multicultural.

We will discuss Mexican schools next. Even though Mexico is our southern neighbor, many Americans know little about its history, culture, and society. We do know that Mexico is influencing American culture. Treaties like the North American Free Trade Agreement (NAFTA) are building new and different economic relationships between the two countries. Immigration from Mexico is changing the demographics of both the United States and that country. Mexico is a third-world nation with unique problems. Like the U.S., Mexico is a multicultural society that has significant social and economic problems. Although Mexicans have been concerned about education for centuries, Mexico's schools have a short history. Mexico is the only third-world country in the world that shares a common border with a wealthy nation.

Last, we will discuss Japanese schools. Teachers in the U.S. probably feel they know a lot about Japanese schools because of the amount of publicity they receive in our media. Japan is an important, international, economic giant that credits its success to its educational system.

Organizational Governance

To help you understand the English, Mexican, and Japanese school systems, we need to first classify schools by the type of governance or control they have experienced. Because schools in our country are controlled at the local and state levels, we assume that is the case worldwide, but it isn't. As we discuss the types of governance—local control, centralized control, national and state cooperation, and national control—you will notice that each has its own special purpose. As a teacher, you may wish to compare these governance structures with the one you are used to.

Local Control.   In countries like the United States and Switzerland, schooling strives to be both egalitarian and utilitarian. While there is a national consensus about educational priorities, education is not driven by specific political ideologies. Americans believe education should be the responsibility of each of the states that make up this country. The states entrust significant educational freedoms and obligations to approximately 14,950 local school districts and their elected school boards. Compared with England, Japan, or Mexico, our federal government exercises minimal power over schools.

Centralized Control.   Some countries, like Japan, have a history of the national government developing educational policies. In countries that have centralized control, the national government has ultimate control over schools. Educational policies are debated thoroughly at the parliamentary or legislative level and do not encourage a specific political philosophy over another.

National and State Cooperation.   Several countries, like England and Mexico, have national school systems that are locally administered. Authority and responsibility for schools are shared by the national government and local education authorities. Each school has its own governing body, and teachers exert significant leverage on educational policies. You will learn more about this as you study the English and Mexican school systems later in this chapter.

National Control.   Although none of the countries you will study in this chapter adhere to national control, you should be aware of this form of educational governance. National control of education occurs when the national government is the ultimate authority in educational policies. The People's Republic of China is an example of a government that has total control of schools. The Chinese political system is an interlocking network of government units and Communist party organizations. Educational policies involve both the government and the Communist party leaders—usually the same individuals. Since the Chinese government is highly centralized, schools are also highly centralized. Under national control, no debates occur over educational policies at the parliamentary level, because the educational policies reflect the current ideological position of the party in power.

English Schools

Schools in England, part of the United Kingdom of Great Britain and Northern Ireland, are a reflection of a conservative society built on social class. Through the centuries, English tradition held that education was a private responsibility. Parents were responsible for the education of their children. Aristocrats did not feel it was their responsibility to educate the lower social classes, nor did they feel that would be desirable.

Educational History

Americans might have difficulty understanding a society headed by an aristocracy. The English aristocracy is a remnant of a time when very few people needed an education. Educational elitism has continued to influence English education ever since.

Pre-Reformation.   From the time of Edward the Confessor (1002?–1066 A.D.) until the Reformation (1500s), little attention was given to *who* should go to school. Most schools were in the courts of the aristocrats, where clergy taught boys how to read the Bible and do elementary arithmetic. (Girls were taught only domestic arts.) Even for this select group, an education was not always required. During this period, the majority of the English population lived on farms owned by aristocrats. For these peoples, formal education simply was not required. Few farmers were able to read or even sign their names, nor did they need to.

The Reformation.   During the Reformation, education of the commoners became more important, as clergy and aristocrats attempted to control their religious beliefs or create religious converts. Martin Luther and other religious dissidents believed the average person needed direct access to the Bible. It was at this point in English history that it became important for common people to learn how to read.

The Industrial Revolution.   By the Industrial Revolution (1850s), even larger portions of English society needed to be schooled. Robert Owen's Infant School and Lancaster and Bell's Monitorial schools attempted to teach workers' children at a low cost.

The Education Act of 1870 established local educational administrative units that were mandated to start primary (elementary) schools throughout the country. This landmark legislation allowed public primary schools to accept local tax monies and monies from Parliament at the same time. The Education Act of 1870 allowed these schools to compete with private or voluntary schools for grants given by Parliament. These grants were called "payment by results," because schools received money from the government based on the number of students who passed standardized year-end examinations. These examinations were monitored by **Her Majesty's Inspectors,** bureaucrats who were sent from London to evaluate the quality of schooling children received.

The Twentieth Century.   The next significant change in education came during World War II (1939–1945). Secondary education had traditionally been reserved for the aristocracy and the middle class, who could afford the heavy financial sacrifice. Boarding schools like Eton, Winchester, Rugby, and Charterhouse—with curriculums steeped in the classics, humanistic studies, and sportsmanship—prepared young boys for leadership roles in government, clergy, academics, and the military. These young men then went on to study at Oxford or Cambridge Universities.

The wartime government under Prime Minister Winston Churchill passed the Education Act of 1944 or, as it became known, the Butler Act. There were many reasons why a new Education Act was needed. English schools did not seem to be educating children for a changing world. Many British critics had noticed, during the war, that American soldiers were able to make decisions more easily than their British allies. American noncommissioned soldiers were able to take command on a moment's notice if no officer was present. These displays of leadership seemed to indicate that American schools did a better job teaching creativity than the class-structured English schools.

The Butler Act changed the purposes of schools. Both Scotland and Northern Ireland, parts of the United Kingdom, were allowed to have their own schools. Traditionally, education was regarded as the private responsibility of families. Parents decided how much education their children should receive. Under the Butler Act, schools were responsible for providing an education children could understand and use. Schools in Great Britain were required to contribute to society just as American schools did.

Schools like Eton and Rugby remain open for children whose parents are able to afford to send them there. But the Butler Act requires English schools to educate the commoner to live in a changing world. England's educational goal today is to contribute to the overall good of the people and country.

A Multicultural Society.   The picture of the proper English gentleman and four o'clock tea does not accurately reflect England today. Beginning in the 1960s, job opportunities, high standards of living, cultural opportunities, and quality health services began attracting large numbers of peoples to England from all parts of the world. Most of the immigrants came from former British colonies in Africa and Asia. These people made new lives for themselves in large urban centers like London and Liverpool. Although many immigrants had received an English-influenced education at home, they brought with them different histories, values, ideas, religions, and family structures. English schools discovered they needed to educate these newcomers into society. As a consequence, English language instruction and multicultural in-service programs are now found in most English schools.

England has not had as long a history of multiculturalism as we have in the United States. Therefore, English schools and society are presently in flux, as peoples of various heritages learn to live together. For example, while freedom of religion is accepted and taught in school, non-Western religions like Hinduism and Islam are becoming increasingly common. In short, English society and its schools are being challenged by nontraditional and non-Western ideas.

Administration

In contrast to our schools, which are administered at the state and local levels, English schools are administered at the national and regional levels. English educational administration is a series of partnerships between the **Local Educational Authorities (LEAs)** and the **Department of Education and Science (DES)** in London.

National Administration.   At the national level, educational administration is the responsibility of the Department of Education and Science (DES). The DES is represented in the Government's cabinet; therefore, its educational policies are a reflection of whichever political party is in power. Some specific responsibilities of the DES include teacher education, teacher certification, educational finance, and curriculum. Much of the day-to-day operations of the Department are run by the Civil Service. These educators and administrators make certain that educational legislation is implemented throughout the country. Through Her Majesty's Inspectors and other agencies, the Department of Education and Science continues operation regardless of which party is in power.

Local Administration.   Local administration of schools is conducted by Local Education Authorities (LEAs). There is no equivalent of the LEA in the United States. Their responsibilities are similar to those of our local boards of education. These include hiring teachers, maintaining school buildings, and identifying special needs of schools. LEAs also negotiate with teacher unions about salaries and working conditions. Since passage of the 1988 Education Reform Act, LEAs have also been responsible for the implementation of a national curriculum.

School Administration.   As in schools in this country, administration of English schools is conducted by educational professionals. **Headmasters** are generally equivalent to principals in the United States. The headmaster is the administrator teachers work with most. They make certain the national curriculum and the various regulations outlined by the DES and LEA are implemented. Teachers, through their national professional unions, affect education through sponsored research and proposals for curricular and examination reform. Unions such as the National Union of Teachers are committed to teacher welfare and present their concerns to the LEAs as well as to Parliament.

As we mentioned, educational administration in England is a partnership between the DES and the LEAs. While this partnership has generally worked well in such areas as developing and administering a national curriculum, educational administrators are given few opportunities to conduct far-reaching change. For example, while financing of schools is shared by the LEAs and the DES, the national Department of Education and Science has little control over monies that come from other agencies within the government.

Organization

English schools are divided into primary and secondary schools. The primary school is further divided, into an early stage and a junior stage. As you become familiar with these schools, notice the similarities to and differences from schools in this country.

Primary Schools.   Children between the ages of 5 and 11 attend primary schools. These are usually neighborhood schools close to children's homes. Primary schools are traditionally divided into two parts. The early stage (ages 5 to 7) emphasizes informal classrooms, while the junior stage (ages 8 to 11) focuses on children's ability to work with others. Like teachers in this country, English primary school teachers concentrate on teaching children how to read and write and use basic arithmetic skills. Teachers also want their children to increase their knowledge of

Students in a British primary school

science, social studies, the arts, and physical education. The English primary school receives international attention periodically because of its commitment to helping children learn in nonthreatening classrooms.

Secondary Schools.   Upon completing primary school, English children attend secondary school. They can stay there until age 18; they are required by law to stay in school until age 16. Unlike primary schools, secondary schools force students to specialize. This is a key difference between American and English secondary schools. While we want our students to become familiar with a wide variety of subjects, English schools encourage their students to concentrate on an area of study.

In the early secondary years, English students continue studying the core courses—English, history, science, and mathematics—that they learned in primary school, but starting at about age 13, students start to specialize. This is very important for students who want to go to the university. Secondary students specialize in either the arts (English, history, foreign language, etc.) or sciences (physics, mathematics, biology). These concentrations prepare students for the General Certificate of Secondary Education, an exam they must pass if they want to graduate.

Curriculum

As we mentioned earlier, England established a national curriculum under Prime Minister Margaret Thatcher. The 1988 Education Reform Act established a national curriculum that would guarantee that students, whether they lived in England or Wales, would receive a broad education that would challenge them physically and academically. The Act also requires schools to give students experiences that prepare them for the problems of adult life.

Mathematics, science and English (or Welsh, in Wales) are core subjects all students are expected to take. In addition, subjects such as history, geography, technology, music, art, and physical education are taught to fulfill the national curriculum's goal of well-educated British citizens. Beginning at age 11, students learn a foreign language. Because there are no laws separating church from state, religion is included in the curriculum.

Examinations.   English examinations are much different than ours. English teachers give far fewer exams or quizzes than American teachers. American teachers want constant feedback about how students are learning; English teachers believe that fewer examinations, given over long periods of time, will do the same thing. But as in any country, the evaluation methods used to find out what their students *know* influence what children *learn* and how teachers *teach*.

The Butler Act (1944) created the **eleven-plus examination,** a standardized test taken by all students at age 11. This examination was designed to measure academic abilities and direct students to subjects in which they could succeed. Although the original purpose of the test was to help children, the eleven-plus examination was one of the most controlling factors in a child's life. Passing the eleven-plus examination was critical to every student who wanted to go to the university or begin a professional career. Failing the examination was disastrous for children and their parents. Failure meant that children had to change their mind about what they wanted to be when they grew up. Failing the eleven-plus examination meant the end of childhood dreams and life goals, if those dreams and goals included a university education.

Because of the public outcry about the restrictive nature of the eleven-plus examination, other examinations were created for students to take at different stages in their academic career. The **General Certification of Secondary Education (GCSE)** is now taken by students when they are 16 years old. It follows other achievement tests that are given to students at 7, 11, and 14. The purpose of these achievement tests is to periodically evaluate students' academic abilities as they proceed through the national curriculum.

Mexican Schools

Only recently has the United States become aware of Mexico's influence on our society. Mexico is important to the United States for both economic and social reasons. The passage of the North American Free Trade Agreement (NAFTA) by Congress in 1993 bound together the economic futures of these two countries. We are also discovering the social impact Mexico is having on our society as greater numbers of Euro-Americans learn Spanish, eat different types of foods, and watch television programs broadcast from Mexico. Americans have now chosen salsa rather than ketchup as their favorite condiment.

Mexico is a developing country that faces many of the same social and educational problems as the United States. But because of lack of economic resources, its ability to succeed is not always guaranteed. Mexico's educational system is hampered more than American, English, or Japanese schools in its ability to employ teachers and purchase necessary classroom supplies and materials. Mexico's school systems are on the frontline of fighting poverty.

Educational History

The history of Mexican education is an excellent example of how the Aztec (an indigenous culture) and the Spanish (a European culture) met and, despite a turbulent history, eventually learned to live together. As you study Mexican education, reflect on what you think each culture was required to learn about the other.

The Aztecs.   The indigenous people of Mexico, the Aztecs, developed a culture to rival that of the Greek or Egyptian civilizations hundreds of years before Europeans landed in the New World. When the Spanish explorer Cortés encountered the Aztecs in 1519, he wrote his king that the Aztec capital, Tenochtitlán (near present-day Mexico City), was larger than the largest city in Europe.

The Aztecs used both oral and written language. The government wrote directives to provincial leaders, children of the nobles learned their alphabet, and friends and relatives wrote letters to each other expressing many of the same feelings and attitudes we do today when we telephone a friend or parent. Aztec writing, like Egyptian, was a kind of picture-writing, in which symbols represented words or ideas. For example, a footprint meant you were traveling, while a tongue meant you were speaking. A figure sitting on the ground indicated one had experienced an earthquake. The laws of the empire, intricate calendars, and important pieces of historical information were written in the same form.

The Aztecs also had books. Many of them had colored pictures drawn on cotton cloth, skins, or maguey (a plant like Egyptian papyrus). Oral tradition, too, was extremely important. Stories, myths, and histories passed from one generation to another orally. Students were expected to memorize this literature so they could understand important facts about Aztec society and pass the knowledge on to the next generation. Aztec schools served much the same purpose schools do today. Almost 300 years later historian W. H. Prescott described an Aztec college:

> In the colleges of the priests the youth were instructed in astronomy, history, mythology, etc.; and those who were to follow the profession of hieroglyphical painting were taught the application of the characters appropriated to each of these branches. In an historical work, one had charge of the chronology, another of the events. Every part of the labor was thus mechanically distributed. The pupils, instructed in all that was before known in their several departments, were prepared to extend still further the boundaries of their imperfect science. The hieroglyphics served as a sort of stenography, a collection of notes, suggesting to the initiated much more than could be conveyed by a literal interpretation. This combination of the written and oral comprehended what may be called the literature of the Aztecs. (Prescott, 1964, p. 69)

The Spanish.   The Spanish Empire in the Americas lasted from 1492 until 1821. Spanish education had two goals. The first was to educate Spanish children who lived in Mexico, and the second was to instill European values in the Aztecs and other indigenous cultures.

Spanish schools in Mexico were controlled by the Catholic Church. Various religious orders, such as the Franciscans, founded primary schools and academies similar to those in Spain. They taught the same curriculum: language, literature, mathematics, and religion. Just as in Spain, the important part of the curriculum was the study of Catholic religious values and church dogma. Consequently, children in Mexico were taught that the culture, literature, and history of the Aztecs and other indigenous societies were the work of the devil.

Spanish boys in Mexico who were interested in studying for the clergy were sent to school in Spain. Girls generally learned how to sew, do tapestry, and look after a home. Some girls, however, were allowed to enter a convent.

The education of Indians was another matter. Usually Franciscan or Jesuit priests organized schools. They served as teachers and were given the responsibility of financing and administering the schools by the Spanish government. Weber (1992) talks about the fervor of the Franciscan missionaries in starting schools. Teachers deprived themselves of everything, jeopardizing their own health, in order to educate Indian children. The curriculum was basic. Boys were taught to throw away the clothes their parents gave them and wear European shirts, pants, and shoes. They were taught how to eat in the European manner. Children were taught how to grow crops such as wheat, take care of animals, and run a farm just as if they lived in Spain. And, of course, the teaching of religion was the most important part of the schools' mission, for the clergy were convinced that believing in Indian gods would keep people from going to heaven.

The education of Indian children was barbaric even by the standards of that day. Students were flogged and physically abused by their teachers for the smallest offense. Some children were placed into virtual slavery. The abuse was so bad that many Indian revolts were staged in an attempt to reject the new ideas forced upon unwilling learners at the mission schools (Weber, 1992).

Looking back, it is easy to see why the Spanish schools did not accomplish their goal of duplicating European life in Mexico. Even though Spain dominated Mexican culture, Indian influence remained strong. Thus began a blended Mexican society of both Indian and Spanish influence.

Mexican Educational History.   Mexico's independence from Spain came in 1821. But it was not until the 1910 Revolution and the present Constitution (1917) that schools became a priority of the federal government. In its infant years, the government did little for schools. In the early 1920s, President Obregon began programs to build schools, especially in rural areas. In 1924, President Calles decreased the Catholic Church's influence in government and society. Both helped Mexican education by encouraging public support of schools.

The Institutional Revolutionary Party (PRI), which has been in power since 1929, has also supported education. Yet its success in achieving universal education is tempered by the number of social and economic problems that plague Mexico. Even though federal law currently requires all children to go to school from age 6 until 14, only two-thirds of the children actually attend school.

As in any country, the history of schools in Mexico is closely tied to the country's economic, political, and social problems. During the middle part of the twentieth century, many Mexicans were extremely poor. Farmers tilled their land as they had in the last century. School children begged for food from American tourists. Mexico's economy suffered because few industries were located in Mexico's cities. Education lagged because there was no money to build schools, hire teachers, or purchase textbooks. Schools also faced major dropout problems. Many children were forced to drop out of school so they could work on farms. During the 1940s, fewer than one in four Mexicans could read or write.

Mexican education began to have brighter prospects in the 1970s. The international oil crisis, which increased oil prices at an alarming rate, was a blessing for Mexico. As an oil-exporting country, Mexico saw the value of its oil increase from $4 a barrel in 1972 to more than $30 a barrel in 1980. (This short-lived financial boom collapsed in 1981, when oil prices fell to $13 a barrel.) During the 1970s, the literacy rate, increased to more than 85 percent.

Today, schools are beset with problems. They are presently overcrowded because of the enormous increase in the nation's birthrate. The population of Mexico is increasing about 3 percent a year. Mexico City, the largest city in Mexico, has a metropolitan population of 16 million, with uncounted thousands arriving each year. For comparison, Mexico's total population is 90 million (Parfit, 1996). As urban areas such as Mexico City and Ciudad Juárez grow, children are coming to school only to discover that their opportunities for an education are limited by a lack of teachers, textbooks, paper, pencils, chalkboards—all the things that help children learn.

Mexico's rapid population growth is also causing environmental problems in both rural and urban areas. Massive pollution is coming from factories, fertilizers, and automobiles. Drinking water in urban areas and irrigation water in rural areas are becoming scarce. As a consequence, diseases such as cholera and typhoid are spreading throughout the population, along with tuberculosis (Parfit, 1996).

Administration

The Mexican Constitution (1917) gave the federal government the responsibility for building and administering schools. It shares this responsibility with the states, especially with regard to funding and supervision. Most schools are financed and administered by the federal government's National Ministry of Education. Because of Mexico's long-standing tradition of church–state separation, the Constitution does not allow religious groups to establish public schools, although churches are allowed to operate private schools. Only 15 percent of Mexico's elementary schools are private.

The Minister of Education is a political appointee. The minister holds cabinet rank and is responsible for the educational policies of the federal government. These policies are usually debated in Mexico City, but because the Institutional Revolutionary Party (PRI) has had the majority vote for more than seven decades, it is the PRI's policies that are instituted through the Ministry.

A major goal of the government has been to increase the number of children who go to school. But, with an average age of 14 in a nation of 90 million, the government is continuing to discover the difficulty of placing all children in school. The vast majority of students are attending the first three grades in elementary school; less than half of this number are enrolled in middle school.

The Ministry of Education is divided into administrative divisions called subsecretaries. Each subsecretary coordinates a program such as higher education, technical education, cultural affairs, or general education. It is at the state and local levels, however, that day-to-day educational administration takes place.

Because of the diversity of Mexico's population, especially in its rural areas, the Ministry of Education has developed a special subunit called the National Service for Cultural Promoters and Bilingual Teachers. These teachers teach the national primary school curriculum in the various languages of Mexico's indigenous populations. They also teach Spanish as a second language. The National Service is also involved with teaching children of parents from other countries, such as Guatemala, who have migrated to Mexico in search of a better life. This international migration, while small, stretches the scant resources of the Ministry of Education.

Organization and Curriculum

Mexican schools are divided into primary schools and middle schools. Middle schools serve the function of secondary education. They are divided into specific academic tracks in which children specialize.

Primary Schools.   Children begin primary school at age 6 and are expected to continue until they are 14. All students, whether attending public or private school, study a national curriculum including Spanish, mathematics, history, geography, natural science, social sciences, the arts, health, and physical education. Textbooks, prepared by the Ministry of Education, are usually free. This helps many children remain in school. Mexican teachers, like their counterparts in England, teach from a syllabus, so that regardless of which primary school you attend, instructional units are the same. Primary school children attend school for eight months each year. Traditionally the year begins in September and ends in July. The year is broken into three trimesters, with vacation periods in between.

The dropout rate in Mexican primary schools is high. Because of a lack of facilities, about 9 percent of children do not attend school. Few villages have schools that go beyond the first four years of instruction. In rural areas, only one in ten children attends primary school and perhaps no more than 10 percent of the students graduate. This means that for every hundred rural children of school age, only ten attend primary school. Of that number, only one or two will complete the entire primary school curriculum.

Students in a rural elementary school in Mexico.

Middle Schools.   Mexican educators have traditionally disliked the terms *secondary education* or *high school,* because of their European connotations. Instead, they use the term *middle school* to mean secondary education. Middle schools in Mexico extend the education of primary school students and prepare them for university. The middle school is six years long. It is divided into two parts, each of which is three years in length. Although current data are not reliable, it is thought that less than 20 percent of elementary students will attend some form of middle school.

In the first three years of middle school, students study Spanish language and literature, mathematics, and sciences. These are the same subjects they learned in primary school, but they are presented in greater depth. Art, physical education, and technical education are also offered.

The study of foreign languages is required: students are allowed to choose between English and French. Of the two languages, English is by far the more popular. Many of the students recognize that English is important to their later careers. In fact, wealthy families encourage their children to learn English so that they can attend prestigious American colleges and universities.

Mexican students take teacher-made exams that they must pass in order to continue their studies. Like the tests in primary school, middle school achievement tests are designed to assess student knowledge.

Students who graduate from the first half of the middle school program are given an opportunity to specialize during their last three years. Study is divided into three distinct majors: General Studies, Vocational and Technical Education, and Teacher Training. Students must choose a major when they enter. This is a serious decision, because what the student studies in the next three years will influence what that student will do with the rest of his or her life.

General Studies is the most prestigious major. Here students specialize in one of several different programs to prepare for the university. In some programs, the curriculum is actually a prep course for entrance to the National University in Mexico City or some other prestigious college.

Vocational and technical schools are gaining prestige among Mexican students. As the nation industrializes, many more students are recognizing the value of a vocational or technical diploma by the salaries it commands. Also, students who perform well in this major can continue their studies at technical institutes, now found in many parts of the nation.

Students who wish to become teachers are able to major in a program preparing them to attend normal schools. The curriculum for primary school teachers is much less rigorous than for those who want to be middle school teachers.

 Japanese Schools

In a post-Cold War world in which economic and technological competition is more important than military strength, Japan stands as a giant among nations. How this happened to a country that was practically destroyed during World War II is considered by many to be a miracle. For the Japanese, however, what happened after World War II fits within a cultural context in which government, industry, and schools cooperate for the national welfare. As you study Japanese schools, you will notice that cooperation among these three agencies is of critical importance. Japanese schools recognize they must cooperate with industry and government so that Japan can reach a common national goal.

Supporting this extremely important concept are two important facts of Japanese life. The first is that Japan is homogeneous society in which each person must be loyal to the group. Schools are expected to stress social cohesion, not individuality. The second is that Japan must have a strong economic system to compete on the international level. Japan has few natural resources, therefore schools are required to develop a work force that will help industry. In fact, schoolchildren are considered to be Japan's primary natural resource.

Educational History

The history of modern Japan began with the opening of that country to the West in 1853 by Commodore Matthew Perry, an American naval officer who sailed into Tokyo Bay in 1853. Prior to that, Japan was a **closed society,** a society that chose to remain culturally exclusive. It has always been important for Japanese society to remain homogeneous. Isolation from countries that might "contaminate" Japan has been a central theme throughout Japanese history.

Pre-Western History.   Japan already had a long educational history before Perry's arrival. Elementary schools taught both boys and girls the rudiments of the three R's. Other schools, reserved for the samurai, or members of the warrior class, taught leadership skills, military proficiency, and Confucian ideals. Pre-Western Japan had a relatively high literacy rate. According to Fägerlind and Saha (1989) this model eased Japan's transition to industrialization.

> After political and social stability had been established during the Tokugawa period, which began in the early 17th century, education in Japan was used as a main unifying force to combat the fragmentation of the previous feudal period. Even though Japan was a closed nation for over two centuries while Britain and Europe were slowly undergoing industrialization, important events took place which made for an easy and rapid transition into an industrial state. Before 1850, it has been estimated that 40 percent of the male population was literate, and in 1872, a universal and unified education system was introduced. When Japan decided to industrialize in the late 19th century, it had a model to follow, for the technology of the West was known and desired. (p. 39)

Modern History.   Beginning with the Fundamental Code of Education (1872), education changed dramatically because of Japan's entrance into international affairs. European and American educational systems were studied by groups of Japanese educators who traveled extensively. Based on their reports on such topics as school organization and curriculum, many Western ideas were transplanted into Japanese schools. The Minister of Education, Arinori Mori, was concerned that

Western ideas would corrupt Japanese society. Therefore, in the 1880s he formulated "three pillars," criteria, that non-Japanese ideas had to meet in order to be accepted in Japan:

1. Schools should enhance the government.
2. Schools should educate the citizenry.
3. Schools should protect the nation from foreign influence.

The Twentieth Century.   During the early decades of the twentieth century, Japanese schools mirrored English and other European schools: elementary education was open to all children, but secondary and higher education was much more selective. By 1930, schools, like Japan itself, had become more strident. In the rush to industrialize, the government developed plans to increase the size of the Japanese Empire by attacking neighboring countries like Korea and China. They reasoned this would increase their access to natural resources. Parts of China and Southeast Asia were conquered, culminating in World War II. During the war, schoolchildren learned a curriculum based on the nationalistic foreign policy of the military government. Schools emphasized absolute loyalty to the Emperor and stereotyped non-Japanese, especially Koreans, as less than human. Children were taught that their emperor was a god and that Japan had the right to dominate Asia.

The Japanese were defeated in World War II. During the Allied occupation that followed, Japanese schools were denationalized and the curriculum was rewritten to remove statements that told children they should follow the emperor without question. Other courses, such as geography and morals, were also drastically changed.

In the American-influenced re-industrialization of the nation, schools took a commanding role in the education of children. The government called upon schools to educate children so that, as they became workers, Japan could compete with other countries around the world. The schools, partnered with the government and industry in rebuilding the nation, totally focused Japanese society on education. All parts of society understood the importance schools played in the life of the country—and in no place was that clearer than in the Japanese family.

Family influence on children is somewhat different than in the United States. In traditional Japanese families the vertical link between parent and child is extremely important. For example, the Japanese middle-class mother is typically more involved in the day-to-day school activities than her American counterpart. It is also typical that the mother–child relationship is more intense. This leads the child to understand that his or her bond to the family is significant and life-lasting (McAdams, 1993).

Japanese educators today face a dilemma. Continuing influences of Western mass culture are seen on television and movies, and many Japanese are threatened by the changing values and attitudes of young people. These groups are pushing for a reform of education, a return to the traditional values of Japan. On the other hand, economists note that if Japan wants to remain a world economic leader, it is important for schools to teach children how to become creative. Many Japanese are questioning whether Japan's economic success rests on the educational elite (as many in the United States think) or on the workers that represent the bottom half of Japanese society.

Japanese education will change, but the impact of that change on society is still unknown.

Administration

The administration of Japanese schools is centralized. All decisions about schools are made in Tokyo. Educational administration is a microcosm of Japanese society at work.

National Administration.

The Ministry of Education, Science, and Culture (MESC) dictates what every Japanese schoolchild will learn. It has authority in many fields beyond education as well. It is in charge of such areas as religious affairs, science, and culture. The Ministry divides its administration of schools into subunits called bureaus. The Bureau of Elementary and Secondary Education oversees pre-university schools. Other departments in the Ministry, such as Higher Education, Science and International Affairs, Facilities and Cultural Affairs, Social Education, and Physical Education, also have responsibilities in education. However, their influence is minor compared to the Bureau of Elementary and Secondary Education.

As in the United Kingdom, the Minister of Education is a political appointee and is part of the government's cabinet. Therefore, educational policies reflect the ideals, values, and philosophy of the central government in Tokyo. Educational policies are debated in the Diet, or parliament. Through these means Japanese education, government, and industry are able to cooperate in developing a strong national economy that competes internationally. The Ministry of Education, Science, and Culture, like other government agencies, has its own budget. It distributes funds equitably throughout Japan, regardless of whether schools are located in urban areas such as Tokyo or in rural areas such as Hokkaido. This is much different than the school financing methods we use in the United States. While our schools operate with differing budgets, depending on the local and state tax base, the Japanese believe giving the same amount of money to all schools gives them identical opportunities to have the same resources and the same quality of teachers.

Local Administration.

The Ministry of Education, Science, and Culture communicates with individual schools through the local prefecture's Board of Education (a prefecture is the equivalent of a county or local governmental unit). It is the Board of Education's responsibility to keep the schools within its boundaries informed of all the Ministry's regulations. Because the Japanese value social conformity and strive for national consensus and unity, local Boards of Education and the Ministry expect that all schools will respond to the policies in the same way with no expectation for local differences.

Curriculum

The Ministry of Education, Science, and Culture is responsible for the curriculum of elementary and secondary schools. It employs professional educators to plan the curriculum and methods that teachers are required to teach and use in the classroom. In addition, they specify the sequence in which the content is taught. The curriculum is divided into specific units of instruction, and teachers are informed how many class periods they should spend on each unit. Seldom are teachers asked for advice on how units of instruction should be taught. In fact, teachers are instructed *not* to deviate from the Ministry's plan. On rare occasions when course content cannot be totally delineated, as in art for example, the Ministry clearly states the outcomes students are expected to reach. That is, while some teachers may become more creative in teaching a unity of study, the results must be the same throughout the country.

Textbooks.

The Ministry evaluates all textbooks based on the national criteria. Like in the United States, local schools may choose a text; however, it must be on the Ministry's approved list. While our texts are large, perhaps three hundred pages or more, Japanese students typically study from books of one hundred pages or less. Usually, Japanese texts have few pictures and little color. The Ministry's expectation is that textbooks should be convenient and easy for students to memorize for examinations.

Examinations.

The goal of Japanese students is to pass the national examinations and college entrance examinations given each January. Examinations are reflective of Japanese society. Classroom teachers assume that because each student is given the same education, students must take equal responsibility to compete for their academic success. That means teachers are committed to teaching for the examination and not student learning.

How students succeed on the these examinations will, to a very large degree, determine the type of education they will receive in future years. Students and their families fear that failure in any part of the examination will ruin the child's chances of attending college and bring discredit to the family. Mothers, particularly, feel they are tainted or praised by how well their child does on the examination, because they are traditionally their children's academic nuturers.

Japanese teachers believe examinations identify the nation's brightest students. Students are tested throughout their school career. Gutek (1993) has aptly compared the examination structure to an escalator: after you get on the escalator, there is little or nothing you can do to advance. In other words, *where you get on* the escalator determines how quickly you advance to the top. Everyone who is on the escalator moves at the same pace, because social and economic success in Japan is determined by examination scores. It is of critical importance to pass the examinations with the highest scores possible. In fact, Japanese students and their parents use the term *examination hell* to describe the pressure they feel.

Organization

Japanese schools are organized into primary or elementary schools and secondary schools. The latter are further divided into two divisions, lower and upper. Each is controlled by the national curriculum and the examination structure.

Elementary Schools.

Elementary schools cover the first six years of a child's education. Beginning at age 6 and continuing to age 12, more than 99 percent of all children are taught the national curriculum, which includes Japanese language and literature, social studies, mathematics, science, music, art and handicraft, homemaking, physical education, moral education, and special activities.

Mathematics and science are the two most important subjects students are required to learn: the Ministry requires 25 percent of all instruction time in the elementary school to be spent on these courses. As children advance in school, the total amount of class time for these subjects increases. It is easy to see how specifying the amount of time students spend on certain subjects feeds into a standardized approach to teaching, learning, and studying for examinations.

By the time students leave elementary school, they have learned how to work together and be contributing members of a group. It is important that students be able to fit into the group, not stand out or be different. Japanese children attend school seven hours a day during the week and three hours on Saturday morning. The school year is 210 days—about 35 days longer than the American school year. The Japanese school year is divided into three trimesters with vacations between.

Secondary Schools.

Secondary schools are divided into two three-year segments. Lower secondary school (ages 11–15) is compulsory, but upper secondary school (ages 15–18) is not. The organization of the lower secondary school and upper

Young Japanese students in school.

secondary school is somewhat equivalent to our junior and senior high schools. However, these schools are used for different purposes than American schools.

Lower Secondary School.   The lower secondary school is a transition for students in several ways. While they are aware of the importance of doing well on examinations, it is here students realize that the more they learn (and the higher their examination scores), the better their lives will be. Lower secondary schools begin to deviate somewhat from the national school curriculum students study in the six years of elementary school. Students are now given a limited choice of electives. For the first time foreign languages are taught. Schools usually give students a wide selection of foreign languages from which to choose. The foreign language most children want to study is English. Japanese children listen to the same songs and watch many of the same movies and television programs as American students, and they are interested in learning the language so they can understand what is happening in western culture. In short, Japanese students study foreign languages for very personal reasons as well as academic reasons.

Upper Secondary Schools.   The upper secondary school is extremely important for Japanese children. Because attendance is no longer required by law, students (and their parents) are now free to choose the school they think will help them most in their career. The single most important reason most often expressed by children for applying to a specific upper secondary school is its ability to help them get into a good university. What students and their parents look for first when they evaluate an upper secondary school is the percentage of its graduates who have been admitted into the nation's most distinguished universities. We can now appreciate why the three years spent in lower secondary school are so important to students: It is there they must study to pass an examination that will qualify them to go into an upper secondary school which, in turn, will prepare them for university. Students know that just passing the examination is not enough. The higher the score students are able to get, the more prestigious the school they will be able to enter.

The upper secondary school's first year has a common curriculum. Attending school for five and one-half days a week, children learn Japanese, contemporary society, mathematics, science, English, physical education, health, music or calligraphy, and other subjects.

In the second and third years, students choose between two majors. Each prepares students for college. Literature majors study subjects such as classical literature, Japanese history, and world history. Science majors study integral and differential calculus, probability and statistics, and physics.

The ultimate goal of the Japanese student is to pass the **Joint Achievement Test.** The Ministry of Education, Science, and Culture administers the nine-hour examination each January. It is the capstone of students' educational experience. Passing with high grades brings families together for a celebration at which the student is praised by parents and relatives. Failing the Joint Achievement Test is emotionally wrenching for students and parents alike. High scores on the Joint Achievement Test allow students to take the university entrance examinations.

These exams, which last usually two days, are administered by higher education institutions. But passing the examinations is not enough: students know the higher their scores, the greater their chances of attending a prestigious university and having a good job later in life.

It is difficult for us in the United States to understand the impact of examinations on Japanese students. Although American students complain about the pressures of grades, they have little experience with the "examination hell" Japanese students live through. One of this book's authors, William Segall, describes some of the horrific emotional fallout Japanese students experience after failing these exams.

> As principal of a preparatory school for Japanese students in the United States, I could easily see the impact of examination failure. Students who had failed the examinations in Japan had great difficulty understanding that American schools could give students a second chance. It was as if failing was permanent. They didn't expect, or perhaps couldn't accept, the idea that failure didn't have to be forever. I remember bright young kids who were willing to throw it all away because they simply couldn't comprehend the idea of individual success. It was as if each person had been told what his or her place in society was and nothing—not even an act of God—could change that.

Other Schools.   The fear of failing examinations has created a unique out-of-school educational system. **Jukus** ("cram schools") are private schools that tutor children. Students usually attend jukus on Saturday afternoon or in the evening after regular school. Sitting in large classrooms that may hold three hundred students or more, teachers reteach lessons taught in regular classrooms that week. Because the curriculum is standardized, students know the juku will teach the same lessons they learned in their school. Students also learn how to take examinations. These juku tutoring sessions improve students' chances of passing important exams.

Recently, students who passed the Joint Achievement Test but were not able to meet the entrance requirements set by prestigious Japanese universities have had the opportunity to study at American university branch campuses in Japan. For students, this is an opportunity to continue to learn English and broaden their understanding of the world. Still, Japanese students know that if they are to succeed in Japan, they must attend a prestigious Japanese university.

What You Have Learned

✔ Comparative education is a specific discipline in the study of education that focuses on analyzing how and what children in other nations learn as well as how schools are organized, financed, and administered.

✔ English schools have a history dating to the Middle Ages. Generally, schooling remained out of reach for large numbers of children until the Butler Act (1944), which created the Department of Education and Science (DES). Schools presently provide all children an education. They are controlled by a national curriculum and examination system.

✔ Today, English schools are confronting new immigration patterns that are challenging the values, ideas, and culture of this traditionally homogenous society.

✔ Mexico is historically a multicultural nation. Its Indian civilizations were invaded by Spain hundreds of years ago, producing a blended culture.

✔ Like most underdeveloped countries, Mexico understands the need for schools. Schools have been consolidated under the federal Ministry of Education, which administers schools and curriculum. Presently, Mexico's schools suffer large dropout numbers, teacher shortages, and funding problems.

✔ Japan is a homogeneous society. Education bolsters specific national or social aims. Schools are part of a three-party partnership with government and industry. This partnership focuses Japan's resources on becoming an international economic giant.

✔ Japanese educational policy is centered in the national Ministry of Education, Science, and Culture, which controls all aspects of schools including curriculum, teaching methods, examination, textbook selection, and finance.

✔ Japanese students learn through memorization. Creativity and experimentation are generally not valued forms of learning. Examinations are the only indicator of student success, a fact that causes much student and parental stress.

Key Terms

comparative education

Her Majesty's Inspectors

Local Educational Authorities (LEAs)

Department of Education and Science (DES)

headmasters

eleven-plus examination

General Certification of Secondary Education (GCSE)

closed society

Joint Achievement Test

jukus

Applying What You Have Learned

1. Mrs. Sugiyama was interested in learning whether Japanese schools had the problems she noticed at Capitol Hill Elementary. What types of questions do you think she wanted to ask her Japanese colleagues? Do you think she was more interested in finding out if the problem existed, or how Japanese schools solved it?

2. The organization and administration of English, Mexican, and Japanese schools have certain commonalities. What are they?

3. During the past decades, Japanese and American schools have taught different things about each other as well as themselves because of social and economic differences. Should schools teach stereotypes when nations disagree with each other? Why?

4. The United Kingdom, Mexico, and the United States are multicultural societies. Japan is not. Can you distinguish specific elements of Japanese education that illustrate this point? Is is possible to transfer those elements to the United States, United Kingdom or Mexico? Why or why not?

Interactive Learning

1. Form small groups of four or five students to discuss the three school systems covered in this chapter. Which would you like to teach in? Why or why not?

2. In small groups compare the four types of organization and governance structures we have discussed. What advantages and disadvantages did you discover about each?

3. Invite several administrators into your class to discuss organization and governance issues in their schools. In what way are their issues different from those of the schools you learned about in this chapter?

4. In small groups discuss the following questions. Of the three school systems discussed in this chapter, which do you feel would have helped you succeed? Which do you think would not have helped you?

Expanding Your Knowledge

Gutek, Gerald L. *American Education in a Global Society: Internationalizing Teacher Education.* New York: Longman, 1993. (An excellent text that investigates international problems from an educational vantage point.)

Osborn, Thomas Noel. *Higher Education in Mexico.* El Paso: Western Press, 1976. (Part of a major series on Mexican–American relations, this text approaches Mexican education through demographics. A good book to own.)

Weber, David J. *The Spanish Frontier in North America.* New Haven: Yale University Press, 1992. (This excellent history book contrasts Spanish and Native American societies, including their education, during the Spanish colonial period, a time of extraordinary stress.)

Part Three

Philosophy and the Classroom

In Part Three you will learn about the philosophical foundations of education. As you continue your studies to become a classroom teacher, you will often question your beliefs about what students should learn or how you should teach. Many of your beliefs are probably part of a specific philosophy of education. Chapter 6 explores educational philosophy, so you can participate in discussions of educational issues. Chapter 6 will help you recognize how you develop your own philosophy of education.

Understanding your philosophy of education is important for another reason. Just as classroom teachers have a philosophy of education, so do schools. Your enjoyment of teaching may depend on whether your philosophy of education complements that of the school in which you teach. In *Becoming a Teacher* in Chapter 6, Jefferson Shibata discovers how diverse teachers' philosophies are as he listens to a discussion about a new student assessement policy. After you read his story, ask yourself whether you would like to teach at a school that has the assessment policies described.

Educational philosophy involves more than just thinking about schools in a broad sense. You will use your educational philosophy every day as a teacher in the classroom. It will influence and shape your curriculum and instructional techniques. For example, in *Becoming a Teacher* in Chapter 7, Bill discovers how his philosophy of education influenced the unit he just taught to his junior high students. As you will see, not all parents appreciate his teaching style. Even his superintendent, Dr. Yates, is not certain of Bill's teaching philosophy.

Your philosophy of education will impact more than the curriculum and your instructional techniques. It will influence the manner in which you learn more about your students and become more aware of their personal, cultural, and ethnic histories. Think about some of the best teachers you had in elementary or secondary school. Can you identify their philosophies of education through their instructional practices?

Putting Philosophy to Work in Culturally Diverse Classrooms

In Chapter 6, we will study how educational theories are derived from diverse classical and contemporary perspectives. Then we will discuss how teachers put these theories into action in their classrooms. Philosophy does not exist only in books. Your personal philosophy of education will guide your classroom instruction.

What are the roles of philosophy? These roles include

- helping us use analytical skills as part of our intellectual tools,
- presenting alternative ways of thinking about situations,
- affecting our perceptions of rational behavior, and
- teaching us how to communicate effectively as we strive to find solutions to problems great and small.

As you learn about differences in philosophical approaches, think about how you will begin to apply them to solve problems in your daily life. As you decide which philosophical approach (or combination of approaches) matches your outlook on life most closely, you can begin to use it to help you address problems in your classroom. Studying philosophy does not guarantee you will know how to solve all problems, but it does provide a constructive foundation from which to make decisions.

No single philosophical approach offers all the answers. Understanding different philosophies will help you clarify your own personal philosophical stance, which will determine how you run your classroom.

What you will learn

- How to begin to speak the language of philosophy.
- The major schools of philosophy and how they relate to education.
- How to begin to develop your personal philosophy of education.
- How you will put educational philosophy into action.
- How an understanding of cultural diversity affects the way you teach.

BECOMING A TEACHER   *To test or not to test*

Walking back to his office after a faculty meeting, Jefferson Shibata, the principal, is thinking about his teachers' reactions to a new school board policy. The board is concerned about the public's perception of the quality of education the students are receiving, and has asked the teachers to develop new testing procedures to evaluate students. These results are to be shared with parents.

In the faculty meeting, Maria Alvarez worried that "What the Board wants is going to force us to return to memorization of material. Some of our students will be penalized because direct instruction/memorization is not the best learning style for them."

John Chin agreed. "I'm not sure parents will understand what the test scores mean. Many will look at the numbers and compare their child to the other children in school. I'm really concerned about how implementing this new policy will impact my teaching."

Martin Jones disagreed, "Over the years the changes in our school have reflected the way the community has changed. Most parents will understand the purpose of the tests, so how can our students be hurt by them? We really need to go back to the basics. That seems to be what the public wants for their money."

Maria shook her head. "I try to be sensitive to the various cultures represented by my students. I think awareness and appreciation of the diverse cultures in our classrooms is crucial for learning. Since I've altered my teaching in response to the diversity in learning styles, my students seem to do better. How will my students' test results be perceived?"

John agreed, "Standardized tests don't always reflect the students' knowledge and information. How will we find the time to assess students other than by the numbers? It won't be easy!"

???   *In a small group, discuss what each classroom teacher was saying. What differences of opinion do you notice in your discussion that parallels the discussion among Maria, John, and Martin?*

Mr. Shibata thought he knew his faculty very well. Many had been at the school for years, some even longer than he. How can professionals concerned about their students, the school, and the community have such different positions about the school board's new testing policy?

Maria, John, and Martin all have very strong ideas. Their viewpoints are consistent with their personal educational philosophies, and each is grounded in a school of philosophical thought. As you study each philosophy, try to match it to each teacher's unique perspective.

The Language of Philosophy

The term **philosophy** comes from the Greek word meaning "love of wisdom."

Through the study of *philosophy,* we explore of the meaning of reality and of life itself. The goal of philosophy is to describe the nature of reality within the limits and scope of our knowledge. Philosophy tries to help us *see* what we say and *say* what we see (Angeles, 1992). Philosophic questioning does not guarantee that we will ultimately become wise, but it provides direction as we search for wisdom. Schools of philosophy differ, but all are interested in three basic questions:

- What is real?
- How do we know?
- What do we value most?

How we answer these questions reveals our own philosophical approach. As educators, we are also involved in helping students find their own answers to the three basic questions. Keep them in mind as we explore the major educational philosophies.

Central Concepts of Philosophy

To help us understand individual schools of philosophy, we need to learn about some concepts that are central to all. These concepts are metaphysics, epistemology, and axiology.

Learning about reality.

Metaphysics: What Is Real?   The aspect of philosophy that asks the question "what is real?" is called **metaphysics.** You may think reality consists only of sensory information, the things that you can see, touch, or hear. However, there are different forms of reality depending on how one defines and describes facts or events and their relationship to each other. For example, reality may be defined in spiritual terms—an objective order apart from humankind—or as a result of people's social and physical interaction with the environment. As teachers, we continually define what is real to our students through the curriculum.

Epistemology: How Do We Know?   The part of philosophy concerned with answering the question "how do we know?" is **epistemology.** The question "how do we know?" examines the process of how we think, understand, and learn. Often, people maintain that knowledge is based on experience and observation. However, at times we believe we know something simply "because." While we are confident of our knowing, we are unable to explain why we are confident. How many of us have answered a persistent three-year-old's barrage of "why" questions with an exasperated, "Just because"? The process of knowing differs depending on our philosophical approach. Some people believe knowledge is derived from reason or cognitive processes, while others require some sensory experience or interaction with the environment as

How do we know?

a prerequisite for knowledge. As educators, our belief in *how* students learn will guide our teaching methods.

Axiology: What Is of Value?   The part of philosophy that seeks to answer the question "what is of value?" is **axiology.** As we discuss "what is of value?" we are really looking at two separate concepts. Those who study *ethics* are concerned with value as it relates to morality and conduct. For example, we discourage cheating and encourage learning in the classroom. Those who study *aesthetics* are concerned with value as it relates to beauty and goodness. What is beautiful to one person may not be beautiful to another. For example, some view beauty as universally genuine in all times and places. Others view beauty as culturally based, an idea that varies depending on the time, place, and situation. As teachers, we model our values every day. Vignette 6.1 is an excellent example of how values differ.

VIGNETTE 6.1   *The Manhattan Country School in New York City*

Last week, in my first eighth grade grammar assignment, I had an ulterior motive. I asked them to name nouns and adjectives that they associated with Manhattan Country School. I did not conceal my reason for such a simple assignment. I simply told them that I had to speak to MCS parents on Tuesday, and I wanted to know what they felt about the school and the world in which they lived.

Their responses, excluding those concrete nouns such as "farm," "friends," "teachers," and so on, evoked the values of the school with such precision that it may be hard for you to believe I did not put words in their mouths. MCS means: "security, trust, union, equality, inclusion, bonds, comfort, diversity, caring." The adjectives they used included: "relaxed, cozy, small, different, kind, protected, and unreal." Some of their words needed explanation: "control—by that I mean I feel in control of myself here"; "specialists—I mean, even the special subject teachers relate to you as a person, not just like a science teacher or an art teacher"; "awesome—I don't mean awesome like cool; I mean what it says in the dictionary; inspiring awe."

Source: "The Road Not Taken" by Augustus Trowbridge in *Manhattan Country School Newsletter, 15,* (1), 8. Copyright © 1992 by Augustus Trowbridge. Reprinted by permission of Augustus Trowbridge.

???   *How did the children respond to Trowbridge's questions about "what is of value?"*

Logic: How Do We Make Decisions?

Another philosophical concept is concerned with logic, the way we use reason to make decisions. There are two basic types of logical thinking—deductive and inductive. The **deductive method** of inquiry moves from general premises toward a specific conclusion. In the study of logic, this involves a formal statement of the premises and the conclusion; this statement is called an argument. In a valid deductive argument, the conclusion must be true if the premises are true; if a premise turns out to be false, the conclusion will be invalid. Or if the conclusion does not follow logically from the premises, the argument is invalid.

The **inductive method** moves from specific observations or facts toward a general conclusion. Scientists use the inductive method in observing phenomena and proposing a hypothesis to account for them. They then test the hypothesis to see whether it is supported by additional observations under controlled conditions that can be replicated by other observers. We all use inductive reasoning in daily life; for example, based on several purchases Mina concludes that a particular store has produce that is especially fresh. Note that in the inductive method the conclusion does not necessarily follow from the observations; the conclusion may be correct, incorrect, partly correct, or incomplete. It is often more a matter of probability, and different people working from the same observations may come to quite different conclusions.

Figure 6.1 gives examples of inductive and deductive methods.

Figure 6.1   Deductive and Inductive Logic

DEDUCTIVE

(Premise 1) All reptiles are cold-blooded.

(Premise 2) All alligators are reptiles.

(Conclusion) Therefore, all alligators are cold-blooded.

The conclusion is supported by the premises, so the argument is valid. Is the following argument valid?

(Premise 1) All alligators are reptiles.

(Premise 2) All alligators are cold-blooded.

(Conclusion) Therefore, all reptiles are cold-blooded.

The argument is invalid; the premises do not support the conclusion. (Just because one group of reptiles is cold-blooded does not mean that all reptiles are. The conclusion may be true, but it does not follow logically from the premises stated.)

INDUCTIVE

(Observations) Whenever Alex is around marigolds, he sneezes and his eyes water.

(Conclusion) Alex could be allergic to marigolds.

The conclusion might or might not be true, but as a premise or hypothesis it could provide the basis for doing more tests (observations). Note that with the inductive method, different observers can reach different conclusions, so in science it is important that a hypothesis be testable and that any test can be duplicated by others. In daily life, we accept that people can have differences of opinion.

Educational Philosophy

As you study the various schools of philosophy, keep in mind that each school has many different branches. We are presenting an overview of these philosophies. If you wish more information about a specific philosophical approach, we encourage you to read other books, some of which are described at the end of this chapter.

Classical Philosophies

Idealism.   Idealism is regarded as the oldest organized philosophy in the Western world, dating back to Plato and Socrates in ancient Greece. **Idealism** contends that the only true reality is ideas, because the world is always changing. Idealists believe that people should seek the Truth because Truth never changes. Idealists maintain that nothing exists except as ideas in human minds or in the mind of God. Idealists you may be familiar with include Plato, Socrates, Descartes, Berkeley, Hegel, Emerson, Thoreau, and Kant. Others are Friedrich Froebel, founder of the kindergarten, and William T. Harris, U.S. Commissioner of Education in the late 1800s.

What Is Real?   Idealists emphasize the importance of mind over the material world. For Idealists, what is real exists only in the mind. What is real, for Idealists, is the ongoing search for Truth. Many Idealists believe that while there are levels of Truth, it is the search for Truth itself that is of paramount importance. Idealism focuses on using our mind rather than just our senses to define reality. For Idealists, gaining insight into ourselves and our universe is the way to answer the question "What is real?"

How Do We Know?   Idealists believe that knowledge is an active process of a rational and substantive mind. They assume we are thinking beings who are capable of seeking Truth through reasoning. Idealists believe it is very important for us to direct our thinking toward universal concepts rather than just the mundane activities of living. Idealists believe the search for insight into the relationship of facts and great ideas will enable us to move to a higher plane of knowledge.

What Is of Value?   Idealists see values as genuine, absolute, and permanent, with a religious base. Idealists place less value on the physical and the concrete and more value on the nonphysical and the abstract. They value self-realization as a part of the whole person, not as an end in itself. In this way, Idealists are very concerned with the enormous potential for growth, both in a person's behavior and reasoning.

Idealism in the Classroom.   Of all the philosophies we will discuss, Idealism has probably had the greatest influence in education. Idealists are very concerned with the presentation of information to students. Idealism focuses on learning using a holistic approach rather than a fragmented one. Idealists want students to have a broad understanding of the world rather than one that is narrow and piecemeal. Thus, the curriculum revolves around broad concepts rather than specific ones. As an Idealist teacher, you would focus on providing an environment where dialogue is the method of instruction. Because of the emphasis on a broad understanding and the search for Truth, Idealist teachers rely on the classics as a central part of their curriculum. Idealist teachers believe ideas can change lives and teach with this thought uppermost in their minds.

Realism.   Like Idealism, Realism dates back to the Greeks. **Realism** contends there is a natural order to events and that this order exists whether or not we, as humans, are aware of it. Realists maintain that reality, knowledge, and values exist independently of our mind. Remember the old question, "Would a tree falling in the forest make noise if no one was there to hear it?" The Realist would answer yes, the noise is not dependent on our hearing it for it to occur.

Realists believe our physical world evolved naturally, without the need of supernatural force, and they maintain Truth can be observed. In other words, Realists maintain that as we observe data, gather information, and analyze it, we will develop principles or knowledge. Realists you may be familiar with include Aristotle, Aquinas, Bacon, Locke, Whitehead, and Russell.

What Is Real?   Realists believe we live in a world of objects. Everything that exists is related and, at the same time, independent of everything else. A critical part of Realism is the belief that objects have matter and form, a structure that gives them a shape and design. For Realists, the answer to the question, "what is real?" is found in the universe of objects and the perception of those objects by people.

How Do We Know?   Realists believe knowledge is the result of direct contact with objects and the laws that govern them. Realists further maintain that we humans can know about the objects we encounter because we have sensory abilities that enable us to acquire information about our environment. Thus, our ability to conceptualize is dependent upon our abilities of perception and understanding. It is these abilities that set us apart from other inhabitants of our world.

What Is of Value?   For Realism, values are permanent and objective. But above all, values are rationally based. In other words, Realists believe values are derived from the natural, physical, and social laws that govern nature. Because these laws are universal, so are the values which are derived from them.

Realism in the Classroom.   Realism emphasizes critical reasoning in the classroom. Realists focus on the scientific method as a way of studying material. It is not just the understanding of facts that is important to the Realists but also how we arrive at this understanding. In other words, a Realist teacher focuses on how a student learns the information. Realists emphasize the importance of scientific research and development. They believe that anything can be measured, even the inculcation of values. For Realists, competency, accountability, and performances can and should be measured.

Contemporary Philosophies

Pragmatism.   Unlike Idealism and Realism, whose roots can be directly traced back to the Greeks, Pragmatism is considered to be the first major educational philosophy developed in the United States. **Pragmatism** is an active philosophical perspective that assumes we will pursue the best possible means to achieve the most desirable resolutions to current problems in our society. Pragmatists believe that we must look at our experiences in terms of cognitive, physical, and emotional development and examine how these interact with each other. For Pragmatists, the use of the scientific method is a major component in solving real-life problems. Pragmatists believe that concepts must be tested through real experiences.

Are you familiar with the three major American philosophers, Charles Peirce, William James, and John Dewey? We will not discuss these three in depth, but some of their concepts have contributed to our educational system.

Charles Peirce was the first to tackle what he called "the duality of mind and matter." He believed that we must verify our ideas through actual experiences. If we did not verify our ideas, then they were nothing more than hypotheses. Remember how the Idealists and the Realists believed that the search for Truth was most important? As a Pragmatist, Peirce believed the search was just the beginning—one had to validate the Truth through actual testing.

William James argued that the heart of ideas was their practical workability in everyday life. James believed that truth was not absolute; in fact it was *made* in actual, real-life situations. He held that experience and truth were inseparable and that each of us might view an experience differently. Because we each experience our world differently, we attach various meanings to similar experiences. This does not mean that one person's experience is better than another. It just means that each experience is distinct.

John Dewey built on the works of Peirce and James and is said to have systematized Pragmatism. He did not view his investigations into experience as conjecture but rather as inquiries into how to solve real-life problems. Using Peirce's concepts about the practical consequences of ideas, Dewey argued that one began with a problem situation, examined it as unique, and studied the consequences of behaving in particular ways upon that problem situation. He maintained that we must be responsive to change and modification, which facilitates an approach of creativity to finding solutions to problems.

Like Peirce, Dewey maintained that ideas were only hypotheses until they were tested by experience, and that actual knowledge was dependent upon observable verification. He believed that human affairs were part of a natural process.

What Is Real?   Pragmatists view reality as everything a person experiences, even though the experiences are forever changing. In Pragmatism, the truth of an idea lies in the terms of its verifiability. What is real are those experiences based on the events of things, ideas, hopes, fears, and joys. For Pragmatists, reality is constantly changing, which is why they consider verifiability as crucial to knowledge.

How Do We Know?   Pragmatism maintains knowledge comes from actively exploring and solving problems. In this process of exploring and solving problems, what we "know" about that problem is subject to the "meaning" we have given to it. Because reality is always changing, how we know is also always changing. Pragmatists view problem-solving as the most effective way of coping with the changing reality.

What Is of Value?   Pragmatism believes values change as situations change. For Pragmatists, individuality and the social world cannot be separated but are interdependent and interrelated. Individuality is seen as the interplay between personal choice (freedom) and objective conditions. Through participation in social groups, we develop moral rules. In this participation, our ideas about morality influence how we interact ethically with one another.

Pragmatism in the Classroom.   Pragmatists believe a broad education is much better than a specific narrow one. They believe that we will have difficulty if we break knowledge into separate and distinct areas and then try to bring these areas back into the whole. A Pragmatist teacher is concerned with teaching children how to solve problems and will use actual, real-life situations in the classroom. Pragmatists see education as changing and fluid, not written in stone. The educational process is seen as experimental, flexible, and open-ended. It focuses on helping students in their capacity to think and intelligently analyze situations and solve problems.

Existentialism.   Like Pragmatism, **Existentialism** is one of the newer contemporary philosophies. It is concerned with how experience, reality, and purpose are pivotal within the lived experience of a person. Unlike other more traditional schools of philosophy, Existentialism has many and varied interpretations. Part of this variety may be due to its spread across several nations and cultures.

The central focus of Existentialism is its emphasis on the individual and self-fulfillment. Existentialism has a profound sense of ethical reservation about individual obligation. Existentialists de-emphasize the idea of the group or individuals working within a group. Existentialism is considered one of the newer philosophies; philosophers identified with it include Kierkegaard, Nietzsche, Buber, Heidegger, and Sartre.

What Is Real?   Existentialism views reality as a process of becoming, an awareness from within one's self. Existentialists believe life has no meaning except what we ourselves give to our lives. In other words, there is no preformulated belief system available from which to draw. It is up to each of us to discover the meaning of life. Existentialists invite us to scrutinize our personal lives and to reject frivolous positions and uncommitted action.

How Do We Know?   Knowledge, for Existentialists, results from free choices we make in the process of becoming and from accountability for the choices we make. Existentialists focus on the search for individual truth by which one could live and die. They believe individuals need to be subjective, not objective, in their search for meaning. This search is to be a personal choice, not dependent on objective proofs. Existentialists maintain that, as individuals, we are confronted with choices in life which we alone can make. Therefore we must accept full responsibility for our choices.

What Is of Value?   Values are individual decisions and are selected. Insisting the individual is a creative being, Existentialists consider their values to be widely divergent. As humans, we enter this world without meaning, and any meaning that occurs is constructed by us. The formation of meaning is an individual matter which we ourselves forge. In other words, we exist without justification from God or science, except for that meaning which we make. Existentialists believe we are totally free and totally responsible for our actions.

Existentialism in the Classroom.   Existentialism emphasizes the creation of ideas that are relevant to each student. It deals with each student as an individual who is unique. In this uniqueness, Existentialists focus on the student as a living, breathing human being in total, not just a mind. An Existentialist teacher emphasizes individuality and works to assist students to see themselves with all their fears, joys, hopes, and concerns. Existentialism argues that the first step in an educational process is to understand ourselves. In understanding ourselves, we are *becoming.* Teachers are to help students explore the world and open up the possibilities of this world for themselves.

Eastern Philosophies.   Four major geographic areas are considered to represent Eastern philosophy: India, China, Japan, and the Middle East. We are going to focus on Chinese and Japanese philosophical beliefs. Many Euro-Americans view these philosophical approaches as having only religious significance rather than being true philosophies. In fact, religious and philosophical beliefs are more intertwined within Eastern philosophical perspectives than they are in Western philosophy.

Chinese Beliefs.   The traditional Chinese philosophies emphasize the individual and his state of mind. They do not emphasize divine injunction but rather the striving of humanity to achieve harmony with the universe and with life. Two major philosophical beliefs held by the Chinese are Confucianism and Taoism.

Confucius, a Chinese philosopher, expected his students to revolutionize any government in which they might participate and to force the government to serve the needs of the people. Confucius believed students' initiative, character, and intelligence needed to be developed to the utmost. **Confucianism** assumes that humans are essentially social beings and are, to a considerable extent, molded by society. Confucius stated that humans could find happiness only as a community of free people. He also believed people could not be free if they followed someone else's beliefs.

Taoism was developed in contrast to Confucianism and greatly de-emphasizes competition. In other words, the best way to get something done is to leave it alone and it will happen. Taoists believe in conforming to nature, not forcing one's personal desires onto the natural course of events. Taoism exhorts us to let things come naturally; striving or straining after competitive goals is nonproductive and only gets in the way. Taoists believe that people should be able to govern themselves and should give their lives to correcting social injustices. While Confucianism stresses the realization of external responsibilities, Taoism concentrates on the necessary evolution of the inner being whereby one becomes ready to meet any difficulty.

The Chinese see Western culture as aggressive and competitive. They believe that excessive competition leads to quarrelsome individuals. Most Chinese philosophers extol the virtue of contentment and most Chinese practice it to a great degree. They find joy and drama in everyday events: family life, a bird, a flower, or a cricket's song. The Chinese value expanding on previous achievements, with an emphasis upon improving quality rather than increasing quantity. The story in Vignette 6.2 articulates the Chinese perspective.

VIGNETTE 6.2   *Chinese perspective*

Years ago when I was in Asia, I watched an old man tend his water clock. I had never seen a water clock, and because I was young, inquisitive, and immature, I asked him why he spent so much time taking care of a water clock when his watch was more accurate. I didn't realize I was bothering him, so I told him why the modern world needed innovations which would help people live better.

The old man patiently listened to me. It was obvious he understood what I was talking about. In fact, I thought he was aware of all the things I told him. Then he said, "My son, even though there are years separating you and me, there is something both you and I should understand. A water clock tells me more than the time. It explains to me the beauty and harmony of nature and the sincerity of life." Pausing, he looked at me and smiled, "I am too old to appreciate the artificiality of inventions—artificiality hides my true character."

??? *How might you apply this perspective to your life?*

___

Japanese Beliefs. Japanese philosophy has its base in **Shintoism.** Although not formally practiced much in modern Japan, the influence of Shintoism continues. This philosophical perspective focuses on recognizing life's pleasures and acquiring an affinity with nature. This means one must strive for peace of mind and the integrity of one's natural character.

Zen Buddhism is practiced by many Japanese, as well as many Indians and Chinese. Zen enlightenment carries a deep and lasting comprehension of one's place in the totality of the universe. Zen philosophers believe that illumination may come in a sudden flash during which one perceives one's self and the rest of the world. Most likely, enlightenment will occur only after an extended period of disciplined personal effort. Zen Buddhists maintain people must engage in a lengthy pursuit to solve the problem of final "knowing." Zen Buddhists proceed with a single-purposed ferocity and all the attendant frustration of a "mosquito trying to bite on a bar of iron." The anecdote in Vignette 6.3 gives the Japanese perspective.

VIGNETTE 6.3   *Japanese perspective*

It was the end of the year and the students were looking forward to graduation. They were looking forward to attending college and felt their most difficult days were past. I was from the United States so Sugi told me there was much I might not understand. Nonetheless, he tried to help me by telling me a story.

"Many years ago a young man entered the woods. He was dissatisfied about himself and felt his life was not in tune with nature. He wanted to think about himself and what his life goals should be. Unfortunately, he discovered living in the woods took much effort. He seemed to always be looking for food and shelter or helping others. He was starting to think he would never have time to think about his problems until one day he made a marvelous discovery. As he lived his day-to-day existence, he found himself becoming in tune with his environment. For him, that meant he truly knew. He left the woods soon thereafter."

What Is Real?   Eastern thought begins with sense experience and carries it back into consciousness. This is opposite of Western thought. Across all Eastern perspectives is the belief that humanity must be in tune with nature. The process of getting in tune with nature delineates what is real. Within the many veins of Eastern perspectives is the need for defining reality within the rules and regulations that codify one's life.

How Do We Know?   Eastern thought emphasizes not only the pursuit of knowledge but also the teaching of this knowledge to others. In Eastern thought, many philosophers were also teachers. Sensory experience is diminished in the role of achieving wisdom. It is believed all paths lead to the achievement of wisdom and from wisdom comes virtue, right living, and correct social and political behavior.

What Is of Value?   A common thread throughout Eastern philosophy is the idea of social stability and peace of mind. Through the respect for families and ancestors and an abiding faith in society, a person can find worth and a place in society. For example, Confucianism states that it is not possible to repay the family for all it has done, yet it is important to work (study) hard for the honor of the family. To fail in anything, such as school, is more of a family disaster than an individual defeat.

Eastern Thought in the Classroom.   Eastern philosophers have historically viewed education as the primary means of achieving wisdom, establishing legal systems, maintaining the family, and supporting social and monetary interests.

Eastern philosophy places great value on the teacher–student relationship, especially as a method for transformation. Remember that for Eastern philosophers, change or transformation is expected both for society and the individual.

Educational methods in Eastern philosophy range from oral history to modern methods of communication. Great attention is given to writings of the great philosophers. Eastern philosophy demands order, regularity, and patience and incorporates those values into educational perspectives. The curriculum emphasizes rote learning and memorization. The teacher is viewed as the authority and is not questioned by students.

Because the teacher is held in such high regard, students are expected to follow the teacher's model of learning rather than learning on their own. Eastern cultures emphasize perfection, not just improvement, in the classroom. Finally, Eastern philosophies have rigid expectations, rules, and regulations for behavior both within and outside of the classroom.

Native American Philosophy.   Native American philosophy has maintained an extraordinary vibrancy in the face of enormous odds. Because of social, political, and geographic dislocations, Native Americans have been forced to continually adapt to new environments. There is no one overarching Native American philosophy, but there are common threads to be found among the various belief systems.

Native American philosophy holds that the world is made up of a social reality in which everything is related. Native Americans believe that because nature has no end, people should not view themselves as ceasing—people are part of a greater whole.

Native Americans believe their world has two experiential dimensions that must be taken together, *power* and *place*. Assimilation of the two dimensions provides a means of making sense of the world. *Power* is defined as the living energy that inhabits the universe; *place* is defined as the relationship of things to one another. When power and place are brought together, they produce personality. The universe is a living being: it lives within us and must be appreciated in that personal sense.

Native American philosophy is akin to Eastern philosophy insofar as it cannot accept the Western believe that the environment is dividable. Because the universe cannot be divided into discrete units, Native American philosophers argue that relationships are important. A person's actions therefore are very important, for the result of those actions may be damaging to the relationships. To illustrate, Native Americans believe killing animals for sport is damaging to the relationship within the universe. However, hunting for needed food is appropriate. Vignette 6.4 illustrates the Native American philosophical perspective.

VIGNETTE 6.4   *Native American perspective*

"How much do you want for your land?" Adam asked Red Deer. Red Deer didn't respond. "Why don't you answer me?" Adam said. "I am willing to pay you a fair price for your land. You know it is good and can produce good crops."

Red Deer felt bad. He had a problem. He hadn't thought about selling the land. In fact, he didn't know if he owned it. It was strange. He recognized so many of the locations on the land. For example, that small house where he was born stood by some trees. The cemetery where his ancestors were buried. He even saw how the land looked before he was born. Red Deer knew the spirits existed on and in the land, and he loved them.

"I don't own this land," Red Deer told Adam.

"But you have the title for the land, Red Deer," said Adam. "You can do anything you want with this land. It's yours!"

Red Deer was now truly confused. How could someone *own* land, when it was here before you were born and would be here after you died? He thought if anything, the land should own him. "I can't sell what isn't mine Adam," said Red Deer. "It would be like me asking you to sell something which was part of you."

??? *How do you think Red Deer defined "power" and "place"? How would you transfer these ideas into contemporary society?*

What Is Real? Individuals cannot own elements of the environment, although they may use those elements with care. Some ideas may exist outside of nature and, therefore, are artificial. For example, the concept of time on a clock may connote punctuality, but because it is outside of nature it should not have bearing on a person's existence. Because they are part of the environment, individuals should think of themselves as part of a group (tribe or clan). Native American philosophy values cooperation within the group and between groups. Competition is valued as long as it does not pit one individual against another. One learns through observation and questioning, in an atmosphere of patience. Because curiosity indicates impatience, a person cannot learn in that environment.

How Do We Know? "How do we know?" implies a personal involvement in the functioning of the natural world. For Native Americans, the universe has a personal nature that requires every one of us to seek and sustain personal relationships. All relationships have a moral content which is not separated from other sacred knowledge. Native Americans believe that relationships must not be left incomplete. To complete relationships, people must focus on the results of their actions.

The Native American perspective attempts to preserve the *whole* vision of the world and asks (1) how does it work? (2) what use is it? and (3) what does it mean? Native Americans believe that people must take their cues about the world from the experiences and evidence the world gives. In other words, knowledge cannot be forced from nature. Rather, knowledge must be accepted in its totality.

What Is of Value? Native Americans believe that our human personalities come from our responsibility to be contributing members of our society. They believe there are unifying principles that can be known through experience and that guide all people's behaviors. Families are highly valued in Native American cultures, but are defined differently than in the traditional Western culture. A family is a multi-generational complex of people, clans, and kinships which extend beyond the grave and into the future.

Native American Philosophy in the Classroom.   Native American teachers understand the lack of competitiveness in their children and encourage students to participate in the learning process without a need for aggressive behavior. For Native Americans, parental involvement in education is very important. Teachers include the families as partners in education; in fact, everyone who has something to do with the schooling of children is an important and valued part of the community. Native Americans expect educational programs to reflect the reality of their culture, community, and history for their children.

Education in the traditional Native American view occurs by example, not by indoctrination. The elders of the tribes are considered to be the best example of what the product of education and life experiences should be. Native Americans believe the elders incorporate both the positive and negative experiences of life, which is critical for younger persons to understand. Native Americans consider successes to be accomplishments of the family, which each member contributes to. Individuality is discounted. Traditional knowledge is important to help people see their place and responsibility within history.

Native Americans believe that curriculum reform is necessary. They want direct control over their educational institutions. Cultural retention is an important issue in this educational reform. Many Native Americans believe that assimilation of the Euro-American educational philosophies has been detrimental to their social, economic, and political well-being. This philosophical approach insists education must be relevant to tribal communities. Not surprisingly, Native American philosophy argues for a holistic approach to education.

African-American Philosophy.   Like Native American philosophy, **African-American philosophy** was born out of traditions that predate European history. Pervasive Euro-American domination has made it impossible to comprehend the total impact of the social, political, and geographic dislocations endured by African Americans since they first entered this country as slaves. As we explore African-American philosophy, we are forced to admit that the vast majority of African people came to America unwillingly, without free choice. They came as slaves and, as you read in Chapter 4, remained in bondage even after being "freed."

For us to understand African-American philosophy, we need to first discuss Africans before they were transported to the United States. The West Coast of Africa was the original location of most African Americans. Although these people have long been depicted as savages by many Europeans, in reality they lived in and with complex social institutions ranging from extended family groupings to village/states and territorial empires (Bennett, 1993).

The family was the nucleus of West African society. In some African tribes, the family was created on a matrilineal basis with the heritage coming from the mother, not the father. African social life was well-organized. The old, the sick, and the infirm were well cared for. Unmarried people were rare and prostitution was unknown. Although there were many different languages, there was a common thread among them. Studies of African tribal languages have shown them to be complex, corresponding in structure to Italian (Bennett, 1993).

Religious beliefs were deeply embedded in West African philosophy. Like people all over the world, Africans wrestled with questions such as: What is a person? What happens to people after death? What is the meaning of life? The answers to these questions formed the basis of African philosophy.

Undergirding all was the basic concept of 'life forces.' West Africans believed in a Supreme Being with several lesser gods. Intertwined with this was ancestor worship and a belief in fate. Life forces were seen as fragments of the Supreme Being or Creator that continued to exist even after a person died. For West Africans, "being" was a process, not a state. A person was thought of in terms of force or spiral energy rather than as a body composed of matter. Every event had religious significance, including death (Bennett, 1993).

African Americans brought traditions of kinship from their homeland. The African family was extended, with far-reaching kinship ties that gave personal meaning to economic, political, social, and religious relationships and functions. Kinship groups were the building blocks that allowed larger social units, such as village/states and territorial empires, to be founded and held together. Historically, Africans lived in agrarian societies in which the kinship group owned the livestock and the land was used communally but not owned. These kinship systems are at the heart of African-American philosophy and are reflected in African-American society today.

Booker T. Washington and W. E. B. Du Bois helped shape African-American educational philosophy. Washington believed African Americans should work hard in menial positions until acceptance by Euro-Americans was achieved. Du Bois argued vehemently against that position, believing that African Americans would gain respect by having access to the same opportunities as Euro-Americans.

Martin Luther King, Jr., and Malcolm X, who both were assassinated during the 1960s, also shaped educational philosophy. Malcolm X believed in radical political action and he called for a socioeconomic program that would give African Americans control of their communities. On the other hand, King advocated nonviolent direct action as the way for African Americans to gain equality. He organized marches, supported equal education for African-American children, and focused the African-American community's attention on achieving equal status with Euro-Americans. The clearest example of King's philosophy can be found in the speech he gave on August 28, 1963, on the steps of the Lincoln Memorial, in front of more than 250,000 Americans. Vignette 6.5 is an excerpt from King's most famous speech; it articulates one important part of African-American philosophy.

VIGNETTE 6.5   *"I have a dream," by Dr. Martin Luther King, Jr.*

I have a dream that one day this nation will rise up and live out the true meaning of its creed: "We hold these truths to be self-evident; that all men are created equal."

I have a dream that one day on the red hills of Georgia the sons of former slaves and the sons of former slaves owners will be able to sit down together at the table of brotherhood . . .

This is our hope. This is the faith with which I return to the South . . . With this faith, we will be able to work together, to pray together, to struggle together, to go to jail together, to stand up for freedom together, knowing that we will be free one day.

This will be the day when all of God's children will be able to sing with new meaning, "My country 'tis of thee, sweet land of liberty, of thee I sing, Land where my fathers died, land of the Pilgrim's pride, from every mountain side, let freedom ring. . . "

And if America is to be a great nation this must become true. So let freedom ring from the prodigious hilltops of New Hampshire. Let freedom ring from the mighty mountains of New York. Let freedom ring from the heightening Alleghenies of Pennsylvania! Let freedom ring from the snowcapped Rockies of Colorado!

Let freedom ring from the curvaceous peaks of California! But not only that; let freedom ring from Stone Mountain of Georgia!

Let freedom ring from every hill and mole hill of Mississippi. From every mountainside, let freedom ring.

When we let freedom ring, when we let it ring from every village and hamlet, from every state and every city, we will be able to speed up that day when all of God's children, black men and white men, Jews and Gentiles, Protestants and Catholics, will be able to join hands and sing in the words of that old Negro spiritual: "Free at last! Free at last! Thank God Almighty, we are free at last."

Source: Copyright © 1963 by Martin Luther King, Jr. Copyright renewed 1991 by Coretta Scott King. Reprinted by arrangement with the heirs to the estate of Martin Luther King, Jr., c/o Writers House, Inc. as agent for the proprietor.

???   *Reflect and discuss in small groups how your dreams have been influenced by the ideas in King's speech.*

The African-American struggle to be free, to be equal, to be affirmed, and to succeed was born from slavery. Most African Americans have a positive sense of racial identity and spiritual strength, derived from the physical and psychological struggles of slavery. These struggles are what shaped a distinct African-American philosophy.

What Is Real?   For African Americans, reality is based in the communal networks of support found in their families and religious and civic institutions. These institutions create a culture of meaning, a feeling of support, and a positive identity for African Americans within the larger culture. This bringing together of loving yet critical affirmations facilitates individual worthiness and allows for the hope for transracial understanding.

How Do We Know?   In African-American philosophy, knowledge is contained within African-American culture and history and their relationship to contemporary living. The Afrocentric way of viewing the world is different from the Eurocentric way. Afrocentricity holds that there is a transforming power involving five levels of awareness. In the first four levels, people share personalities, interests, and concerns with other African people in the global community. The fifth level of Afrocentricity is achieved when people struggle against acceptance of dominant cultures as replacements for their own culture and ways of knowing.

What Is of Value?   African Americans emphasize self-love and love of others as methods by which people can enhance their personal lives and encourage political change. They place value on the family and individual differences. It is important for people to understand their own cultural heritage and to be accepted as they are, not as less than others.

African-American Philosophy in the Classroom.   In a pluralistic society, it is important to create a culturally inclusive curriculum. For African Americans, this means learning about African-American children and their culture and incorporating this knowledge into the curriculum. African-American philosophy holds that African-American children need to have their culture and customs acknowledged in conjunction with the reality of their history. This philosophy encourages the idea that all people have individual and unique profiles of intelligence. Children learn differently and must not be made over to reflect any one specific image. It is important for teachers to recognize differences to facilitate learning. African-American philosophy does not want people to be color blind, rather it wants us to appreciate the diversity of our nation.

Not surprisingly, African-American educational philosophy has viewed education as the key that can unlock both knowledge and power. African Americans see education as a struggle to free the mind. In this struggle, they believe it is necessary to understand that who you become is a result of the obstacles you have overcome. All of us have to make our way out of nothing. It is this process of *becoming* that African Americans see as crucial to the educational process.

Educational Theories in Action

Educational theories are based on the general schools of philosophy which we have just studied. Educational theories put the various schools of philosophy into action. Teachers choose what they think is the most effective method of presenting information to students.

Contemporary Theories of Education

Perennialism.

Perennialism is based on the educational philosophies of Idealism and Realism and, like these philosophies, views Truth as constant and never-changing. Perennialists believe it is our ability to reason that makes us different from the nonhuman inhabitants of our world. They advocate the cultivation of intellect, because it is critical to our understanding Truth. Perennialism argues that we must develop our intellect by learning how to focus our instinctual and emotional energies in the pursuit of rational, logical, thought. The main purpose of education, for a Perennialist, is to nourish a person's intellect.

Values.   Perennialists promote the study of the great books, because they believe this study will develop reasoning and analytic abilities that can then be put to use in solving current societal or world problems. Value is placed on training the intellect through the use of difficult mental exercises, such as grammar, logic, and rhetoric. Perennialists believe the classics incorporate unequivocal facts and exemplify the foremost knowledge that has been created by the great thinkers of our world. This learning, they argue, will develop excellent reasoning powers in students.

Curriculum.   The curriculum of a Perennialist teacher relies heavily on studying the classics in the European tradition. These are the best and most significant works created by humans. The criterion for a curriculum is: Are students learning information which represents the most lofty accomplishments in that area? A traditional curriculum of arithmetic, reading, and writing is the core for elementary schools. Secondary schools are to focus their energies on the intellectually gifted. Those students who are not pursuing advanced education will be put into a vocational education program.

Teaching Style.   A Perennialist teaching style focuses on extensive reading in the classics. A Perennialist teacher asks questions for the purpose of eliciting students' views. A teacher's job is to help students reach their own conclusions through the uncovering of consistent underlying principles. Perennialism is authoritarian in its approach to learning, with the teacher as the dispenser of knowledge and the students as the recipients.

Essentialism.   Like Perennialism, **Essentialism** assumes that a core of common knowledge students need to learn exists. Essentialists believe this knowledge needs to be transmitted to students in a methodical, orderly manner. This core of common knowledge and skills is crucial for students, so they can become productive members of society. Unlike Perennialism in its search for Truth, Essentialism understands that knowledge can and will change because information changes. Through the development of basic skills, a greater understanding of this information will occur.

Values.   Essentialists value the transmission of our cultural heritage to students. Worth is placed on the learning of good study habits, mental discipline, respect for authority, and a fundamental core of knowledge so that students will become good citizens.

Curriculum.   Essentialists believe the curriculum should be practical and provide students with sound instruction by which to live their lives. However, Essentialists are opposed to a curriculum that emphasizes or attempts to influence social policies. An example of the Essentialist philosophy is the back-to-basics movement that began in the 1970s. This movement stresses reading, writing, and mathematics.

Teaching Style. The Essentialists stress traditional teaching in the classroom. They emphasize the teaching of facts and give little place to the arts and humanities. The Essentialist teacher is one who believes school is a place for students to learn a core body of knowledge. In other words, students are in school to learn from the teacher. The Essentialist teacher is authoritarian and emphasizes required readings, lectures, memorization, and examinations as a major part of the learning process.

Progressivism.

Progressivism is based on Pragmatism and is the counterpoint to both Essentialism and Perennialism. **Progressivism** emphasizes educating the cognitive, social, physical, and moral aspects of the student, using what is called the whole-person approach. Human experiences are believed to be the basis of knowledge, thus Progressivism strives to teach students *how* to think, not *what* to think. Progressivists contend that while truth and/or knowledge may be factual today, it may change in the future. They also maintain that people are basically good and can be trusted to act in their own best interests.

Values. Progressivists embrace a student-centered approach and stress the *process* of learning rather than the *result.* Progressivists value change and advocate preparing students to cope with change. Rather than focusing on a specific body of knowledge to be taught in the classroom, Progessivists emphasize flexibility in educational styles.

Curriculum. This curriculum emphasizes the integration of children's needs and interests with the resources necessary to guide the students' learning. Progressivists do not believe in teaching by drill, memorization, or use of authoritarian powers. Their curriculum accentuates a cooperative, problem-solving approach in which both teachers and students learn together. This approach is congruent with the concept that children are basically good and the school needs to provide an environment in which this basic goodness can be nurtured.

Teaching Style. A Progressivist teacher uses the scientific method to have students examine social experiences, projects, problems, and experiments. This process helps students develop a functional knowledge base derived from all subjects. Books are seen as just one of the tools available to teachers to facilitate student learning. Perhaps most importantly, teachers work with students in planning the lessons to be learned.

Social Reconstructionism.

Social Reconstructionism has two major premises: (1) society is in constant need of change, and (2) this social change involves the use of schools. The concept of change means involving people in making life better than it currently is. Social Reconstructionists are generally thought of as social and educational activists, and concentrate on how social and cultural conditions can be enhanced for all of humanity. Not surprisingly, Social Reconstructionists see society in a serious struggle for survival. They believe that educators are social activists and that school is a change agent.

Values.   Social Reconstructionists believe that the primary struggle in modern society occurs between those who advocate and work for radical changes and those who advocate maintenance of the status quo. Social Reconstructionists see themselves as radical educational reformers who are involved in societal as well as educational change. In fact, Social Reconstructionists argue that educational reform requires teachers to be deeply immersed in societal change movements. They are adamant that educators are agents for action within and without the classroom.

Curriculum.   Social Reconstructionists favor curriculums that emphasize student involvement in societal and world issues. They advocate the integration of cultural pluralism and multicultural education in educational programs. They believe that education in the United States has overlooked the cultural diversity of its citizens, and that society has suffered as a result. Finally, Social Reconstructionists contend educators must teach how current social issues will affect our future.

Teaching Style.   Social Reconstructionists are generally critical of the current methods used in schools, because they believe these methods reinforce traditional values and attitudes and make it difficult to change. They assert that most textbooks are chosen because they are noncontroversial, or because they contain subtle forms of stereotypes that preserve the dominant culture. Social Reconstructionists endorse teachers focusing on critical social issues in the classroom. In this way, students will develop critical and analytical thinking skills. They will become an actual part of the process of formulating the objectives, methods, and curricula used in their educational process.

Cultural Inclusivity in the Classroom.   **Cultural Inclusivity** refers to the need to understand and incorporate diverse cultures in our classrooms. Cultural inclusivity acknowledges the need to learn about the various race/ethnicities and attendant cultures that comprise our nation. By practicing cultural inclusivity, we turn ethnic diversity into an educational advantage for all. For example, we learn about different national holidays that relate to various cultures. By celebrating these different holidays, we enhance the diversity of our classrooms and decrease the level of stereotyping and prejudice. Vignette 6.6 suggests a way cultural diversity can be used to enrich all students' education.

VIGNETTE 6.6   *Kwanzaa*

Most of the students were becoming restless. After all, it was Friday afternoon and everyone was ready for winter vacation. Christmas was coming soon and most of the students were more interested in their gift lists than in world geography. Even Dela Moore, the teacher, had to agree.

"What will you do during vacation besides eat a lot of turkey?" Ken asked Larry as they were putting away their books.

"Oh, I think I'll sleep as much as my parents will let me. But I'm really looking forward to seeing my grandparents when we celebrate Kwanzaa."

"Kwanzaa? What's that? Some new age religion?" Ken sneered.

"No," said Larry. "It isn't really a religion."

"Well," said Ken, "it's hard for me to believe people would celebrate something that isn't a religion. It sounds silly."

Larry was becoming ruffled. "Kwanzaa is a celebration of a lifestyle that's . . . "

But before he could say any more, Miss Moore, who had overheard, joined their conversation. "Our neighbors have been telling me about Kwanzaa. I didn't realize it wasn't a religion. I also learned Kwanzaa is not an African holiday."

"That's right," said Larry. "Many people who are not African Americans don't understand Kwanzaa. But, if you like, I would be happy to take pictures of our celebrations and have my Dad and little sister come to school to talk about it after the vacation."

Miss Moore realized she had an opportunity to promote cultural awareness in her classroom and quickly agreed.

???   *How could you incorporate a culturally inclusive perspective into your teaching style?*

Values. When we are culturally sensitive, we are willing to incorporate diverse values into our perspective. Some people value a human-relationship centered world; others a person-centered one. For some, reliance is placed on hierarchical and formal relationships, for others informal relationships work best. In either case, cultural inclusivity requires an emphasis on personal duty, a respect for authority, and a concern for group harmony.

Curriculum. A culturally inclusive curriculum works to include all students using a cooperative method of learning. For many students, motivation is derived from a concern for how their group will be perceived. For these students, identity is group-based not individually based. The content of the curriculum needs to be culturally inclusive rather than exclusive, so that all students, whether from the mainstream culture or a different culture, will learn new and different ways of solving social problems.

Teaching Style. A teacher who is culturally inclusive provides opportunities for all students to display their skills, aptitudes, or talents to their classmates. This facilitates the students' acceptance of each other. Teachers who are able to establish close personal relationships with students using approval and support will be able to use these relationships to reinforce children's accomplishments. For example, teachers may give step-by-step instructions for carrying out specific tasks because some students may function best in a highly structured learning environment. It is important to keep in mind that a highly structured classroom is different from a strictly disciplined classroom. Students often learn through modeling and emulation. This learning style is important for teachers as they develop the best method for instruction in their classroom.

Your Personal Philosophy of Education

Developing your personal philosophy of education requires an awareness of education as more than just school or classroom activities. Education occurs throughout our lives on a continual basis. Our view of this process of education is part of our own personal philosophy. When you enter the classroom, it can become very easy to focus on only those activities which directly involve you as a teacher. It is very easy for school administrators to be only concerned with the daily, monthly, and yearly concerns of administering the school in an efficient manner. Yet it is impossible to separate education, or the school, from the social and cultural environment in which it exists. Education is the passing on of cultural and social heritage from one generation to another. It also is the process of learning new and different ways of doing things by utilizing our skills, abilities, and knowledge as the global community continues to change.

Philosophy provides a comprehensive view of education. Philosophy is a discipline that enables us to develop a coherent understanding of education. As you review each of the educational philosophies and educational theories in this chapter, think about how your beliefs influence what you do, how you think, and how you best learn.

Developing Your Personal Philosophy

These questions will help you develop your personal philosophy. Remember, education must fit in with your values if you are to be happy—and good at—teaching.

VALUES

- What are your personal values?
- Do you value individuality and an ongoing quest for knowledge? Or do you like and value change?
- Is structure in a learning situation important to you, or would you rather learn in a loosely structured environment?

CURRICULUM

- Are you more comfortable with traditional methods of doing things? Or are you willing to experiment with new and different techniques?
- Is it important for you, as a student, to have a core or base of knowledge? Or are you more interested in gathering information about a variety of subjects that you can weave together?
- Do you learn best in a situation where you can work on your own? Or do you work best in a cooperative group setting?

How Your Learning Style Influences Your Teaching Style

Reflect on several instructors you have had during your college years. Which of their teaching styles made you most comfortable? Did they use the lecture method in which the teacher is in a position of authority, asks for minimal feedback, and relies on memorization and examinations? Or did they actively involve students in discussions and cooperative work sessions? Your learning style is indicative of your teaching style.

As you review the educational philosophies we have discussed in this chapter, keep in mind that you will be building your educational philosophy over a period of time. You have just begun the process. The development of a personal philosophy of education requires continual research, study, and reading in the area of educational philosophy. You must be actively involved in education if your personal educational philosophy is to continue to evolve.

What You Have Learned

✔ The study of philosophy asks three basic questions: (1) What is real? (metaphysics), (2) How do we know? (epistemology), and (3) What is it we value most? (axiology).

✔ Idealism contends that only ideas are truly real, because the world is forever changing.

✔ Realism believes that facts and information are autonomous, not dependent upon the mind.

✔ The deductive method of inquiry moves from the general to the specific, while the inductive method of inquiry moves from the specific to the general.

✔ Pragmatism is a philosophy that assumes people will pursue the best possible means to achieve the most desirable resolutions to current problems in society.

✔ Existentialism holds that the attributes of experience, reality, and purpose are pivotal within the lived experiences of a person.

✔ Eastern philosophy has common threads of social stability and peace of mind. This approach maintains that through a respect for families and ancestors and an abiding faith in society, a person can find contentment and a place in society. Eastern perspectives view education as the primary means of achieving wisdom, estab-

lishing legal systems, maintaining the family, and supporting social and monetary interests.

✔ Native American philosophy holds that knowledge of facts cannot be separated from knowledge about spiritual realities. The Native American perspective attempts to preserve the whole vision of the world and asks (1) how does it work? (2) what use is it? and (3) what does it mean?

✔ African-American philosophy holds that a positive sense of racial identity, in combination with spiritual strength, is critical. The African-American perspective views education as the key to unlock both knowledge and power.

✔ Perennialism maintains that it is the rationality of humans that sets us apart, and it is the cultivation of the intellect that is critical to our understanding of the Truth.

✔ Essentialism maintains that a common core of knowledge must be transmitted to students in a methodical, orderly manner.

✔ Progressivism holds that education should address the whole person: the cognitive, social, physical, and moral aspects of the child.

✔ Social Reconstructionism has two major premises: (1) society is in constant need of change and (2) this social change involves the use of education.

✔ Development of a personal philosophy of education is important as it directly affects your teaching style and what you consider important knowledge for your students.

Key Terms

philosophy
metaphysics
epistemology
axiology
deductive method
inductive method
Idealism
Realism
Pragmatism
Existentialism
Confucianism
Taoism

Shintoism
Zen Buddhism
Native American
    philosophy
African-American
    philosophy
Perennialism
Essentialism
Progressivism
Social
    Reconstructionism
Cultural inclusivity

Applying What You Have Learned

1. Reread *Becoming a Teacher,* then break into small groups. Identify a new teacher and an experienced teacher. What are the philosophic similarities between them? What are the differences?
2. Identify which educational philosophies the teachers in Question 1 reflect. Support your conclusions with examples. What are some implications for the students in their classrooms?

Interactive Learning

1. Outline your own philosophy of education, including logic, metaphysics, epistemology, and axiology. Share your personal philosophy with your small-group members. What type of classroom will you be most comfortable in? How will you include all your students?

2. Why do you think Idealism focuses on using a broad approach to learning? How does idealism intersect with the search for truth? Discuss with a small group of students how you (or they) would use this approach in your classroom.
3. Do you belong to a fraternity, sorority, or other social group on campus? In what way have you developed rules of morality through these groups? Observe others in your social group to confirm your findings. How might your rules of morality affect you as a teacher?
4. As you read this chapter, you learned that the cultural history of students can be seen in the philosophies and values they bring with them to school. How could you incorporate a culturally inclusive perspective into your teaching style? Interview several teachers and ask them if they were able to solve this problem. Compare their thoughts with yours.

Expanding Your Knowledge

Josephy, Alvin M., Jr. *America in 1492: The World of the Indian Peoples Before the Arrival of Columbus.* New York: Alfred A. Knopf, 1992. (A wonderful and exciting exploration of the Americas prior to 1492. It includes both North and South America and brings to life the vast array of native societies that inhabited this area.)

Ozmon, Howard, and Samuel Craver. *Philosophical Foundations of Education,* 5th edition. Upper Saddle River, NJ: Merrill/Prentice Hall, 1995. (An excellent discussion of the major philosophies in education, including a critique of each perspective.)

Pai, Young, and Susan A. Adler. *Cultural Foundations of Education.* 2d ed. Upper Saddle River, NJ: Merrill/Prentice Hall, 1990. (An excellent discussion of the many ways cultural factors influence education. Pai and Adler include case studies of African-American, Asian-American, Hispanic American, Native American and Euro-American perspectives, which enhance their examination of educational philosophy.)

Chapter 7

Learning and Teaching in the Classroom

In this chapter, you will learn about curriculum and how teachers deliver it to their students. For classroom teachers, this is the most important part of their professional lives—helping students learn. Classroom teachers know the purposes of schools are based on many factors, such as the cultures and ethnicities of the students as well as their own educational philosophy. They realize the purpose of the curriculum must be consistent with the purpose of the school.

As you study the different purposes of the school and curriculum, think about the type of schools in which you would like to teach. This is an opportunity for you to begin thinking about what kind of instructional leader you want to be.

What you will learn

- There is a relationship between the purposes of the school and the curriculum.
- Factors in the school and classroom influence how a curriculum is organized.
- There are various learning and teaching styles; all are influenced by technology.
- Tests and measurements are an essential consideration for developing a philosophy of grading.

BECOMING A TEACHER   *When is a massacre called a victory?*

"I don't understand it," Bill says. And in case he hadn't been heard, he raises his voice, "I just don't understand it!!" He is standing in the hall at Dunbar Junior High waiting to be called into a meeting with the superintendent and principal at which a group of irate parents are to present a petition demanding his teaching contract be cancelled.

Bill is a first-year social studies teacher, and what had at first been a wonderful idea about teaching a history unit on the Indian wars has turned into a nightmare. Bill had not even wanted to teach about the Indian wars, but it was a required part of the curriculum, so he decided to do the best he could.

Although Bill had learned about the Indian wars in college, it wasn't until he spent a summer after graduation working on a ranch in western Oklahoma that he understood what the wars really signified to both Euro-Americans and Native Americans. He could understand why many of the parents of his eighth-grade students were upset when they learned what he had taught about General Custer's military successes and failures throughout the west. Yet he thought there must be many other parents who understood about Custer and what had really happened. "Surely," he thought, "they wouldn't ask the superintendent to fire me over something so trivial as the Battle of the Little Bighorn."

As Bill's students had studied the Battle of the Little Bighorn, they had questioned why that specific battle was referred to as a "massacre." Ken asked the question first, "Why is it that when whites win a battle, it's called a victory, but when Indians win a battle, it's called a massacre?"

Other students picked up on Ken's point. Maryann said it the best. "When General Custer fought the Indians in Oklahoma, he purposely killed men, women, and children. But Sitting Bull gets a bum rap when he only fought against soldiers. He didn't kill women and children."

And Natalie asked, "If Sitting Bull was the leader of his army, why don't we call him General Sitting Bull?"

At the meeting, Bill hears the parents' side of the story. "It's absolutely disgusting to think you took the Indians' side in this lesson," one of the parents says.

"If this is the type of teacher you are, you shouldn't be allowed to give these crazy ideas to our children," says another.

Finally, one mother, a Native American, speaks. "I have really tried to remain quiet in this meeting, but I have something I want to say. When I was young I lived in South Dakota on an Indian reservation. I remember whites telling my father that his family deserved to live in poverty because he was lazy. I also remember that when he had a job, he was underpaid because whites said he didn't deserve the same amount of money as a white man—they said he would only spend his money in a bar. My father was a hard worker who struggled against great odds because he was not able to finish high school. And," she adds, almost as an afterthought, "I never saw him take a drink once in his life."

Dr. Yates, the superintendent, is shocked by the heartfelt emotion of the parents on both sides, but he realizes it is important not to take sides. Diplomatically, he says, "I know this is an important issue for many of us in this community, but I talked with several history professors at the state university. They agree that Bill's lesson plans are correct historically. Why do you want me to fire Bill?"

???   *Bill and Dr. Yates are facing a dilemma. Some parents are concerned that the traditional history of the Battle of the Little Bighorn will be lost if history is put in the hands of teachers like Bill. Others believe the battle should be put into proper context. Write a letter to Dr. Yates explaining your views about what Bill should teach about the Battle of the Little Bighorn.*

 ## Purposes of Schools

When you become a teacher, you will want to know what your students have learned in your classroom. Do you want them to know a lot of facts and information about the subjects you are teaching? Or are you interested in what they learn about themselves? Perhaps, if you are like many other teachers, you will want your students to learn about themselves *and* your subject matter.

This is the source of disagreement between Bill and several of his students' parents. They believe the purpose of Dunbar Junior High School is to teach students Euro-American information about the Indian wars. Bill believes schools should help students learn how the Indian wars impact their lives. He knows the United States is a multicultural society in which students represent diverse views and traditions. Let's look at several purposes of schools before learning about curriculum.

Schools for Social Conservation

Some educators, such as Bloom (1987), Hirsch (1987), and Schlesinger (1992), believe schools should conserve society's treasures and masterpieces. Classroom teachers, they believe, are like curators. They open the museums' doors so students can learn about society's great treasures. When the schools' purpose is to conserve society, it is easy to evaluate what students know and how well they are taught. Allan Bloom says schools have moral goals:

> Every educational system has a moral goal that it tries to attain and that informs its curriculum. It wants to produce a certain kind of human being. The intention is more or less explicit, more or less a result of reflection; but even the neutral subjects, like reading and writing and arithmetic, take their place in a vision of the educated person. (1987a, 26)

Bloom believes the proper purpose of the school is to recreate the Euro-American heritage in each student, regardless of personal heritage. This is what he means by the "vision of the educated person."

Schools for Social Change

At the opposite end of the spectrum, some educators (Counts, 1962) believe the purpose of schools is to change society. Society, they say, is filled with problems and schools should try to correct them. They believe classroom teachers should teach children how to improve their lives and, thus, society will be improved. For example, because medical science has discovered the harmful effects of tobacco, classroom teachers are obligated to encourage children not to smoke.

The most famous educator who believed that schools could change society was John Dewey. In his book, *Democracy and Education* (1916), Dewey said schools should help students recognize that the experiences they have will allow them to control the types of experiences they will have in the future. He believed experiences are either active or passive.

> On the active hand, experience is *trying*—a meaning which is made explicit in the connected term *experiment*. On the passive, it is *undergoing*. When we experience something, we act upon it, we do something with it, then we undergo the consequences. (p. 139)

Dewey is telling us schools change society when they allow students to take responsibility for their learning.

More recently, **reconceptionalists,** like Paulo Freire (1970), have discussed the role of schools in social change from another perspective. Freire and others believe schools should help students become active citizens so they can change society. Some reconceptionalists believe students should not be educated in the traditional Euro-centric tradition. Rather, students should learn how to cooperate with others to eradicate social problems such as racism and poverty. Other reconceptionalists, called Neo-Marxists, believe schools are expressions of Euro-centered capitalism. They contend students are the unwilling pawns of corporations who have little desire to help the individual. We will learn more about this later in the chapter.

Sergiovanni (1994) and Etzioni (1988) believe many of society's problems stem from the breakdown of families and neighborhoods. They point out that neighborhoods were, at one time, like large families, in which each member helped the others. Today, they contend, many people live in crowded neighborhoods isolated from each other. They believe the purpose of schools is to give students experiences in community building. In this changing society, children may be part of dysfunctional agencies, such as the family and the neighborhood, but schools have the ability to bring society together.

> Why is community building important in schools? Community is the tie that binds students and teachers together in special ways, to something more significant than themselves: shared values and ideals. It lifts both teachers and students to higher levels of self-understanding, commitment and performance. . . . Community can help teachers and students be transformed from a collection of "I's" to a collection of "we," thus providing them with a unique and enduring sense of identity, belonging, and place. (Sergiovanni, 1994, p. xiii)

Purposes of the Curriculum

Now that we have become familiar with different philosophies about the purposes of schools, let's look at curriculum—what children should learn. *Curriculum* is a term used by almost everyone, but it may mean something to one group of educators and something totally different to another.

The word *curriculum* is loosely translated from the Latin term *currere,* which originally meant to run a course, as in a race. The word *currere* is appropriate for schools, because we expect students to participate in prescribed subjects and have specific educational experiences. Educators disagree about what knowledge and experiences should be included in the curriculum. Let's look at various curricula and how they reflect the purposes of schools.

Curriculum for Social Conservation

A **curriculum for social conservation,** advanced by such scholars as Bloom (1987), Hirsch (1987), and Bestor (1985), focuses on students learning a structured sequence of courses that are organized into individual subject units. The subjects are standardized so all students learn the same content. A curriculum for social conservation is more likely to teach English than language arts, or history than social studies. Classroom teachers protect their students from learning "watered-down" information by organizing a series of agreed-upon facts that students are expected to learn.

Curriculum for Social Change

The **curriculum for social change** comprises the ideas of such educators as Dewey (1916), Freire (1970), and Sergiovanni (1994). These educators are interested in helping students learn to become productive members of society. For example, Sergiovanni (1994) describes how schools can teach students to become valued members of society while still in school:

> One way to instill the spirit of generosity, to teach caring, is by calling upon students to become actively involved in service projects. Even kindergartners and first-grade students can be called to service. High school students might teach residents of the local nursing home to use computers; younger children can clean their classroom, water the flowerpots in front of the school, or phone classmates who are ill. The Japanese are further ahead of us on this count. They routinely call upon students to share responsibility for caring for their schools with wonderful results. (p. 131)

Sergiovanni's point is that curriculum can teach students to be committed to important ideas that are beyond themselves. He wants students to be less self-centered. The ideal of contributing to the community or neighborhood helps students know they are important and that others care for them. Of course, Sergiovanni realizes his curriculum only can exist in schools that have social change as their purpose.

In the same fashion, Freire (1970) believes poor people in his native Brazil are trapped because they cannot control their lives. In an experiment, he taught them how to read. Then he required his students to list the problems they saw in their neighborhood. Next, he had them analyze the problems, so they could understand their social and economic consequences. Finally, he required his students to develop possible solutions. Freire demonstrated that educated individuals are active and willing to take social and economic risks.

 ## Organization of the Curriculum

Schools, of course, have different purposes at different levels of education. Curriculum organization, too, varies at different levels of education. Figure 7.1 lists the basic goals of different schools. As you look at it, think about what kind of curriculum organization works best at each level.

Figure 7.1 Curriculum and the Purposes of Schools

Elementary School	Curriculum designed to develop basic skills and knowledge.
Middle School	Curriculum designed to assist students in exploring their personal and academic environment.
Junior High School	Curriculum designed to assist students in exploring their personal and academic environment and preparing academically for senior high school.
Senior High School	Curriculum designed to prepare students for continued · education in college or to enter the world of work.

Single-Subject Curriculum

You may remember the **single-subject curriculum** from your school days. In it, you took courses in specific subjects such as math, science, literature, and history. The oldest form of curriculum organization in the western world, it emphasizes uniform learning of facts, information, and knowledge by students. It has philosophical foundations in Idealism and Realism. It originally came from Europe, where it began in the Medieval period. It was first known as the trivium and quadrivium. The trivium (meaning three subjects) focused on grammar, rhetoric, and logic. The quadrivium (meaning four subjects) included arithmetic, geometry, music, and astronomy.

The content of today's single-subject curriculum is much different, but the idea is still the same. The single-subject curriculum's success has come from the ease in which it has been used by state departments of education, classroom teachers and students alike. Facts, information, and knowledge are emphasized, so classroom teachers can easily test students' knowledge.

Some educators, like Schlesinger (1992), believe the single-subject curriculum alleviates the problems of tracking. Single-subject curriculum does enhance tracking, by identifying bright students for advanced placement programs, or less-capable students for remedial classes.

Single-subject curriculums do present problems. The most obvious problem is its rigidity. Students are required to learn the curriculum in a prescribed manner, regardless of personal learning style. Most single-subject curricula encourage students to learn through the lecture method, classroom discussions, essays, and projects. Of course, this is especially difficult for children who represent cultures or ethnicities that foster other types of learning styles. It is also difficult for classroom teachers, because they have few teaching strategies from which to choose.

Competency-Based Curriculum

Competency-based education (CBE) assumes the competencies students learn are first defined by classroom teachers. A relatively new curriculum organization, competency-based education, sometimes called **outcome-based education (OBE)** or mastery learning, is intended to help students learn specific pieces of knowledge from fragments of the curriculum. Rooted in Realism, competency-based education requires that facts or skills be specific, identifiable, and measurable. Students learn beginning with the simple and moving to the complex.

Competency-based education is not without its critics. It has been attacked by fundamentalist Christian parents (Schlafly, 1993) as being in opposition to what they want their children to learn. Others are critical because it requires subjects to remain isolated from each other. Even state legislatures have debated its value.

Broad Fields Curriculum

The **broad fields curriculum,** or **fused curriculum,** was developed to correct problems created by the single-subject curriculum. Its purpose is to imitate real life in the classroom by combining selected single subjects into larger curricular fields. A common example is social studies. In social studies, students learn how history, geography, sociology, economics, and other subjects are interrelated. Another example is language arts. In language arts, students are taught that communication is both written and oral.

Supporters of the broad fields curriculum insist it emphasizes critical thinking, because students do not learn isolated facts. Because the broad fields curriculum is rooted in Pragmatism, subject matter is integrated, logical, and useful. Proponents of the single-subject curriculum believe this represents a watering down of the curriculum.

Activity Curriculum

The **activity curriculum,** or **child-centered curriculum,** is dependent on students' interests and their motivation to learn. Like the broad fields curriculum, it has its roots in Pragmatism. It was popularized by John Dewey, who wanted students to be actively involved in what they learned, rather than be passive receptors of knowledge as they were in the single-subject curriculum. Dewey assumed that if students were responsible for learning a curriculum based on real-life issues, they would be motivated. In fact, he felt students should be actively involved with teachers in planning their learning.

Several flaws were readily apparent in Dewey's curriculum. For example, he wanted classroom teachers to continually change and modify the curriculum as their students' needs changed. This made the curriculum impractical. As a Euro-centered philosopher, he wanted students to learn through the problem-solving and inquiry methods. It would be interesting to see how John Dewey would develop his curriculum today, in a multicultural society. Perhaps he would change some of his views.

Students learning together.

Core Curriculum

The **core curriculum,** like the activity and the broad fields curriculums, is a reaction against the single-subject curriculum. Proponents, such as Goodlad (1984) and Banks (1991a), believe the core curriculum helps students understand that information is interrelated.

Banks (1991a) discusses the core curriculum from a "transformational approach." He says students should learn different types of information so they can understand ideas from various points of view. This is what Bill was attempting to do in *Becoming a Teacher.* Some of the more common advantages of the core curriculum are:

- Students reinforce their learning with related information.
- Students understand ideas and knowledge from different points of view.
- Students relate what they learn in the classroom to contemporary social problems and ideas.
- Students participate in their own learning.

Although the core curriculum has many advantages, critics like Bloom (1987) believe it does not give students opportunities to learn specific information, as the single-subject curriculum does. There is no guarantee all children will learn the same thing. Other critics point out that the core curriculum is difficult to teach. They believe many teachers have not been prepared to integrate new and differing academic content in their classrooms. For example, Schubert (1986) questions whether students are sufficiently mature to develop a balanced curriculum for themselves. He believes the core curriculum, in practice, amounts to nothing more than a list of courses students must take.

Humanistic Curriculum

The **humanistic curriculum** is based on Existentialism and client-centered psychology. **Client-centered psychology** is based on theories of Carl Rogers (1983) and others. They advance the concepts of openness, honesty, and uniqueness of the individual. Rogers insists facts make sense only when they relate to other information. Humanistic classroom teachers encourage students to learn information in relation to the whole. Rogers believes that when this happens, student behavior will change.

Like Dewey's activity curriculum, the humanistic curriculum is student-centered. Basically, classroom teachers are monitors or guides who supervise or oversee students' learning. Consequently, the classroom teacher and the students develop a close personal relationship based on trust and mutual respect. Both students and classroom teachers personalize what they are learning.

As early as the 1980s, critics of the humanistic curriculum believed it was doomed to failure. How can students learn when there are few objectives, they asked. They believed the humanistic curriculum would promote chaos in classrooms.

Classroom Factors Influencing Curriculum

The **explicit curriculum** is the public statement of what knowledge and skills students are expected to learn. The curriculum is affected by many factors: physical plant, student schedules, attitudes and values of students and classroom teachers, and other factors that may not be obvious. Let's look at some factors that may modify curriculum.

School Buildings and Class Schedules

Two factors that traditionally influence the curriculum are the school building and student schedules. School buildings, or school plants as they sometimes are called, create the physical environment in which learning takes place. If the school building is designed according to the traditional factory model, with standardized classrooms, halls, and assembly areas, some curriculums will not succeed. Many classroom teachers complain about schools built this way because the floor plan allows teachers and students to remain isolated.

A school in rural America.

Student schedules, too, influence the curriculum. Such factors as the length of the school year and the extent of course offerings impact what students learn. While some scheduling factors are beyond the control of the classroom teacher, others are not. For example, how much time students spend learning and the length of class periods are within the grasp of the classroom teacher and the school system.

Hidden Curriculum

There is another part of the curriculum that is seldom talked about and poorly understood. The values and ideals students and teachers espouse impact what students learn beyond the explicit curriculum.

The **hidden curriculum** (sometimes called the implicit curriculum) is a series of informal, unspoken demands placed on students to act in a prescribed manner. It includes the way students interact with others including classroom teachers. It even includes the way classrooms, halls, and lunchrooms are decorated.

Two examples of what students learn in the hidden curriculum are the value of competition and the importance of grades (Eisner, 1985). Students learn the importance of grades from their friends and classroom teachers. They understand that competition results in rewards and respect, such as that given to athletes by students, teachers, and the community. Eisner believes children's self-worth is influenced by the types of classes in which they are placed. In fact, what the hidden curriculum teaches is what the culture of the school really values.

Extracurricular Activities

Extracurricular activities, a traditional part of the school experience, comprise another curriculum. Typically, extracurricular activities include athletics, music, theater, student government, and various social clubs. The purpose of extracurricular activities is to give students social and intellectual experiences that support the classroom curriculum. In fact, some educators believe these experiences are so important they should be thought of as co-curricular activities equal in importance to the curriculum taught in the classroom. Sergiovanni (1994) believes extracurricular activities can also create a bonding among students and classroom teachers in the community called the school.

There are critics (Gifford & Dean, 1990) who believe that extracurricular activities have no educational value. In fact, many parents today question how extracurricular programs can help their children prepare for college entrance exams. As a consequence, extracurricular activities have been de-emphasized by state departments of education and legislatures. For example, the Texas legislature enacted the no pass/no play rule, but recently modified it because so many players were being punished. The legislation requires students to maintain a specific grade point average in order to participate in extracurricular activities.

Null Curriculum

So far you've studied what students should learn in school. But equally important is what students are *not* taught, what has been left out of the curriculum. Eisner (1979) refers to that missing information as the **null curriculum.** The null curriculum is found in every classroom.

Small communities support school activities.

Because students are in school for a limited time, classroom teachers have to prioritize what students learn. For example, in Language Arts classes, it may have been decided that students need to learn more short stories and poetry because they are emphasized on college admissions tests. Because of time constraints, other parts of the curriculum will be de-emphasized. Students may have less class time to learn creative writing or improving their spelling skills. Other parts of the Language Arts curriculum may be lost entirely.

Many times the null curriculum is a focus for special interest groups. You will become more familiar with this later in the chapter, when you study textbook adoption. In short, the null curriculum illustrates the continuing professional debate about the purposes of the curriculum and the classroom.

Instruction

In this section you will learn how teachers implement the curriculum. As you learned in Chapter 6, it is important for classroom teachers to develop an effective instructional philosophy. As you develop your instructional philosophy, ask yourself these questions:

- What do you want your students to learn?
- What results do you expect of your students?
- What instructional methodology will you use?
- How will you know that the students have learned what you intended?

Instructional Objectives

Curriculum purposes are the long-range aims classroom teachers have in mind when they teach their students. For example, teachers may want their students to read more books or understand how literature helps them become part of a Euro-centered society (curriculum for social conservation). Or teachers may want students to understand how society's problems influence the quality of their lives (curriculum for social change).

Curriculum purposes may also be expressed by the school board, the state department of education, or other professional groups. School boards may express the curriculum purpose that students should learn more about specific topics so they score higher on state and national achievement tests. You will become more acquainted with curriculum purposes when you study Chapter 13.

As classroom teachers understand curriculum purposes, they develop instructional objectives that help students have positive learning experiences. **Instructional objectives** are the anticipated results of instruction, usually stated as behavior objectives. Classroom teachers understand that students have different learning styles that are influenced by many factors, including their social, cultural, and ethnic heritage. Teachers need to develop instructional approaches that meet students' learning styles.

Specific Learning Objectives

Just as long-range goals are intended to help you arrive at your instructional objectives, **specific learning objectives** are the outcomes classroom teachers expect to meet in each instructional unit. Learning objectives should have three basic components:

- The specific class assignment.
- Intended observable student behavior.
- Minimum level of acceptable outcomes by each student.

For example, if you are teaching junior high school French, your specific learning objective might be whether each small group can translate an assigned Molière play from French to English without error.

Learning Styles

Just as classroom teachers need instructional and specific learning objectives, they also must recognize that all students have individual learning styles. Some students learn quickly, while others seem to plod along. Some students may learn visually, while others are more comfortable listening. Some students enjoy the security of learning in small groups, while others find comfort in being concealed in large classes. Students also bring their primary learning patterns with them to school.

As early as the 1970s, educators were researching differences in how children learned. Castaneda and Gray (1974) believed these were two kinds of learners: field-dependent and field-independent. Field-dependent learners enjoy learning with others; field-independent learners enjoy learning by themselves.

More recently, some educators believe students' learning styles are subject to various stimuli. For example, Dunn and Dunn (1993) have identified five stimuli that impact learning style. The first, environmental, is concerned with activities that surround the student who is studying. The second, sociological, focuses on how students may be swayed by the attitudes and feelings they have for others. The third, physical/perceptual strength, relates to *where* students study and *when,* during the day or week, they are required to learn. The fourth, emotional, relates to the learner's own set of values about the importance of the material being learned. The fifth stimuli, psychological, focuses on the attitudes students may have about learning in general.

While Dunn and Dunn believe students are influenced by five stimuli, others such as Reiff (1992), believe students are influenced by two. Reiff believes some students are reflective learners, who like to dissect problems or question why something is as it is. He believes these students enjoy learning by themselves. The other type identified by Reiff is the impulsive learner. These students like to take chances and are curious. They usually interact with fellow students and teachers, but lose patience easily if their studies do not give them immediate satisfactory results.

In short, learning styles are influenced by the student's history and culture, the subject matter, and the classroom's learning environment.

Instructional Approaches

By now, you realize that no single instructional approach is perfect for all students. Because student learning is based on many things—including culture, race, ethnicity, and gender—classroom teachers acquire a broad set of instructional approaches. Because students interpret the curriculum differently, good teachers are eclectic in their choice of instructional approaches.

Mastery Learning.

Benjamin Bloom (1976) has developed a concept called mastery learning to account for students whose abilities differ or who learn at different rates. While you may expect all students in your classroom to achieve the same specific learning objective, mastery learning allows them a greater degree of flexibility in which to learn by giving low-achieving students sufficient classroom time to successfully learn and teachers who are willing to help (Levine, 1988).

Mastery learning assumes classroom teachers will distinguish between the time students need to learn and the time available for learning (Carroll, 1989). Student learning styles determine the amount of time needed, but the classroom teacher controls the amount of time allotted. Mastery learning requires teachers to be realistic in their expectations of how much time students require to learn. Its goal is the success of each student.

Critical Thinking Skills.

To become independent thinkers, students are taught **critical thinking skills.** They learn how to ask questions, explore divergent viewpoints, examine evidence, and draw conclusions. Critical thinking skills challenge students to think about why they have formed an opinion rather than learn the information necessary to answer the questions on a test.

Critical thinking skills were once thought to be acquired informally. But more recently, critical thinking skills are being introduced through formal instruction by classroom teachers. These skills allow students to become more responsible for their own learning, and critical thinking skills transfer from school to other life situations. Vignette 7.1 shows how critical thinking skills shape—and are shaped by—personal experience.

VIGNETTE 7.1   *Ito: Coming to America*

I remember coming to the United States as if it were yesterday. I came because I wasn't allowed to go to college in my own country. Even though I was young, I knew I needed a college education to succeed in life. I didn't realize then how coming to this country would change my life. Eventually, I become an American citizen and a classroom teacher.

Throughout the years, I've seen foreign students. As they learn about the United States, they remind me how I learned. For example, their study habits are the same as mine when I arrived. Many memorize the lessons whether they understand them or not. I also watch the American students. They study just as hard, but they have a different attitude about learning.

After years in this country, I believe I better understand the differences. The reason foreign students study so hard is that they appreciate the opportunity to learn. It is a privilege. For Americans, learning is a right. Having the opportunity to go to school is not something American children think about. They know going to school will help them become anything they want to be.

??? *What skills was Ito using to reach his conclusion?*

Individualized Learning.   Many times classroom teachers encourage students to work at their own pace. This is referred to as **individualized learning.** Most individualized learning relies heavily upon a structured curriculum in which the student controls how much time is spent on each lesson or unit. The student and teacher work together, with the teacher monitoring learning.

One of the most common individualized learning programs is the Personalized System of Instruction (PSI), or the Keller Plan. This program uses students who have already learned the content to help beginners. The Program for Learning in Accordance with Needs (PLAN) encourages students to learn in specific time blocks; you may recognize it in the individualized block scheduling found in some schools.

All individualized learning programs incorporate the following steps:

- Test the student to discover what information she or he already possesses.
- Help the student understand the specific learning objectives.
- Test the student at the completion of the instructional unit.
- Move to the next instructional unit and begin the process again when the student meets the specific learning objectives.

Cooperative Learning.   The purpose of **cooperative learning** (Johnson & Johnson, 1991; Slavin, 1995) is to help students learn in nonthreatening environments. Cooperative learning discourages competition, so students do not label themselves as winners or losers. It is designed to enhance leadership and cooperation among students. Cooperative learning can only succeed when every member understands the assignment and contributes to the benefit of the group.

Classroom teachers require students to learn appropriate skills in communication, leadership, trust, decision making, and conflict management before they actually form work groups (Johnson & Johnson, 1991). Groups must also analyze themselves to understand how they are functioning (Slavin, 1988). Cooperative learning is a positive instructional approach if it is used properly by the classroom teacher.

Inquiry Method.   Like the scientific method, the **inquiry method** (Dewey, 1938) focuses on students investigating problems. Although the inquiry method has many variations, such as discovery learning, all require students to take control of their own learning (Eggen & Kauchak, 1988). Classroom teachers empower students to become active learners who define problems, hypothesize, test, and draw conclusions. The inquiry method allows students to learn on several levels. On one level they may be solving social, scientific, or academic problems, while on another, they may be evaluating their feelings, attitudes, and knowledge.

Many classroom teachers like the inquiry method because it provides opportunities for students to learn outside the classroom. For example, social studies students who are studying local government may find themselves interacting on a personal level with government workers about real-life issues.

But the inquiry method can also create problems for some students. For example, a student who is studying the effects of poverty on families may discover his or her basic beliefs about what causes people to fall into poverty challenged. If the student believes only lazy people live in poverty, the shock of discovering how difficult it is for people to escape poverty may force the student to question basic beliefs learned at home.

Teacher-Directed Learning.   Teacher-directed learning is probably the teaching approach you have encountered most as a student. This instructional approach has many variations; in all, the teacher determines the curriculum and its delivery.

One of the oldest forms of teacher-directed learning is the lecture. The lecture approach is effective when professors present curriculum content to large classes. It allows classroom teachers to question students to obtain immediate feedback about their learning. When students ask teachers questions in class, it gives other students the benefit of clarifying and extending their knowledge. It also provides a central focus of authority for students who find this important to their learning styles.

But there are disadvantages to the lecture. Students learn at different rates. While the lecture may be too fast for some students, others may be bored. Because the lecture is highly dependent on listening, visual learners cannot take advantage of their optimum learning style. The lecture is also sedentary: students are required to be passive rather than hands-on and active. And giving an entertaining and thought-provoking lecture is very difficult—it requires the classroom teacher to become, in part, an actor.

Textbooks

Textbooks have been part of school life for centuries. Instructional innovations have come and gone, but textbooks are still the major instructional tool for most teachers. How are textbooks chosen for classroom use? Typically, representative groups of classroom teachers review books in their curriculum specialty at the state level. Usually, these adoption committees review large numbers of textbooks before arriving at a list of chosen books, from which textbook committees at the local level chose books. Depending on a school district's finances, teachers may also use other books from the adoption list to assist students' learning about a particular issue. Private schools usually pay close attention to the state adoption list if their goal is to remain accredited by the state department of education. However, private schools recognize the importance of expanding their textbook list to meet curriculum requirements specific to that school. To illustrate, most private Christian schools require students to read the Bible, while in public schools that book may be used for specific curriculum issues only.

Although some adoption criteria may appear to be superfluous, experienced classroom teachers understand the importance of textbook evaluation, especially when rising educational costs and shrinking school budgets force classroom teachers to use textbooks for as long as seven years. Teachers know students appreciate textbooks that are attractive, colorful, and that communicate concepts effectively. Textbook adoption committees also evaluate the quality of ancillary materials such as overheads, computerized test banks, posters, videotapes, teacher manuals, workbooks, and CD–ROMs or laser disks. These are usually excellent teaching aids that help classroom teachers use different teaching techniques. Of course, textbook content is the most important consideration.

Adoption committees try to gauge whether specific information might offend special interest groups within the community. These special interest groups represent all segments of society. While most groups are passive, others demand that schools adopt textbooks that are sympathetic to their educational philosophies. It is in this way that special interest groups influence the curriculum. Classroom teachers and school boards are well-aware that citizens have legal rights to express their convictions about what children should learn. Vignette 7.2 shows how special interest groups can influence curriculum.

VIGNETTE 7.2   *School board blasted for* Catcher in the Rye

Last evening's school board meeting lived up to its top billing, as opponents expressed their opinions about the school board's adoption of J. D. Salinger's novel, *Catcher in the Rye.*

"We told them if they forced our kids to read that dirt we would organize a protest group tonight," said Martha Addams. Her daughter, Jerri, attends Dunbar Junior High School. "If they don't listen to us we'll physically throw that book out of the library," Mrs. Addams said.

School Superintendent Kyle Yates said, "I realize many of the parents are concerned, and I sympathize with them, but there is nothing wrong with the book. It is a state-adopted text and we are planning to keep it in our curriculum. I should mention that not all teachers are using this book in their classroom. Classroom teachers have the option of using *Huckleberry Finn* if they wish."

Questioned about why he thought some parents were upset about *Catcher in the Rye,* Dr. Yates said, "You know, I really don't understand it myself. Mrs. Addams mentioned to the school board this evening that she has not read the book because she refuses to read trash."

???   *Mrs. Addams and Dr. Yates represent different views about what books should be allowed in the classroom. In a small group, discuss why Mrs. Addams doesn't want her daughter to read* Catcher in the Rye. *Why is Dr. Yates reluctant to remove it from the reading list?*

Technology and Computers in the Classroom

Technology and computers are revolutionizing education in the United States. Every part of the school, from kindergarten to the superintendent's office, has felt the impact. For example, most schools today keep their student attendance records on computers rather than in file cabinets. Not long ago, classroom teachers were aided only by the chalkboard. Today, teachers have access to CD–ROMs, laser disks, LCD projection screens, interactive TV, and more.

Classroom Teaching and Management.
Some of the traditional work of the classroom teacher—such as grading papers, creating lesson plans, and filling out report cards—can now be done quickly and accurately with computers. Not long ago, these time-consuming activities required classroom teachers to work after school and on weekends.

For many classroom teachers, however, the best thing about the computer is how it can help students learn. Using **computer-aided instruction (CAI)** software programs, students complete assignments on a computer prior to interacting with teachers. Foreign language software programs, for example, help students to learn vocabulary through games such as crossword puzzles and hangman. After students learn their vocabulary, teachers can use class time to improve their conversation skills and give them more individual instruction. Another computer application, electronic mail or e-mail, allows students and classroom teachers to interact throughout the week rather than for a short period during the school day. Students can hand in homework assignments, ask classroom teachers questions, and work with other students on class assignments.

Distance Learning.
A technological breakthrough many classroom teachers are now experiencing is **distance learning.** Interactive television programs, many of which emanate from colleges and universities, feature professors or other experts who teach high school students special topics or advanced subjects in such fields as foreign languages, mathematics, and sciences. Distance learning helps schools expand their curriculum. Students are given the opportunity to learn in a nontraditional "classroom." As professors become better educated in instructional approaches, these programs will continue to improve.

The Information Explosion.
In a technological world, information is power. Just as it is important for students to communicate verbally and mathematically, it is as critical they be able to access information through computers. Because computers increase the amount and rate of data flow, teachers have to be aware that speed is not always a good thing. Many students do not have time for reflective thinking. Teachers may have to make a special effort to provide opportunities to synthesize information.

Tests and Measurement

For the beginning classroom teacher, constructing tests can be an intimidating experience. Tests represent a moment of truth for both teachers and students. Obviously, tests require students to demonstrate their knowledge. But for the professional classroom teacher, testing has other purposes as well.

Student Evaluation.   The purpose of tests is to help classroom teachers discover how well their students are learning. As a teacher, therefore, you will want to apply test and measurement theories so the examinations you construct reflect the curriculum you teach. Teachers usually create **criterion-based tests,** tests designed to discover how much students know about a certain portion of the curriculum, such as a unit. Sometimes classroom teachers use standardized tests. While the tests inform them about what students know, they are also designed to compare students' knowledge with others who have taken the same test. These are called **normative tests.** College entrance tests, like the ACT and SAT, are normative tests.

Perhaps the most difficult part of the classroom teaching experience is grading students. Teachers usually wrestle with several issues when they assign grades to their students. Tests give teachers information upon which to base a grade, so it is very important that tests actually measure what the students learn.

Teacher Evaluation.   When classroom teachers evaluate their students, they are also evaluating themselves. Because of different learning styles, cultural backgrounds and personal histories students bring to the classroom, teachers know that not all of their students will learn the curriculum the same way or at the same rate. Teachers use tests to help them focus on how well they are communicating with students. Test results help classroom teachers identify instructional deficiencies they need to correct.

What You Have Learned

✔ Purposes of curriculum reflect the purposes of the school.
✔ Different curricular organizations are influenced by the classroom and school.
✔ Classroom instruction is dependent on many factors, including students' cultural and ethnic histories and the purposes of the curriculum.
✔ The technological revolution is changing the way teachers teach and manage their classrooms.

Key Terms

reconceptionalists
curriculum for social conservation
curriculum for social change
single-subject curriculum
competency-based education
outcome-based education
broad fields curriculum
fused curriculum
activity curriculum
child-centered curriculum
core curriculum
humanistic curriculum
client-centered psychology
explicit curriculum
hidden curriculum
null curriculum
instructional objectives
specific learning objectives
critical thinking skills
individualized learning
cooperative learning
inquiry method
computer-aided instruction
distance learning
criterion based tests
normative tests

Applying What You Have Learned

1. Read the education section of your local newspaper or educational magazines in your college library. Which two major purposes of schools seem to be most prevalent?

2. Bill, in *Becoming a Teacher,* wanted his students to learn about the Battle of the Little Bighorn from various cultural viewpoints. Do you think he was correct in doing this?

3. In a small group, explain what you think are the purposes of the curriculum you will teach. Ask group members to list the instructional objectives you have given in your explanation.

4. Ask several classroom teachers to explain their instructional philosophy to you and detail how it has changed throughout the years.

Interactive Learning

1. If your instructor had assigned you the responsibility of teaching this chapter to your classmates, how would you test them? Develop a test.

2. In this chapter you learned about various forms of curriculum and how they conflict. To understand the seriousness of such conflicts, ask several teachers to explain their philosophies of curriculum organization. In what ways do their philosophies conflict?

3. Talk to several classroom teachers about their schools' curriculum. What factors might induce them to modify their curriculum? Center your discussions around classroom factors mentioned in this chapter which influence the curriculum.

4. In this chapter you learned about the null curriculum. Teachers often think the null curriculum exists because of a lack of

class time. Consequently, some educators suggest increasing the time students attend school. Form a small group and develop a plan to increase the school day and school year. What part of the curriculum would you expand to fill the additional time?

Expanding Your Knowledge

Banks, J. A. *Multiethnic Education: Theory and practice,* 3rd edition. Boston: Allyn and Bacon, 1994. (This book gives you important insights into curriculum issues as they relate to race, culture, and ethnicity. A must-read book.)

Gollnick, D. M., and P. C. Chinn. *Multicultural Education in a Pluralistic society,* 4th edition. Upper Saddle River, NJ: Merrill/Prentice Hall, 1994. (This book provides an overview of the different cultures to which children belong. The text is designed to examine group memberships and ways in which teachers can develop educational programs to meet the needs of those groups.)

Sergiovanni, Thomas J. *Building Community in Schools.* San Francisco: Jossey-Bass, 1992. (This slim book is typical of Sergiovanni—a well written book with a lot of good ideas. He believes gangs are substitutes for families and neighborhoods, and proposes substituting the school for the gang.)

Sleeter, C. E., and C. A. Grant. *Making Choices for Multicultural Education: Five Approaches to Race, Class, and Gender,* 2nd ed. Upper Saddle River, NJ: Merrill/Prentice Hall, 1994. (An excellent discussion of the definition of teaching and the conceptual base of multicultural education.)

Part Four

Educational Governance, Organization, and Funding

In Part Four you will learn about the organization, administration, and financing of schools. These topics are important to classroom teachers because they serve as the basis for what happens in the classroom. In fact, some will concern you prior to teaching. For example, in *Becoming a Teacher* in Chapter 8, Lorna is frustrated with the interview process for a classroom teaching position because she doesn't know about educational organization. Lorna does not understand how schools are accountable or what specific responsibilities they have to society.

Like students, teachers have rights and responsibilities. In Chapter 9, you will learn about some of the rights and responsibilities you have as a teacher. Because of schools' responsibility to the public, you will quickly discover the importance of the federal and state constitutions and court systems as they relate to the classroom. In *Becoming A Teacher* in Chapter 9, Carl is asked by Mrs. Snyder to lead the class in prayer. The prayer itself was selected because it didn't support any particular church or religion. Yet Carl doesn't want to read it. He feels trapped. Is Carl obligated to lead the class in prayer? Does he have a right to refuse to carry out the assignment Mrs. Snyder gave him?

Chapter 10 discusses school revenue and expenditures. Educational finance is becoming more controversial. Who should pay for schools? Some taxpayers believe only parents of children in school should be responsible. Others believe state and local governments should finance childrens' education. Some parents are concerned that private schools receive public money to educate their children. Regardless of who finances schools, it is clear that the money we spend affects the quality of education.

The Organization of Schools and How They Are Governed

In Chapter 8, you will discover how schools in the United States are governed, organized, and administered. As the legal framework upon which our schools were founded, governance is an important concept for you to understand. You will realize the federal government's effect on school governance is less than many think. State governments have direct control of schools. Legislatures develop state school policy and establish state departments of education that oversee many aspects of the educational process, such as hiring teachers and defining the curriculum. At another level of governance, local school boards are intended to reflect the demography and values of their community. Members are locally elected or appointed. Yet many local school boards are much different than the diverse society they represent.

Our nation's schools reflect the complicated demands of a culturally diverse society. In some countries, a dual school system gives different school experiences to different students. Our country maintains it is vital to have various cultures, ethnicities, and social classes represented in a single school system that gives equal opportunity to succeed to all children.

We will also examine how schools are established within the community, from the oldest form of school organization, the neighborhood school, to one of the more recent innovations, school consolidation.

As a new teacher, you may be unsure how the governance of the school affects you personally. Because schools are legally accountable to the public, you may find the school's organization confusing and the roles of the principal and superintendent mysterious. In this chapter, we will focus on governance, organization, and administration, so your transition into teaching will be smooth and rewarding.

What you will learn

- The U.S. Constitution, President, Supreme Court, and Congress affect schools.

- State governors, state legislatures, state supreme courts, and state departments of education have responsibility for schools.

- Local boards of education and their various educational officers, including the superintendent and principals, have the primary responsibility for running schools.

- In the U.S., both nonpublic and public schools have a role in educating children.

- International and multicultural changes within society are impacting the governance, organization, and administration of schools.

BECOMING A TEACHER   *The interview*

Graduation from college was Lorna's dream. She was anxious to get into the real world and begin teaching. She'd enjoyed math for as long as she could remember and wanted to share her love of mathematics with others as a teacher.

Lorna had discovered that looking for teaching positions was more complicated than she'd realized but, with the help of her college placement office, she had been able to narrow down a list of schools she was interested in.

Nonetheless, Lorna is now frustrated. Her interview with the assistant superintendent of personnel for the Woodside school system, Mrs. Gray, had gone well, but Lorna had not been offered a teaching position. Mrs. Gray had asked many questions about Lorna's certification, experiences, motivation, letters of reference—but she had asked nothing about math, teaching methods, or classroom management. All the assistant superintendent said was, "Please talk with Dr. Karpov, the principal at Horace Mann Middle School. He will interview you. He may ask you to meet the math department head as well."

Lorna shares her experiences with her roommate, Kerry. "You know, you'd think they would want the best math teachers possible. It seemed as if the assistant superintendent didn't even care whether I would be a good or bad teacher. All she did was ask me a lot of technical questions and then pass me along to the principal. I don't understand it," Lorna says. "If they can't make up their minds without a lot of fuss, this may not be the school I want to teach in."

"I don't understand it either," says Kerry. "You know, our professors never told us we would have to go through this to teach. Anyway, what does an assistant superintendent of personnel do?"

???   *If you had been Lorna, what would have been your reaction to the interview process?*

Lorna and Kerry's introduction to teaching is a common one. It is easy to understand their confusion. We generally do not think of schools in this country as a big business, yet schools employ in excess of 4.4 million people. In fact, our nation's 2.6 million classroom teachers represent only 59 percent of all school employees. Support staff such as librarians, psychologists, nurses, cafeteria workers, bus drivers, and administrative professionals make up the difference (Ogle, 1990, 88, 174; National Center for Educational Statistics, 1995).

We will begin with the governance of schools, starting with the federal and state governments and finishing with the local community. You will then study the various ways schools are administered and different methods of organization for schools.

The Federal Role in Education

Educational **governance** defines the legal responsibilities of schools. Schools in this country are not controlled by the central government. Our schools are the responsibility of each state. You need to understand how governance works from the federal, state, and community perspectives.

Amendments That Affect Education

The Constitution of the United States makes no mention of schools and educational governance; its framers were concerned with the responsibilities and parameters of the federal government. Ten amendments, collectively called the Bill of Rights, were added to the Constitution in 1791. Since that time, 16 additional amendments have been approved. Of those 26 amendments, three are pertinent to educational governance.

The First Amendment.
The **First Amendment** guarantees citizens freedom of speech, freedom of religion, freedom of the press, and the right to petition the government. You can read the First Amendment and the other amendments that pertain to education in Figure 8.1. The First Amendment protects children who attend public and nonpublic schools. It provides for the separation of church and state, and has been the basis for many Supreme Court decisions regarding religion in the schools. The First Amendment has protected all citizens, including children, when public schools have become the battleground for people who have different ideas about what children should learn and/or teachers should teach.

Tenth Amendment.
The **Tenth Amendment** transfers responsibility for education to each of the states. Each state constitution has specific stipulations for the provision of education to its students. For example, one state may stress the financing of education, another state may underscore a ban on discrimination, another may emphasize freedom from sectarian control, and another may combine all of the above points.

Figure 8.1   Amendments and Education

FIRST AMENDMENT

Congress shall make no law respecting an establishment of religion, or prohibiting the free exercise thereof; or abridging the freedom of speech or of the press; or the right of the people peaceably to assemble and to petition the Government for a redress of grievances.

TENTH AMENDMENT

The powers not delegated to the United States by the Constitution, nor prohibited by it to the States, are reserved to the States respectively, or to the people.

FOURTEENTH AMENDMENT

All persons born or naturalized in the United States, and subject to the jurisdiction thereof, are citizens of the United States and of the State wherein they reside. No State shall make or enforce any law which shall abridge the privileges or immunities of citizens of the United States; nor shall any State deprive any person of life, liberty or property without due process of law; nor deny to any person within its jurisdiction the equal protection of the laws.

Fourteenth Amendment.   The **Fourteenth Amendment** became part of the Constitution after the Civil War. Its immediate purpose was to protect African Americans, whose new-found rights as citizens were often restricted by various states. However, its overall purpose was to protect all citizens. The Fourteenth Amendment guarantees all citizens equal protection and due process. Therefore, while states have the responsibility to educate children, they do not have the right to say one child should have a better opportunity to receive an education than another. *Brown v. Board of Education* (1954), a Supreme Court case that overturned the legality of separate but equal schools, was based on this amendment. The Fourteenth Amendment remains extremely important as children from different cultures, ethnicities, and social classes are attending school. As Vignette 8.1 demonstrates, some difficult issues still arise that must be resolved according to the precepts of the Fourteenth Amendment.

 VIGNETTE 8.1   *Other people's children*

The system has the surface aspects of a meritocracy, but merit in this case is predetermined by conditions that are closely tied to class and race. While some defend it as, in theory, "the survival of the fittest," it is more accurate to call it the survival of the children of the fittest—or of the most favored. Similar systems exist in every major city. They are defended stoutly by those who succeed in getting into the selective schools.

The parallel system extends to elementary schools as well. A recent conflict around one such school illustrates the way the system pits the middle class against the poor. A mostly middle-income condominium development was built close to a public housing project known as Hilliard Homes. The new development, called Dearborn Park, attracted a number of young professionals, many of whom were fairly affluent white people, who asked the school board to erect a new school for their children. This request was honored and the South Loop Elementary School was soon constructed. At this point a bitter struggle ensued. The question: Who would get to go to the new school?

The parents from Dearborn Park insisted that, if the school is attended by the children from the projects—these are the children who have lived there all along—the standards of the school will fall. The school, moreover, has a special "fine arts" magnet program; middle-class children, drawn to the school from other sections of Chicago, are admitted. So the effort to keep out the kids who live right in the neighborhood points up the class and racial factors. The city, it is noted, had refused to build a new school for the project children when they were the only children in the neighborhood. Now that a new school has been built, they find themselves excluded.

The Dearborn parents have the political power to obtain agreement from the Board of Education to enter their children beginning in kindergarten but to keep the Hilliard children out until third grade—by which time, of course, the larger numbers of these poorer children will be at a disadvantage and will find it hard to keep up with the children who were there since kindergarten. In the interim, according to the *New York Times,* the younger children from the project are obliged to go to class within "a temporary branch school" in "a small, prefabricated metal building surrounded on three sides by junkyards."

Source: From *Savage Inequalities: Children in America's Schools* by Jonathan Kozol, pp. 60–61. Copyright © 1991 by Jonathan Kozol. Reprinted by permission of Crown Publishers, Inc.

??? *Do you think these children are protected by the Fourteenth Amendment? Are the poor children receiving the same education as the middle-class children? What would you do if you were teaching in this school?*

Congress

Because the Constitution limits the federal government's powers, Congress has no authority to compel schools to teach a national curriculum, set mandatory teaching standards, or establish an examination structure.

Although the responsibility for education rests with state governments, the federal government does have some educational responsibilities. Congress funds the District of Columbia school system. The Department of the Interior is responsible for the education of children in U.S. territories and possessions such as Samoa, the Caroline Islands, and the Marshall Islands. This department is also accountable for educating the children of National Park Service employees and overseeing the Bureau of Indian Affairs, which supports many Native American schools. The Department of Defense is responsible for the education of military families, military personnel, and the four military academies.

Department of Education.   In 1867, Congress established the first federal agency concerned with schools and called it the Bureau of Education. It was renamed the Office of Education in 1869 and became part of the Federal Security Agency in 1939. This agency later became part of the Department of Health, Education, and Welfare. Congress created the **Department of Education** in 1979. With a Secretary of Education and cabinet status, the department's responsibilities rest exclusively in the area of helping schools educate children. In other words, public monies granted by Congress or other departments for such programs as school lunches, special education, and grants-in-aid are intended to help children learn without influencing what they learn (curriculum), how they are taught (classroom methodology), or their evaluation (national testing standards).

President

Like Congress, the President does not have constitutional power to control schools. However, he may attempt to influence education by advocating specific theories or policies. The President can influence the educational views of state legislators, board of education members, citizens, and others who are directly involved with school governance. For example, President Bush established the Goals 2000 agenda (1990) and President Clinton campaigned for the Educate America Act (1994).

Supreme Court

The educational role of the Supreme Court is much greater than other branches of the federal government because of its responsibility to interpret the Constitution. The role of the Supreme Court and other appellate courts is to resolve disputes in such areas as religion, finance, free speech, and student expulsion. The Supreme Court's decisions explain the outcomes in each case the judges choose to review and guide the behavior of others who may wish to avoid similar controversies in the future.

 # The States' Role in Education

State Constitutions

As we mentioned earlier, states have specific constitutional provisions governing education. Usually state constitutions empower legislatures to establish and support a state-wide school system. For example, Kentucky's constitution certifies:

> The General Assembly shall, by appropriate legislation, provide for an efficient system of common schools throughout the state. (1792: 35)

The Pennsylvania constitution (1776) confirms schools should be opened in each county and the state should pay teacher salaries. Figure 8.2 is an organizational chart of public education at the state level.

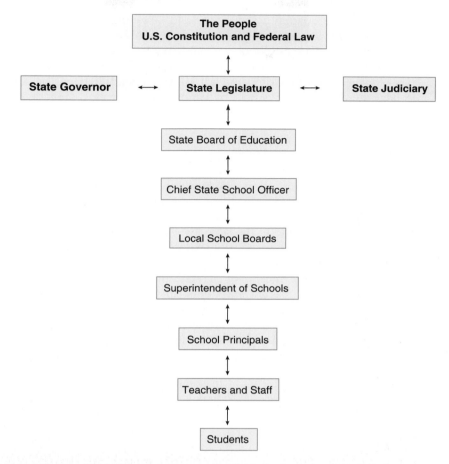

Figure 8.2   Organizational Chart of Public Schools at the State Level

State Legislatures

The responsibility for education in each of the states typically rests with the legislature. In the broad sense, these policymakers are responsible for the financial support of public schools, the organization of the curriculum, and the certification of all school personnel, including teachers and administrators. They are responsible for nonpublic schools as well.

Because of the political process, state legislatures are usually bombarded by lobbyists and other vested interest groups that, for their own reasons, want to influence schools and teachers. For example, lobby groups such as school administrators' associations, state school board associations, teachers' associations, and higher education associations have a vested interest in the education of children, teachers, and schools. Lobby groups such as manufacturers' associations, chambers of commerce, business associations, agricultural associations, and labor unions have a vested interest in products or services specific to school needs. Lobby groups with an interest in the curriculum or welfare of school-age children include churches, religious groups, and various charity organizations. Civil rights groups function as lobbyists in the protection of legal rights of children and school personnel. While legislatures are expected to hear the differing views held by various public groups, they are constitutionally obligated to generate legislation that will benefit children.

State Boards of Education

Every state except Wisconsin has a state board of education. These are separate from the boards of education which oversee colleges and universities within each state. The state board of education is the most powerful state agency concerned with education. The state board of education often functions in an advisory position to the governor and to the state legislature. As shown in Figure 8.3, most state boards of education are responsible for the establishment of procedures necessary to implement legislation related to education. They are involved in (a) setting the qualifications for, and the hiring of, state department of education personnel; (b) setting standards for teacher and administrative certification and school accreditation; (c) managing state educational funds; and (d) collecting data about education. Some state boards of education are responsible for representing the state in educational matters, acting as a judicial body in hearing grievances about state educational policies, and creating advisory groups, such as textbook selection bodies.

State Board Membership.   In some states, members are elected to the state board of education, while in others they are appointed by the governor. The demographic composition of state boards of education is changing to include more

Figure 8.3   State Boards of Education Duties and Responsibilities

LEGISLATION

- Develop regulations to implement legislative acts
- Establish committees as required by law
- Give advice to the legislature and governor regarding educational policy
- Administer state monies as required by law

EDUCATIONAL ADMINISTRATION

- Develop and maintain accreditation policies for individual schools in the state
- Discuss and publicize policies and procedures to improve schools on a state-wide basis
- Develop certification policies for officials within the state department of education
- Act as the state's representative with the federal government and other agencies

women and minority members to reflect the characteristics of the states. The composition is moving away from Euro-American male-dominated boards to include women and members of various minority groups.

Textbook Selection.   In many states, textbook selection has become an extremely controversial subject. For example, recently in California, *all* science and mathematics textbooks under consideration were rejected because they did not academically challenge the students. The Texas state board of education requires biology textbooks to include a discussion of creationism. In many states, textbook selection is influenced by testing procedures that, many argue, work in opposition to the enhancement of education for children.

The Chief State School Officer

The **chief state school officer** is the chief executive officer of the state board of education. In 27 states, the office is filled by appointment by the state board of education; the governor makes the appointment in 8 states; and in 15 states, the person is elected to this position. In 1990, one of these officers was African-American and nine were women (Directory of Chief State Officers, 1991).

The duties of the chief state school officer vary somewhat but generally include the following:

- Serve as the chief administrative officer of the state department of education and the state board of education.
- Select personnel for the state department of education.
- Ensure conformity with state laws and regulations concerning education.
- Make recommendations regarding improvements in educational legislation and regulations.
- Hold responsibility for the studies, committees, and task forces necessary to identify problems and recommend solutions.
- Report to the state legislature and the governor on the status of education within the state.

State Departments of Education

State departments of education, sometimes known as **cabinets of education** are established by state legislatures to oversee that state's educational enterprise. Departments employ professional educators as outlined by the state board. They implement educational legislation, administer various tasks outlined by the legislature, and advise legislators on educational matters when asked. Specifically, state departments of education are mandated to certify teachers, principals, superintendents and support personnel; to distribute public monies; and to audit local school district financial records.

State departments of education fund schools and are empowered to administer compulsory education laws, which require children to remain in school until the age of 16. State Departments of Education are perhaps best known today for their regulation of state curriculum-reform legislation. While curriculum-reform legislation differs among the states, all state departments of education attempt to incorporate the expertise of teachers, administrators, parents, and others at the local and state levels of decision-making, so legislative goals can be met.

Finally, state departments of education have the responsibility for school accreditation. **School accreditation** is that process by which state departments of education evaluate school programs, teachers, and other areas important to the education of students. Accreditation ensures that schools have met specific standards. Lack of accreditation means that, though schools may remain open, students suffer. For example, graduates from nonaccredited schools are usually not viewed by colleges and universities as equal to graduates from accredited schools. Both public and nonpublic elementary and secondary schools can be accredited and can have that accreditation removed.

Intermediate Units

Intermediate units are agencies that function between the state department of education and the local school district. The chief executive officer of the intermediate unit may either be appointed or elected. The primary purpose of the units is to provide services that schools districts would be unable to provide alone. For example, intermediate units may provide special education, counseling, and psychological services to a number of small rural districts. These services would be cost-prohibitive if each district had to provide the services separately. Other intermediate units provide in-service training for teachers, centralized audiovisual departments, legal services, laboratory facilities, and instructional materials. Approximately 30 states have some form of intermediate units.

Governors

Like the President, governors often attempt to articulate educational policy. In fact, many gubernatorial candidates campaign on educational issues. Think about your governor's educational stance and the ways in which she or he has tried to impact education in your state. Governors are responsible for vetoing or signing educational legislation passed by the legislature. Like the President, governors cannot implement educational issues through executive order.

State Supreme Courts

State supreme courts interpret the constitutionality of state laws, just as the United State Supreme Court interprets the constitutionality of laws for our country. For example, in June 1989, the Kentucky State Supreme Court ruled that the entire state system of elementary and secondary education in Kentucky was unconstitutional, because rural students had fewer opportunities than students in the larger cities to get a quality education. The state high court held that the General Assembly of Kentucky had to create a new system of common schools in the state, which it did in the Kentucky Education Reform Act of 1990. In any state, laws that directly impact schools, curricula, teachers, and children may be heard by the state supreme court. Decisions rendered at the state level may be appealed to the United States Supreme Court, which has jurisdiction over all 50 states and the territories.

The Role of Local School Districts in Education

Local Boards of Education

Most teachers in the United States understand governance at the community level. The **local board of education,** with its elected or appointed members, is charged with the legal responsibility to operate local schools. Figure 8.4 illustrates the placement of the school board in the structure of the local school district.

Board of Education Members.   Local board of education members are representatives of the state, even though they have been elected at the local level. Each member brings with him or her specific ideas about what children should learn (curriculum), how teachers should teach (methodology), and other factors

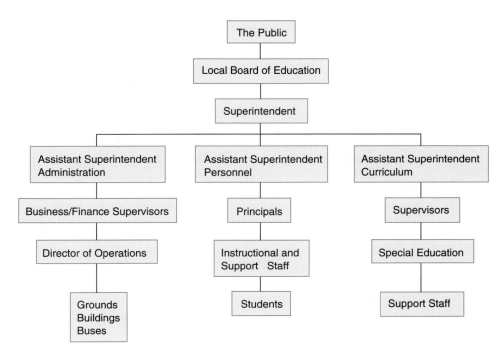

Figure 8.4 Organization of Local Public Schools

they think constitute a good education. Some citizens run for the school board so they can advance educational philosophies or causes they think are important. Some have gained office for the sole purpose of radically changing the curriculum, firing the superintendent, or overseeing their own children's education. Fortunately, most school board members soon discover that power is vested in the school board, not in each member. That is, the powers some board members may perceive as theirs, in fact belong only to the board as an entity. Vignette 8.2 is an example of an abuse of power.

VIGNETTE 8.2   *Abuse of power*

Sharon Mays, an advanced placement high school English teacher, has several school board members' children in her class. Everyone, including other teachers, her principal, and parents, thinks very highly of Sharon. They know she is a demanding teacher with a reputation for being fair.

One of her students, a junior, is the son of the president of the school board. Jim had some difficulty completing his assignments, and told Mrs. Mays he would just hand in the assignments late. Mrs. Mays told him she did not accept late assignments; consequently, he would receive a zero for each uncompleted assignment. Jim left her room very angry, and said he was going to tell his mother, the school board president.

Now, Jim's mother has come to speak with Mrs. Mays, and has threatened to not have her contract renewed unless she gives Jim an opportunity to hand in the assignments late with no penalties.

???   *If you were Mrs. Mays, what would you do? What advice would you give Jim's mother about the difference between being a school board member and being a parent? If you were Jim's mother, how would you have handled this situation?*

Typically, school board members are elected to office. In most states, school elections do not require candidates to identify their political affiliation; therefore, elections are traditionally waged on educational issues. In a small number of communities members may be appointed by the mayor or city council. In either case, the selection process is intended to get qualified board members who are truly concerned about children's education to represent the citizens. Since local board members are usually paid honorariums, most consider their time spent on the board community service.

Because of the diversity of our society, there is no typical school board member. Yet some characteristics are worth mentioning. Cameron, Underwood, and Fortune (1988) found the average board member was a middle-aged married male who owned his own home, earned between $40,000 and $50,000 per year, and was in his second four-year term on the board. He was also white, a college graduate, and a manager or professional. During the same year, only 3.6 percent of school board members were African-American, 1.5 percent were Hispanic, and fewer than half were women. In fact, school boards seldom accurately reflect the gender, race, and social-class composition of their communities.

The Role of Boards of Education.   Generally, the role of boards of education is directed at (a) maintaining schools through taxation of local citizens, (b) constructing school buildings, (c) purchasing materials and supplies, (d) hiring teachers, administrators, and others to operate academic or support programs, and (e) assigning students to specific schools. While the roles of boards of education may differ throughout the United States, all are responsible for school governance according to the laws of the state and the federal government.

The School Superintendent

Local boards of education employ administrators. Administrators and their staffs are accountable to the board for the day-to-day operations of the school district. It is important to understand the relationship between the school board and its administrators.

Although the school board is the administrator's employer, its purpose is not to micromanage. That is, school boards authorize administrators to conduct the affairs of the school so that the boards do not have to become involved in the details of educational administration. School boards are legally responsible for the implementation of various state and federal mandates. Ultimately the board is responsible for the education of the community's children. School boards establish an educational bureaucracy that is responsible to the superintendent who, in turn, is responsible to the board.

Because the superintendent is the chief executive officer of the school system, school boards consider her or his appointment the most important decision the board will make. It is the superintendent's responsibility to keep the school board fully informed of the school district's activities, so the board can make sound policy decisions. Board members, who are not expert educators, rely on the advice of the superintendent before arriving at any major decision.

While state department of education regulations differ by state, superintendents are typically required to be certified classroom teachers with teaching and administrative experience. Usually, the superintendent also has experience as the principal of an an elementary, junior high, middle school, or high school. Some states also require experience in district-wide administration, such as director of special education or supervisor of instruction. In any case, superintendents usually need a variety of district-wide administrative and classroom experiences to be able to understand the complexity of the school system. States usually require superintendents to hold a minimum of a master's degree in the field of educational administration. It is not uncommon for superintendents to hold an Ed.D. or Ph.D. degree. Superintendents are required to have a broad understanding of schools, curriculum, teaching methods, finance, and educational leadership.

The pressures placed on superintendents are extraordinary. Perhaps that is why superintendents often change positions every three to four years. Constituents representing conflicting social views actively lobby superintendents just as they lobby school boards or state legislatures. While some taxpayers may pressure the superintendent to reduce the costs of education, others are pressuring her or him to add specific academic or support programs.

Superintendents are increasingly aware of the need to meet the social challenges of an increasingly diverse population. The continued curricular modification caused by a more culturally diverse society has created cultural stresses that continually challenge the superintendent's ability to articulate the purposes of the school in relation to the demographic and cultural changes within the community.

Central Office Staff.   Most school systems have a central office staff to assist the superintendent. Generally, the staff's role is to advise the superintendent, conduct studies for school improvement, implement the superintent's directives, and respond to the various mandates of the state department of education, state legislature, and federal government. Let's compare several types of central office organizations.

In very large school systems, the central office houses associate and assistant superintendents, directors, coordinators, and others who are specialists in finance, personnel, maintenance, and other areas. Many times these departments are large, employing dozens of individuals.

Another form of central office organization found in larger communities is the **subdistrict organization.** In this case, the central office divides the community into zones, or subdistricts. The purpose of the subdistrict is to bring the school's central office closer to local citizens, so the administration can be more responsive to the needs of the people it serves. The subdistrict office is under the direction of the central office and is headed by an assistant superintendent. There is conflicting evidence about the effectiveness of the subdistrict organization. Some superintendents believe it will only add another administrative layer on top of already large administrative staffs. On the other hand, most superintendents understand the need of citizens to communicate easily and effectively with the central office. Subdistricts have the ability to gather information, react to problems, articulate the policies of school board and central office, and respond to the immediate concerns of citizens. This is especially important as communities become more diverse. Evidence continues to mount about how important it is for parents to be directly involved with the education of their children. Subdistricts, which are better able to understand a community's demographics on a first-hand basis, can help schools become more responsive to the unique needs of diverse cultures within the community.

A third type of central office can be found in small, rural schools. While the superintendent is required to fulfill the same functions as superintendents in large urban centers, the process can be implemented with fewer assistants. It is not uncommon in small rural communities for the central office functions to be performed by the superintendent, a secretary, and the school principals.

Principal

The principal is the school's chief administrative officer, and the superintendent's representative in the school. The principal is responsible for the school plant, teachers, students, and programs. The principal is the administrator teachers interact with most. Most of the information originating in the superintendent's office is distributed through the principal.

A principal's meeting.

The principal has responsibilities in the areas of management, curriculum, and instruction. Elementary principals are usually more concerned than secondary school principals with curriculum and instruction. (Secondary school principals typically have department heads who are curriculum leaders in specific subject areas.) Principals conduct the school's operations, from assigning teachers classrooms to developing class schedules. Principals are vitally concerned about the school buildings, faculty, students, educational finance, curriculum content, and community relations.

Principals render a vital service to the superintendent by offering advice and assistance. Principals call upon superintendents, too, whenever school board policies are not clear or when specific problems require central office action. Principals are in a unique position to influence the education of their schools' children. If the principal is committed to quality education and demonstrates an accepting attitude to children who come from different social and cultural backgrounds, that attitude will permeate the school. If the principal has difficulty understanding the cultural uniqueness of children, learning may suffer.

School-Based Management

School-based management is a new form of school administration. The idea of school-based management is that schools will be more effective learning environments if teachers have shared control over how schools are administered. School-based management assumes teachers should be actively involved in the decision-making process on such topics as staff development, teaching assignments, and other areas. As you might guess, this administrative model is controversial. Proponents believe teachers are an untapped administrative resource. They also believe school-based management increases teacher loyalty, because teachers no longer receive top–down administrative orders. School-based management requires teachers to be knowledgeable about school board policies and state and federal mandates. In other words, school-based management requires teachers to increase their professional maturity. Vignette 8.3 highlights some of the advantages of school-based management.

   VIGNETTE 8.3   *School-based management*

The pride of Riply is its community high school. McCloud High School is noted for its fine football team. It has consistently played in the regional and state finals for the last seven years. In fact, last year it won the state football championship in Division B against Delhart High, a much larger school. The state athletic association has designated McCloud High as one of the smallest schools in the state. Its student population is only 250, counting Grades 9 through 12.

McCloud High is a reflection of Ripley. More than 58 percent of McCloud's students are classified as needy under the state's free lunch program. Ripley's unemployment rate of 14 percent is above the state average. McCloud High has no science lab for its students. When it rains, the band practices in a large upstairs hallway because the regular band room and gymnasium flood.

But what makes many Ripley parents happy is that they know their children receive the best education possible when they attend McCloud. Most parents know McCloud is known throughout the state for its efforts in helping students succeed. They speak with pride that every senior on the football team was also on McCloud's Academic Bowl team.

What's happening at McCloud is happening at many schools throughout the state, say teachers and administrators. McCloud is succeeding because parents, students and teachers have developed a tradition of classroom accomplishment. In brief, they have developed a working model of school-based management. McCloud has a council made up of two parents, three teachers, and the principal. They develop policies relating to curriculum, personnel assignments, student support services, instructional materials, and other aspects of school management.

Critics insist teachers are too busy in the classroom to spend time solving administrative problems. They argue that some teachers want to become part of a school-based management team in order to carry out personal grudges against the principal or other teachers. They see school-based management as destructive to children's education, because it can lead to teachers involved in open conflict with the principal or with each other.

Neighborhood Schools

No discussion of school organization would be complete without an understanding of the controversy over **neighborhood schools,** sometimes called **attendance centers.** Traditionally, neighborhood schools encompass a specific geographic area within a community. School lines or boundaries are designated by the local school board. In very small communities, the neighborhood school may be the only school within the community. Larger communities may have as many as 500 schools. Proponents of the neighborhood school believe children learn more effectively because they are already acquainted with the values expressed in the neighborhood. They contend neighborhood schools allow teachers to understand their students better, because the students represent a specific socio-economic area within the community. It is also thought children will receive a more personal education. Some administrators support the neighborhood school because it is easy to administer.

Opponents of the neighborhood school seldom argue against these advantages. However, they point out that neighborhoods are seldom integrated. In fact, neighborhood schools in many communities are *de facto* segregated. That is, housing patterns cause the school to be segregated on the basis of race/ethnicity, culture, or social class. Further, they charge neighborhoods differ socioeconomically. As a consequence, the quality of a child's education may depend on which school he or she happens to attend. Opponents further assert that children who have opportunities to learn about and interact with various ethnicities and cultures are, in fact, receiving a superior education, which will help them live in a culturally diverse nation. They believe that educating children only with those who are like themselves does not allow students to understand the totality or complexity of life in this country.

School Consolidation

For a long time, educators have disagreed about the most effective size for a school or school district. Years ago, it was argued that larger high schools and bigger school districts were more effective and efficient (Conant, 1959). More recently, educators have stated that small schools and smaller districts are better for the community, the students, and the teachers. However, as you will learn from the following discussion, the disagreement continues. During the last half century, the demographics of rural America have changed dramatically. Many small towns are losing their young people to larger cities or to other states, and many rural schools are faced with decreasing student numbers. Rural educators are torn between the community's desire to keep the school open and the need to give children quality education. Many small communities in rural areas are painfully aware that they offer young people few reasons to remain, and they fear that school closure will mean the death of the community itself.

These emotional arguments are easy to understand. Besides the obvious contribution of educating children, schools give a community status and entertainment. State school boards have attempted to solve rural school problems through **consolidation,** in which several rural school systems join together to make a

A Southwest rural school.

larger school district. For example, several communities may join an agreement under which each town maintains an elementary school and several towns pool resources to support a high school. Through consolidation, children can experience academic diversity in their education, while continuing their education close to home. Yet there's always sadness when a school closes due to consolidation, as illustrated in Vignette 8.4.

VIGNETTE 8.4   *The closing of a rural school*

"I don't care what they say! McCook is one of the nicest towns in the state and my family has always lived and gone to school here!" The crowd, made up of long-time residents of McCook, stood up and applauded. The meeting was heated and noisy; tempers were hot. "The problem with you guys," said the speaker, "is you don't want to understand all the good things that small towns give kids."

Thus ended the community meeting with visiting members from the state department of education. They had been invited to come to McCook to explain why McCook children would not be able to go to high school in their community. It was difficult for them to hear the state officials mention that the opportunity to receive a better education could only come about if McCook was willing to consolidate with Ardmore, its neighboring town. It sounded as if the school would be closed because McCook was not a good place to live.

In fact, students would attend McCook *Elementary* School, the state officials said. It was only McCook *High* School that would close. But many of the parents knew that if McCook High closed, the community would suffer. Mr. Berry said it best. "I was on the McCook football team 35 years ago. My son played football 15 years ago, and in 8 years my grandson will play for McCook High. I think McCook will disappear without its high school."

"Well," said Mr. McNeal, "as principal of McCook High, I am torn between what is best for the students and the community."

"They never explained why the school should close," responded Mr. Berry.

??? *What might be the outcome if these schools are forced to consolidate? If you were teaching at McCook High, how might the consolidation affect you? How might you feel about the consolidation?*

School Deconsolidation

Unlike small rural schools that are forced to consider consolidation, large urban schools sometimes undergo **deconsolidation.** Educators and researchers are concluding that large urban schools can breed violence, increase the probability of students dropping out, increase likelihood of academic failures, and foster alienation among students. They have found that students, especially those identified as at risk, do much better in smaller schools. Poor children, too, do much better in smaller schools than they do in large schools. Advocates of small schools believe that they do more than reach out to adolescents; they also can be agents and models of school improvement. Vignette 8.5 profiles a small high school.

VIGNETTE 8.5   *You have to think*

In John Steinbrink's social studies class, students are laughing as they play parts in a play that mimics Shakespeare. The play was written by the class as a way of learning about social change. In Bruce Petty's class, students are learning about different uses of technology.

This is the way it is with students at Willard High. Students are not allowed to memorize. "You have to understand it," says David. "If you can't explain it, Mr. Yellin says you don't know it."

"That's right," says Kay. "I know you have to study, but you also have to think. Thinking isn't always fun. Sometimes it's hard. But it's better than memorizing."

David and Kay are in a special program at Willard High. They are eligible because they dropped out of school because of personal difficulties. Kay had a baby and David's dad died unexpectedly. Both had to support others. Now they have a chance. "I was afraid to come to Willard," says David. "I wasn't a good student before, but now I love school. I know I will graduate."

??? *What is happening to the students in this school—many of whom would be expected to fail in other schools? What can we learn from this?*

Nonpublic Schools

As we stated earlier, the United States Constitution gives states the responsibility for education. It also gives parents the right to send their children to private schools or to educate them at home. Nonpublic schools and home instruction are bound by the same compulsory education laws as public schools. Parental involvement in nonpublic schools and home instruction must meet the same academic requirements as public schools.

Religion and Private Schools

Private schools have always been part of the United States and are protected by the Tenth and Fourteenth Amendments. For example, the Boston Latin Grammar School (1635) was a private school with a religious curriculum, controlled by the church. Spanish missions and schools utilized a religious curriculum under control of the church. Schools for Native Americans and Hawaiians were controlled by missionaries who taught a curriculum imbued with religious ideals aimed at the conversion of these indigenous peoples.

Religion continues to play an important role in schools today. As more and more students ask their teachers to help them define moral codes of conduct, public and nonpublic schools alike are finding it increasingly necessary to answer such questions as "Who am I?", "How do I relate to others?" and "How should I live?". This means governance issues about vouchers, tax credits, and other incentives to encourage religious private schools are wrapped in vital theological questions. These questions are asked by people regardless of their religious beliefs or cultural heritage. As a future teacher, you should be thinking about what type of school you will feel comfortable teaching in. How will you with your world view work with children who represent differing theological histories?

While private schools have traditionally taught approximately one in every ten students, they have seen a recent surge in parental interest. Private school enrollment increased from 7.3 percent of the total number of children enrolled in schools in 1920 to a high of 13 percent in 1983. In recent years, while the percentage of students attending private schools has remained fairly constant, enrollments in charismatic and fundamentalist Christian schools have increased significantly (National Center for Education Statistics, 1995). Because private schools are required to teach the approved curriculum to meet state certification requirements, the major issues presently surrounding nonpublic education rests on whether (or how) public funds can be used to support nonpublic schools.

One method that is being advanced by private schools as well as those in public education is the voucher system. The voucher system is based on the premise that public monies should be given to private as well as public schools. Parents should be allowed to place their children in any type of school they believe will give them the best education possible. Opponents of the voucher system counter that public funds for education are now so limited that the voucher system would simply stretch scarce money even further, thereby causing more students to leave the public school. Regardless, educators are aware of the basic question which is, Can the United States have a common culture while maintaining the parents' right to educate their children?

Home Instruction

Home instruction, like private schools, is part of United States educational history. Teachers (and courts) agree the home is the first school children attend. Therefore, home instruction may meet state department of education regulations as long as instruction is carried out in good faith. This means, in all states except Iowa and Michigan, that parents are not required to be certified teachers. However, they must teach the state-mandated curriculum and obey compulsory education laws.

The advocates of home instruction insist children can receive a quality education at home because the parent (teacher) knows the child best. They maintain that their family philosophy, theology, or values can be articulated, and children can learn at their own rate. Opponents insist children may receive a poor education, insofar as they do not have the benefit of teachers who are expert in such diverse academic fields as physics and English grammar. Further, they contend most homes do not have the supplies or equipment required to teach laboratory work in such areas as science. Most of all, opponents insist children will not have the opportunity to expand their social skills that public and nonpublic schools supply. School experiences, they contend, allow children to become well-rounded citizens who can function in a multicultural, multiethnic society.

Education in a Changing Society

Paul Kennedy (1993) believes specific global economic and social events are changing and testing the manner in which nations, societies, and individuals react to each other. He maintains that the ability of education to introduce a deeper understanding of global trends will be severely limited by the inhibition of open debate, by blaming ethnic minorities for society's problems, and by the media's trivialization of serious issues. Kennedy points out education and schools must be more than retooling centers for laborers and workers. His concern centers on the way in which societies sometimes stop people from thinking freely and use ethnic groups as scapegoats for negative events.

As teachers, it is important for us to understand Kennedy's concern about what and how we educate our children. Thoughtful administrators are expressing concern about whether the present form of educational governance, administration, and organization is adequate to educate children who will live the majority of their lives in the twenty-first century. Some educators are questioning whether our nation should have state educational systems or even a national system. While the local school board is still considered important for the day-to-day affairs of the school, administrators are pondering their ability to develop policies that will improve the quality of education for children. If Kennedy is correct, legislators, school boards, and administrators may succumb to the lobbying efforts of those who are more interested in using schools for their own economic advantage than for the education of children

What You Have Learned

✔ Educational governance in the United States is different than in other countries, in which schools are agencies of the central government. The United States Constitution does not mention schools or education, thereby giving the states and people control of the schools.

✔ The First, Tenth, and Fourteenth Amendments recognize the importance of education in the lives of peoples. But in each case, the Constitution does not interfere with schools except as they impact on the rights and responsibilities of children (citizens). It is for this reason that the United States Supreme Court hears cases concerning schools.

✔ State legislatures have responsibilities to enact legislation creating schools that describe their governance, organization, and administration.

✔ School organization assists students in learning and addresses the specific cultural and social needs of the community.

✔ Neighborhood schools have traditionally been a part of school organization. Because many fostered segregation, other forms of school organization have been instituted to achieve racial equity.

✔ Declining enrollments are causing schools to consolidate in rural America.

✔ Local boards of education are state agencies. Members only have authority when they meet in session as a group.

✔ Superintendents, as chief executive officers of the school district, have specialists assisting them in central or subdistrict offices. Their certification is specific to exercising educational leadership within the district.

✔ Principals are educational leaders within the school plant, concerned with curriculum and management.

✔ School-based management includes teachers, parents, principals, and others in the decision-making process.

✔ Concern about the problems of governance, organization, and administration is being voiced by thoughtful administrators. Some administrators are questioning whether the present form of school organization is adequate to help children to live in the twenty-first century.

Key Terms

governance
First Amendment
Tenth Amendment
Fourteenth
    Amendment
Department of
    Education
chief state school
    officer
cabinets of education
school accreditation
intermediate units

local board of
    education
subdistrict
    organization
school-based
    management
neighborhood
    schools
    (attendance
    centers)
consolidation
deconsolidation

Applying What You Have Learned

1. Lorna and Kerry in *Becoming a Teacher* have little understanding about how to interview for a teaching position. Do you think they understand how schools are governed or administered? What advice would you give them so they can understand schools better?

2. As a school board member, you have been contacted by several Asian-American parents who insist their neighborhood school has fewer academic programs than other neighborhood schools in the community. They consider this *de facto* segregation. Describe the problem as they understand it. What should you as a school board member do to change it? What types of arguments would you expect to hear from others in your community?

3. Some scholars, such as Paul Kennedy, state the United States is not prepared to enter the twenty-first century with our present educational system. Do you agree? Using what you've learned in this class, develop a new school organization. How would you administer this new school?

Interactive Learning

1. Your school board has instituted a school-based management program. Your principal is very leery about teachers forming a committee to oversee her actions. You have a high regard for her administrative abilities, and find it difficult to understand why she is concerned. Develop a list of no more than four points outlining why she may be opposed to school-based management. What do these points tell you about your principal? Do you feel your principal has a high regard for the faculty's leadership ability? Would you like to teach in this school? Why?

2. Do you think it is important to have separation of church and state? If your religious beliefs were different from others, what would be your response if you were forced to participate in others' religious activities? Talk to several parents about why they are concerned about schools teaching values.

3. Why do you think the selection of textbooks is so controversial in some states?

Research how the process of textbook selection occurs in your school district or state.

Expanding Your Knowledge

The Constitution of the United States. (An extraordinary document, written in the form of an eighteenth-century contract. Teachers should understand the Constitution because their work is people-oriented. A remarkable piece of literature.)

Chubb, J. E. & T. M. Moe. *Politics, Markets, and American Schools.* Washington, D.C.: Brookings Institute, 1990. (Excellent book about how school's actions and policies are impacted by the federal government.)

Etzioni, Amitai. *A Comparative Analysis of Complex Organizations.* New York: Free Press, 1961. (While this is an old text, it is excellent for understanding how schools can or should be organized. Etzioni makes the reader think.)

Hoy, Wayne K. & Cecil G. Miskel. *Education Administration: Theory, Research and Practice.* New York: Random House, 1987. (An excellent general introductory text. It discusses basic administrative topics such as organizational perspectives, leadership, decision making, and communication. This book gives the beginning teacher an idea of what superintendents, principals, boards of education, and others within the governance structure actually do.)

Kennedy, Paul. *Preparing for the Twenty-First Century.* New York: Random House, 1993. (Kennedy attempts to outline significant problems for the United States and how we should react to them. Some of the problems he discusses are ethnicity, international migration, and environment.)

Sergiovanni, Thomas. *Educational Governance and Administration,* 3rd edition. Boston: Allyn and Bacon, 1989. (This text is much like the Hoy book. The section on cultural view of schooling and administration is very well done. The text informs teachers about the everyday life of the principal and superintendent.)

Teachers and Students as Citizens: Rights and Responsibilities

In Chapter 9 you will study the rights and responsibilities of teachers and students. At this point in your teacher education program, you are probably more interested in learning how to be a good classroom teacher than in studying legal issues. After all, what could a well-meaning classroom teacher do that would be terrible enough to cause a lawsuit? Surprisingly, a lot. You need to know about the legal rights you and your students enjoy as well as the responsibilities you each have.

As our society becomes more complex, and as we continue to redefine the role of children in our schools, courts have become increasingly involved in the rights and responsibilities of students and teachers. Schools today are developing relationships with students that are different than they were when you were a student. Classrooms are, in many ways, cultural frontiers at which society's values are tested.

In this chapter you will study how our schools are changing and the different ways we look at students and teachers. Once we thought of children as less than adults, half-persons who should be seen and not heard. Today, we recognize their constitutional rights as citizens. It is much the same for teachers: We once thought of teachers as role models who should live flawless lives, but we are now redefining their rights and responsibilities.

The United States Supreme Court has highlighted students' and teachers' rights and responsibilities with regard to such major social issues as desegregation (*Brown v. Board of Education,* 1954) and how long pregnant teachers should be allowed to remain in the classroom (*Cleveland Board of Education v. LaFleur,* 1974).

Some teachers feel overpowered by the judicial system. They see the courts as complicated, mysterious, and confusing. This chapter will help remove the mystery of the court system, so you will be able to recognize its influence in your classroom and your life. After all, good teaching—and unhampered learning—can occur only when we understand our rights and responsibilities.

What you will learn

- The First and Fourteenth Amendments are concerned with student and teacher rights and responsibilities.
- Teachers have specific rights and responsibilities guaranteed by the Constitution.
- Schools are confronted with many controversial church–state issues today.
- The legal implications of tort liability and negligence apply to classroom teachers.
- Students have specific rights and responsibilities guaranteed by the Constitution.
- Copyright laws have an important role in schools.

BECOMING A TEACHER   *A prayer*

Today is Monday, and Carl is happy as he walks into his Spanish class. He feels he is on a winning streak. He likes his teacher, Mrs. Snyder. She's lived in both Spain and Mexico and has been able to make things come alive for him.

"Carl, I would like you to help me start the class today by leading us in prayer," Mrs. Snyder asks, handing him a small piece of paper.

Students bow their heads and Carl begins to read, "Almighty God, we acknowledge our dependence upon Thee, and we beg Thy . . ."

Carl isn't able to finish. "Why should I read this stupid prayer?" he thinks. "It doesn't have anything to do with Spanish and it doesn't say anything to me. Besides, it sounds like mush."

Everyone waits for the next line, "Thy blessings upon us, our parents, our teachers, and our country."

"Someone else can read this prayer if they want to. I think it's a waste of time, and it makes me feel like I am supposed to be religious," Carl says. He slides into his desk, half-mad and half-embarrassed. "There, I've said it. I hate that prayer. I don't want to pray and they can't make me!"

Some of the kids laugh. Others snicker. In the back of the room, Jerry whispers loudly, "Just because Carl is a Jew he thinks he's special. Why can't he smarten up and be like us?"

"Class—stop it!" Mrs. Snyder rises to her feet.

"Jerry, I know you wanted everyone to hear you." Mrs. Snyder is shaken. "What you said is not fair and it's wrong. Carl has every right to refuse to read this prayer. When the school board wrote the prayer it said if a student didn't want to participate he didn't have to."

Carl knows his winning streak is over. He can tell Mrs. Snyder's is preoccupied with the prayer. "Is she mad at me for what I did?" Carl wonders. Now he knows the rest of the day is going to be a drag.

???   *Mrs. Snyder responded to Carl and Jerry's values and ideals as well as a directive from the school board. If you had been Mrs. Snyder, what would you have done? Why?*

The Constitution and the Court System

Do you know what issues can be taken to court? Why are there different court systems? How do judges or juries arrive at decisions? What is the law based on? As you can see, there is a multitude of questions about the law and the courts. Let's remove some of the mystery, so you can appreciate the court system as a protector of our individual rights and responsibilities.

Dual Court Systems

There are two court systems in the United States. The federal court system is based on the United States Constitution and is nationwide. State court systems are based on state constitutions. Each court system has specific powers given to it by federal and state constitutions. Federal and state court systems are separated into criminal and civil divisions. The majority of cases involving schools fall under the jurisdiction of the civil court. In both state and federal court systems, the United States Supreme Court is the court of last appeal. Let's look at these court systems to see how they operate.

State Court System.
Each state has a court system whose purpose is to settle disputes within its borders. The court derives its authority from the state's constitution. State court systems may vary because of differences in their constitution. What is legal in one state may be illegal in a neighboring state. In short, state courts are expected to rule on cases that involve state laws. Because schools are a state responsibility, educational issues are tried at this level.

Civil Courts.   The lowest court, sometimes called the court of original jurisdiction, such as a municipal or a superior court, is the court that will first try a case. It is here the plaintiff enters a grievance and submits evidence to the court. Trials are structured procedures based on ancient law. The person bringing a charge is known as the plaintiff. The person charged is referred to as the defendant. Both the plaintiff and defendant submit evidence in support of their position. The judge or jury weighs the evidence, interprets the law, and renders a decision.

The American legal system allows for an appeal of the verdict by the person who loses a civil case. In other words, a person has the legal right to appeal the decision to the next-highest court. These courts, called appellate courts, review the case to make certain the verdict was within the law and that each party's constitutional rights were upheld. The state supreme court, the highest court of the state, hears cases that are appealed from appellate courts. The United States Supreme Court is the final arbiter of any case appealed from a state supreme court. While these processes *are* slow and complicated, it is through this extraordinary legal process that citizens' rights and responsibilities are defined, defended, and guaranteed.

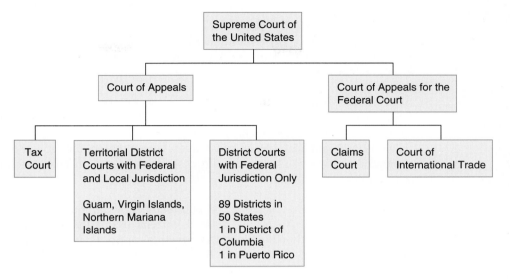

Figure 9.1   The Federal Court System

Federal Court System.   The purpose of the federal court system is to apply the United States Constitution to legal questions that come before it. These come through appeals from state supreme courts and lower federal courts. Not all issues go before a federal court. Let's look now at the structure of the federal court system (see Figure 9.1).

District Courts.   This is the lowest court at the federal level. District courts serve specific geographical areas, usually several states. In this way, the federal court system attempts to stay as close as possible to the people. If a plaintiff or defendant is not satisfied with the district court's decision, it may be appealed to the circuit court of appeals.

Circuit Courts of Appeal.   Several district courts in a geographic area make up the circuit court of appeals. The circuit court acts as a court of appeals, hearing only cases from lower courts within its geographic borders. Circuit courts, like state appellate courts, are concerned that lower court rulings are within federal law and each party's constitutional rights have been upheld.

U.S. Supreme Court.   The United States Supreme Court is the court of last appeal. It hears cases only if four of its nine judges believe the state supreme court or circuit court's decision should be reviewed. If fewer than four justices agree to hear the case, the lower court's ruling is upheld. If the case is heard, a majority of the justices must agree on a decision in order to overturn the lower court's ruling.

Constitutional Amendments

The two most important constitutional amendments that pertain to you and your students are the First and the Fourteenth Amendments. The Eighth and Tenth Amendments are also important. Each defines specific rights and responsibilities.

First Amendment.   The First Amendment guarantees you and your students freedom of speech and religion. You have the right to express your personal views, read uncensored books and magazines, publicly express and practice your religious and political ideals and values, and petition the government if it has attempted to stop you. Several court cases that hinged on First Amendment rights are pertinent to educators.

Fourteenth Amendment.   The Fourteenth Amendment asserts that states may not abridge any of the rights granted citizens under the U.S. Constitution. The court has consistently maintained that an equal opportunity to learn is one of these rights. For example, in *Brown v. Board of Education* (1954) the court ruled that color of skin was not a reason to deny any child equal educational opportunity.

Religion and Public Schools

The United States Constitution separates church from state. **Church–state separation** is a constitutional method of guaranteeing religious freedom. This means state-supported schools are not allowed to advance any specific theology or religious set of values.

Church–state separation and free speech are important for teachers to understand. At what point does expressing one's religious beliefs interfere with the rights of others to learn in the classroom? The prayer Carl read in the *Becoming a Teacher* was a prayer used in a New York school district in 1962. Because the community was multicultural and reflected different religious beliefs, the school board had tried to write a prayer that would not insult the beliefs or values of the children or their parents.

Engel v. Vitale.   In the ensuing Supreme Court case, *Engel v. Vitale* (1962), the school board asserted that the prayer was religiously neutral. They believed that, because it was nondenominational, it offended no religious group. Because the students were not required to participate in the prayer, the school board argued that it should be allowed. The Supreme Court ruled that the prayer was unconstitutional. Free speech was not an issue. Rather, the court found that the school board, as a government agency, had no right to be involved in religion at all. Freedom of speech does not allow government agencies to support religion in any way, for that would violate the principle of church–state separation.

Pierce v. Society of Sisters.   In 1922, the Oregon state legislature passed the Oregon Compulsory Education Act. This act said parents were required by state law to send their children to the state's public schools. The Society of Sisters challenged the legislation, and in the ensuing *Pierce v. Society of Sisters* (1925), the Supreme Court struck down the Oregon legislation. The Court ruled that parents had the right to send their children to either public or private schools. The First Amendment was not specifically discussed, but its commitment to religious liberty was crucial to the court's decision.

Wisconsin v. Yoder.   This 1972 case dealt primarily with the Amish. The Amish are a religious sect who are opposed to secondary education, because they question the value of much that is taught there. The Amish want their children to master the fundamentals of education, but it is important to them that parents retain control over what children learn or are exposed to. The Supreme Court ruled that Wisconsin's constitutional requirement of educating Amish children past the eighth grade was less important than preserving religious liberty. It reaffirmed parents have the responsibility to educate their children.

School District of Abington Township v. Schempp.   Many believe, erroneously, that the *Engel v. Vitale* ruling banned the Bible, as well as all types of prayer, from public schools but it did not discuss how the Bible could be used in the classroom. In *School District of Abington Township v. Schempp* (1963), a Pennsylvania school district allowed classroom teachers or students to read ten verses from the Bible each morning as part of an opening exercise. The Pennsylvania law clearly stated children were not required to attend the morning exercises if they were offended by the Bible reading. The Supreme Court ruled that the Bible could be read in classrooms when children were learning great literature, studying the history of religion, or attending a class in comparative religion but objected to the use of the Bible as an opening exercise in a public school.

Lee v. Weisman.   In a similar case, the Supreme Court held that prayer at public school graduation ceremonies was unconstitutional. In *Lee v. Weisman* (1992), a Rabbi in Rhode Island delivered a prayer at a public middle-school graduation. The Supreme Court ruled that children should not be compelled to participate in a religious exercise in order to graduate. The majority opinion, written by Justice Kennedy, supported this ruling with the additional comment that the Establishment Clause of the First Amendment disallows the state from forcing religious involvement in a required educational activity.

Mozert v. Hawkins County Board of Education.   In 1986 Christian fundamentalists sued Hawkins County school board in Tennessee for suspending their children from school. The parents did not want their children unduly influenced by what they considered anti-Christian beliefs in *Macbeth, The Wonderful Wizard of Oz,* and *Rumpelstiltskin*. Each book, the fundamentalists stated, would influence their children with secular humanistic values and disrespect for the Bible.

The district court ruled in favor of the Christian fundamentalists, because Hawkins County school board could not give compelling reasons why the three books were essential to prepare children for citizenship. In fact, the district court ruled that when the school suspended the children, it had denied them their right to an education because they had exercised their freedom of speech. In 1987, the district court's decision was overturned by the Sixth Circuit Court of Appeals. The Sixth Circuit Court ruled that the state's interest in educating children far outweighed the children's freedom to exercise their religion. Upon further appeal, the United States Supreme Court refused to hear the case. In effect, it agreed with the Sixth Circuit Court.

Religious values and ideas in schools will continue to be controversial for a long time. It is becoming increasingly clear that classroom teachers must understand students' constitutional rights regardless of whether their students are Christian fundamentalists, Moslems, Hindus, Jews, or agnostics.

Lemon v. Kurtzman.   The "Lemon Test" is used as a method to evaluate how public funds can be distributed to private schools. Based on the *Lemon v. Kurtzman* (1971) case, nonpublic schools may receive public funds if:

- excessive entanglement between church and state does not occur,
- the assistance is used only for secular purposes, and
- the specific assistance does not help or hinder religion.

In *Lemon v. Kurtzman,* the Supreme Court held that monies may be given to schools if children are able to maintain their constitutional rights.

Unresolved Issues

There are still many questions about religion and public schools left for society to debate. The Supreme Court has yet to rule on whether meditation, as used by some religions, should be allowed in classrooms. For example, if you are given a period of time for meditation or prayer as part of an opening exercise, what stops you from using your moment of silence to think about which excuse you should give your teacher because you forgot your homework? What happens if a group of students decide on their own to hold a Bible study during their lunch hour?

It is clear the Supreme Court will continue to hear cases about the teaching of religious values in the future. As society becomes more multicultural, religious beliefs become more diverse, and more people fear their religious values will disappear.

Christian fundamentalists are one of the most vocal groups concerned that schools are teaching their children values contrary to their religious beliefs. Classroom teachers, they charge, are teaching **secular humanism.** They believe that children are being taught to be responsible for their own decisions and actions rather than to rely on religion (Nord, 1995). Vignette 9.1 illustrates how special-interest groups can impact your future work as a classroom teacher.

Teaching secular humanism?

Yolanda Chad graduated from college last year with a major in English and a secondary school teaching certificate. She loves English. She especially likes Shakespeare. This year she was thrilled when she read that the state-approved book list included *Macbeth* and her personal favorite, *Of Mice and Men*. She developed a series of lesson plans to acquaint her students with George and Lennie's struggle to survive in a hostile social environment.

She was surprised when her principal told her several parents were concerned about her teaching *Of Mice and Men*. "Please don't take this personally, Yolanda," Mr. Deneal told her. "The parents told me you were a good teacher. It's just that they believe *Of Mice and Men* teaches values that are opposite of those they want their children to learn. They say this book teaches secular humanism."

As Yolanda tried to understand what Mr. Deneal was telling her, she heard him say, "They also are going to the school board about your teaching *Macbeth*. They want it removed from the curriculum, too."

???   *Interview a member of the clergy to learn why these two books might be considered by some Christians to advance the ideas of secular humanism. Try to learn why some people believe parents have a right to stop teachers from teaching children values that are against their beliefs. Interview an attorney or law student to find out what legal considerations this case represents.*

Tort Liability and Negligence

In the last section we dealt with how people's beliefs influence their right to an education. This section is concerned with how courts decide whether a person has been hurt and who is responsible.

A **tort** is a civil wrong. Tort law concerns individuals who have suffered physical or verbal harm because of the action of another. A person may go to court for the purpose of correcting such a wrong. The concept of tort law comes from old English law. By tradition, if you were injured either on purpose or by accident, you could take the individual who hurt you to court. In other words, you could sue. It was generally assumed, in old England, that you could not sue the government or the king. This legal tradition was brought to the United States. However, most states today allow citizens to sue the government. This means classroom teachers, administrators, and others, as employees of the school, may be sued by students and their parents.

Tort law is based on the idea of **reasonableness.** That is, what would a typical, reasonable person who was prudent do under the same circumstances? Reasonableness is not a hard-and-fast concept. It can change according to circumstances.

Tort law applies only to situations in which a person has been injured because of another individual's negligence. **Negligence** is a legal term that describes a civil wrong that is caused unintentionally. Three criteria must be satisfied for negligence (in the legal sense) to occur:

- There must be a duty to exercise care
- There must be a breach of that duty
- There must be **proximate cause** between the breach of duty and the resultant injury

For example, teachers are required to maintain safe environments for students. Schools traditionally have policies that require teachers to assume specific responsibilities which will protect the learning environment. Injuries may be physical or nonphysical. In the following example Mrs. Markham has not maintained a safe learning environment.

MRS. MARKAM

Mrs. Markham is introducing her seventh graders to a new unit in chemistry. Because she believes the class is mature for its age, she does not stress how the students should handle the new chemicals. Consequently, two students suffer chemical burns.

Mrs. Markam has demonstrated one of the elements of the definition of negligence: she has neglected her duty to exercise care. Mrs. Coogan, in the next case study, illustrates what Mrs. Markam should have done.

MRS. COOGAN

Mrs. Coogan is introducing her seventh graders to a new unit in chemistry. Because the students will be using chemicals that could potentially hurt them, she explains how the chemicals could injure them and demonstrates how they should be handled. She also tells the students not to use the chemicals without her monitoring their actions. As a safety measure, she keeps the chemicals at her lab desk. Later, as Mrs. Coogan answers questions about the assignment, several students remove some chemicals from her desk without her permission and are injured while using them.

In this case, Mrs. Coogan has informed the students about the chemicals and, most importantly, kept them from their reach. Even though several students were injured, it was not her fault. She had exercised reasonable care by keeping the chemicals in her lab desk and had been present.

MR. CHESSMORE

Mr. Chessmore is an eighth-grade physical education teacher who is teaching students how to climb ropes. Students, he knows, typically like to learn rope climbing, so when Sarah tells him she is afraid of heights, he does his best to change her mind. Sarah is nervous when it is her turn. As she climbs the rope, she falls and sprains her ankle.

Mr. Chessmore's intent was to help Sarah gain confidence in herself and meet the challenge of climbing a rope. In this case, it is apparent that Mr. Chessmore should have understood Sarah was at risk of being injured because of her fear of heights.

Strict Liability.

These three examples illustrate types of problems students and teachers have in the classroom. During the last several years, courts have tended to apply a standard of **strict liability.** That is, they are less willing to accept "reasonable precautions" as a defense. Classrooms are complex environments, and it is important for teachers to understand the significance of the equipment, activities, and environment. Never assume that your students will understand the dangers or follow the procedures you tell them to. Your principal will probably inform you of school policies and procedures you are expected to use to safeguard your students. Usually the policies are written where you can refer to them often.

Parental Consent.

Some teachers think that asking parents to sign a parental consent form will release them from legal responsibilities. This is not the case. Parental consent forms are used for several reasons, including informing parents of where their children are and what they are learning. Just because parents sign a form does not cancel their right to sue the classroom teacher or the school over questions of negligence. As a classroom teacher you are still responsible for the safety of your students.

Liability Insurance.

We hope you now recognize the need for **liability insurance,** insurance that will provide legal assistance and pay your legal fees and damages if you are sued. In all likelihood, your professional organization or an approved insurance company will explain the coverage available to you at the professional development workshop held during the first several days of each school year. This insurance is especially important to you if you are a physical education instructor, vocational teacher, science instructor, or extracurricular activities sponsor. However, no teacher should be without insurance.

Your Rights and Responsibilities as a Teacher

Not long ago it was assumed classroom teachers had few constitutional rights. Teachers could easily be dismissed from their positions for such trivial offenses as refusing to teach Sunday school or being seen in taverns. Over the years, teachers have had their constitutional rights clarified through the court system. In fact, the Fourteenth Amendment guarantees all citizens the same constitutional rights, regardless of the positions they hold—it applies to teachers as well as students. Figure 9.2 is a sampling of Supreme Court decisions pertaining to teachers' rights and responsibilities.

Figure 9.2   United States Supreme Court Decisions Regarding Teacher Rights and Responsibilities

---

Pickering v. Board of Education (1968)   A teacher was dismissed because he had written a letter to the local newspaper criticizing the school board. The Court reinstated him, saying the school board had not recognized his rights as a citizen under the First and Fourteenth Amendments

Cleveland Board of Education v. LaFleur (1974)   A pregnant teacher was required to take mandatory maternity leave. The Court struck down the school policy because it was arbitrary.

Lehnert v. Ferris Faculty Association (1991)   Union dues were being used for political purposes that were not related to the union's collective bargaining agreement. The Supreme Court stated employees who are not union members are not required to pay dues for these purposes.

Board of Regents of State Colleges v. Roth (1972)   A teacher who had a one-year contract sued because he said he had a property interest that qualified him for procedural rights under the Fourteenth Amendment. The Supreme Court stated that, because he was still in the probationary period, he did not have a property interest.

Steelworks v. Weber (1979)   The question was whether employers could use affirmative action plans to include more minorities. The Supreme Court stated employers, including school boards, could develop affirmative action plans.

North Haven Board of Education v. Bell (1982)   Several female teachers asserted that they had been discriminated against because of their sex. The Supreme Court stated they were protected through Title IX.

Russo v. Central School District No. 1 (1973)   A teacher was dismissed because she would not take part in the daily flag salute. The Supreme Court ruled she had a constitutional right to her beliefs and should be reinstated.

Academic Freedom

Academic freedom is one of the most misunderstood terms in education. There are three types of freedoms classroom teachers should recognize. They deal with free speech and conduct in your classroom, working conditions within your school, and your private life outside the school.

Inside the Classroom.
Exactly what freedoms do elementary and secondary teachers have in the classroom? As you probably know from your own experience, teachers do not have unlimited license to say or teach anything they wish. The two examples in Vignette 9.2 emphasize teachers' rights and responsibilities inside the classroom.

Freedom of speech in the classroom

Example 1:   Maribel wanted to teach *The Catcher In The Rye* to her junior literature class. She remembered that, when she went to school, Salinger's book had created a real storm of protest by parents and students alike. "That's probably the reason I read it," she thought as she prepared for her first lesson of the day.

When Mrs. Yacono, her principal, told her it was not a good idea to teach the story, she was surprised. "Don't do it," she said. "Even the superintendent is opposed to you teaching this book."

"What's the matter with this book?" Maribel asked.

"It's dirty, if you want to know," said Mrs. Yacono. "These kids are too immature to understand what the author is trying to say."

Example 2:   The next week, Maribel's literature class was coming to the end of the period. In order to make a point, she wrote a taboo word used by the author on the board. "Let's discuss what the author meant by this term to see if we can identify a more socially acceptable term."

Several students appeared to be uncomfortable as she asked them questions about how the term could be changed.

Mrs. Yacono was not sympathetic when she talked to Maribel in her office. "Didn't you think some parent would complain about you using that word in class?" she asked.

"I really didn't think there was a problem," Maribel said. "After all, the students hear that word every day in the halls and on the street. They use that word in their daily lives."

"That may be true, Maribel," said Mrs. Yacono, "but you don't expect me to tell the parents you have the approval of the school board to use that word in class, do you?"

???   *Each example is concerned with freedom of speech in the classroom. Help Maribel answer each of the following questions. (a) Is the information appropriate for the age of the students? (b) Is the content related to the curriculum for the course? (c) Is the content and methodology approved by other members of the profession?*

In the first example in Vignette 9.2, the issue was whether a specific novel was appropriate for students. Teachers' First Amendment rights state the principal and superintendent must prove the novel is inappropriate for the age level of the students and is disturbing the educational process. That is, Mrs. Yacono must prove that *The Catcher In The Rye* is not appropriate for 16- and 17-year-old students to read. They must prove the book is dirty according to legal definitions, not just their own values.

In the second example in Vignette 9.2, the issue is whether the content—in this case a taboo word—is an integral part of a lesson. A second issue is whether the manner of classroom presentation is acceptable to other members of the profession. In summary, freedom of speech issues inside the classroom relate to students, teaching methods, and curriculum.

Inside the School.   Like any classroom teacher, you will be interested in your school's governance. What are your responsibilities when the school and your students are in conflict? Do you have specific constitutional rights that allow you to publicly express your professional judgment? Let's follow Maribel to see how she reacts to her school board's decision to reduce her classroom budget in Vignette 9.3.

VIGNETTE 9.3

Rights of teachers in relation to school boards and administrators

Maribel received a memo saying that the English program budget had been cancelled by the school board, effective immediately. She read: "Upon the recommendation of the superintendent, the board voted 8–2 to reduce classroom expenditures in secondary English programs, so the monies can be used more effectively to purchase new helmets for the football team."

Maribel was disgusted! This meant she had to give up her request for a VCR so students could watch the new Shakespeare tapes she had received from the state Department of Education.

Mrs. Yacono, her principal, said "Maribel, I know you don't like what the school board did, but what can I do about it? They are the final authority on how monies are spent in the system. Even the superintendent couldn't change their mind—and, in this case, he wants the team to have new helmets."

Disappointed, Maribel went home. "It just isn't right!" she thought. "My students are going to suffer because of the school board's decision. They didn't even wait until next budget year—they took the money away in mid-semester." In a fit of disgust, Maribel wrote a letter to the city newspaper outlining her feelings. Two weeks after Maribel's letter was printed, Mrs. Yacono stopped her in the hall.

"Maribel, I have some terrible news! The school board is having a special meeting tonight, and they want you there. They want to fire you for going to the newspapers with your story."

Maribel was stunned. "Oh no! Not only have I lost the money for the VCR, but now they want to fire me."

??? *Does Maribel have a right to tell the taxpayers in her community how the school board and superintendent are planning to spend the money? Was there another way she could have expressed herself to the school board? What might you suggest?*

A similar situation happened to a classroom teacher in Illinois in 1967. A teacher named Pickering wrote a letter to the city newspaper complaining that the superintendent was trying to stop teachers from criticizing a local bond issue and criticizing the manner in which the school board was allocating monies between academics and athletics. Mr. Pickering was fired by the school board for writing the letter.

In a landmark case, *Pickering v. Board of Education* (1968), the United States Supreme Court stated that Mr. Pickering had specific rights guaranteed by the First and Fourteenth Amendments. The fact that he was a classroom teacher under contract to the school board did not give the school board the power to remove those rights. The Court ruled that Mr. Pickering had been fired unjustly and required the school board to reinstate him.

The Court did place a limit on freedom under certain circumstances, however. The Supreme Court stated that problems involving a close working relationship (like that you will have with your principal) must be resolved within the school system through grievance procedures. Obviously, the public airing of disagreements between subordinates and immediate superiors can undermine the working relationship between them and harm the learning environment.

Outside the School.   Beginning teachers used to worry about how their out-of-school actions would influence their chance to be rehired for the next school year. Vignette 9.4 looks at out-of-school freedoms.

 VIGNETTE 9.4   *Out-of-school freedoms*

Lorna isn't sure how she feels. She's outraged, sad, and confused all at the same time. Marnie is her best friend. They met in college and this is their second year together at Carter High School. Mr. Deneal has just told Marnie her contract will not be renewed for next year.

"I just don't get it, Lorna," Marnie sobs. "I did a good job teaching. I know the kids like me, and the parents are complimentary of my work. Even Mr. Deneal said I was one of the best beginning social studies teachers he had seen at Carter in years."

"What did Mr. Deneal say when he told you your contract would not be renewed?" asks Lorna.

"He said that because I went door to door distributing religious tracts, the school board felt I was demeaning the role of the teacher and embarrassing the school," says Marnie. "But you know, that's part of my religion as a Jehovah's Witness—I have to be able to practice my religion."

In this difficult situation rests a Constitutional question: whether teacher activities outside school influence the learning environment in the classroom. In New York, a high school teacher was dismissed because she would not take part in the daily flag salute ceremony. She would stand quietly while another teacher performed the ceremony. In *Russo v. Central School District No. 1* (1973) the Supreme Court upheld a circuit court's ruling that, as a citizen, the teacher was allowed to express her freedom of conscience. That is, her out-of-school activities, which included selling religious books, had no bearing on her in-school responsibilities. In another case, *Board of Education v. James* (1972), a teacher who wore an armband in the classroom had been dismissed by his school board. The school board appealed the case to the Supreme Court. It upheld the teacher's right to his own beliefs.

You do not lose your constitutional rights when you become a teacher. In fact, there is great similarity in how the court system treats student and teacher rights and responsibilities.

Teacher Contracts

In general, states require teacher certification applicants to pass specific curriculum tests and to hold at least a bachelor's degree. States may also require you to be of good moral character and in good physical health.

A teacher's certificate is like a driver's license: both are privileges, and both can be withdrawn by the state with cause. Unlike a driver's license, however, a teacher's certificate is concerned with *minimum* requirements. States may allow school districts to require additional qualifications, because of specific features of that school district. Courts consider a teacher's certificate to be a **property interest;** that is, the certificate belongs to you. It cannot be taken from you without due process. **Due process** is a legal procedure, guaranteed by the Fourteenth Amendment, which stipulates that the school district must prove its allegations against you in a fair and timely manner.

Terms of Employment.   Your contract outlines the terms of your employment, what your teaching assignment will be, whether you will be required to periodically pass competency tests, other duties (such as extracurricular responsibilities), how much you will be paid, and how you will receive your salary. You will be required to sign the contract. The school board is your legal employer. Traditionally, school boards will enter into a formal contract with you upon the recommendation of the superintendent.

Tenure.   As a beginning teacher, you will become aware of tenure and all its implications when you sign your first teaching contract. Usually, your principal or another administrator will inform you of the requirements you must meet in order to receive tenure. Tenure is a legal concept and is defined at the state level; it differs from state to state. Basically, **tenure** is conferred on teachers after a probationary period to protect them from arbitrary dismissal.

Tenure is frequently misunderstood by teachers and the public alike. It was developed about a century ago to protect the academic freedom of teachers and remove them from political patronage. In the 1800s, teachers were often hired by school boards because of who they knew, rather than how good they were. Good teachers were sometimes fired because an influential individual in the community disliked them.

Tenure is favored by school boards because it helps keep quality classroom teachers in the school district. Sadly, it sometimes protects a few teachers who are lazy or unwilling to spend the effort in helping children learn. Tenure is not an ironclad guarantee. It is not true that once you are tenured, you will never be fired. Tenured teachers *have* been fired—for cause. That is, you may be dismissed if you are proven to be incompetent, immoral, insubordinate, or neglectful in your duties. How these terms are legally defined depends on state laws.

Due Process.   If a tenured teacher is fired, the law guarantees him or her due process. Figure 9.3 outlines the steps generally required for due process. Even though state legislation may differ slightly, due process requires the school district and the teacher to be fair in their relations, even during the dismissal period.

Due process requires schools to submit extensive documentation or evidence to establish their case. The fired teacher, too, must be prepared to submit extensive evidence on her or his own behalf. The panel before whom the case is first tried is, traditionally, the school board.

What happens if a teacher believes a school board is prejudiced? According to *Hortonville Joint School District v. Hortonville Education Association* (1976), it is the teacher's responsibility to submit evidence the school board is prejudiced. In the event an impartial school board supports the firing of a tenured teacher, it is the teacher's legal right to appeal his or her case to a state court.

Probationary Period.   One of the requirements of tenure is usually that you have served a school system for a period of time. During this probationary period, usually two or three years depending on the state, teachers are expected to demonstrate quality classroom teaching ability. You should expect your principal or another administrator to evaluate your classroom teaching several times a year.

Figure 9.3   Steps Required for Due Process

- You must be given a notice of dismissal in which the charges are clearly stated. The notice must be written and given to you promptly.
- You have a constitutional right to meet your accusers at an official hearing at which you may be represented by an attorney.
- You have the right to present witnesses, give oral and written evidence, cross-examine witnesses, and dispute evidence given by the school.
- You have the right to a fair hearing before an unbiased panel, which must supply you with a written transcript of the proceedings.
- If the panel finds for the school, you have the constitutional right to appeal.

You should also understand that successful teaching evaluations during your probationary period do not necessarily guarantee you a tenured teaching contract. For example, if your probationary term is three years, and you have received satisfactory teaching evaluations for the first two years, the school district is not obligated to offer you a third-year contract. Beginning teachers should realize that school districts may dismiss them for any reason and are not required to give an explanation why they will not be rehired. If you are offered a fourth contract, usually called a continuing contract, you may expect to teach during the following years unless the school district indicates otherwise.

Traditionally, tenure is conferred by the district. That is, it does not necessarily transfer to another school district within the state or to a school district in another state. Obviously, if you are transferred from one school to another within the same school district, tenure will follow.

Unions and Teacher Rights and Responsibilities

At one time, school boards informed teachers who were rehired what the terms of their contract and salaries for the school year would be. Today, many states have statutes which allow as many as 75 percent of all classroom teachers in the country to bargain collectively. However, state laws vary greatly. Some states, such as North Carolina and Virginia, forbid any type of collective bargaining between school boards and teachers. The remaining 48 states view collective bargaining differently. For example, Maryland's law permits school boards and teachers to enter into binding arbitration if they are not able to agree. Kansas considers negotiations between school boards and teachers to be fact-finding exercises. Generally, the states consider collective bargaining to mean both sides should be able to meet and discuss their differences.

Teacher Strikes.   States view striking teachers differently. For example, are teachers workers? Do they provide an essential service? Can public employees legally withhold services? Some states—such as Alaska, Hawaii, Montana, New Hampshire, Oregon, Pennsylvania, and Vermont—permit teachers to strike. In other states, school boards usually obtain a court injunction to force teachers to remain in the classroom if they threaten to strike. Some states punish striking teachers. For example, New York's legislation declares teachers will lose two days' pay for each day they are on strike. Florida and Minnesota forbid striking teachers to receive pay increases for a year after the strike. One thing is clear: states consider classroom teachers to provide a essential service, like firefighters or police officers.

Drug-Free Workplace Act.   Some schools require prospective teachers to submit to drug tests. While the *Drug Free Workplace Act* (1988) is the basis upon which schools may test teachers, teacher unions in New York and Georgia have questioned the school's right, under the Constitution, to require drug testing of all teachers. They believe teachers should submit to drug tests only if there is a reasonable suspicion of drug use. Indiscriminate drug testing, they contend, is a violation of individual rights. Presently, the Supreme Court is hearing specific cases involving indiscriminate drug testing of student athletes. Regardless of its ruling, it is clear schools want their classrooms to be drug-free. Other school districts are testing employees for diseases such as tuberculosis.

 ## Students' Rights and Responsibilities

As a beginning teacher, you will probably teach students whose parents are living and working in this country illegally. You may also be aware of parents who are United States citizens, but who are not able to send their children to your school because they live in another school district. This seemingly contradictory situation illustrates a pillar of American society: the right of a child to attend school is based on residency, not citizenship.

We are aware that children, regardless of citizenship, must attend school. But what is their relationship to schools and classroom teachers? Until the 1960s, schools considered themselves to serve *in loco parentis*. That is, they had the same legal authority over students during school hours that parents had after school. Teachers and other educators thought children needed continual parental nurturing and guidance during the school day. But society's concept of children has changed. Today, we recognize that students have specific rights and responsibilities guaranteed them by the Constitution. That recognition has come through various Supreme Court cases.

Free Speech

The issue of what constitutes free speech has always been controversial in the United States. Although everyone is for it, it is many times confusing and threatening. It is sometimes difficult to know the difference between free speech and libel. Is it legal to be able to say anything you wish about another person? Is flag burning a free speech issue? The nation's courts will have to continue to redefine *free speech* just as they have in previous generations.

Tinker v. Des Moines Independent School District.   During the height of the Vietnam War in the late 1960s, several students in Des Moines, Iowa, chose to wear armbands to high school to peacefully demonstrate their opposition to the war. It is important to understand how these students felt. The war was very controversial and was reported on all television nightly news programs. Male high school students were especially concerned about the war, because they knew they would be eligible for the military draft when they became 18. When the Des Moines Independent School District school board heard of the students' planned, peaceful demonstration, it immediately reacted by writing a policy that stated that wearing armbands was not allowed on school property. Students who wore them, the policy said, would be suspended.

The parents of the children who wore the armbands sued the school district when their children were suspended. The case eventually ended up in the United States Supreme Court. In *Tinker v. Des Moines Independent School District* (1969), the Court ruled that students were citizens of the United States, free to express their political views as long as they did not disrupt the learning environment. Because the Des Moines Independent School District could not prove that wearing armbands caused the school's learning environment to degenerate, the Supreme Court ruled that the students' constitutional freedom to speak must be allowed.

Hazelwood School District v. Kuhlmeier.   *Tinker v. Des Moines* only protected the right to free speech if it did not disrupt the learning environment. In this case, several journalism students at Hazelwood East High School in Missouri had written articles for the student newspaper in which they outlined the sexual lives of students they had interviewed. The principal objected to the articles because they were poorly written. He judged that there was not sufficient time for the articles to be rewritten for publication in the next edition of the student newspaper, and the articles were not published. The students sued.

This extraordinary case, known as *Hazelwood School District v. Kuhlmeier* (1988), was heard by the Supreme Court. The question was whether the principal had limited the students' free speech. The Court ruled that the principal had the constitutional right to remove the articles from the newspaper. It stated the students' right of free expression was modified in this case because the newspaper was part of the curriculum. That is, the newspaper existed only for the purpose of teaching and learning—it was not a public forum.

The Supreme Court went further. It ruled that schools could develop policies that regulated student newspapers and obscene literature. The Court pointed out that the obscenity had to be legally defined, not based on personal values. To guarantee students due process, the Court insisted schools develop procedures in which students could participate in their own suspension hearings.

Bethel School District No. 403 v. Fraser.   The Supreme Court had already placed limitations on students' free speech. In *Bethel School District No. 403 v. Fraser* (1986), the Supreme Court ruled that a student who had used socially taboo words and sexual innuendos at a school function was not protected by the First Amendment. In fact, the Supreme Court insisted that schools, as instruments of the state, could not fulfill their duty to teach children manners and civility if they allowed students to use offensive speech.

Residency

Residency has become a controversial issue recently. In California, Texas, Arizona, New Mexico, and Florida, school districts have complained they are not able to give students a quality education because of the ever-increasing numbers of children whose parents are illegal aliens. This frustration was highlighted in 1994, when Californians passed Proposition 187. This Proposition, which is presently in the courts, was intended to deny public services, including schooling, to illegal aliens. Proposition 187 required teachers to verify the citizenship status of all children in their classroom.

Phyler v. Doe.   In Texas, children of illegal aliens were told it was against state law for them to attend public school. In *Phyler v. Doe* (1982), the Supreme Court overturned the Texas law, stating it forced undue hardship on children because of issues over which they had no control. That is, children should not be punished because their parents illegally moved to the United States. Further, the Supreme Court ruled the Texas law was unintentionally creating a specific social subclass which, because of its illiteracy, would increase financial costs to society.

Search and Seizure

As our society becomes increasingly complex, crime has made inroads into schools. Schools throughout the nation are reacting to violence in the classroom by installing metal detection devices. Alcohol breath analysis and the removal of weapons, beepers, and portable telephones are other attempts to minimize crime in the halls. In the fight against crime, schools also search students and lockers. But is search and seizure in school subject to the same regulations as when police come to your house with a search warrant?

The Fourth Amendment declares there should exist a probable cause for police to search your premises. That is, in order to receive a search warrant, police are required to demonstrate to the courts that evidence probably exists at a specific location.

> The right of the people to be secure in their persons, houses, papers, and effects, against unreasonable searches and seizures, shall not be violated, and no warrants shall issue, but upon probable cause, supported by oath or affirmation, and particularly describing the place to be search, and the person or things to be seized. (Fourth Amendment of the United States Constitution)

School administrators, on the other hand, must only demonstrate they are reasonably suspicious that illegal objects are within the school. In *New Jersey v. T.L.O.* (1985), the court asserted that the limits of reasonable cause include the constitutional right of students not to be strip searched, touched by trained police dogs, or be part of a general search in which school officials do not have evidence of a specific crime.

Verbal Abuse and Sexual Discrimination

What at one time seemed to be the prerogative of adults in controlling children's behavior is, in recent years, being viewed as abuse. You may remember teachers from your own personal experiences in school who yelled and used socially taboo terms to embarrass or control you or other students. They may have referred to students in negative, derogatory fashions. This type of abuse is illegal today.

Courts have generally upheld school boards who fired teachers who used insulting, derogatory, abusive words to address students. Classroom teachers are becoming familiar with court cases in which families are suing schools and teachers alike for personal and physical injury. These families—rightly—are using criminal or civil liberty laws to support their claims.

Student Privacy

Not long ago, administrators and teachers did not want students to see their school records. These files, which followed the student from grade to grade, were usually stored in secure offices and used by administrators, teachers, and counselors. Mostly, they contained attendance reports, health documents, and teachers' appraisals of student performance. But, too often, mistakes, misinformation, and social and gender bias were written into records and never corrected. Regulations governing school records include:

- All parents, regardless whether the child lives with them or not, should be allowed to see their child's school records.
- Administrators must inform parents as to how they can inspect school records.
- Schools must obtain parental permission to show a child's records to any group other than school officials, teachers, and others who have a legal right to know.
- Students who are eighteen years and older have a right to see their own records.

Buckley Amendment.   The Buckley Amendment of the Family Educational Rights and Privacy Act (1974) stated that individuals 18 years of age or older have the right to see their records, and that parents have the right to see the records of their children. Also guaranteed is the right to challenge information found in the file and ask that it be corrected.

The Buckley Amendment shocked many classroom teachers when they realized students and their parents now had access to their evaluations. Because of this amendment, teachers today are very careful what they write in student files. Regardless of the law, it is expected teachers will be professional in their use of student records. As you enter the classroom as a teacher, your principal or department head will undoubtedly inform you of how student records should be kept, stored, and used. It is important you be continually cognizant of the importance of student records. What you write in your students' files will follow you as long as it follows them.

Discipline in Schools

Disciplinary problems are defined differently among school districts. In truth, teachers disagree about what constitutes a discipline problem. A discipline problem, we believe, is that which occurs when students engage in actions that disrupt the learning environment. The most common discipline problems reported by teachers and administrators range from tardiness, to vandalism, to selling drugs, to destroying private property. Throughout the years, schools have developed policies that govern student behavior. While policies may differ, students are informed what the consequences for breaking the rules are, and how the punishment will be administered.

Spankings.   Spanking is a traditional method of maintaining discipline that has recently become controversial. Most good teachers today understand that physically hurting students hurts the learning environment. In fact, many classroom teachers are debating whether paddling students amounts to physical abuse. Some school districts have banned spanking, even in states that allow corporal punishment. Other states have developed extensive, complicated codes outlining the offenses that warrant corporal punishment and the exact procedures regarding who can spank students and how spanking is to be done.

Expulsion/Suspension.   Another method of controlling student behavior is removal from school. This can take several forms. One is **suspension,** the forced removal of a student from the classroom for a short period of time, such as several days. **Expulsion** is the forced removal of a student from the classroom for a longer period of time, such as a semester. In either case, forced removal of a student from the classroom cannot occur without the advice of the superintendent and the school's legal authorities. As you are aware, education is a guaranteed right. Students cannot be forcefully removed from the learning environment without due process.

Most administrators are aware of *Wood v. Strickland* (1975), in which a school board summarily expelled several girls because they had spiked the punch at a school-sponsored party. The Supreme Court found the school board guilty, even though they did not know the girls were entitled to due process.

In another case, *Goss v. Lopez* (1975), the Supreme Court ruled that students could not be removed from school if they had not been given an opportunity to explain their side of the story. In this case, several students were told by the school board they were suspended from school. The students had not known that the school board met privately to discuss how they were to be disciplined. The Supreme Court ruled that school boards cannot forcefully remove students from school without due process. In this case, the board should have informed the students of the charges against them and, if the students denied the charge, explained or shown them the evidence. Further, the students should have been allowed to meet with the school board. The Supreme Court ruled that the school board had arbitrarily taken away the students' right to an education.

Teacher Malpractice

The Supreme Court has yet to rule on the rights of students who may be forcefully removed from school for academic reasons. For example, at what point is the failure of a student to learn the responsibility of the teacher? Let's look at teacher malpractice in this section.

The term *malpractice* is used in the medical profession when patients allege physicians have caused them injury. In the case of teacher malpractice, graduates allege their ex-classroom teachers did not teach them well enough for them to get a job. They sue the school because job openings for which they should be qualified are closed to them, because of their lack of academic qualifications. For example, a high school graduate who is not able to read the simplest directions may be disqualified for employment, while other graduates from the same school district compete in the job market. So far, courts have favored teachers and schools in these highly emotional cases, simply because they are not able to differentiate between a student who is not motivated to learn and a teacher who is incompetent. Courts presently do not want to become involved in the day-to-day activities of the classroom.

Hoffman v. Board of Education.   A student, tested on the Stanford–Binet Intelligence Test at age 5, scored below the national average. As a consequence, the school placed him in a special education class. He remained there until he graduated from high school. When he retook the intelligence test at age 18, the boy was shocked to learn his IQ was above the national average, and as a consequence, he would lose his federal assistance for the disabled. He recognized that the school had not educated him in a manner that gave him other life alternatives. He did not have enough education to get a job or go to college. This very complicated case eventually ended up in the New York Supreme Court. In *Hoffman v. Board of Education* (1979), the court reversed various lower court rulings that had required the school to pay the ex-student.

Legal Provisions for Children with Special Needs

Extraordinary court cases have been fought on behalf of children with special needs to allow them equal access to America's classrooms. Although many cases are significant, we want to draw your attention to three that illustrate the importance of understanding special education.

Diana v. State Board of Education.   Studies have shown that children who are brought up in Hispanic or Asian-American homes, having different cultural norms and relationships, can score lower on tests that were composed for children who have a Euro-centered cultural history. In *Diana v. State Board of Education* (1970), the plaintiffs contended that there were countless children who received a poorer education because of the labeling imposed on them and because of their placement in special education classes.

One of the more important consequences of this extraordinary case—which was settled out of court—was that children whose primary language was not English should be tested in their own language. That is, children should not be forced to translate test items in order to pass the test. All children in special education classes were required to be retested, and all the school districts in California had to explain to the court how children wrongfully placed in special education classes

Everyone can learn.

would be mainstreamed. *Diana v. State Board of Education* was a template for other cases. Many, like *Diana v. State Board of Education,* were settled out of court.

The Pennsylvania Association for Retarded Children v. The Commonwealth of Pennsylvania.

In *The Pennsylvania Association for Retarded Children v. The Commonwealth of Pennsylvania* (1972), the plaintiffs alleged that the state of Pennsylvania's policies led to specific practices that denied an appropriate education to schoolchildren with mental disabilities. Pennsylvania, like several other states during this period, had school codes that could exclude trainable mentally retarded children. The result of the case was that schools had to provide an appropriate education program for these children, that education should be understood by teachers and administrators as more than the acquisition of academic knowledge, and that education for these children could begin prior to age 5. Like the *Diana* case, *The Pennsylvania Association for Retarded Children v. Pennsylvania* was settled out of court.

Mills v. The Board of Education of the District of Columbia.

Unlike the *Pennsylvania* case, *Mills v. the Board of Education of the District of Columbia* (1972) dealt with *all* children with disabilities. The *Pennsylvania* case only applied to trainable mentally retarded children. This case set a principle that required schools to expand their curriculum for *all* children.

Education for All Handicapped Children Act.

None of these court cases had the far-reaching effect of the **Education for All Handicapped Children Act** (1975), better known as PL 94-142. This historic act established the basic tenet that children with disabilities have the same constitutional rights as all other children. That is, education should be conducted in the **least-restrictive environment** in which their constitutional rights, such as due process, can be guaranteed and their learning assessment can be conducted fairly by the school.

The Education of the Handicapped Act Amendments of 1986, PL 99-457, provided for early intervention services for infants and toddlers (birth through age 2) and for preschoolers aged 3 to 5. Amendments in 1990 specified replacing references to the *handicapped* with *individuals with disabilities* and retitled the act the **Individuals with Disabilities Education Act.** The 1990 changes also expanded the definitions of disabilities, recognizing AIDS as a disability, for example.

PL 94-142 and succeeding legislation address two major issues about children with disabilities. One is that children should be placed in the least-restrictive educational environment possible. Each child, after individual analysis, should be removed from the regular classroom only if her or his disabilities are of such a magnitude as to require special classrooms or separate schools. Many teachers mistakenly believe that PL 94-142 requires all students with disabilities to be mainstreamed. In fact, removal from the classroom is dependent on the extent of the disability. What PL 94-142 does require is that we should not assume all children with disabilities must be excluded from a typical classroom comprising children from many walks of life. The second issue is that students with disabilities should be taught through **individualized educational programs (IEP).** That is, each student is evaluated and his or her educational experiences are tailored to meet specific needs.

Gifted and Talented Children's Act.

In 1978, Congress passed the Gifted and Talented Children's Act, which provided federal monies to states for improving programs for gifted and talented children. Like all the other legal provisions for children with special needs, its requirement was simple: teachers must develop educational programs that meet the needs of each child. This requirement simply focused on good teaching.

Copyright Laws

Teachers are becoming more aware of copyright laws, now that photocopiers, video recorders, and computers have become more commonplace in schools. Supplementary materials such as poems, short stories, videotapes, television programs, music, and anthologies are enticing because they appear beneficial to your students and curriculum. Unfortunately many teachers do not realize that making unauthorized copies of copyrighted materials can have serious legal implications for themselves and their school.

What is a copyright? **Copyright** is the legal right to reproduce, distribute, and sell a created work, such as a book, poem, play, movie, video, choreography, audio recording, or computer program. For an unpublished work, copyright remains with the author, composer, or creator. Once a work is published, copyright is often transferred to the company that reproduces and distributes it. A copyright notice that identifies the copyright owner and date of publication should appear in a reasonable location (in a textbook, for instance, the copyright notice usually appears on the page following the title page).

Teachers should know that the Copyright act of 1976 made provisions for **fair use**, which allows you, under certain conditions, to make copies of copyrighted materials for educational and other specified purposes. In judging whether copying is fair use or copyright infringement, the law looks at (1) the purpose of the use (whether commercial or educational); (2) the nature of the copyrighted work; (3) the amount of the work used in relation to the whole; and (4) the effect of the use on the potential market for the work.

Under fair-use guidelines, you are allowed to make one photocopy of a printed work for personal use in teaching or research. But multiple copies must be limited to the number of students in the class and must carry the copyright notice. In addition, the copying must meet the tests spontaneity, brevity, and cumulative effect. *Spontaneity* means the copying was the teacher's idea (not a supervisor's), and there wasn't time to request permission. *Brevity* means the copy cannot be more than 250 words of a poem or more than 1000 words (or 10 percent, whichever is shorter) of a longer work. *Cumulative effect* limits the amount of material a teacher can copy from one author or work. It also limits the number of times that copies can be used in a class, and so on (McCarthy & Cambron-McCabe, 1992).

At one time, it was common practice for classroom teachers to collect materials and arrange them in book form for class use. Usually, teachers asked a copying service to duplicate the materials, and students were asked to pay the duplicating costs. In a 1991 court case, however, a U.S. district court ruled that a Kinko's copying service was violating fair-use standards by duplicating materials without obtaining permission from the copyright holders.

Taping a program or movie from a television broadcast and replaying it for students may also be a violation of copyright. Guidelines for fair use issued by Congress in 1981 include showing the tape only once within 10 days of taping and destroying the tape after 45 days. Taping a program to avoid paying the purchase price or rental fee is not allowed.

Computer software is also covered by copyright laws. When you buy a computer program you are allowed to make one copy as a backup in case something happens to the original. However, it is a violation of copyright to duplicate a program to avoid paying for it. To discourage copyright violations, many companies assign numbers to purchasers so they can upgrade programs at minimum cost. Also, many software companies have developed special programs that teachers can share inexpensively and legally.

For more information about copyright regulations, check with your principal's office, technology center, or school library.

What You Have Learned

✔ Students and teachers are citizens, and they maintain their rights as citizens in school. Students and teachers have rights guaranteed by the Constitution.

✔ Student and teacher rights are tempered by the learning environment. Specific types of freedoms are limited so teachers and students have a classroom in which they are able to teach and learn.

✔ The Constitution allows schools to use the Bible to teach *about* religion but will not allow it to be used to teach students *to become* religious.

✔ Education is a state responsibility. School law is forged in state courts. The federal court system gets involved with education and schools when the rights of its citizens appear to be threatened.

✔ Elementary and secondary teachers do not have academic freedom. Rather, they have freedom of speech. This freedom is tempered by the interests of the state.

Key Terms

church–state separation
secular humanism
tort
reasonableness
negligence
proximate cause
strict liability
liability insurance
property interest
due process
tenure
suspension
expulsion

Education for all Handicapped Children Act
least-restrictive environment
Individuals with Disabilities Education Act
individualized educational programs (IEPs)
copyright
fair use

Applying What You Have Learned

1. The *Engle v. Vitale* (1962) ruling by the Supreme Court is one of the most controversial decisions handed down in decades. It said government officials, such as school boards, cannot write prayers for students to read. The Bible *can* be read in school as part of a comparative religion, history, or literature class. Develop a lesson plan in your discipline which would use the Bible as a learning tool rather than as a tool to teach children to become religious.

2. From your reading, you understand that the purpose of tenure is to protect classroom teachers from personal vendettas by people who disagree with them. What part of the curriculum will you teach that might be controversial? What would you do if you were told by your principal to teach something you knew to be false?

3. Teacher liability is an obvious issue in classes like chemistry and physical education, because students can be physically injured. How can students be hurt in *your* classroom?

4. You are a teacher who sees a student cheating on the final exam. You are angry because while other students have studied, this student is trying to take the easy way out. You want to stop him from cheating and also make him an example of what happens to cheaters in your class. What do you do? Review the court cases in this chapter to help you develop a response to the student.

Interactive Learning

1. Copyright laws protect the intellectual property of composers, poets, authors, and other creative people. Investigate how you would copyright a song, computer program, or poem you have written.

2. In a group, reread and discuss the prayer from Mrs. Snyder's class in *Becoming a Teacher*. Does it support church-state separation or freedom of speech? Debate this with others in the group. What were your group's conclusions? Compare them with those discussed in the chapter.

3. What would you do in this case? As a journalism teacher, you assign your class to interview fellow students for the purpose of writing human interest articles. One story is interlaced with sexual innuendoes and punctuated with socially taboo words. Ask several journalism teachers what they would do. Have them critique your ideas about what you would do.

4. Have you known a teacher who enjoyed calling you names, or who felt comfortable discussing your gender or how much you weighed? Interview a principal and ask what guidelines the school board has on such topics as verbal abuse and sexual discrimination.

Expanding Your Knowledge

Fischer, Louis, David Schimmel, and Cynthia Kelly. *Teachers and the Law*. New York: Longman, 1995. (If you are a teacher and have never taken a law course, this book will make you want to enroll in one. It is concise and makes the law understandable.)

Nord, Warren. *Religion and American Education*. Chapel Hill: The University of North Carolina Press, 1995. (An excellent text that describes the dilemma schools face as they attempt to deal with religion.)

Zirkel, Perry. (This frequent contributor to *Phi Delta Kappan* writes a column, "De Jure," that helps you become more aware of educational law as it applies to schools and teachers.)

Educating Children Takes Money: Financing Schools

In Chapter 10 you will learn how schools are financed. If there is a single educational issue taxpayers have strong opinions about (other than what children should learn), it is how much they should pay for schools. Taxpayers have criticized the increasing costs of schooling and have complained they are not getting their money's worth. They are worried because they believe schools are costing more and delivering less. For example, many people do not want to pay for the education of children whose parents are illegal immigrants. Others are offended by the teaching of cultural diversity in the classroom and are resistant to paying for it through taxes. Teachers feel the brunt of taxpayer anger when they are accused of working nine months out of the year and receiving three months' "paid vacation." Many taxpayers are angry at schools for many reasons.

This chapter will focus on how schools spend their monies and how revenues are raised. It will help you understand how educational finance affects your professional teaching goals.

What you will learn

- There are many different types of educational expenditures and many purposes of school budgets.
- States collect different types of revenue and have various methods of funding schools.
- School districts collect local revenue.
- The federal government distributes resources to schools and states.
- The United States Supreme Court and the various state supreme courts equate educational finance with equal educational opportunity.
- How nonpublic schools relate to the national, state, and local educational enterprise and how public monies can be used for nonpublic schools.
- How changing social needs and the emergence of more and different cultural groups and ethnicities can lead to various funding problems for schools.

"Well, it finally happened! Have you read the paper?" Jack Marteniz stomped into the faculty lounge, waving a newspaper in his hand. "I just can't believe it—I've been a teacher for fifteen years in Hooverton and they've finally pulled the plug on schools!"

Governor Announces Huge Cutback—Schools Hard Hit

CAPITAL CITY: Governor Lillian Chain announced today that state revenues for this fiscal year would be much less than expected.

"We knew the economic slowdown was going to cause us to reduce our budget this fiscal year," Governor Chain told reporters in a prepared statement. "Our concern increased when Augatube International announced they were closing their production plants in Capital City and Hooverton. We anticipate a minimum 5 percent decrease in revenue through sales taxes alone," said the governor.

The usually-upbeat Chain stated she expected the present all-time high unemployment rate of 8.7 percent to skyrocket to between 9.2 percent and 9.7 percent.

Hooverton Mayor Andrew Swart said he expected the Hooverton unemployment rate to be more than 10 percent. Mayor Swart, visibly shaken, acknowledged that Hooverton had real financial problems.

"With Augatube International moving to Romania, we anticipate an additional 1,500 unemployed. The downtown merchants will really suffer. Governor Chain has guaranteed economic assistance to Hooverton, but it certainly is not going to be enough to get us through this winter," said the mayor.

Governor Chain supported Mayor Swart, with the comment that the state's fiscal health had been jeopardized by plant closings and unexpected high unemployment.

Kurt Raines, president of Augatube International, stated he was sorry Augatube International was leaving Hooverton.

"We started our business here in Hooverton more than 80 years ago—we never thought we would leave. But, the reality is, we cannot continue to compete in a global economy without reducing our costs. Labor just got too expensive for us in Hooverton. Although Augatube International doesn't require skilled labor, we just can't afford to pay even minimum wages. Another expenditure we found too high was the property tax."

Mr. Raines mentioned that Romania has promised not to tax the company for ten years.

"I couldn't believe it when I read the paper this morning at breakfast," Martha Bush groaned. "Ralph and I were so happy to move to Hooverton. But we were told last week his job at the assembly plant was finished at the end of the month. We're hoping the money I make from teaching will carry us through until he finds another job."

"You know," said Ben Goodman, "I've seen this happen before. You just wait and see, all the administrators in the school system will keep their jobs. We teachers are always the first to go when times get tough."

"It's crazy," groaned Jack. "I was talking to some administrators at the central office last week. They said that even if the economy is slowing down, the real reason for much of this trouble is the amount of money we are paying for welfare— and a lot of it goes to foreigners!"

The intercom came on. "I know many teachers have heard about the cutbacks announced in the morning paper," said Connie Lee, the principal. "I'm having a special faculty meeting this afternoon as soon as school is out, and would like all faculty to be present. It's not as bad as the newspapers said it was. We are *not* anticipating severe financial cutbacks."

"Isn't that just like an administrator?" sneered Ben, "They know their jobs are safe, so they can look at the bright side."

???   *Why would the closing of Augatube have such dire results for Hooverton? How might Augatube's leaving affect schools?*

Martha, Ben, and Jack reveal many of the attitudes teachers display about educational finance. Because we teachers spend most of our professional lives in a classroom teaching children, it is easy to put aside educational controversies that do not seem to immediately touch us. It's easy for us to think that the financing of schools is someone else's business, while ours is to teach in the classroom. Yet, because we receive a paycheck at the end of the month and purchase supplies, equipment, and materials needed to teach our students, finance is indeed our business.

Moreover, schools are everybody's business. In 1994, approximately $265 billion were spent on elementary and secondary schools in the United States. This extraordinary financial outlay represented more than 4 percent of the gross national product during 1994. Schools are big business.

Purpose of Budgets at Local Level: Educating Children

A budget is the key to living within your means. Your budget, regardless of its size, expresses many things about you personally. The manner in which you prioritize your purchases, activities, or savings reflects what you value. Budgets also give you power. They assist you in planning for the future, allow you to live at a realistic level in the present, and help you make decisions.

Budgets have two components: revenues and expenditures. **Revenues** are incoming monies, such as your monthly check from a school district in which you teach. **Expenditures** are those monies you spend for rent, car payments, insurance, clothing, food, and entertainment.

Schools, too, have revenues and expenditures. They receive monies (revenue) in order to educate children, keep schools operational, and pay your salary (expenditures). Let's start by discussing how schools budget for expenditures.

How Money Is Spent

Educational expenditures are extremely complicated. Simply because of the size of the educational enterprise and the diverse needs of the school, it is difficult to illustrate in one simple model how schools spend their monies. Schools reflect the various cultures and economies of the communities in which they reside, so there are countless formulas for spending monies.

Local schools receive money from the state because education is a state responsibility. The amount of money they receive varies, depending on how important citizens and legislators consider education to be as well as the state's economic health. For example, in Figure 10.1 the average amount spent per pupil in the 1995/1996 academic year was projected to be $6,300 (National Center for Education Statistics, 1995). Notice that the states have continually spent larger amounts of money on students. Many times, the money has been used to improve the ratio of students to teachers. That is, greater numbers of professionals have been employed as classroom teachers, counselors and other experts who help children learn. Yet, public monies must also pay many expenses that do not have an immediate impact on the quality of education children may receive. For example, monies spent for busing, maintenance, and security may not help children learn immediately but are important to the welfare of the school and community.

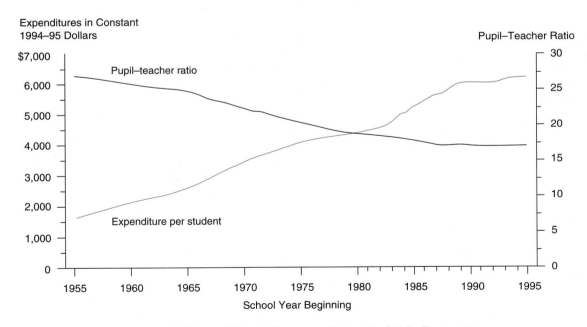

Figure 10.1   Pupil–Teacher Ratios and Expenditures per Student in Public Elementary and Secondary Schools: 1955–56 to 1995–96

Note: Expenditures per student not available for 1960–61.
Source: U.S. Department of Education, National Center for Education Statistics, *Digest of Education Statistics,* Indictor 30, Pupil/Teacher Ratio and Expenditures per Student, 1995.

Teachers' Salaries.   Teacher salaries are usually a school's greatest expenditure. Most school budgets show that teacher, administrator, and support personnel salaries and fringe benefits equal more than 75 percent of the monies dedicated to education. Education is labor intensive. Learning requires a close classroom relationship between students and teachers.

Teachers are paid according to a salary schedule. Table 10.1 is an illustration of a salary schedule from a typical school district in a small, rural state. Usually teachers receive a state-mandated base salary. Local communities, depending on their economic ability, sometimes increase this amount. Federal or state programs may also augment salaries. For example, special education teachers and some types of reading teachers receive increased salaries for the very specific professional work required of them. Athletic coaches have traditionally received additional monies. In recent years, Academic Bowl coaches have begun receiving additional pay for their work with advanced placement or honors students.

Fringe Benefits.   Fringe benefits differ throughout the nation as well. Some school districts pay all of the teachers' retirement and medical plans, while others contribute partially. Some districts consider fringe benefits to include sabbatical leaves, purchase of professional books, and travel to professional conferences. Just as communities differ, so do teacher salaries and fringe benefits.

Curriculum.   Monies are also spent on the curriculum. Obviously, supplies and equipment are needed by teachers and students for learning. Some parts of the curriculum cost more to deliver to students than other parts. For example, senior high school science courses typically are expensive because of the lab experiences students are expected to have. Some parts of the curriculum use more supplies than others. As any kindergarten or first grade teacher knows, the amounts of construction paper, tape, glue, and similar materials used during a week may equal what a junior high school class would use in a nine-week grading period. Classroom equipment, such as maps and bunsen burners, is intended to last for much longer periods than supplies, but the initial outlay and replacement costs will be more expensive.

Table 10.1
A Typical Teacher's Salary Schedule (over 25 years) in a Small Rural State

Step	BA/BS	BA/BS +16	MA/MS	MS/MA +16	EDD/PhD
0	20,460	20,757	21,882	22,678	23,919
5	22,838	23,038	23,953	24,830	26,201
10	24,165	24,865	26,238	27,207	28,720
15	25,798	27,246	28,761	29,831	31,501
20			31,546	32,729	34,573
25			34,622	35,927	37,963

+16 means the person has 16 hours of credit toward the next degree.

Students learning together.

Guidance centers, libraries, audio visual and technology centers, student organizations, and intramural and extramural sports are included in curriculum costs. Costs for these programs vary. For example, schools that maintain large athletic programs that are used to enhance their reputation within the community will have greater costs than schools that focus on intramural athletics. Guidance centers, libraries, and technology centers are costly because of the tremendous investments in personnel and high-technology equipment.

Buildings and Physical Facilities.   Few teachers are aware of the tremendous investment buildings and physical facilities represent. While many buildings and physical facilities are built with funds raised through the issue of bonds, the maintenance and repair of these structures are part of the yearly budget for each school building. Unfortunately, repair costs are soaring because of vandalism, the overuse of structures, and other reasons which we will discuss at the end of this chapter.

Transportation is also included in a school's budget. American schools have the responsibility of transporting children to and from school. While some taxpayers resent schools for taking on this role, most children and their parents understand the need for busing. Purchasing, maintaining, servicing, housing, and operating buses are becoming increasingly expensive. Vignette 10.1 describes what can happen when school bus drivers strike in a small rural community.

VIGNETTE 10.1   *Striking school bus drivers*

It was in all the newspapers and nobody was happy about it. Clarington school bus drivers finally did what they said all summer long they would do if they didn't get a raise—they went on strike the day before school opened. Everyone was mad. Teachers were angry because they were ready to start school. Students were angry because they were bored at home and wanted to be with their friends at school. But the angriest were the parents. They had enjoyed their children for as many days as they wanted. "It's time they went back to learning and gave me a rest," was a common statement in the small town.

"We know you are all mad at us, and that's good. We've asked for a raise this year to help us feed our children and keep our families together," said Ken Wyndom, a bus driver for fifteen years. "We haven't had a raise in four years, and it's our turn," he said. "This is the only way you will listen to us."

The superintendent had no choice. Dr. Davis was forced to close the school. He also called an emergency meeting of the school board. How were they going to find the money to increase bus driver salaries by 8 percent?

???   *What impact do you think the strike will have on the school's budget? Is it appropriate for employees of the public school system to be able to strike? Why or why not?*

Administration.   Like Ben, Jack, and Martha in *Becoming a Teacher,* many teachers believe that administrative costs are disproportionate to their function. However, schools require professionals who are expert in various administrative capacities. Costs for staff, computers, travel, supplies, and other activities related to administration in most school districts are low compared to other parts of the budget.

How Budgets Are Developed

School district budgets are developed the same way your personal budget is developed. The budget process for schools, though, is a yearly event that is time consuming and involves the entire school district. At its heart, a school budget is an instrument to help a school identify objectives and arrive at its goal of educating children.

Educational Objectives.   In the budget process, boards of education, administrators, and teachers must ask themselves, "How can we best deliver a quality education to our children within the financial constraints given the school district?" In order to answer this question, administrators, teachers, and the board of education must identify objectives for the curriculum, teaching, staff, and support services that will enable the district to meet specific goals set by the state department of education and the state board of education. Many times this is done through mission statements. A **mission statement** is a statement of philosophy or intent that explains how a curriculum or other supporting activity lends support to the central purpose of the school. Such issues as school accreditation and teacher and

The budget process: A school board listening to a parent.

administrative certification play a leading role in mission statements. The ability of those involved in the budget process to articulate the specific educational objectives of the school is critical. Without vision, little can be accomplished, and the education of children will suffer.

School Needs.   Budgets, like individuals, do not remain static. Budget changes occur continually because of new and different demands placed on the school by the community or lobby groups. For example, some communities have experienced a significant increase in unemployment because of the loss of private industry or federal defense contracts. Because of the extraordinary stresses created by unemployment, schools may find it necessary to develop counseling programs to assist children through a family crisis. You can see that, while state department of education requirements are a significant part of the budget process, community needs are a major component as well.

Prioritizing Monies.   The dream of most superintendents, boards of education, and teachers is that schools will have an unlimited amount of money so all budgets can be funded. The fact is, no school has ever had that experience. Therefore, the most difficult part of the budget process is prioritizing the school district's specific educational needs. The most important criterion is the importance of the program in relation to the central goal of the school district. Other criteria for evaluation may include:

- whether a program can be delayed until further funding can be identified,
- whether there is federal, private, or state aid available to fund specific projects, and

- whether the program can be restructured so it can be implemented over several budget periods.

This task is very difficult: every program is considered by some specific group to be the most important item in the budget. For example, a budget request by an elementary school faculty to develop a foreign language curriculum for students is, undoubtedly, a legitimate request. Yet its funding may be in question because monies must be spent to support a new secondary graduation requirement mandated by the state department of education. Most budgets go through many, many revisions before specific amounts of monies are assigned to each item.

School Boards.   Construction of the budget is often the specific task of the superintendent, who will request input from principals and teachers. The school board's job is to make certain all state and federal mandates have been recognized in the budget and funded as required.

As a representative of the community, school boards are also concerned that the schools meet community needs. Special needs of the community are usually debated by the school board, especially if the budget has not been explained adequately by the superintendent, or if a specific community group is lobbying for or against a budget item.

Local and State Revenues

By now you are becoming aware of how schools *spend* their monies. How schools raise revenue varies depending on the type of school. We will discuss how non-public schools raise revenue to operate their programs later. First, let's examine how public schools receive their revenue.

Traditionally, public schools receive monies from three sources: (1) local communities, (2) state governments, and (3) the federal government. They may also raise revenue through bonds or from industrial or private foundations.

Local Revenues

Property Taxes.   Property is the oldest form of private wealth. The ability to own land, or property, was the enticing element which brought many immigrants to this country. Historically, taxation at the local level has been on property (wealth). Governments (and schools) usually divide property into two types. One type, **personal property,** broadly refers to items we own such as cars, television sets, and jewelry. The second type, **real property,** refers to property we own such as land or homes. State laws govern how much a person's property can be taxed. Usually, property tax is assessed on an ***ad valorem*** basis. *Ad valorem* is Latin for "according to the value." Thus, an *ad valorem* tax is levied as a percentage rate of the value of a good or property. Usually the tax rate is expressed in mills. A **mill** is one thousandth of a dollar (one tenth of a cent): one mill for every dollar of assessed valuation is equal to one dollar per $1000 assessed valuation.

Historically, property taxes have served schools well. Because property is stable (it does not change value radically over a short time), schools can generally judge how much money they will receive each year. During a recession, when revenues from taxes on goods fall, property generally holds its value.

A shortcoming of property taxes is that some assessors may play politics to remain in office. Some states have found that where county property assessors are elected, they have delayed property reevaluation for years, thereby depriving schools of large sums of money. Another inequity of property taxes is that communities with large commercial enterprises may receive more revenue per capita than rural schools or inner city schools.

So while property taxes *are* stable, they do not guarantee school districts their fair share of revenues. Nonetheless, property taxes are vital to schools' economic well-being. Vignette 10.2 describes a community's reaction to a proposed increase in property taxes.

VIGNETTE 10.2   *Plan to increase property taxes*

Monday night's school board meeting was packed with retirees. "We all decided to come out and protest the proposed property tax increases," said Mrs. Phillips. "It's getting really hard to live in Templeton. Every time you turn around, someone wants more money."

The proposed increase of 19 cents for each $1,000 of assessed value would mean a $19 increase for an owner of a $100,000 home.

Other retirees spoke out against the increase, too. "It seems to me school teachers make enough money these days." One person spoke sharply about the superintendent using a school car as her personal vehicle. "If she needs a car so badly, why doesn't the superintendent buy one like everyone else?" said Mrs. Scott.

"It's time to stop this foolishness. I want the school board to live within its means like we do, or we will vote them out next election," said Mrs. Davidson. "My taxes have gone up 20 percent since I moved to Templeton."

??? Are these objections to a property tax increase logical? What might be short- and long-term consequences to a no vote on the tax increase? How would you respond if you had attended this meeting?

Bonds.   Property taxes cannot cover one-time, big-ticket expenses like building schools, remodeling classrooms, or buying school buses—they cover only operating costs. These items, usually referred to as *capital projects,* are the types of expenditures school boards and administrators expect will take several years, or even decades, to pay off. Because these projects are nonrecurring, boards usually finance them through capital bonds. **Capital bonds** are a way of borrowing money from the public. Schools cannot go to a bank for a loan like you can. With a capital bond, taxpayers pay off the bonds and interest. Of course, bond issues must be approved by the voters, and such elections usually create community concern. If the election is successful, schools are allowed to sell the bonds. If the election is not successful, schools are not able to finance long-term projects. As you would expect, states control bonds carefully.

Business Foundations.   Unfortunately, local taxes and bond issues cannot always fully meet local school needs. In some states, local businesses have joined in a partnership with schools. These business foundations meet regularly with school boards to evaluate school needs. Usually, through agreed-upon procedures, the foundation will finance needed programs. For example, a foundation comprising several private companies might, in partnership with the local school board, finance computer labs for students in elementary, middle, and high schools. Typically, the schools would hire the necessary computer specialists and the foundation would purchase the computers and provide maintenance.

Business foundations make other kinds of contributions that aren't financial. Many ask their employees to volunteer their off hours, vacations, and weekends to assist teachers. Some programs, for example, encourage engineers to help mathematics students with their homework. In other partnerships, executives are encouraged to attend elementary schools to read to children. In any case, these school–business partnerships offer many advantages. Besides helping the schools financially, these citizens/volunteers are reminded of the importance of the school

Learning together with a computer.

and teachers in the lives of children. Their support in the classroom is, in many cases, even more valuable than their economic support.

States' Revenues

States, too, play a major role in educational finance. States are concerned about education for a number of reasons. First, they are constitutionally responsible for schools. Second, many communities could not afford to fulfill state mandates without state financial assistance. (As you may know, schools in most communities in the United States are able to, at best, finance half of their needs.) Third, state legislatures are involved in educational funding in order to equalize the quality of education and educational opportunities throughout the state.

Not all communities have the same type or amount of resources. The money states commit to schools has a direct bearing on the opportunity children have to receive a quality education. Let us look at how states collect revenue to assist in financing schools.

Income Tax.   Many states receive the largest portion of their revenue from income taxes. These taxes are received from individuals and corporations. An advantage of the income tax is that it is easy to administer and easy to change. An income tax, unlike other taxes, is responsive to the economy; that is, tax collections rise and fall with the health of the state's economy. Another advantage of the income tax is that it is progressive—it is based on the financial ability of each taxpayer to pay.

State Sales Tax.   A sales tax is collected from customers by merchants and returned to the state each quarter. While sales taxes are certain, they have a disadvantage in that they are very responsive to the economy. For example, if a state's unemployment increases, fewer taxable goods and services will be sold. Furthermore, sales taxes are regressive—all people have to pay sales tax whether they can afford to or not. A good example is a sales tax on energy. During cold winters, both rich and poor pay equally. In fact, because poor people usually live in poorly insulated homes, they may actually pay more.

Other Taxes.   Additional revenue sources for states include turnpike fees, license plate fees, driver's license fees, and many other types of user fees. Although states also have jurisdiction over property taxes, the majority of states have given this right to communities so they can finance schools.

Many states tax natural resources such as oil, coal, lumber, and natural gas. Approximately half the states generate monies through the legalization of gambling. Games of chance, like lotto, require no skill other than buying a ticket and tantalize people with the chance of becoming instant millionaires. Another type of state sales tax is the sin tax. These taxes, usually levied on tobacco and alcohol, seldom are questioned by citizens because most would like to think these products are luxuries. Most of these taxes and user fees are placed in the state's general revenue fund along with income tax revenues. Some, however, are earmarked for specific funding purposes such as roads, prisons, or schools. Few of these alternative revenue sources have consistently returned large amounts of money.

The Taxpayer Revolution.   During the last several decades, taxpayers have voiced strong opposition to increased taxes. Beginning in 1978, with California's Proposition 13, state legislatures have become increasingly aware that taxpayers do not wish to pay more for their present services. One of the latest tax revolts was held in Oklahoma in 1993. The revolt, led by a lobby group called STOP (Stop Taxing Our Property), removed the right of the legislature to raise taxes. In this state, taxes can now be raised only by public referendum. As a consequence of these taxpayer revolts, many schools are not able to purchase books, materials, or supplies. In some communities, school buildings condemned by fire departments are still in use.

There is a bright side to the tax revolt. School boards are now legally bound to inform the taxpaying public of the intent to raise the tax rate. Through the use of public seminars, meetings, and demonstrations, school boards are educating citizens about their needs. In short, schools, as public institutions using public monies, are being held accountable to the citizens for their actions.

State Aid to Schools

Now that you are aware of how states receive their revenue, let's look at the formulas states use in funding schools.

The Flat Grant Model.   The oldest method of funding schools is the flat grant model. Basically, a **flat grant** is a formula by which states give money to the schools based on the number of students enrolled in each local school. During the early part of the century, this method was generally equitable. Schools were small, located in rural communities, maintained only basic curriculums, and were supported by an agrarian economy.

Now the flat grant is less than equitable. Most people live in large urban centers with diversified economies. Many states require complex curriculums to help educate students to live in a competitive, global market. Perhaps the greatest difference between the early part of this century and now is the diverse cultures and ethnicities represented in our schools. Schools in urban areas, particularly, have greater demands placed on them to meet the needs of a diverse student population. Obviously, this creates a need for more money. Students who live in the inner city find it increasingly difficult to escape a life of poverty. As Bennett and LeCompte state;

> [flat grants ignore] the reality of how unequally distributed economic resources are in this country, and how difficult it is for minority groups in this country to gain access to them. (1990, p. 211)

Weighted Student Plan.   Some states use a **weighted student plan** to distribute revenues among districts. Schools receive monies according to the types of children enrolled. For example, schools may receive larger amounts of money for students who are disadvantaged, handicapped, or bilingual than for students who are not so defined. The problem with this formula is the difficulty of setting priorities in regard to classroom instruction. What type of child is more worthy than another?

Foundation and Matching Plans.   Two other plans are also used by states to fund schools. One plan, called the **foundation plan,** assumes there is a minimum cost to schools that the state provides. According to this plan, school districts are to add to this basic state-supplied money in order to develop quality schools. The other plan, referred to as **matching funds,** distributes monies to school districts on a dollar-for-dollar basis. That is, for every dollar a school district spends on schools, the state will give an equal amount. While both plans seem to support education, there is a problem for poor schools. Because of their poor tax base (property taxes), the amount of matching monies designated by the state is simply not sufficient to even minimally fund the schools. In truth, tax monies required for schools are simply not available from *within* poor communities. Many of these communities would be delighted just to be able to afford schools others consider average.

State Supreme Court and School Funding

Many states are searching for new methods of state funding that will be equitable both for schools and the children who attend them. Several major court cases have helped clarify the problem for state legislatures and school officials.

Beginning with *Serrano v. Priest* (1971) in California, that state's supreme court found the difference in financial support between wealthy and poor school districts astronomical. Specifically, it found wealthy districts did not burden their taxpayers with high taxes, yet were able to spend up to twice as much as poor districts on schools. Poor districts taxed their citizens to a greater extent, yet were only able to collect sufficient resources to give students a minimum education. The California Supreme Court, therefore, found California's educational financing methods to be unconstitutional.

The *San Antonio Independent School District v. Rodriguez* (1973) case was also significant. In this instance, the United States Supreme Court reviewed the Texas court's decision and found that educational funding was the constitutional responsibility of the states. Further, the U.S. Supreme Court declared the use of property taxes as a revenue source for schools.

Perhaps the most striking case was *Rose v. Council for Better Education* (1989). The Kentucky Supreme Court ruled that children in rural Kentucky did not have an equal opportunity to receive the same quality education as children in larger communities, such as Lexington and Louisville. In its decision, the Kentucky Supreme Court gave the Kentucky legislature two years to equalize educational funding. Tossing out the property tax as a method of funding schools, the court gave the legislature the responsibility of raising sales taxes, corporate taxes, and local taxes. The Court also required that at-risk preschool students be identified for special educational programs and that elementary students be grouped according to their progress in the curriculum rather than by age.

In Texas, *Englewood Independent School District v. Kirby* (1989) attracted national attention. The Texas Supreme Court overturned that state's method of funding schools because it concluded the funding methods were inherently unequal. Some districts were extremely wealthy and others were abjectly poor. As in Kentucky, the disparity among Texas school districts was striking. In 1989, the Texas Supreme Court ruled that wealthy districts must share their resources with poor districts. Poor districts, many of which comprise large numbers of Hispanic-Americans, are unable to finance schools at the same level as wealthy districts because of high unemployment rates and social bias.

In *Abbott v. Burke* (1990) the New Jersey Supreme Court cited major discrepancies in funding between wealthy and poor counties and declared the state funding formulas unconstitutional. Using the wealthy districts as a model, the New Jersey Supreme Court held that wealthy school districts should help fund poorer districts to the point of equity. Poor school districts were required to establish special compensatory programs that would immediately help children. As a consequence, preschool programs, smaller elementary classes, and adult literacy programs were funded.

The Kentucky and New Jersey decisions have had a significant impact on schools throughout our nation. At last count, more than 14 states had legislation to improve or close at-risk schools. Fourteen state supreme courts, including Arizona, Arkansas, Connecticut, Montana, Minnesota, New Jersey, Washington, West Virginia, and Wyoming, have ruled on educational funding. Oklahoma's House Bill 1017 (1990) identifies at-risk schools in many of its major cities and rural counties. Educators and state legislators are becoming increasingly aware that economic disparity, like segregation, has caused American society to polarize. State supreme courts are clear in their intent in equating equal educational opportunity with educational funding.

Federal Revenues

The federal government has no constitutional authority over schools. The First, Tenth, and Fourteenth Amendments guarantee schools to be a state responsibility. Yet, as you remember from Chapter 3, the Colonial Congress passed the Land Ordinance of 1785 and the Northwest Ordinance of 1787 prior to the Constitution's ratification. These acts advocated education "as necessary to good government and the happiness of mankind," and detailed a division of land to provide monetary support for schools. The Land Ordinance of 1785 stipulated that the sixteenth section of each township be reserved for the support of schools. Since then, hundreds of millions of dollars have flowed from Washington to local communities and schools. Figure 10.2 lists some of the more important pieces of federal legislation that have impacted schools. The argument continues about how much influence Washington should have in educating the nation's children.

Constitutionalists

Constitutionalists believe the Constitution gave schools to the states so the federal government could not promote certain political views in the teaching of children. It is their contention that the further schools are removed from the federal government, the safer the nation will be. Some presidents who have held this philosophy are James Buchanan, Herbert Hoover, Ronald Reagan, and George Bush.

Figure 10.2   Federal Assistance to Schools

Morrill Act (1862).   This historic act gave 30,000 acres of land per United States Senator to each state, for the purpose of developing and building agricultural and mechanical colleges. These "people's colleges" were revolutionary, because the typical college in those days taught only the classics. President Buchanan had vetoed the same bill in 1859 because it conflicted with his view of the constitution, but President Lincoln gladly signed it.

Smith–Lever Act (1914).   This act, passed prior to World War I, focused federal resources on preprofessional education of teachers. It was to help students become secondary school teachers in agriculture and domestic economy (home economics).

Smith–Hughes Act (1917).   Congress passed this Act to help states establish vocational education programs in secondary schools. While the program was not as successful as some had hoped, it was able to introduce new ideas about what children could learn in school.

National School Lunch Act (1946).   At the end of World War II, the federal government expressed a concern that children were not eating nutritiously. First through school milk programs, and later through financial support for those who could not afford to eat, the National School Lunch Act improved the health of the nation's youth.

National Defense Education Act (1957).   The NDEA was passed during the Cold War, when this country and the Soviet Union were involved in a space race. Congress passed the NDEA, to, among other things, improve the teaching of math and science in schools, give loans for college tuition, develop vocational programs, improve audiovisual techniques in teaching, and improve the teaching of foreign languages.

Public Law 94-142 (1975).   This act gives states monies to establish educational programs for children with disabilities at all levels of precollege education. This act gives federal assistance to schools for the purpose of developing, establishing, and maintaining educational programs for children with disabilities. The Act is important to educators because it has forced schools to learn new ways of teaching children who had been largely forgotten.

The Tax Reform Act (1986) is an excellent illustration of the constitutionalists' position on school funding. Passed at the beginning of President Reagan's second term, the Act's intent was to remove portions of state sales tax as a deduction on IRS forms. While it was hoped this would create more revenue for the federal government, states found their revenues for schools decreased. This is one reason many states are presently experiencing difficulty supporting schools. In hindsight, the Tax Reform Act may be viewed as part of the tax revolt discussed earlier in this chapter.

Neo-constitutionalists

The neo-constitutionalists agree with the constitutionalists that schools should not be under the control of the federal government. They support local and state control of schools as defined in the First, Tenth and Fourteenth Amendments. Yet they argue that schools are important to the nation's welfare, and, because each of us must rely on others, it is important all children have a good education. In short, they assert that just as states are concerned about equal educational opportunity within their boundaries, we should be concerned about equal educational opportunities within the United States. Examples of presidents who have held this view are Abraham Lincoln, Franklin D. Roosevelt, John Kennedy, Lyndon Johnson, Jimmy Carter, and Bill Clinton. The most striking example of the neo-constitutionalist position on school funding is the Elementary and Secondary Education Act (1965). Passed during President Johnson's administration, the Elementary and Secondary Education Act was a focused attempt to help children who were poor and disadvantaged. It gave assistance to state departments of education, bilingual education programs, reading programs, and other programs to improve the educational experiences of all children (Sullivan, 1973). It is this same concept that underlined the creation, in 1979, of the United States Department of Education as a cabinet-level department.

Methods of Federal Funding

The federal government does not support schools in the same way that it supports federal agencies like the Department of State or the Department of Transportation. Historically, federal aid to schools has been through categorical grants. That is, monies were focused on specific programs to attain specific results. The Elementary and Secondary Education Act, as you read in the previous section, is an example of categorical aid. Yet local community educators noticed difficulties in implementing the Act. At times it seemed unfair. For example, pencils and paper purchased for use by children in one activity were not allowed to be used by other children in other activities. Most categorical grants generate exasperating bureaucratic problems. Strict accounting measures require large numbers of forms to be filled out and sent to Washington.

The 1981 Educational Improvement and Consolidation Act was intended to give local and state authorities more leeway in spending federal monies. Specifically, block grants, as these federal monies were called, were intended to give local and state authorities more authority in making decisions about how federal dollars should be spent. Because it was thought local people understood local problems better than people in Washington did, everyone expected monies would be used more efficiently and wisely. While decision making was undoubtedly easier, many teachers now feel that the omission of important parts from the Act—such as education for those with disabilities, vocational education, impact aid, and other programs—has been detrimental to the overall education of children.

The Educational Improvement and Consolidation Act, like the Morrill Act, gives greater autonomy to states and local units; however, serious questions are being asked. For example, are federal tax dollars being spent wisely and efficiently in the various states? Has the money helped those it was intended to help, namely children? Are all children being helped equally? Let us hope the Act lives up to its goals of improving schools through staff development, curriculum development, counseling, gifted student programs, early childhood programs, and programs to reduce cultural and racial isolation.

Public Funding of Nonpublic Schools.   The use of public monies for non-public schools has always been a thorny issue. Approximately one out of every ten children is educated in nonpublic schools. Nonpublic schools lift a tremendous financial burden from local school districts. The amount of monies private churches, groups, foundations, and individuals spend on schooling is enormous. No good accounting exists of the financial savings nonpublic schools represent to taxpayers.

Public sentiment supports Jefferson's belief that a wall must separate church from state. But the controversy over public funding of nonpublic schools is much more complex. Educational legislation and court cases used to assert that no public monies should be spent in nonpublic schools. Today, such debate focuses on

- What activities do children in nonpublic schools engage in that are equal to activities children in public school engage in?
- How can children be best served without hindering or helping those who control nonpublic schools?
- At what point can taxpayer funds be given to nonpublic schools so children will benefit, not the church, agency, or school?

Figure 10.3 outlines several significant United States Supreme Court cases that have attempted to answer these questions.

Educational Vouchers.   One plan for assisting nonpublic schools through state monies is the educational voucher system. Basically, the idea is that parents should have a choice about which school their children attend. If parents are dissatisfied with the school their children are attending, they have the right to transfer them to another public or nonpublic school. To help parents bear the financial burden of moving their children, the voucher system gives parents a financial rebate, or voucher, to be used to pay the new school. On the surface, the educational voucher system appears to place direct control of children's schooling in their parents' hands.

Proponents argue that parents should have the right to determine what type of education their children receive. If the local school district, beset with problems, is not teaching children on behalf of their best interest, parents should be able to choose another public or nonpublic school. Implied in this statement is the belief that children will receive a better education if schools are forced to compete. If schools had to compete with each other, teachers would improve their classroom instruction and children would learn more. Because public schools are a monopoly, supporters of the educational voucher system insist, there is no incentive for teachers to improve.

However, public school teachers, administrators, teacher unions, and others argue that parental choice is not the issue. They wonder whether competition will actually improve schools, whether the voucher system is simply an underhanded way to give public monies to nonpublic schools, and whether it is a disguise for segregation. Let's look at each of these arguments.

Competition may be good for business in a free society because, through advertising, sales, and other means, businesses can improve their profit margins. However, schools, unlike businesses, cannot have sales or advertise what is taught in the classroom. The purpose of schools is not to make a financial profit but to

Figure 10.3   Selected Supreme Court Cases
Concerning Public Monies and Nonpublic Schools

Emerson v. Board of Education (1947).   The Supreme Court held using public tax monies for reimbursing parents for transporting their children to private schools did not violate the First Amendment.

Lemon v. Kurtzman (1971).   A Pennsylvania case in which public monies were provided to nonpublic schools for teacher salaries, instructional supplies and textbooks. The Supreme Court ruled the legislation was not constitutional because of the entanglement between government and religion.

Wolman v. Walter (1977).   The question was whether providing nonpublic school students with diagnostic, therapeutic, and remedial service was constitutional. The Court stated this did not violate the First Amendment.

Agostini v. Felton (1997).   The Supreme Court ruled public school teachers are allowed to enter private schools to teach remedial students. Overturned *Aguilar v. Felton* (1985), which barred public school teachers from teaching private school students as part of their normal classroom duties.

educate children. Therefore, the voucher system pits one school against the other with no benefit. Public schools will suffer financially because the voucher system will drain tax dollars from public schools and give them to nonpublic schools. In effect, the voucher system will develop a two-tiered educational system, in which children of the wealthy will attend elite private schools and the poor and minorities will attend public schools. This form of segregation, educators argue, is contrary to the principles of equal educational opportunity.

Tuition Tax Credit.   Like the voucher system, tuition tax credits give parents a choice in the schools their children attend. In this case, parents may claim a deduction on their income tax for part or all of the tuition paid to nonpublic schools. One quarter of the state legislatures have investigated tuition tax credits. Minnesota is the only state so far that has developed tuition tax credit legislation. Proponents insist the tuition tax credit is a way to give parents the right to decide what type of education their children should receive. Opponents argue that the tuition tax credit, like the voucher system, is an attempt to remove public tax dollars from the schools, support nonpublic schools with public monies, and divide American society both economically and racially.

The tuition tax credit has several problems. Few states are willing to reduce their revenue and, at the same time, continue to fund public schools. Legislators are also concerned that as their states' populations become more diverse, schools will need larger amounts of money to meet the special needs of immigrant or disadvantaged children. Finally, legislators are concerned that the tuition tax credit is unconstitutional insofar as it may deny equal educational opportunity to the poor who do not pay taxes.

State Financial Problems

The tuition tax credit is an excellent example of the type of revenue dilemma many legislators, school board members, administrators, and taxpayers are facing. While some legislators may consider the tuition tax credit a good idea, the threat of losing revenues causes most to reconsider.

States are burdened with economic problems few dreamed possible a few years ago. The hoped-for "peace dividend" caused by the collapse of the Soviet Union has changed the nation's economic structure in unforeseen ways. Military base closings, reduced federal and industrial funds for military research and development, smaller standing armies, and less need for a global military presence will be felt in the national and state economies for decades to come. States are also concerned about how their economies will survive in an international economy in which their industries must compete globally. Many states are suffering volatile economic swings as once-stable industries move to other nations to remain competitive.

Loss of industries and increased unemployment reduce the amount of taxes the state will receive. The ripple effect of unemployment will be felt by other businesses in all sectors of the economy, compounding the problem. Unfortunately, many states find they must increase services such as welfare to help citizens in need.

The financial impact on schools can be devastating. Schools are unable to maintain buildings or purchase much-needed equipment and supplies. In many communities, schools are eventually forced to lay off administrators and teachers. The losers, of course, are the children. The long-term impact is visible in many school districts. Aging buildings that are expensive to maintain or are condemned by local fire departments are still in use. Inadequately ventilated classrooms and administrative offices are common throughout the nation. In the northeast, for example, during the winter, schools are cold and drafty. In the south and southwest during spring and fall months, children sit in rooms that have temperatures hovering above 90 degrees. In many schools, textbooks are out of date or worn beyond recognition. It is commonplace in many school districts for teachers to purchase books for their students with their own money. Segall (1985) reported that in one southwestern high school during the 1980s, teachers had contributed more than $4,500 of their own money to purchase books, supplies, and other classroom materials. Many school boards have developed **financial retrenchment policies** that prioritize which services and materials should be cut so that children will suffer less.

Teacher layoffs are becoming increasingly common. Usually, boards are reluctant to institute R.I.F. (reduction in force) policies because of the impact on teachers, children, and the community. One of the tactics school boards use to keep teachers is to reduce the number of administrators, secretaries, and others not immediately involved in the classroom. Through these cost-saving measures, school boards hope the learning process will continue.

School Funding and Equal Educational Opportunity

A 1990 study (Hayes-Bautista, Schenk, & Chapa) found that in California in 1980, the average educational level was 13.5 years for Anglos and 10.4 years for Hispanics. The average educational level of California's total workforce was 12.9 years. Hayes-Bautista et al. forecast that if all factors remain equal and population trends remain the same, California's work force in 2030 will have an educational level of 12.1 years. That is, California's work force will be less educated in 2030 than it was in 1980. Hayes-Bautista et al. further observe that workers will be required to perform in a more complex workplace. Obviously, California's 60 percent Hispanic dropout rate is dangerous to that state's economic and social future. As you probably have concluded already, California's present goal must be to decrease the number of Hispanic dropouts and increase educational opportunity. Implied in this challenging economic and social look at California's future is the knowledge that California schools may have even less money to operate on because of the lack of a qualified work force. In other words, as industries leave the state and unemployment increases, California will have even less money to fund schools.

A national study conducted by the General Accounting Office (1993) found that poverty is rising among young preschool children throughout the United States. It found that a large number of children will not be socially or academically prepared for kindergarten in the foreseeable future.

In another study, the U.S. Department of Commerce reported that 21.2 percent of all students live below the poverty level. The study also found that 43 percent of these children were children of color (U.S. Department of Commerce, Bureau of the Census, 1994).

The General Accounting Office study and the U.S. Department of Commerce report specifically highlight the difficulties of educating children in a diverse society in which so many children are poor. Both studies show that children from minority backgrounds, cultures, races, and ethnicities are slipping through the cracks of our society and our school systems.

Yet it is important to understand the financial and social costs associated with providing equal educational opportunity for these children. If all children who start school are to be ready to learn, revenue from many sources will need to be identified. The General Accounting Office indicated in its study that increasing numbers of disadvantaged Americans could overwhelm existing local preschool budgets. Government programs like Project Head Start increased their budgets to more than $3 billion dollars during 1994, yet few believe that amount will help solve this present and future financial crises.

To place the importance of education funding and equal educational opportunity in perspective, Ronald Takaki explains it thus:

> Most of today's immigrants, however, come from Asia and Latin America. Over 80 percent of all immigrants have been arriving from these two regions, adding to America's racial

diversity—a reality charged with consequences for our nation's work force. By the year 2000, there will be more than 21 million new workers. They will be 44 percent white, 16 percent black, 11 percent Asian and other groups, and 29 percent Hispanic. (1993, 421)

What You Have Learned

✔ The budgeting process is important because it identifies local schools' goals and objectives and prioritizes school needs.

✔ Local schools spend most of their monies on teachers, curriculum, physical facilities, and administration.

✔ Local schools raise revenue through *ad valorem* taxes on property and through bonds.

✔ States generally raise revenue through sales taxes and income taxes. States have several methods by which they distribute monies to local schools. While every state attempts to equalize educational opportunity, none are completely successful.

✔ State supreme courts have equated equal educational opportunity with the methods by which local and state governments distribute monies to schools. Kentucky and New Jersey declared their state schools unconstitutional because of the methods those states used in financing schools.

✔ Federal influence on schools is controversial. Constitutionalists insist the federal government should not assist schools. Neo-constitutionalists argue that the federal government has a constitutional role to play in assisting schools.

✔ Parental rights to control their children's education have been expressed legislatively and financially through the voucher plan and tuition tax credits. There is heated controversy over whether these plans use public tax monies to support nonpublic schools and potentially threaten state revenues for public schools.

✔ States have recently experienced major social and economic dislocations caused by economic problems. Local plant transfers to foreign countries, increased unemploy-

ment, and the collapse of the old Soviet Union have all had a part in reducing revenue for schools.

✔ The continued migration of people to the United States is causing educators and legislators to focus on how schools and teachers will meet the needs of a diverse society.

Key Terms

revenues	flat grant
expenditures	weighted student
mission statement	plan
personal property	foundation plan
real property	matching funds
ad valorem	financial
mill	retrenchment
capital bonds	policies

Applying What You Have Learned

1. Many teachers think their salaries are very low for the amount of work they are required to do. Do you think teachers should receive higher salaries? What reasons can you identify?

2. Property taxes are becoming more controversial as a source of revenue for schools. What other sources of revenue should be used for school funding? For example, should the federal and state governments pay property taxes for the buildings they own? Should there be a national sales tax?

3. You are asked to speak at a tax revolt rally! What arguments could you use to convince your audience that schools need more money?

4. State supreme courts have found that equal educational opportunity may be

defined by the amounts of monies given to schools within states. Do you agree? What exceptions can you identify to cause you to disagree with the decisions listed in this chapter?

5. Assume you are a United States Supreme Court justice. The case argued before you is the following. A state has passed legislation that will give a $1,000 tax credit to all parents who send their children to private schools. The state argues parents should be reimbursed because they are paying taxes to support public schools while they are also financing their children's private education. Opponents argue that the United States Constitution requires church–state separation. How would you interpret the Constitution? Do you think Jefferson is correct about the wall separating church and state? What would be your decision? Why?

Interactive Learning

1. Educational vouchers and tuition tax credits are two possible results of *Agostini v. Felton* (1997). What are the educational consequences you foresee? Interview a school principal to discover how vouchers would affect public schools.
2. Find out how much money your state spends on education. Is it more or less than you expected? In a group discuss why your state should spend more money on schools and how that money should be spent.
3. Find out from your local school district the fringe benefits package offered to teachers.

Are these benefits state-mandated or does the district have a choice in offering specific benefits? What fringe benefits are you most concerned with? Why?

4. You are a member of a school board which has been informed that the school must reduce its expenditures. A colleague suggests the school reduce the amount of money spent on supplies and materials in the kindergarten classes and cut out girls' lacrosse. At the same time, the same board member wants the school to buy new uniforms for the football team. In a small group compare and discuss your reactions to this request.

Expanding Your Knowledge

Hartman, W. T. *School District Budgeting*. Englewood Cliffs, NJ: Prentice–Hall, 1988. (Discusses the various perspectives of budgeting at the local level, including how budgets impact the teacher in the classroom.)

Ward, J. E. and P. Anthony. *Who Pays for Student Diversity?* Newbury, CA: Sage-Corwin Press, 1992. (The point of this text is to give a human face to educational finance. The school budget is the mechanism by which children have the opportunity to receive a quality education.)

DeYoung, A. J. *Economics and American education: A Historical and Critical Overview of the Impact of Economic Theories on Schooling in the United States*. New York: Longman, 1989. (This text is concerned with the influence of philosophers like Adam Smith and Karl Marx on the contemporary school. While much of the text focuses on reform, DeYoung's understanding of school funding is insightful.)

Part Five

The Worlds in Which Children Live

In Part Five you will learn about the two worlds in which children live. As a classroom teacher you will quickly become aware that the lives children lead outside the school influence how well they learn in the classroom. In fact, you will become increasingly aware that children's private lives are extremely complex, confusing, and sometimes dangerous. Because we live in a diverse society, not all of your students will have the same type of childhood experiences you had. Chapter 11 describes private lives of children that are filled with despair. It catalogs some of their more significant problems, such as poverty, homelessness, literacy, suicide, and pregnancy.

Bakari Clay, in *Becoming a Teacher* in Chapter 11, explains in her own words what her neighborhood is like. Although Bakari, an eight-year-old, doesn't tell us about her family life, she describes her thoughts about going home from school. Even though her grammar, punctuation, and spelling are faulty, it is easy to understand her: she is afraid. Bakari's dreams of a safer tomorrow are all she has.

Chapter 12 describes how children bring the experiences catalogued in Chapter 11 with them into the classroom. It focuses on what classroom teachers can do to help students learn. For example, in *Becoming a Teacher* in Chapter 12, Mrs. Baxter meets one of her students, Mario, at home. Only by learning about Mario's world is she able to understand him better. Mrs. Baxter learns that the problems students encounter in their private lives are part of the school experience, too. This chapter is meant to help you develop strategies to help students in your classroom.

Chapter 12 describes two schools in which teachers are making a difference. In one, the Benjamin Franklin Day School, teachers and students are able to come together to help each other learn. The results are extraordinary, especially because teachers and students reflect different values in a multicultural society. The second, the Manhattan Country Day School, shows that children who live in different cultures can, if given opportunities, learn about themselves, others, and the neighborhoods in which they live.

The Child's World
Beyond the Classroom

In Chapter 11 we will discuss how experiences outside the school alter your students' education. Students bring diverse perspectives of childhood to school. To many, the word *childhood* conveys the image of a carefree time spent with friends, activities at school, going to movies, doing chores at home, and having few responsibilities. While this image is accurate for many students, a sizeable group of children will not experience childhood in this way. Their childhood is fraught with gangs, violence, drugs, poverty, and/or abuse.

In this chapter, you will learn that children do not live within the four walls of your classroom. Rather, children bring to their classroom the world in which they live. To help you better understand some children's experiences, we will introduce you to several children as they describe their inner-city neighborhood. As you read their stories, think about how you, as their teacher, could help them.

What you will learn

- Great changes in family structure are taking place today.
- Children today express social values that may be different from yours.
- Poverty and other social problems influence school children.

BECOMING A TEACHER   *My neighborhood*

Hi My name is Bakari Clay an I'm going to tell you all about my neigborhood. The neiborhood that I live in wasn't bad until about a year ago. It use to be safe and clean until they started to sell drugs and do drive bye's and stick people up. I think that people are so dumb for killing each other over drugs, coats, shoes, chains, and other material items. Some days I'm scared to even walk to school by myself thinking that I'm gonna get killed, kidnapped, or just plain kicked around by some older guys who wanna have a little fun before school. Then there's even more fear when walking home because face it I live a block away from school but in this world we live in today that's a long walk home anything could happen. But I just take a deep breath and keep my head to the sky hoping that the police or someone can make my neiborhood safe to live in again someday. There's trouble anywhere you go so I'm gonna do all I can to help my neiborhood be the cleanest and safest place I can but I'm only 8 years old. I can't do it all by myself. When I grow older I'm gonna be the best I can be so I can make a difference some day.

??? *Even though most teachers have not had childhoods like Bakari Clay, they will meet students like her in their classrooms. Think about the friends you had as a child, and compare their attitudes to Bakari Clay's. Interview several teachers about their "Bakaris" and what happened to them.*

The Child's World Beyond the Classroom

Children experience the fallout from the rapid social, demographic, and economic changes America has endured in the last several decades. In the world outside the school, more than 26 percent of U.S. children live in poverty—an increase of more than a third since 1970. The overall health and well-being of our children has declined, although some children are doing better. Twice as many teens attempted or committed suicide in 1990 as in 1970. Homicide rates among young people have been steadily increasing since 1985. On the other hand, illegal drug use among teens is down from the 1970s, and the percent of college graduates is as high as it ever has been.

What does all this mean for you as a classroom teacher? Most classroom teachers seldom experience the everyday problems their students encounter. Few really comprehend how some of their students live when they leave school at the end of the day. Because you will experience the results of our country's rapid change in your classroom, we want to help you prepare to effectively meet the needs of all your students in your classroom.

Poverty

Since the mid-1970s, both absolute and relative poverty have consistently increased. While 26 percent of all children live in poverty today, 35 percent of children of parents under 30 live in poverty. During the decade ending in 1987, the total income of the poorest one-fifth of America's families declined 10 percent. During that same period, the bottom one-fifth of African-American family income declined 20 percent. Today, 75 percent of children who live with a single parent exist in poverty (Eisenberg, 1996). A growing underclass of poorly paid workers earn significantly less than comparable workers in other countries. Most of these workers exist at or below the **poverty line,** which is the minimum amount of money the U.S. government estimates an average family needs to exist.

If you have been poor, you know you were a part of an environment over which you had no control. You know you can't be lazy when you are poor. Every member of a poor family is committed to making money, simply to survive. Even so, many poor people lack the skills that would allow them to live better. Table 11.1 shows the designated poverty line for different-sized families.

Table 11.1
Federal Poverty Line 1995

Poverty line by family size	Minimum income level
Family of two; e.g., one adult and one child	$9,137
Family of three; e.g., two adults and one child or one adult and two children	$11,186
Family of four; e.g., two adults and two children or one adult and three children	$14,335

Source: Data compiled by authors from 1995 U.S. Government Welfare Guidelines.

Let's examine the growth of poverty a little closer. The Bureau of the Census reported (1994) that 82 percent of all African-American children who lived with a single female head of the house in 1994 were poor. This is compared with 46 percent of Hispanic and Euro-American children who lived with a single female parent. Poor children are more likely to have academic difficulties and are absent more. Some students drop out of school to find full-time work to support themselves and/or their families. Others try to work part-time and stay in school, but often find it difficult to balance school and work.

The consequences of poverty are varied. Poor children endure both short- and long-term effects of a lack of medical care and adequate nutrition. They are more

Children in poverty face problems such as poor clothing, lack of housing, inadequate food, and—most important—hopelessness.

susceptible to colds, flu, and other diseases found in crowded classrooms. You may even wonder, as many others do, whether some of the children in special education programs are there because of the effects of poverty.

In a study of children in Chicago's federal housing projects, Levine and Havighurst (1992) described children as being prisoners in their homes when they returned from school. James Baldwin, a well-known African-American author, compared his life as a poor child to that of a captive.

Anyone who has ever struggled with poverty knows how extremely expensive it is to be poor; and if one is a member of a captive population, economically speaking, one's feet have simply been placed on the treadmill forever. One is victimized, economically speaking, in a thousand ways. (Baldwin, 1961)

Illiteracy

Literacy is the ability to read, write, and use basic math skills. A national study (U.S. Department of Education, 1996) examined a group of 13,600 individuals who were 16 years and older in 12 states. Included were 1,100 inmates. The study found that 41 to 44 percent of all adults could not perform at the lowest literacy levels, compared to 4 to 8 percent who performed at the highest literacy levels. It was also noted that 70 percent of adult inmates operated at the lowest levels of literacy. Not surprisingly, the study concluded a direct relationship between reading and economic success.

Another study (Oklahoma Department of Libraries, 1995) examined nongraduation patterns of adults 25 years or older and found that students who were unable to read or write dropped out of school before graduation. Emmy Bell, head of the Literacy Coalition for the state of Nevada, states, "there is a direct correlation between income level and education, so we are probably safe in assuming that people who earn the least may be hampered by reading problems" (1994). That means young adults who are not able to read are likely to be poor.

What does it mean to be illiterate? For many, it means reading pictures rather than words, listening to others more intently to find out hidden meanings, relying on television for information, and learning how to bluff others into thinking one can read. Illiteracy is something adolescents feel they can deal with. But as the illiterate enter adulthood, they find it humiliating. Job opportunities pass them by.

Homelessness

The homeless are the most invisible people in America. Our stereotype of a homeless person is a dirty, disheveled, middle-aged man who refuses to work and begs or sells flowers at intersections. We tend to think of homeless people as winos, social misfits, and/or bag ladies who sit in doorways.

As a society, we are becoming more aware of the homeless, and we are discovering that our stereotypes are not correct. The homeless pass us quietly on the street every day, mostly without our noticing them. As a group, they tend to be poorly educated and impoverished: more than half did not complete high school

Our home: A family meal at a homeless shelter.

and their monthly median income is about $100, a figure that is less than one-fourth of the federal poverty level for a single person (Levitan and Schillmoeller, 1991).

How do schools, states, and the federal government respond to problems of this magnitude? Unfortunately, the difficulty schools and governments have helping homeless children is that they and their parents are difficult to locate.

Runaways

Runaways are usually junior high and middle school children who have decided they no longer want to live with their adult parent or parents. They leave home for a multitude of reasons, some of which are child abuse, alcoholism, pregnancy, and poverty. Some runaways are children who have been pushed out of the house by a parent.

A runaway's life is difficult and dangerous. Many juveniles are forced into prostitution. They work the streets and give their money to pimps who, in return, give them an allowance and a place to sleep. Because of poor eating habits over a period of time, these children are susceptible to even the most minor diseases. Many have perpetual colds and runny noses. Because they share living space in shelters with others, these children frequently find themselves in demoralized environments. They are often physically and sexually abused by the adults they live with.

We don't know how many runaway children have learning disabilities. We do know, however, that some return home or live with relatives. Unfortunately, we don't know how many runaways decide to stay on the streets, or for how long, or whether they attend school. Runaways usually live in downtown areas of cities, where they roam the streets begging for money during the day and soliciting in the evening. You may even see them on the outskirts of your university campus, where they beg for money from students and professors alike. Eventually, they become part of the developing underclass we call the homeless.

AIDS

If there is one single thing that separates your students from previous generations, it is the disease acquired immunodeficiency syndrome (AIDS). AIDS is the nation's leading killer of people between the ages of 25 and 44. Because the disease can be acquired by adolescents, its impact has yet to be felt by our schools. AIDS is often stereotyped as a disease of homosexuals and I.V. drug users; however, it is clear that this epidemic encompasses all populations.

Since 1981, 441,000 Americans under age 26 have contracted AIDS, of whom 250,000 have died (Centers for Disease Control, 1995). In 1993, for every 100,000 people, 35 people died from AIDS, compared with 32 who died from accidents. The Centers for Disease Control report that 20,000 AIDS cases are discovered every three months in the United States.

While AIDS is a medical and social problem throughout the nation, its impact is greatest in urban areas. For example, one-third to two-thirds of all deaths among young adults aged 16–25 in New York, Miami, and Atlanta are AIDS-related. AIDS

Which child has AIDS?

is also the leading killer in Omaha, Nebraska; Springfield, Illinois; Raleigh, North Carolina; and Tulsa, Oklahoma.

Teen Pregnancy

Educators have learned a lot about teen pregnancy during the last several years. The average adolescent mother is white and in her late teens. Childbearing among teen-age girls is not an epidemic. In fact, the birth rate is lower than it was in the 1950s. For every 1,000 females between the ages of 15 and 19, there were 90 births in 1955, 68 births in 1970, and 51 births in 1986.

So why do we consider teen pregnancy to be a more serious problem now than we did during the 1950s or 1960s? There are two reasons. First, during the 1960s, the average age at marriage for girls was approximately 20. Pregnant 18- and 19-year-old girls were not far from the norm. In fact, many of the teens who were having children prior to the 1970s were married. In 1980, approximately 55 percent of women between the ages of 15 and 19 who had children did so outside of marriage. In 1991, that figure had risen to 68 percent (U.S. Bureau of Census, 1993). Adolescent childbearing was not considered a problem in the 1950s because pregnant teens tended to get married, to establish stable families, and to live relatively prosperous lives. Men with little formal education could find good-paying jobs in factories or mills. Young people with the same level of education today are faced with low-paying service jobs. The economic situation is much different for young families today than it was in the 1950s.

Teen mothers face increased economic pressure.

While many social workers and educators believe the majority of babies born to adolescent girls are fathered not by teenage boys but by men older than 20, it is difficult to study male involvement, because many are not identified. Therefore, it is difficult to describe the characteristics of fathers of out-of-wedlock children.

Teen Suicide

Another form of victimization is teen suicide. Studies estimate that as many as 5,000 adolescents and young adults take their own lives each year. It is difficult to know the exact number of teenagers and young adults who make that fatal decision because of the manner in which they choose to end their lives. For instance, we do not know how many single-car automobile accidents are intended to be suicides. We have yet to understand why teenagers who live in rural America commit suicide more often than teenagers in urban settings. We know Native American adolescents kill themselves at a rate ten times greater than white teenagers. Yet studies indicate that white teenagers commit suicide five times more often than African Americans.

There are many reasons why adolescents and young people commit suicide. Changes in family structure, despondency over grades and teacher relationships, or personal problems beyond their control contribute to suicide. The clustering of teen suicides has been witnessed in many schools, when one teenager's suicide has sparked others. Researchers wonder how well teenagers understand death and dying: Influenced by the casualness of murder on television and movies, teenagers may not understand the permanence of death or the agony of death (and its aftermath for survivors).

 ## Juvenile Violence and Crime

Violence and crime have become a way of life for many school-age children. During the 1950s, we thought of breaking windows and stealing cars as serious violent offenses for children. Now we understand that violence can take deadly forms, even for schoolchildren.

Juvenile Justice System

How does society react to young people who break the law? Traditionally, communities are flexible with children in trouble. Schools use special support services designed to counsel students. Community teen centers also help troubled children under 18 years of age.

However, when adolescents continue to commit crimes, they are taken into custody and charged with an offense. At that time, adolescents are classified as juvenile delinquents and, if convicted, placed in institutional settings, such as jails.

Juvenile delinquents are people 18 years of age or younger who commit a crime or statutory offense. They are not charged as adults.

Juvenile delinquency proceedings differ from criminal proceedings. Allen and Simonsen (1992) explain that the courts make repeated attempts to help adolescents succeed. Figure 11.1 defines the terms used in juvenile delinquency proceedings.

Kids as Delinquents

We don't usually imagine criminals as children. However, in a recent study by the U.S. Department of Justice (Sessions, 1990), 27.3 percent of all crimes in this country were committed by children 17 or younger. In fact, 11 percent of all arrests for crimes were of children 14 or younger. Table 11.2 is a partial listing of offenses for which school-age children are brought before the court system.

Figure 11.1   Terminology in Juvenile Proceedings

Absence of legal guilt.   Legally, juveniles are not found guilty of crimes but are found delinquent. Juveniles are not held legally responsible for their acts. Juvenile status, like insanity, is a defense against criminal responsibility. It is not, however, an absolute defense—it is possible for certain crimes to be bound over to adult criminal court.

Treatment rather than punishment.   Whatever action the court takes following a finding of delinquency is done in the quest for treatment or community protection, not punishment, as is the case for adult felony offenders.

Absence of public scrutiny.   Juvenile proceedings and records are generally closed to the public. What goes on in court is presumed to be the business only of the juveniles involved and their families. This position is part of the child-saving mission of the court. Hearings for serious juvenile offenders are now being opened to the public.

Importance of a juvenile's background.   Juveniles' needs and amenability to treatment can, it is widely presumed, be deduced from their social history, prior behavior, and clinical diagnosis. This presumption is used to justify the wide discretionary powers granted to probation officers in screening petitions, to the court in deciding fitness and making dispositions, and to youth correction agencies in deciding when a ward should be released.

No long-term incarceration.   Terms of confinement for juveniles are considerably shorter than those for adults.

Separateness.   The juvenile system is kept separate from the adult criminal justice system at every point: the place of detention, the identities of the officials who handle the case in court, and subsequent placements.

Speed and flexibility.   Delinquency cases are disposed of more quickly than comparable adult criminal cases, and the juvenile court judge has a broader range of disposition alternatives.

Source: Corrections in America, 6/E by Allen and Simonsen, © 1992. Adapted by permission of Prentice-Hall, Inc., Upper Saddle River, NJ.

Table 11.2
Parial List of Juvenile Arrests, 1989

Offense	Ages under 15	Ages under 18
Murder/nonnegligent manslaughter	290	2,208
Forcible rape	1,699	4,706
Robbery	8,895	30,810
Aggravated assault	14,134	47,008
Burglary	45,017	113,754
Larceny–theft	162,402	359,732
Motor vehicle theft	20,462	74,729
Arson	4,356	6,360
Percentage distribution of type of crime		
Violent crimes	4.7	15.8
Property crimes	12.8	30.7
Total	11.0	27.3

Source: William Sessions, *Uniform Crime Reports: 1989* (Washington, D.C.: U.S. Department of Justice, 1990), p. 182.

Gangs

Our society sends mixed messages about gangs. Sometimes we glorify them, such as in movies about the Old West. Sometimes we romanticize them in song and dance, as in "West Side Story." In the 1950s, movies such as "Blackboard Jungle" implied that gang members went to school and did their homework at night.

Gangs are not a recent criminal occurrence. Gangs, sometimes called crews, have been part of our urban landscape for decades. Recently, though, gangs have begun appearing in small towns throughout the nation. Gangs, which have traditionally maintained their territories in inner cities of large metropolitan areas, are now found in communities of less than 250,000. Sociologists and criminologists still are not certain how or why gangs are spreading throughout the country. Some believe gang recruiters follow the interstate highway system to establish new chapters, or that the recruiters are attracted to a community because of its special makeup. We do know gangs are strong in areas where adults are uncertain of their economic future and where elementary, middle, and junior high school students find their school and family life unsatisfactory.

Why do school-age children join gangs? The reasons are varied. Many children join because their life in and out of school is not satisfying. Gangs become substitute families for many children. Children gain social approval, love, and respect from other gang members. Gangs are like extended families, allowing children and adolescents to travel the country knowing there is a gang-family close by to help if they are in trouble. Here are some common reasons children join gangs.

- Lack of social approval by peers
- Abusive home life
- Inability to make money
- Poor success in school
- Opportunity to buy and sell drugs

But there are other reasons children join gangs. For example, members feel gangs are better prepared to protect them from social problems than schools. A study of inmates between the ages of 21 and 51 years old reported that while 85 percent of both men and women offenders identified a teacher they admired while they were students, they believed their classroom was not a "safe haven" for them (Segall, 1994). Years later, these offenders continue to believe the problems they had as children were more easily solved by gangs than by teachers.

While we may think incarceration is punishment, some inmates find jail life comforting because they don't face the same problems as they did on the outside. Their life in jail has order, and they are not required to make decisions. They do not worry where their next meal is coming from, or where they will sleep that night. Many adolescents learn more about how to develop relationships in jail than at school with teachers or home with parents. Increasingly, jails are creating new and different types of families unheard of a generation ago (Segall, 1994).

Usually, classroom teachers think they do not know anyone who has been in jail when, in fact, they do. In Vignette 11.1, the authors interview a young man to find out what he thinks about school and what his chances are of remaining out of the criminal justice system.

VIGNETTE 11.1   *The importance of schooling for Mark: An interview*

Authors: *Mark, Mr. Benson talked to you about why schools are important. Why do you disagree with him?*

Mark: *I like Mr. Benson, but he is an old man. Maybe not in years, but in ideas. He thinks everyone has a mom or dad at home waiting for you. I know he thinks I have my own room at home. Well, I don't!*

Authors: *There are a lot of kids who go home to an empty house because their parents are working, Mark. And even if Mr. Benson thinks you have your own room, it's nothing special to have to share it with others in the family.*

Mark: *Boy, you don't get it. The reason I didn't have my homework done the other day was because I need to make money for my mom. Her money doesn't go far enough to pay the rent. Besides, I don't like living there! She has too many boyfriends and they don't want me hanging around.*

Authors: *Mark, we're sorry to hear that! But, what about your teachers? Don't you think they want to help you?*

Mark: *You're just like my teachers. You don't understand! They don't live in my world—they live someplace else. They like to read and things like that—I can't read and I don't need to. If they were as smart as me, they would see I have succeeded without having to read. It's easy to make money if you know the right people. I can sell drugs at school and at Lincoln Elementary and make enough to buy me a car and enjoy life. Besides, I get my hits free.*

Authors: *We think we understand what you mean. But what's going to happen to you after you graduate?*

Mark: *Graduate? Those teachers aren't going to let me graduate—no sir! Even though they smile at me and use their nice voices, I know they don't like me. Oh, I don't mean me personally. They just don't like people like me. They think we're too dirty . . . we talk different . . . we don't have manners. They just put up with us. It's like Mr. Benson. He wants to teach people like him. He and I have something in common . . . we both want out of this school . . . and I'll get out before he does.*

???   *Obviously, Mark is evaluating his school experiences with values he developed outside the classroom. Think about the values that helped you remain in school and led you to become a teacher. What are some of the differences between you and Mark? What will Mark need to learn to survive in school?*

Mark is not unusual. In fact, Mark is an excellent example of one out of every six boys who will appear in a juvenile court by the time he is eighteen. Counting girls, one out of every nine adolescents will be required to attend a court case on their own behalf. Reported crimes committed by youths 18 and younger have increased at an alarming rate. Allen and Simonsen (1992) believe there are several reasons for this. One is that young people have a tendency to commit crimes in groups. When they are arrested, several will go to jail rather than one. Not surprisingly, many adult felons were first incarcerated while they were adolescents.

A Child's Family

There are many types of families. Each may be a positive or negative force in a child's life.

Traditional Families

Have you ever watched television reruns of 1950s family sitcoms like "Leave it to Beaver" or "The Donna Reed Show"? In all likelihood, the family consisted of a working father who, when he came home, was greeted by his wife and two or three children. You may have been raised in a family like that yourself, and you may believe that these shows present a fairly accurate picture of a typical family.

Actually, these television shows perpetuate several myths that surround U.S. families. Throughout most of history, families have needed more than one bread-winner to survive. Either both parents worked or one parent and the children worked. It wasn't until the 1920s that a small majority of children lived in the breadwinner-plus-homemaker family.

A traditional family?

Families with One Wage-Earner.   During the 1950s, television programs depicted family life as it was supposed to be, not as it actually was. Even though these shows never did reflect the realities of family life, many people today still hold them as models of the way family life should be. But these are difficult models to have. In 1955 only 11 percent of mothers of preschoolers worked outside the home. By 1987, 70 percent of mothers of preschoolers worked outside the home. In 1993, only 7.4 percent of mothers of children under six did not work outside the home (U.S. Department of Labor, Bureau of Labor Statistics, 1993).

The mothers who worked outside the home in the 1950s typically held jobs that allowed them to maintain a nearly traditional home life. For example, women often became teachers so they could spend summers and school vacations at home with their children. Teachers could come home in the afternoon in time to be with their children and have dinner ready for their husbands.

In the traditional family model of male breadwinner/female homemaker, children are likely to have more time with a parent, more supervision, and more help with homework.

Families with Two Wage-Earners.   Because of the rapid economic changes occurring in our society, many families find it necessary for both parents to work outside the home. Not surprisingly, families with two wage-earners have less family time together and are more likely to quarrel over housework.

These families, as well as the families with one wage-earner, have the advantage of having more than one adult available to help the children. Parents can back each other regarding discipline, compensate for each other's weaknesses, spell each other in tasks, and model healthy conflict resolution or negotiation.

Nontraditional Families

For many children, a nontraditional family structure best describes their living situation. In some cases, parents divorce and one parent becomes the primary caretaker. In other cases, a parent chooses not to marry and is the primary caretaker.

Single-Parent Families.

A family structure classroom teachers are becoming more aware of lately is the single-parent family. Single-parent families come about for many reasons. For example, after a divorce, a mother may raise her children herself. Or the parent may be a woman who dropped out of school as a teenager to get a job so she could keep her baby. Of course, there are many other reasons for single-parent families, such as the death of a spouse. Regardless, sociologists and educators are attempting to understand the implications of the single-parent family for schools and children. We know the majority of single-parent families are headed by young women. They are usually poor. Levine and Havighurst (1992) found that many of these families are concentrated in poor neighborhoods. In fact, as many as 90 percent of all families in poverty neighborhoods are headed by a parent who is a young, single, woman.

What does this mean for children of single parents in your classroom? Many of these children feel isolated from the rest of society. What they see on TV represents middle-class life and values, not theirs. Commercials hype middle-class products that are too expensive for them to buy. For their parents and other members of the family, isolation is also expressed in frustration, as the jobs they want move out of their neighborhoods. Technology causes adolescents to feel further isolation. Assembly line jobs they qualify for are now performed by machines, robots, and computers. Technology has increased the unemployment level of teenagers who have dropped out of school.

A single parent and his child.

Children of Divorce.   Divorce is another factor changing your students' lives. Although divorce is viewed differently today than it was in previous generations, it is still acknowledged as a difficult period for children. In fact, the 1990 census informs us that more than half of all young working or college-age women will undergo at least one divorce in their lifetimes.

The question many divorced parents ask themselves is whether the trauma of divorce is greater for their children than living in a dysfunctional family would be. Regardless, divorce is an emotionally draining experience in which two adults redefine their lives. While it may be liberating for some adults, its impact on children may be different.

Classroom teachers are all too aware that divorce disturbs children. It is, for the more than 1 million children each year, an emotional period they will remember for the rest of their lives. Prior to divorce, children become aware of the frailness of their family. They don't know what their lives will be like if their mother and father separate. It is bewildering for many children, even though they have friends who have gone through the same experience. It is common for children to try to save the family by taking the blame for its apparent failure.

Children of divorced parents have major adjustments to make regardless of age. Beyond the economic problems divorce usually highlights, children and parents find their relationship changing. It is common for parents and children to redefine each other's role in their lives. As Lipsky and Abrams mention:

> You learn they don't have, as they say, all the answers. When your parents aren't divorced, you think they have all the answers. But that's because they aren't being asked that many questions. Or the hard questions, anyway. When they're married, it's all the same questions. Divorced, you see them as people with certain kinds of tastes in men or women with certain kinds of habits. And because there isn't another person there, they seek you out. (1994, p. 99)

Latchkey Children.   If you were a child in a working family, you know how difficult that was, and how important it is that teachers understand the life and particular problems shared by children of working parents. How will you recognize these children as a classroom teacher? They are the elementary school kids who are dropped off in the morning by a parent or neighbor on their way to work. Regardless of the weather, you may find them playing in the schoolyard hours before classes begin. If the student is in middle school or older, he or she may work, or go to the mall with friends after school to wait for parents. If they have younger brothers or sisters, they are usually required to take care of them after school.

Many children return to empty homes after school. They let themselves in with keys tied around their neck with a string. These so-called latchkey kids obey specific instructions their parents give them. They are told to lock the door as soon as they enter and call their mothers at work to let them know they are home. Then they eat a snack left for them. Typically, they are allowed to watch TV, but not answer the telephone or open the door if someone knocks.

Parents and schools have experimented with programs to provide alternatives for these latchkey kids. In one study, 10.5 percent of all children were participating in some form of extended-day school activity in 1996. It was found that 12.6 percent of children in the central city and 10.0 percent in urban fringe or suburban areas remained in school. Only 8.1 percent of students in rural areas remained in school. The same study discovered that 18 percent of students in private schools remained in extended-day programs (U.S. Department of Education, 1996).

Not all children react negatively to returning to empty homes. Some cope very well by doing their homework, cleaning the house, or setting the table for dinner. In any case, the realities of our society's economic structure are causing children to become more self-reliant regardless of their age.

Jamie, in Vignette 11.2, is a typical latchkey kid. He follows his mother's instructions to the letter but doesn't tell her how he feels about coming home because it might worry her. Many working parents feel guilty about this daily period of unsupervised time. While mothers want to talk on the telephone with their children longer, they are afraid their employers will object. Some mothers worry if their productivity goes down they might lose their jobs.

VIGNETTE 11.2 *The life of a latchkey kid, 3:43 P.M. to 5:25 P.M.*

When Jamie gets off the school bus, he remembers exactly what his mother told him. "Jamie, I want you to go straight home. Don't play with your friends. As soon as you get home, make sure the door is locked and telephone me so I know where you are." Jamie doesn't like this part of the day. He doesn't know why he has to do these things, except that it's what his mother says. He assumes all elementary school kids do this.

When Jamie enters the apartment, he locks the door. Then, carefully, he tiptoes through the apartment. Jamie is afraid. He has never told his mother he does this, he just knows he has to make sure nobody is hiding in the closets or under the beds. Then he calls his mother.

Jamie: *Hi, Mommy—I'm home!*
Mom: *Hi, Jamie. Did you have a good day at school?*
Jamie: *Yeah. But Mrs. Chad says we've got to collect some bugs for our science class. Mommy, will you help me collect some bugs?*
Mom: *Sure! It sounds like fun. Now, Jamie, I left a glass of milk and a couple of chocolate chip cookies for you in the refrigerator. I have to go back to work now, so don't call unless you need help."*

Jamie puts down the phone. With his cookies and milk, he goes into the living room and turns on MTV. Jamie feels better after he talks to his mom. "But I don't like being by myself," he thinks.

??? *Were you a latchkey kid? What memories does Jamie's story bring to mind? Ask a friend who had a different family experience to share his or her memories. How do you think your personal experiences will make you a better teacher? What resources are available in your community and schools for latchkey children?*

Invisible Families

The invisible family is another family structure that is becoming more common, although few teachers are aware of its existence. Unlike traditional and nontraditional families, invisible families have no legal arrangement other than an informal agreement among people who have personal, social, and economic needs to be with others. Invisible families are not permanent. They remain active only as long as the members feel they are receiving help. Invisible families are found among runaways, the homeless, gang members, juvenile prisoners, and adult prisoners.

Family Violence

We are only now understanding the extent of child abuse in our society. Abuse can include physical, verbal, psychological, or sexual mistreatment of a child. Recent studies point out that abuse is usually inflicted on children by parents, older brother and sisters, grandparents, or other adult or adolescent relations. In fact, it is suspected that 80 percent of abused children know their abuser intimately (National Center on Child Abuse and Neglect, 1988). As a society, we like to think that abuse happens to only a few children. The truth is that child abuse happens everywhere in our society, regardless of race, religion, culture, ethnicity, wealth, or geographic location—and it happens a lot (National Center on Child Abuse and Neglect, 1988).

Abused children are hurt and lonely.

It is important for teachers to understand that abuse—in any or all its forms—is not a new phenomenon. In previous generations, it was sometimes respected or described euphemistically as in, "He sure has firm control over his children" or "That family certainly has well-behaved children." In these examples, the point being admired is not the behavior of children, but the power adults and adolescents have over children, who have no one to protect them.

Children are abused by those who are older or have control over their lives: parents, brothers, sisters, or teachers. Abuse, no matter what form it takes, is a way of controlling another.

How do adults become abusers? Many researchers believe abuse is a learned behavior. That is, children who are abused by their parents are more likely to abuse their children when they become parents.

Child abuse is an emotional issue for classroom teachers. Many teachers fear reporting a suspected child abuse case. They may value the rights of families to live private lives. Other reasons are more personal and include:

- The teacher may be unsure what comprises abuse. For example, what is the difference between spanking and hitting a child?
- The suspected adult abuser may be a friend of the teacher.
- The teacher may be concerned about what the abuser will say.
- The teacher feels it is the child's legal right to maintain secrecy.
- The teacher may be uncertain about what information should be reported and to whom.
- Child abuse forces some teachers to recall a time they were abused themselves.

Some teachers are afraid to become involved with families of abused children, because they are not sure governments have a right to regulate the relations between family members. In fact, our government does have the responsibility to become involved with families in order to protect its citizens. Based on that premise, the Child Abuse Prevention and Treatment Act (1974) was passed. This act was intended to help each of the states develop child abuse prevention and treatment programs. Although the states have different types of programs, they all require teachers to report evidence of child abuse to their immediate supervisors. As a classroom teacher, you are required by law to inform your department head, principal, or superintendent when you suspect a child is being abused.

Consequences for Schools

As a teacher you will notice how the problems your children face outside your classroom interconnect. For example, sexually abused children become runaways or commit suicide more often than others. Poverty figures largely in the problems your children bring with them to your classroom, but these problems do not cause poverty. In fact, the reverse is true.

In the world of "Father Knows Best," poverty was thought to be caused by people who did not want to work. This is understandable, because earlier in the century, people could escape poverty by working in steel mills, on farms or assembly lines, or at other types of semi-skilled labor.

The world in which our children live is much more complex than that of our parents. Today's children are victims of our changing social values and economy. In the next chapter, we will look at how children live *in* the classroom.

What You Have Learned

✔ Children bring the society in which they live to school, even if they do not understand its significance.

✔ Violence, within and outside the family, touches children in our schools.

✔ There are many types of families. Each may be a positive or negative force in a child's life.

✔ Sexual behavior among teenagers has a multitude of consequences, including pregnancy and disease.

✔ Poverty is a common base upon which many of our social problems rest. Schools and children are influenced by the changing attitudes caused by increased poverty in the United States.

Key Terms

poverty line   juvenile delinquents
literacy

Applying What You Have Learned

1. Watch a television program produced in the 1950s or early 1960s, such as "The Donna Reed Show" or "Father Knows Best." What messages is it giving children about what to expect in life? Do you think life is really like that now?

2. Why is teen pregnancy a problem now, even though teen-age girls are having fewer children now than they did in the 1960s?

3. What resources are available in your community for homeless or runaway children? Do you think it is society's responsibility to solve this problem?

4. This chapter discussed children as victims of society. Do you think schools have a responsibility to help children who are victims?

Interactive Learning

1. Have you listened to people talk about divorce as a cause for society's problems? Talk to some of your friends who come from divorced families. Do they agree or disagree? What resources are available in your community for children of divorce?

2. Talk to a juvenile probation officer in your local community. For what crime are most juveniles arrested? What services are available for juvenile delinquents?

3. Did you grow up in a family with one or two wage earners? Compare your family with a friend's whose family structure was different. Together, develop a list of how each family structure can help or hinder teachers' understanding of children in their classroom.

Expanding Your Knowledge

Golden, Harry. *Only In America*. New York: World Publishing Company, 1958. (This delightful book of essays by the editor of the *Carolina Israelite* explains how poverty changed him as a child. Carl Sandburg, his friend, liked the book because it describes the human condition. You will like it because it shows how children have changed.)

Hobsbawm, Eric. *The Age of Extremes*. New York, Pantheon Books, 1994. (This eminent historian attempts to give historical meaning to our times.)

Hunter, James D. *Culture Wars: The Struggle to Define America*. New York: Harper Collins, 1991. (This is a must-read book for teachers, because Hunter discusses many of the social issues raised in this chapter from a social–historical perspective. He wants classroom teachers to think about what our legacy will be.)

Mankiller, Wilma, and Michael Wallis. *Mankiller: A Chief and Her People*. New York: St. Martin's Press, 1993. (The autobiography of Wilma Mankiller, who rose to fame in the Alcatraz sit-ins and later became the first woman chief of the Cherokee Nation. Mankiller describes a world classroom teachers must know about.)

Santoli, Al. *New Americans: An Oral History of Immigrants and Refugees in the U.S. Today*. New York: Viking Press, 1988. (This is a book of interviews with recent immigrants to the United States. The author tells a wonderful story about why immigrants live in poverty and why they want their children to go to school.)

Chapter 12

The Child's World of the Classroom

Children bring to your classroom values, ideas, and experiences from their world beyond the school. We hope you now understand how your children's world is complicated by various family structures, social problems, and economic crises. Children are not able to control or understand many of the problems society presents to them, regardless of their gender, culture, or ethnicity. As a teacher, you must appreciate that your classroom is on society's frontier. We are mistaken if we think classrooms are quiet places in which children and teachers are sheltered from the cares of the world. As teachers, many of us want to think of our classrooms as safe havens in which children leave the problems of their private lives behind and enter an oasis of learning. But that is not the case. In this chapter you will learn how successful classroom teachers learn who their children are.

What you will learn

- Our students reflect greater diversity than our classroom teachers do.
- Children are influenced in school by social problems and how classroom teachers help them learn.
- Teachers influence students beyond the limits of the classroom.
- School culture will influence you as a teacher.
- Classroom culture helps children learn.

BECOMING A TEACHER   *Guns in the classroom!*

"Mario!" Mrs. Baxter was beside herself. "I don't understand why you did this! They told me you were in Juvenile Court yesterday! They said you were carrying a gun when you came to school!" Mrs. Baxter was absolutely terrified. She was in Mario's home on the sixth floor of the housing project and felt as if she was in a foreign country.

　　This was the first time she had been in a project. As she was coming up the stairs, she thought, "I can't believe I am doing this. How could anyone live here? Like this?" She had originally thought she would take the elevator, but she wasn't sure it was safe. A couple of young adolescents were in it when the door opened. They just looked at her, and they didn't make any attempt to get out.

Mrs. Baxter couldn't get over the smell, although she recognized it from Mario. The dirt was everywhere. Yet it wasn't the type of filth she thought it would be—it was the leftovers of too many people living too close to each other. There was a stickiness to everything she touched. "Obviously, someone has tried to clean but gave up," she thought.

Mario was standing by the kitchen table with his mother. "I am happy you're upset about my boy, Mrs. Baxter," Mario's mother said. "You know, it's tough making sure everything goes O.K. for him, but I am busy much of the time." She had already told Mrs. Baxter she had a day job at a fast-food restaurant downtown and an evening job cleaning offices in one of the government buildings. "It's hard looking out for him as it is now. He is only in the eighth grade. I am not sure how it will get better as he grows up—there are a lot of bad kids in the project he can get in trouble with."

Mario looked glum, "It's O.K. I don't know what the fuss is about. Lots of guys carry guns or knives to school. You have to protect yourself. You know, when gangs are walking the halls looking for you, you need to protect yourself. I knew the school couldn't protect me."

Mrs. Baxter was beginning to understand what Mario had been telling her all along. "Life is tough, isn't it, Mario?" Mrs. Baxter said. "I don't know how to help you, except I know you will never have a chance for a better life if you don't get an education."

??? *List the values, ideas and attitudes expressed in this vignette by Mario, his mother and Mrs. Baxter. Do you notice that Mrs. Baxter admits to Mario she doesn't know how to help? All she can tell him is that schools will help him escape his life in the projects.*

The Child's World of the Classroom

In *Becoming a Teacher,* Mario and his mother describe the world in which they live to Mrs. Baxter. They work long hours and, at the same time, cope with all of life's problems. Mario, Mrs. Baxter is learning, lives by his own wits. Because his mother works several jobs, she is not available to emotionally support him as much as she would like. The family support Mario needs comes from a gang, not his mother. Mrs. Baxter understands that classrooms must be more than places where students learn an academic curriculum. The classroom, she sees, must help children learn how their lives matter to themselves and others.

Differences Between Teachers and Students

In *Becoming a Teacher,* Mrs. Baxter is learning how different her life is from that of her students. She knows she needs to understand the differences so she can help Mario. This is typical—many classroom teachers do not reflect the same cultural values as their students.

How different will you be from your students? Let's look at some of the probable differences. The first and most obvious difference you may notice is your education. Through your academic ability, and perhaps your parents' financial help, you are in college. This may not seem like much, but it shows that you are able to control your environment so you can succeed. Many of your students will not have the same cultural or social experiences you had. They may not be receiving a quality education and they may even be considering dropping out. You discovered that schools helped you succeed. But for every 100 students in Grades 10–12, 4.4 percent will drop out. While that figure may not seem large, it represents 383,000 students. However, beginning in 1980, the proportion of all 16- to 24-year-old dropouts has continued to decline. By 1994, for example, the dropout rate for African-American students fell 6 percentage points, from 19 percent in 1980 to 13 percent. The percentage of Hispanic dropouts has remained the same, 30 percent—the largest of any group. Dropouts among Euro-Americans continued to decline, from 15 percent in 1980 to approximately 7.5 percent in 1994 (U.S. Department of Commerce, Bureau of the Census, 1996).

Although most teachers are Euro-American, female, and middle-class, your students will come from a rainbow of cultures, races, and ethnicities (Smith, et al., 1994). These are not the only differences between you and your students. Therefore, it is important for you to understand the relationships you will have with students in your classroom.

Teachers in a Child's World

What concerns will you have about your students when you enter the classroom as a teacher? If you are like many teachers in today's classrooms, you will be disturbed by students who come to school from families torn by domestic violence and economic problems. You will notice children coming from homes in which they are not valued members of the family. You will meet children who have parents who do not have the interest, or the time, or the skills to help their children. You will see these children come to school with shorter attention spans and a lessened ability to concentrate on their studies. Children's performance can suffer even before they come into the classroom.

Today's teachers are concerned about the quality of life children experience outside school. When children receive inadequate family support, their schoolwork suffers. Some teachers believe children coming from single parent or working families are the only ones who have problems in school. But we now know the *quality* of family life is the most important factor in a child's educational well-being. While teachers are aware that the *quantity* of time children spend with their parents is important, they are aware that their interactions with children of similar ages, adults, and others within the family and community are also significant to their growth and welfare.

If children are to be successful, teachers must understand how their world influences the learning environment. Let's look at how schools and classroom teachers help children who bring their world into your classroom.

Poverty's playground.

Gangs and Violence in the Classroom

Violence in the school has been a topic of conversation among classroom teachers for decades. Student violence became a serious educational issue in the 1960s and 1970s. Recently, the character of violence in the classroom has changed. At one time, violence was described by classroom teachers as students trying to settle disagreements by fighting. However, as our society has changed, so has the type of violence in the classroom. Drugs, gangs, and **transgressors**—nonstudents who come to school without legitimate reasons—have turned many schools into battlegrounds.

Vignette 12.1 is an excellent example of how violence outside the school has entered the classroom. Not long ago we thought classroom violence was the problem of inner-city schools. We blamed poverty and minorities for the violence. Although Mario, in Vignette 12.1, is an eighth-grade student in an inner-city school, this type of violence is found in classrooms throughout the country. In fact, schools have discovered that as many as one out of every five children come armed with some type of weapon.

VIGNETTE 12.1   *Help me!*

"Help me! Help me!" Mario was running in the halls to the counselor's office. "Help me—I'm bleeding!" Marked with welts on his face, Mario's nose and mouth were bleeding. Students he passed looked on passively. They had seen these things before. They didn't want to get involved—they had seen the work of gangs and were afraid they would get hurt if they interfered.

Officer Suarez, the school policeman, was hurrying and shoving students aside so he could help Mario. "Are you O.K., son? Let me help you! Tell me what happened!" All his questions came at once.

Mario knew he was hurt. He would learn at the hospital that his nose was broken. As Officer Suarez helped Mario, he asked, "Who hurt you Mario? What's his name?"

"I don't know his name," Mario stammered, "he's a big guy, he has a gun, he doesn't go to school. He's too old to go to school."

??? *To understand what is happening to Mario, reread "Becoming a Teacher" at the beginning of the chapter. What should Mario's school do to protect him?*

Schools are reacting to violent behavior in many ways. Some schools are becoming **closed campuses:** once students come into the school building, they are not allowed to leave until the end of the day. Another method schools are using is to restrict the number of entrances students, visitors, and others may use to enter the building. Metal detectors are another technique some schools are using to disarm students. In Mario's situation, a metal detector might have caught the transgressor. It is projected that between 40,000 and 50,000 handguns are confiscated from students each year. The use of police on campus has also helped.

Yet the problem of violence in schools has not been solved. There is a need for larger numbers of student support services, such as professional guidance and career counselors, doctors, and nurses. Schools are also experimenting with programs that attack social problems such as drugs, suicide, teen sex, and pregnancy. Schools are experimenting with programs that provide nurseries and preschools for the babies of junior high and high school students. In these schools within schools, nurses are able to evaluate the health of the newborns and, at the same time, teach teen mothers parenting skills. Intergroup counseling programs have also proven important for students who are alcoholics or are experimenting with drugs. Other schools are experimenting with programs that counsel abused children.

Teachers recognize that the violence entering our classrooms is a symptom of other social problems children face. We should not think violence is a problem in itself. Let's look at how you will be involved in some of the problems your students face.

Recognizing Child Abuse in the Classroom

As a classroom teacher, it is important for you to know how child abuse can influence student learning. Many students find it difficult to focus on their work because they have learned to not trust adults, including teachers. Some abused children will have discipline problems that demand much of your class time. Others may be very quiet in class, not attracting attention from anyone, including yourself.

You may be hesitant about reporting a suspected abuse case, but your legal responsibility is to report any suspected abuse to your principal or department head. Figure 12.1 lists some of the common indicators of child abuse.

What happens if you make a mistake and report a child as abused when he or she has not been? You and your school are protected from criminal or civil prosecution as long as you report the case honestly. Figure 12.2 details your responsibilities as a teacher when you suspect a child is abused. You will learn more about child abuse and become knowledgeable about reporting procedures during staff development workshops in your school. Vignette 12.2 reveals some stereotypes held by many people about child abuse.

Figure 12.1   Physical and Emotional Signs of Child Abuse

Does the child . . .
- indicate a sudden change in learning behavior?
- seem to be overly suspicious, or seem to interpret events to be dangerous?
- have unexplained bruises? Or have unreasonable explanations about how he or she received the bruises?
- seem overly willing to please everybody?
- show lack of parental care?
- express a strong willingness to remain at school rather than go home?
- seem to behave differently?
- go without needed medical assistance, even after the parents have been informed?

Figure 12.2   Educators Must Act

Educators, counselors, and administrators are required to report suspected child abuse or neglect. The identification of abused children, even those without visible bruises, should be viewed as a priority. In reporting suspected child abuse, educators should:

- Know and understand the school's policies and procedures governing abuse.
- Document or establish an unbroken chain of custody for the evidence.
- Document the behavior that prompted the action.
- Cooperate with law enforcement agencies.

Regardless of the outcome, teachers and school officials are not usually held liable as long as they can prove their actions were prompted by good faith.

Source: Adapted from Office of Educational Research and Improvement, U.S. Department of Education, Contract Number OERI88062004

VIGNETTE 12.2   *Carla's abuse case*

"Well, it's obvious to me! Carla has to be abused—just look at her," Mr. Camps told his principal. "She's the classic case of an abused child."

Mrs. Gomez, who had been working on her computer, turned and, without a smile, asked, "How do you know Mr. Camps? What are some of the symptoms of abuse Carla is displaying? How long have you noticed these changes?"

"Well, just look at the facts." Mr. Gomez listed them on his fingers. "First, she lives in a poor neighborhood. Second, her mother is single, and I am sure she has men friends over. Third, she hangs around in the mall—I am sure she is being picked up by strangers."

Mrs. Gomez raised her hand to cut off Mr. Camps. "Just a minute. You haven't given me one piece of solid evidence Carla has been abused by anyone. All you have given me are myths, stereotypes, and your feelings."

In a firm voice, Mrs. Gomez said "I realize you have the best interests of Carla in mind. But don't you know the difference between stereotypes and symptoms of child abuse?"

???   *Mrs. Gomez has challenged Mr. Camps to name the differences between stereotypes and symptoms of child abuse. What symptoms would you list for Mrs. Gomez?*

Obviously, Mr. Camps is lucky he has a principal who knows the symptoms of child abuse and is knowledgeable in applying them to students. Even though Mr. Camps had Carla's best interests in mind, he had stereotyped her.

While it is easy to stereotype adults who abuse children, it is also easy to forget the trauma children suffer because of abuse. Feelings of guilt and low self-esteem may cripple and follow children into adulthood. The more you know about child abuse, the better you will be able to help your students.

Literacy and the Classroom Teacher

In the eighth grade, Mario believes he is a success because he is able to make people believe he can read. As Mario grows older, his inability to read will act as a wall he will have difficulty climbing. He will become separated from mainstream society and less able to find adequate employment.

As a teacher, what are your responsibilities to help students learn how to communicate? Some secondary teachers consider teaching reading to be beyond their professional obligations. They believe their job is to teach specific courses such as mathematics and social studies, and they think reading should be left to reading teachers. Actually, children learn best when *all* teachers are attentive to their reading abilities. Regardless of what you teach, if your students are not able to read or write, they will have difficulty learning.

In one school's reading program (Mabbett, 1990), literacy is based on a cooperative effort of all the students' teachers and parents. There, teaching reading is everyone's responsibility. For example, Mabbett says there are many ways to read and that teachers should help students learn based on their reading styles. Learning how to read is an educational experience that continues throughout school.

Recognizing Chemical Abuse in the Classroom

How would you like to teach a class in which one or several of your students were drunk? Alcohol is the most serious chemical abuse problem in our classrooms today and is found in both elementary and secondary schools throughout the country. Drunk students become unruly in class, are loud, or fall asleep at their desks. They are not interested in what you teach and are, in many cases, interested only in disturbing fellow students who want to learn. Vignette 12.3 describes the impact a student's drinking problem can have on the classroom—and on teachers' attitudes.

VIGNETTE 12.3   *Drunk in class—again!*

"Well, I guess everybody knows about Danny coming to school drunk," Mrs. Willards said as she came into the teachers' lounge.

"Can you believe it?" It was Janice McIntyre talking. Janice was planning on retiring at the end of the year. "I am glad to retire from teaching. I don't understand kids or their parents anymore. When I was in the sixth grade I wouldn't have dreamed of getting drunk! My father would have paddled me!"

"You're right," said another teacher. "It's disgusting the way parents let their kids run wild these days—someone should tell them to pay more attention to their children."

???   *It's always easy to blame someone else for their shortcomings. Write a letter to these teachers explaining their responsibilities to Danny.*

The physical characteristics of intoxication are easy to recognize. Usually, the person's face is flushed and eyes are less focused. An intoxicated person may not be able to walk a straight line, and her or his speech will be slurred. But more importantly, judgment is impaired. An intoxicated person will make decisions based on emotions. His or her attention span will be short and he or she may have wild mood swings. We don't know how many children drink, but one study (Portner, 1993) indicates 20 million seventh- to twelfth-graders drink occasionally, 8 million drink weekly, and about a million are binge drinkers. Figure 12.3 lists symptoms beyond physical characteristics to help you identify students in your class who are dependent on alcohol or other substances.

Figure 12.3   Symptoms of Chemical Abuse

Do you know students who have changed:
- Work habits?
- Clothing styles?
- Social reputation?
- Relationships with friends?
- Relationships with teachers?
- Relationships with family members?

What do you do if you discover a student is drunk or on drugs in your classroom? You should immediately notify your department head or principal. But beyond that, be prepared to talk to your student at a time when she or he can understand your concerns. Although the student may not want you or the principal to talk to her or his parents, they should be informed.

Classroom teachers are becoming more involved with various types of school-sponsored drug and alcohol intervention programs. Many of these programs are run in partnership with local community groups. Classroom teachers realize that asking students to "just say no" to alcohol and drugs is not enough. You as a classroom teacher must understand that students will not learn in your classroom without your commitment to making your school alcohol- and drug-free.

Teen Pregnancy

The problems of teen pregnancy are much more complicated than many adults first believe. Teen pregnancy may result in emotional problems. Scholars such as Males (1994) who have studied prevention programs in the United States have generally concluded such programs do not work. It is important that you understand the educational implications of teen pregnancy and learn how schools can help teen mothers. This means helping them understand the risks of sexual promiscuity. Males (1994) concludes that schools should develop programs that will help young parents graduate. Let's discuss two such programs designed to keep teen mothers in school and help them understand the consequences of their sexual behavior.

Children-of-Children Nursery Schools.   One method of retaining teen mothers in school is to develop quality in-school nursery care facilities for them and their babies. Some junior and senior high schools have developed Children-of-Children Nursery Schools, in which teen mothers bring their babies to school. While the student–mothers attend classes, their babies are cared for by nurses and childcare givers. These professionals help the mothers learn about raising their babies by teaching classes in nutrition, child development, and medical needs. The mothers learn about the demands babies place on them. The programs are

A fifteen-year-old mother does homework while watching her child.

designed to help teen mothers appreciate themselves, so another pregnancy becomes less likely. As the Children-of-Children Nursery Schools help teen mothers learn about raising their children, they also help them live healthier, safer lives.

Sex Education.   Sex education has been a controversial topic for decades. One group, comprising mostly parents and clergy, believes sex education is a family concern and should not be taught in schools. The opposing group, comprising parents, teachers, and medical doctors, agrees that parents *should* take responsibility for teaching children about their sexual nature, but they point out that many parents find the topic of sex embarrassing and have difficulty telling their children the facts of life. Therefore, they say, children learn about sex from experience and their friends on the street.

It is easy to rely on old myths and misinformation, to stereotype students' sexual behavior. Do not assume all students are heterosexual and live in a nuclear, family in which they are able to talk to a mom and a dad. In fact, 10 percent of your students are living in inner turmoil, trying to come to terms with their sexual orientation and the implications of being lesbian or gay (Krueger, 1993).

Many adults assume that all students are sexually active. Perhaps this message is sent to us by television. Yet many students are *not* involved in sexual activities, because of personal reasons or religious values. Many adults believe teenagers

Friendship versus sex.

who *are* sexually active consent to sexual involvement. Unfortunately, studies estimate that 27 percent of girls and 16 percent of boys are sexually abused before they reach age 18 (Krueger, 1993). In fact, the typical form of adolescent abuse is sexual, with 50 percent of all rape victims being between the ages of 10 and 19.

Sex education is a complex and emotional issue. Only 17 states require children to take a sex education course in school. The other states are divided on their attitudes about sex education. Some encourage schools to teach sex education, while others discourage it. Regardless, it is clear that teen pregnancy and sexually transmitted diseases (STDs) are taking a tremendous toll on today's students.

What should be taught in sex education courses? Usually, courses are taught either as part of the health–biology or psychology–sociology curriculum. Courses include such topics as family life and parenthood, dating and marriage, socialization between men and women (especially in relation to abuse), and reproduction and childbirth.

Schools also try to ensure that children learn about the cultural and ethical aspects of sexuality and human sexual behavior. For example, how do culture and ethnicity impact the relations between men and women? How do views about family planning and relations between children and parents differ depending on religious values and cultural and ethnic heritage?

At one time, sex education courses were aimed at adolescents. Therefore, most textbooks are written for junior high school students. However, students now encounter social and sexual problems at a much earlier age. Now schools are teaching sex education courses in the elementary grades. The fifth grade seems to be the most common time to begin sex education courses, but some schools are beginning as early as in the first grade.

AIDS Education.   AIDS education is an exception in the sex education controversy. Parents and teachers agree children should learn about AIDS as soon as possible. Most parents and teachers agree that education is the only way presently available to arrest the spread of this disease.

Recognizing the emotional ramifications of this dread disease, Holland and Tross (1985) have developed a series of cautions teachers should consider. Some of them speak to the human perspective of AIDS, such as being aware of their personal emotions and prejudices and exhibiting compassion and caring. Beyond this, schools must be prepared to teach AIDS awareness, including recognizing myths, how the disease is transmitted, and the various forms of protection and testing.

Students With AIDS

Perhaps the greatest heartbreak you will experience as a teacher is when you become aware of a student who has contracted a life-threatening disease that has no apparent cure. The emotions you encounter will range from grief to questioning why someone so young should have his or her life shortened.

As AIDS becomes more common in our schools, teachers are finding their emotions tested. AIDS is an emotional issue throughout the country. Our society has not reached a consensus about how people should react to people with AIDS. AIDS is a relatively new disease, and the public's knowledge of it is still growing. As a consequence, you will notice various attitudes about AIDS among your students and their parents. In some communities, parents are still concerned about whether their children should be required to attend school with HIV- (human immunodeficiency virus) infected students.

Current medical research has found that AIDS can only be transmitted through infected blood or semen. Obviously, this means you and students in your classroom will not be at risk from ordinary contact with children who have HIV or AIDS. Yet, as you will read in Vignette 12.4, the emotional issues AIDS raises are many.

VIGNETTE 12.4   *Anita and AIDS*

"I don't care what you say, or what those doctors tell you about AIDS and how you can get it! You are the principal of this school. Kick her out!" Mr. Reynolds was upset. "I don't want my child being close to that kid with AIDS. It's contagious. I don't want her touching my kid!"

Mrs. Gomez was frustrated. Her superintendent had telephoned her last night to tell her Anita was HIV-positive. She didn't know the circumstances—in fact, she didn't want to know. Most of the evening she had cried. Anita was a bright girl and an excellent student. Her first reaction was to visit Anita and her parents, but it had been too late in the evening. Now she had to deal with an irate, scared parent who knew little or nothing about the virus.

"I understand how you feel, Mr. Reynolds, but right now Anita does not have AIDS. She isn't a danger to anyone. She . . . ."

Mr. Reynolds broke in, "I don't believe you, Mrs. Gomez. I want Anita out of this school now or I'm going to the school board!"

???   *Assume you are a member of the school board. Would you vote to remove Anita from school? Why?*

Not surprisingly, communities and school districts have reacted differently. In 1987, Ryan White, a 13-year-old hemophiliac, became infected with the AIDS virus through a transfusion. The Kokomo, Indiana, schools refused to let him return to his classroom. Ryan's parents were forced to move to Cicero, Indiana, where he was warmly welcomed by teachers and students in a highly publicized media event. In Arcadia, Florida, the Ray family home was burned because their three HIV-positive children attended the local school. Each child was a hemophiliac.

What should your attitude about AIDS be, as a classroom teacher? First, remember that all parents are required by law to educate their children. Second, schools have a responsibility for children's health. It is for that reason parents are required to have their children immunized before they enroll in school. HIV-infected children are citizens of the United States, and have the same constitutional rights to an education as all citizens. Communities and schools that refuse to allow children with HIV/AIDS to attend school are acting illegally.

Nonetheless, AIDS still represents a problem to your students' parents if they are uninformed. The best way to help people like Mr. Reynolds understand HIV/AIDS is through education. Parental AIDS education programs are usually held in schools or homes of children who have AIDS. An excellent example of an AIDS education program was conducted by the Pilsen Academy in Chicago, Illinois. After learning about AIDS, parents who had previously expressed the same fears as Mr. Reynolds welcomed an AIDS-infected student into the school.

Teen Suicide

We often have difficulty understanding the extraordinary tensions that compel a young person to commit suicide. Students, like adults, are worried about what their lives will be like in the future. Young people often feel under immense pressure from society, which influences their thoughts about what their future will be like.

There are many warning signs of suicide by teenagers. While the following is a sample, you should become familiar with others as well.

- Teenagers become involved in crime, vandalism, drugs, alcohol, and sexual promiscuity.

- Teenagers have feelings of anger, confusion, and low self-esteem.
- Teenagers lose interest in school, classmates, and teachers.

Young people respond to teachers who take an active and personal interest in them. As a classroom teacher, you should reach out to students and learn about their world beyond the classroom. For many students, you may be the only adult in their lives who is not threatening them or their future.

Teaching Runaways and Homeless Children

We do not know the actual number of children who run away from home or become homeless each year. Some speculate that 273,000 school-age children roam our streets. Others estimate there may be as many as 750,000 children living on the streets (Quint, 1994). Vignette 12.5 is a verbatim transcription of a tape recording Quint captured at a homeless shelter.

VIGNETTE 12.5

What homelessness means to me:
The words of an eleven-year-old girl

You think you know what homeless mean but you don't know nothin' 'bout homeless. You think homeless mean you ain't got no apartment, you ain't got no bed for yourself, ain't got no place to wash off when you soil or you be sweaty. Well, bein' homeless mean more than all that.

I mean you don't got no next-door neighbor, no best friend no more. You don't got no favorite place to play or hide your candy money. You don't even got your own seat in your own classroom, you be movin' so many time. Don't know the teacher name. So who care? She don't know your name either.

You ain't got no good memories of holidays or the movies or even rides. You ain't even got yourself bad memories. You know why? You bet you don't! Cause one shelter look like the next, and soon you can't remember how long you been in this one or that one. Anyway, it don't make no difference. Not after a whiles it don't. You know why? Cause you be doublin' up so many nights in the same bed covers, sharin' the same potty so many night, that one mornin' you wake up and you ain't sure who you is anymore. Maybe you still you, maybe you turn into the other person.

So don't tell me you knows 'bout homeless kids. And don't ask me if I understand what happenin' to my family bein' we got no home. They invisible and so is me. I not here anymore. I died three year ago. Hey, you wastin' your time talkin' to a dead person.

Source: Schooling Homeless Children: A Working Model for America's Public Schools by S. Quint, p. 13. Copyright © 1994 by Teachers College Press, Columbia University. Reprinted by permission of Teachers College, Columbia University.

??? *You may have 'heard' many emotions in this transcription. What do you think the speaker's feelings are? If you were her teacher, what would you do?*

Obviously, schools and teachers can't solve all the problems of homeless families and runaway children, but they can help. Some teachers work with agencies to help children enroll in school. Others work with community shelters where schoolchildren are identified and enrolled in school. Still others assist in the tedious but important task of having children's school records found and sent to the appropriate school. Some teachers meet after school with children so they can have a quiet, secure place to study or participate in cultural events that are meaningful to them. It is common for teachers to mentor students—tutor them so they can catch up on the schoolwork they may have missed during the past weeks or months. Some teachers help parents of homeless children find jobs, homes, clothing, food, and other necessities. If you don't know how to help, go to your local community center and volunteer your services.

Schools in a Child's World

We've discussed how teachers can help students learn in the classroom. Let's look at what legislatures and schools are doing to help children.

Legislation

As crime in the classroom has increased, both federal and state governments have passed legislation aimed at making our schools safer places for students and teachers. In 1994, Congress passed the **Safe Schools Act.** This Act allocated federal monies to states for the development of programs that would prevent crime in the school and decrease the use of drugs and alcohol by students. Some programs are located in schools, other programs counsel students about the hazards of firearms, and others help students learn to live and work together.

States have also passed legislation to improve the safety of children in the classroom. Some states have made it illegal for any person to carry or fire a weapon close to a school. These **gun-free zones,** as they are called, are modeled after the federal Gun-Free School Act of 1990, which prohibits anyone from carrying or firing a weapon within 1,000 feet of a school. The Act, as amended in 1994, requires schools to suspend for one year students who bring guns to school. While states are not required to comply with the federal legislation, the government has indicated it will refuse to distribute federal school monies to those that do not. Some states have also passed legislation in which schools have been declared **drug-free zones** as well. This legislation makes it a criminal offense for any person to buy, sell, or use drugs on, or within a certain area around, school property.

Violence Prevention Strategies

Throughout the country, many school boards have adopted violence prevention strategies as well. The most widely used strategy is student patrol programs, in which students are escorted to and from school buses by fellow students or teachers. Other

Using words: Talking about violence.

school districts, such as Washington, D.C., have developed programs in which students are encouraged to inform on classmates who come to school armed. In this case, student–informers' names are not made public for fear of gang reprisal.

Many schools have dress codes, so gang members cannot advertise their colors and clothing styles. Others have removed public telephones so students cannot make drug deals between classes. Some schools arrange partnerships in which college students mentor elementary and secondary students, in order to give younger students role models so they will understand the benefits of staying in school. These programs are especially beneficial for teacher education students, because they give real-life experiences of life in schools and the community.

All these strategies are designed to create safe havens within schools, so students will feel they are beyond the reach of crime or danger. Their success depends to a great degree on the commitment of classroom teachers and the community to helping children.

School Culture

The first responsibility schools have to their students is to guarantee a safe learning environment. But does that mean students will learn after their environment has become safe? A number of studies (Achilles and Smith, 1994) show that students learn best when they are properly treated and shown proper respect by teachers and administrators. Schools have an obligation to create an environment in which students are appreciated and recognized as individuals and human beings.

School culture can be defined in many ways. Some teachers think of it as school spirit or the sensitivities students, teachers, and administrators have about the school. Other teachers think of it as the mood or personality of your school. Still others think it is the way students, teachers, and administrators think about themselves.

Creating and maintaining a positive school culture is everyone's business. But, as a teacher, you will notice it is the responsibility of the principal to set the tone of the school. Principals are the instructional leaders of the school. Just as you will be expected to set the climate of your classroom, principals are expected to set the tone of the school. It is through the principal's leadership that school culture is developed. Positive school cultures aim at helping children and teachers learn and teach to the best of their ability. A positive school culture also gives parents and caregivers opportunities to become involved with teachers, counselors, and others in the school who help their children learn. That is, school culture fosters a sense of community.

Classroom Culture

Just as the school's culture is the principal's responsibility, the **classroom culture** is your responsibility as a classroom teacher. How can you build a positive classroom culture? Of course, there are many ways. One way is to communicate your respect for the cultures and ethnicities of your students. Try to appreciate the wealth of cultural experiences your children represent, and use them as a resource in your classroom.

For example, Asian children are taught that teachers are authority figures. Consequently, some students find it difficult to ask questions. If you want your students to change their behavior in your class, it is important that you change first. Vignette 12.6 is an illustration of a classroom teacher who is not able to appreciate the culture of one of her students.

VIGNETTE 12.6   *Kenny Patu's smile*

Kenny Patu is a new student in Janice Smith's English literature classroom. He transferred to Carson High from Samoa when his father was relocated by his company.

"I tell you, Marie, it gets on my nerves," Janice says. "All he does is smile—nobody can be that happy."

Marie teaches history across the hall from Janice. "I have Kenny in my second-hour World History class. He's a good student, and I like the way he has blended into the class. In fact, I've noticed he's made friends easily."

"Oh, I've noticed the same thing," says Janice. "But I want him to take his literature more seriously—and he'll have to change if he wants to get through my class!"

??? *Can you describe Janice Smith's classroom culture? Will Kenny Patu learn as well in Janice's classroom as in Marie's?*

What can you do to make your classroom culture a positive learning environment? Purkey (1992) describes classroom cultures as either Inviting or Disinviting. He believes classroom teachers create the classroom culture based on their personal and professional attitudes. Using Purkey's theory, we can describe Janice Smith's feelings about Kenny Patu as Disinviting. She intends to have him change to meet her expectations, regardless of his cultural background. In fact, she is demeaning him. Professionally, Janice is Disinviting. She wants to use her power as a classroom teacher to have Kenny learn the way she wants him to.

As you become more aware of how your classroom culture influences your students' learning, it will change your classroom management. Let's look at classroom management in relation to your students' expectations, the physical layout of your classroom, and your relations with students.

Student Expectations.   Students should have a clear idea of what you, as a teacher, expect of them. You can help students learn by helping them understand your teaching philosophy. They should know your goals, the parameters of behavior in your class, and how you will enforce your rules. This helps students see their classwork as important to their learning.

Classroom.   Your classroom should be a reflection of your students as well as you and your teaching philosophy. The classroom should be a physical acknowledgment of the cultural heritage of your students, and it should facilitate your instructional style. That is, the physical arrangements of your classroom should allow you to monitor student learning and interact with students individually or in groups. This means you will be able to help students who are having difficulty learning or are confused about what they are supposed to do.

Teacher/Student Relationships.   An enjoyable part of teaching is learning about your students, who have much to offer. As a teacher, you will learn about your students' learning styles, what their interests are, and how and what they expect to learn in your class. Your students will evaluate your classroom culture by how you treat them in public and in private. They don't want you to publicly embarrass them or become emotional over classroom problems. They expect your classroom management style to be fair and understanding of them.

Two Schools in a Child's World

You might wonder whether it is possible for schools and classrooms to have positive cultures in which children of different cultures, ethnicities, races, and economic status can learn. We are going to look at two elementary schools to see how they incorporate their children's lives into the school and classroom cultures.

The Manhattan Country Day School is a nonpublic school in New York City with students from many different cultures. The Benjamin Franklin Day School is a public school in Seattle with students from poor and homeless families. Even though the types of students and teachers at these two schools are different, the schools' cultures are very similar.

Manhattan Country Day School

The Manhattan Country Day School is a nonpublic elementary school founded in the 1960s. Its beginning was influenced by the civil rights movement. Its founder, Augustus Trowbridge, envisioned a school in which children could learn how to live together in a multicultural society. The school's location was purposely chosen to be close to Central Park, the cultural border between midtown New York and East Harlem. This location allows the school to be a laboratory for children representing the various races, cultures, and ethnicities. In 1992, the school enrolled 185 students, with two of every three children receiving financial aid.

Students at Manhattan Country Day School are required to participate in many common experiences outside their regular classrooms. To build a sense of community, students are encouraged to visit or work in community action groups and recycling and pollution control projects. They are encouraged to visit local senior citizen centers or other community projects.

Because of the large Puerto Rican population, all students are required to learn Spanish. The school believes it is important that its children understand the political, religious, and racial diversity of the Hispanic world. Students have experiences in becoming culturally tolerant. Other common experiences are in traditional areas, such as art, physical education, and shop. Manhattan Country Day School has a farm in the Catskill Mountains where children gain new experiences.

In order to maintain small, intimate classes, Manhattan Country Day School has divided its students into Upper and Lower Schools. The Upper School comprises Grades 5 through 8. The Lower School comprises Kindergarten to Grade 4. Each student is given a placement test when he or she enrolls, to assist the school in placement of students.

Each classroom reflects the school's climate. Each student is encouraged to believe that he or she has a voice in what happens in the classroom. In the Lower School, children are encouraged to voice their opinions. It is here that they begin to learn who they are. Upper School teachers are continually emphasizing students' critical thinking skills. Students are encouraged to think about situations and draw conclusions they are able to support. For students, this classroom culture allows them the security to be wrong and/or to defend their ideas.

One teacher explained classroom culture as an environment:

> What's important about the environment is that each child has a voice, and that they learn they have a voice. Unless they can share who they are, I don't think they can go on to listen to who everyone else is. With the very youngest children, you're creating an environment where they feel open to expressing themselves about who they are, in whatever form that might take. (Bennett, 1992, p. 86)

Manhattan Country Day School's purpose is to help students relate to others in their school and in their neighborhoods. Classroom teachers and students know what they are supposed to teach and learn at Manhattan Country Day School. While the teachers understand they are part of a professional group, they also know their students are resources who can help them.

Benjamin Franklin Day School

In her book, *Schooling Homeless Children,* Sharon Quint describes a time when Benjamin Franklin Day School was dysfunctional. This public school in Seattle was controlled by a small group of ten to twelve boys who threatened fellow students and teachers alike. Day after day the same students were sent to the principal's office. Vandalism, absenteeism, and physical threats to teachers were counterbalanced by teachers' rejection of students.

Then Carole Williams became principal. Williams changed the school by changing its classroom and school cultures. Previously, Benjamin Franklin Day School teachers assumed their students' learning disabilities were caused by their poor social and economic level. Williams acknowledged that many of the children were homeless, lived in poverty, came from single-parent homes, or were dependent on welfare, but it was important to her that these circumstances not describe *who* the children were.

Benjamin Franklin Day School's school culture changed. At one time teachers felt excluded and separated from each other. Now, they were part of a team, each helping others. As one teacher stated,

> The truth is that we all need help at one time or another, whether we are courageous enough to admit it or not. From that day on, I didn't think twice about saying the "H" word—Help! (Quint, 1994, p. 24)

As teachers learned how to become part of a professional instructional group, they were able to establish a sense of community. That is, they understood and appreciated the importance of other teachers, neighborhood volunteers, and support workers. Benjamin Franklin Day School's teachers became aware of the world their children brought to the classroom. Through field trips, teachers learned about the dismal reality of their children's world.

> Although such trips were not mandated, most teachers did in fact accept the responsibility and challenge of learning about the neighborhood. It was this face-to-face encounter with painful ghetto reality that formed a bond of morality and purposeful interaction between and among students, teachers, and parents. (Quint, 1994, p. 123)

As parents and others within the neighborhood joined Benjamin Franklin Day's volunteer group, their attitudes about the school changed. Parents understood the teachers' dedication and difficulties and their need for help. Teachers understood the need to allow parents to be equal partners in the education of their children.

Williams believed all children come to school ready to learn. She wanted children to be responsible for part of their learning. Classroom teachers changed their instructional methods to include self-paced or self-directed learning. Many of the worksheets teachers photocopied for student use were replaced with classroom assignments students found interesting. Rote learning was replaced with students and teachers talking and interacting with each other. This led teachers to helping students in their critical thinking and communication skills. For the first time, children were learning something beyond the basics.

What Makes These Schools Successful?

As you read about the Manhattan Country Day School and the Benjamin Franklin Day School, did you notice at first how different they were? After reading about the schools, did you notice how similar they really are? To help children learn, both schools look at their students in a unique way. Students are treated as individuals worthy of respect. Classroom teachers understand that if their students are to learn, they are going to have to change first. Teachers are willing to share with their students the responsibility for learning. Classrooms are exciting places for students and teachers alike. In both schools, classroom teachers and administrators are part of a team. The school cultures encourage teachers, administrators, and support personnel to be personally and professionally committed to the welfare of students. Finally, both schools help children by incorporating the community into each student's learning experience. The Manhattan Country Day School does this by encouraging students to become familiar with the various neighborhoods surrounding the school. The Benjamin Franklin Day School invites parents, many of whom are school dropouts, to become involved with their children's education. In each case, the schools are successful because the students understand that their education requires more than just passively sitting in a classroom. Students recognize that what they learn in the classroom helps them live better lives in a complex society.

What You Have Learned

✔ Teachers mostly represent middle-class, Euro-America, while their students represent a diverse, multicultural society.

✔ Teachers understand that if they wish to teach children in a diverse, multicultural society, they must learn about the world outside the classroom.

✔ Schools have discovered that if they want to help children learn, they must develop strategies to keep them safe in school.

✔ Classroom and school cultures are ways schools and teachers can help children learn.

✔ There are numerous examples of schools in the United States that have developed strategies to help children who come from different cultures, ethnicities, and levels of income learn successfully.

Key Terms

transgressors
closed campuses
Safe Schools Act
gun-free zones

drug-free zones
school culture
classroom culture

Applying What You Have Learned

1. Mrs. Baxter in *Becoming a Teacher* learned a valuable lesson when she visited Mario. Why do you think she would make a good teacher at the Benjamin Franklin Day School?

2. *School culture* refers to the attitudes teachers, students, and principals have about their school. Interview several principals about how they influence the culture of their school.

3. You are a classroom teacher who believes there is strong evidence one of your students is being abused by her father. What is your strategy to help your student? Interview a school counselor to check how well you answered the question.

4. In Chapter 11 you were asked whether schools have a responsibility to help children who are victims. After studying this chapter, how would you answer the question? Have you changed your mind? Why?

Interactive Learning

1. Ask several teachers if they will let you observe their classrooms for part of a day. Observe students working independently, with others, and with the teacher so you can observe classroom culture in action.

2. In a small group, discuss the warning signs of suicide. Interview several teachers and ask them how they helped students who had a friend commit suicide.

3. Interview several principals and teachers about how they developed the culture within their schools and classrooms. Compare their answers.

4. Visit a mall or major street in your community. Pay close attention to children who appear to be without adult supervision. Do you think these children are homeless? What characteristics do they exhibit which make you think they are homeless?

Expanding Your Knowledge

McLaren, Peter. *Life in School*. White Plains: Longman Publishing, 1994. (A compelling text about what life is really like in school. Analyzes the underlying political and social factors that influence our classroom practices.)

Perkinson, Henry J. *Teachers Without Goals—Students Without Purposes*. New York: McGraw-Hill, 1993. (The author wants teachers to think about students learning by building on past experiences. He believes schools should be responsible for more than teaching students a fixed body of knowledge.)

Quint, Sharon. *Schooling Homeless Children: A Working Model for America's Public Schools*. New York: Teachers College Press, 1994. (It will be difficult to put this book down until you find out what Carole Williams does at Benjamin Franklin Day School to help homeless and poor children learn successfully.)

Part Six

Effective Classrooms, Professional Teachers

In Part Six you will learn how schools and classrooms are changing and what your first years as a classroom teacher will be like. Chapter 13 describes some of the recent controversies about what students should learn and how teachers should teach. Matt Walkingstick, in *Becoming a Teacher* in Chapter 13, represents the crux of the controversy about school reform. He is angry because Mrs. Ivers, his foreign language teacher, advised him to improve his French if he wants to go to college. Because Matt speaks a Native-American language he feels degraded. He already knows a foreign language: English.

Some support Mrs. Ivers. These "first-wave reformers" want the school to focus its curriculum on America's European heritage. They believe Matt and students like him must know the nation's Euro-centered heritage, or society will suffer. They believe this heritage will help the nation improve its ability to compete economically in an international marketplace. It is for this reason, they say, that Matt will be employed when he becomes an adult.

On the other hand, "second-wave reformers" believe that forcing students like Matt to forsake their heritage will damage them and the country's pluralistic traditions. They believe schools should educate students to live fuller lives and help them become employable. Both reform waves try to dictate how classroom teachers should test students and what type of teaching methods are best.

As a classroom teacher, you will be bombarded with studies, reports, and news releases about what parents, the public, and other educators expect you to accomplish in your classroom. How will you choose which is best? To prepare yourself for studying Chapter 13, outline some of your ideas about the shortcomings of schools. Briefly explain how you would correct them. As you read Chapter 13, evaluate your answers to discover if you are a first- or second-wave reformer.

As you will learn in Part 6, teaching is not confusing so much as it is complex. This is what Laurie Ferriri is learning in *Becoming a Teacher* in Chapter 14. Laurie (who, you may recall, nervously began her first day as a classroom teacher in Chapter 1) is finishing her final class at the end of the same day. She is on the first step of becoming a professional when she grasps the social, cultural, and academic interplay between students and teachers. She even recognizes the significant role parents play in the lives of students.

In studying Part 6, you will become aware that classroom teaching is a way of life. If you are like Laurie, you will never stop growing and learning as a classroom teacher. As you relate to other teachers, the curriculum, and your students, you will learn more about yourself. You will develop a philosophy of education that will guide your actions both in the classroom and out.

Chapter 14 gives you helpful advice about how to find the right teaching position. While you may have several years of study left before you graduate, you should begin thinking about what and where you would like to teach. Now is the time to begin building your resume for your first interview.

Educational Reform and Effective Classrooms

In Chapter 13, you will learn about the excitement the new pluralistic society is presenting to schools and teachers. You will learn what some of our most respected educators and teachers are saying about educational reform. Reform can be an emotional issue for teachers and students alike. This chapter will increase your understanding of what teachers and educators are saying about schools, so you will be better able to grasp the changes in teaching.

American society is changing rapidly, and the classroom is changing along with it. If you were to visit your elementary school or high school, you would see differences in what students are now learning compared to when you were a student. You probably would see a noticeable difference in the types of students who are attending your old school. Not only do these students represent different cultures and ethnicities, but they face different social problems, express different values, and have different personal goals than you did during those years.

What you will learn

- The educational reform movement illustrates social conflict about what students should learn in school in our multicultural society.

- The educational reform movement will continue to change as our nation becomes more diverse.

- The educational reform movement has emphasized teacher effectiveness as well as curricular change.

BECOMING A TEACHER   *What is a foreign language?*

Matt Walkingstick is mad. It isn't right to be so angry, he tells himself, but things just aren't right.

"Here I am," he tells himself, "a junior in high school, and they tell me I'm dumb." Slamming his books down on the kitchen table, he tells his mother, "Mom, remember the tests I took last month from the state department of education? Well, I flunked!"

"Matt," his mother says, "You can't fail those tests. They are only supposed to tell you how good an education you are getting. After all, if you want to go to college, you will have to know what the teachers are talking about."

"I know, Mom," Matt mutters, "but Mrs. Ivers said this was all part of school reform, whatever that means. And Mrs. Ivers told some of us Native Americans we were responsible for not doing well, because of our poor background."

"Did she really say that, Matt, word for word?" His mom's voice sounded hurt.

"No, not word for word, but that's what she meant. She said we did poorly on the test because we didn't know such things as what the Mayflower Compact was. Well, I bet she doesn't know what the Iroquois Confederacy was about—and that's just as important!"

"You know, it's sort of sad," says Matt, "Mrs. Ivers said if I wanted to go to college, I needed to do better in my French. She said knowing Kiowa wasn't the same thing, because most colleges don't count that as a foreign language. Sounds stupid to me. Kiowa was spoken in this country before the Puritans came. I told her that for me, English is a foreign language."

??? *When Mrs. Ivers told Matt the tests were part of reforming schools, she meant schools should become better equipped to give students a quality education. Why do Mrs. Ivers and Matt not seem to understand each other? What would you tell them if you were there?*

Reasons for Educational Reform

Americans have always taken education seriously and, once again, society has become interested in the quality of education students are receiving. One reason is the tremendous social changes caused by technological advances such as the computer. Another reason is the economic dislocations caused by the internationalization of industry and America's entrance into the international marketplace. The most significant reason for society becoming interested in schools is the speed and manner in which the nation is becoming increasingly pluralistic. The United States is becoming a cultural and ethnic reflection of ideas and values held by peoples throughout the world.

Teachers

Classroom teachers pay close attention to the types of problems students experience. During the 1980s, they became concerned about whether schools were preparing students to succeed in an increasingly complex society. Many teachers, like Mrs. Ivers, felt some students would not succeed when they left school. Students, they insisted, had little or no comprehension of such basic skills as reading and writing or speaking a foreign language. One report, the *National Assessment of Education Progress,* administered by the National Center for Education Statistics, reaffirmed what many classroom teachers already knew. For more than 20 years, the NAEP has quantified the achievements of American students.

> When the NAEP results are taken as a whole . . . the result is a bleak portrait of the status of student achievement in the United States. Large proportions, perhaps more

than half, of our elementary, middle school, and high school students are unable to demonstrate competence in challenging subject matter in English, mathematics, science, history, and geography. . . . Fewer than 10 percent appear to have both an understanding of the specialized material and ideas comprising the curriculum area and the ability to work with these data to interpret, integrate, infer, draw generalizations, and articulate conclusions. (Mullins, Avens, & Phillips, 1990)

Teachers are aware that how well students learn is a reflection of where students live and the home lives they have. Children with well-educated parents have an increased opportunity of receiving a better education than children whose parents are less educated. Students whose parents have steady jobs have a greater opportunity to succeed than children whose parents are chronically unemployed. Further, Mullins and Jenkins (1990) found a wide discrepancy among children of different ethnic and cultural groups in their ability to read. For example, they stated that white 9-year-old children were able to read almost as well as 13-year-old African-American and 17-year-old Hispanic-American children. This is because of economic and social backgrounds of the children, not because of their culture or ethnicity.

An extension of the NAEP study in 1993 found students knew more mathematics than before, although 40 percent of all 17-year-olds still did not demonstrate a basic proficiency in mathematics. Perhaps one reason is that students do not get much class time to solve mathematics problems. Mathematics tests traditionally stress giving the right answer, not the method of arriving at the right answer.

Ask a friend to solve this fourth-grade mathematics problem given by the NEAP study:

Jose ate half a pizza. He had eaten more pizza than his friend Ella, who had also eaten half a pizza. How could Jose have eaten more than Ella?
(*Answer:* Ella's pizza was smaller than Jose's.)

Only 23 percent of all fourth-graders in the United States were able to give a satisfactory answer. Nearly half of the students gave an incorrect response, and 7 percent felt the question was too difficult for them.

Students

Students in the 1980s were also dissatisfied with their educational experiences. For example, Hafner, Ingels, Schneider, and Stevenson (1990) studied Asian, African, Native, Hispanic and Non-Hispanic White eighth graders, or 13-year-olds, in 1988. They discovered that approximately one-fourth of Asian Americans and Non-Hispanic Whites were below the basic math level eighth graders were expected to know. Approximately half of Native Americans, almost 60 percent of Hispanics, and 70 percent of African Americans were below the basic math level. Students representing all ethnic groups did less well than Non-Hispanic Whites, who scored 26 percent on the test.

Increasing numbers of students dropped out of school because they found no satisfaction in learning and seldom succeeded in the classroom. They felt what they learned (or didn't learn) there was separate from their out-of-school lives. Throughout their study, Hafner et al observed students who had experienced social and academic failure. It was shocking to her to notice that the percentage of 17-year-old high school graduates declined beginning in 1970 (U.S. Department of Education, 1990). In that year, 76 percent of all 17-year-olds graduated from high school. It would be 1990 before that same percentage would graduate from high school again.

To help place these figures in perspective for you, Kennedy (1992) reported that Japan was much more successful in having students complete high school. He states that more than 90 percent of all Japanese students graduate from high school. This rate is greater than the United States or European countries. Only 0.7 percent of Japanese citizens are illiterate.

The Hafner study and the National Assessment of Educational Progress reflect a diverse society, in which many cultures, ethnicities, and races participate. Kennedy was reporting educational results from a homogeneous society that relies on group consensus. With this in mind, let's look at educational reform and discover how it is changing our schools.

Educational Reform

Educational reform is an emotional issue. You may have heard your friends or education professors voice specific—but contradictory—ideas about how education should be reformed. You may be puzzled about what you should expect students in your classroom to learn when you become a teacher. To help you overcome any confusion about the reform movement, we have divided it into several segments, or waves.

The **first-wave reform movement** is concerned with improving the academic qualifications of students and classroom teachers by reinforcing the traditional Eurocentric curriculum. The first wave wants classroom teachers to teach students— regardless of their ethnicity or cultural heritage—how to live in a Euro-centered society.

The **second-wave reform movement** is also interested in the quality of education children receive in our classrooms, but it wants classroom teachers to help students learn how to live in a pluralistic society. The second-wave reform movement emphasizes a multicultural curriculum in which children learn about different cultures as well as their own.

Each reformer, regardless of her or his philosophy, is attempting to make you a more effective teacher, but in different ways. It is important for you to become aware of some of the major education reform programs and their advocates before you become a classroom teacher; that is what this chapter attempts to do.

First-Wave Reports

At the beginning of the 1980s, many industrial leaders and legislators were concerned that the United States could not economically compete in a global society in which nations compete economically, socially, and educationally. Prominent politicians and business executives blamed schools for industry's problems, because they contended classroom teachers were not producing educated workers. The first wave of educational reform, therefore, is known for its reports that criticize schools and classroom teachers for their inability to educate students. Figure 13.1 describes two of the first wave's most devastating reports. Notice they identify schools' problems and offer solutions.

A Nation At Risk (1983).   The reports in Figure 13.1 are important because they illustrate why industrial and political leaders wanted school reform. But it was the report, *A Nation At Risk* (National Commission on Excellence in Education, 1983) that struck a chord with classroom teachers and the public alike. The report called for the total reform of schools in the United States. Unlike reports written for scholars, *A Nation At Risk* was an open letter to the American people. It strongly criticized teachers for not demanding more from their students and issued a dramatic warning. As you read the report's introductory paragraph in Figure 13.2, notice its powerful language.

The recommendations of *A Nation At Risk* focused on core curriculum, elementary school standards, student expectations, time, teaching, and leadership and fiscal support. Because of the report's tremendous impact on educators at the federal, state, and local levels, each of the areas is briefly described here so you can reflect on how it may influence your own philosophy of teaching.

Figure 13.1   Selected First-Wave Education Reform Reports

Action for Excellence: A Comprehensive Plan to Improve Our Nation's Schools (1983).   This report was written by the Task Force of the Education Commission of the States. It urges state legislatures to become increasingly involved in schools. It suggests schools should be more accountable to local and state authorities. Classroom teachers should be better trained and paid higher salaries. Most important, the schools' curriculums should be academically demanding. The report stresses teachers are not challenging students, and therefore, they are not working to their full potential.

What Matters Most: Teaching For America's Future (1997).   Written by the National Commission on Teaching and America's Future, this report is extremely critical of America's teachers. It places the blame for low student performance on unenforced teacher standards, poor teacher preparation, and school district recruitment procedures. While it points out few rewards for teachers, it does discuss how schools are structured for failure. The report offers several solutions, including developing academic and professional standards for teachers and establishing standards boards in all states. In short, the only way students will receive a better education is to have better trained teachers.

Figure 13.2   *A Nation at Risk*

Our nation is at risk. Our once-unchallenged preeminence in commerce, industry, science, and technological innovation is being overtaken by competitors throughout the world. This report is concerned with only one of the many causes and dimensions of the problem, but it is the one that undergirds American prosperity, security, and civility. We report to the American people that while we can take justifiable pride in what our schools and colleges have historically accomplished and contributed to the United States and the well-being of its people, the educational foundations of our society are presently being eroded by a rising tide of mediocrity that threatens our very future as a nation and as a people. What was unimaginable a generation ago has begun to occur—others are matching and surpassing our educational attainments.

Source: The President's Commission on Excellence in Education, *A Nation at Risk: The Imperative for Education Reform* (Washington, D.C.: U.S. Department of Education, 1983): p. 5.

Core Curriculum.   *A Nation At Risk* recommended that English, mathematics, science, and social studies courses be more rigorous, to better prepare students for college or the workplace. Computer literacy and the study of foreign languages are encouraged because of the impact of technology and international economic competition. The report emphasizes that the core curriculum is important because it teaches about a complicated Euro-centered society struggling to retain its international influence.

Elementary School Standards.   Although *A Nation At Risk* is more concerned with secondary education, it recognizes that if high schools are to change, then elementary schools must change too. The report states that the elementary school's major purpose is to prepare students for high school. It reasons that student enthusiasm for learning in high school can only come from a firm academic foundation received in elementary classrooms. This means the basic high school core areas also need to be taught in the elementary school, along with the arts and foreign language. The report recommends students study foreign languages for four to six years beginning in elementary school.

Student Expectations.   *A Nation At Risk* issued a wealth of recommendations about student grades, textbooks, and college entrance requirements. Reacting to public criticism that classroom teachers graded students too easily, the report spoke out against grade inflation. The report asserts that grades should reflect only what students have actually learned in a classroom, not what the teacher assumes they have learned.

The report states that most textbooks are not distinguished for their academic content. Therefore, noted scholars should become more involved in writing high school textbooks. In the area of college entrance requirements, *A Nation At Risk* challenged four-year colleges and universities to accept qualified students while they are still in high school. Bright students who are not academically challenged by high school courses should be encouraged to attend college.

Time.   *A Nation At Risk* notes that students do not have adequate class time to learn. Unlike Japanese students who are in school for 220 days each academic year, American students, on the average, attend school for only 180 days. To make up for lost classroom time, the report encourages classroom teachers to give students more homework and teach them better study skills.

Teachers were delighted that the report acknowledged the amount of classroom time they spent policing unruly students. The report encouraged school boards to impose strong codes of conduct on students who cannot learn in normal classroom settings. Knowing many students will drop out, the report recommended school boards build alternative schools in which students study at different times during the day and classroom teachers use a wider variety of teaching methods.

Teaching.   The report acknowledged that classroom teachers are overworked and underpaid. Therefore, it wants teachers to be employed for eleven months each year instead of the traditional nine months. The additional two months, the report states, can be used to give teachers the much-needed opportunity to work on curriculum development and participate in faculty development activities. The report is in favor of higher teacher salaries in conjunction with more rigorous teacher preparation programs at the college level. Teacher education majors, the report states, should be required to meet the higher academic standards found in other college departments.

Leadership and Fiscal Support.   Because *A Nation At Risk* is not a piece of legislation, it relies on state and local political, educational, and business leaders to achieve its goals. State legislatures and governors are encouraged to pass reform legislation that can be implemented by state departments of education. But the critical leadership, the reports states, has to come at the local level with superintendents and principals persuading classroom teachers to change.

First-Wave Reformers

Supporting the ideas proposed by *A Nation At Risk* is a group of distinguished authors, many of whom you probably recognize by name. While their philosophies about educational reform differ somewhat, what binds them together is their belief that the traditional Euro-centered heritage is no longer being taught in our classrooms. It is their contention that America's cultural past will be forgotten as students become more aware of the cultural and ethnic diversity of our society. They are concerned that present Euro-centered values will be polluted by the values, ideas, and histories of immigrants from other nations and other cultures. The reformers do not believe classroom teachers are well prepared to give students the education they consider essential.

Allan Bloom.   Allan Bloom, author of *The Closing of the American Mind* (1987), is convinced that classroom teachers have failed the nation by giving students an increasingly poor education. He sees students as disinterested in their education. They are unchallenged in the classroom, he believes, and are committed to their own personal pleasures. He says:

> Students these days are, in general, nice. I choose the word carefully. They are not particularly moral or noble. Such niceness is a facet of democratic character when times are good. Neither war nor tyranny nor want has hardened them or made demands on them. The words and rivalries caused by class distinction have disappeared along with any strong sense of class (as it once existed in universities in America and as it still does, poisonously, in England). Students are free of most constraints, and their families make sacrifices for them without asking for much in the way of obedience or respect. Religion and national origin have almost no noticeable effect on their social life or their career prospects. Although few really believe in "the system," they do not have any burning sentiment that injustice is being done to them. The drugs and the sex once thought to be forbidden are available in the quantities required for sensible use. (Bloom, 1987, p. 82)

To combat this social and educational decline, Bloom proposes that colleges and universities teach a **great books curriculum,** a series of Euro-centric texts that teach European history, literature, philosophy, and culture. This, he says, should bring students of differing cultural and ethnic backgrounds into the mainstream of American society.

E. D. Hirsch, Jr.   Hirsch's best-selling book *Cultural Literacy* (1987) supports Bloom's fear that schools don't teach students how to survive in today's world. He lists terms (such as *Huns, dark horse, "I am the state,"* and others) that he believes every good American student should know regardless of cultural or ethnic background.

Hirsch believes well-educated students must have a strong Euro-centered academic background to survive in our culture. Students who have different cultural or ethnic backgrounds will only succeed when they become Americanized and reflect the Euro-centered culture. Figure 13.3 presents a list very different from Hirsch's—one that is not Euro-centered. Can you match the terms on this list?

Arthur S. Schlesinger, Jr.   Schlesinger, too, strongly believes our Euro-centered heritage is threatened. The theme of his text, *The Disuniting of America: Reflections on a Multicultural Society* (1992), maintains that the United States may unravel like a multicolored cloth if classroom teachers teach children about the diverse cultures they represent. He believes European culture and traditions are the glue that holds the United States together, and without this glue, our society will collapse. Like Bloom and Hirsch, he wants students whose families are not originally from Europe to be taught a Euro-centered curriculum so they can be assimilated. He says:

Figure 13.3   Can You Match the Term with Its Meaning?

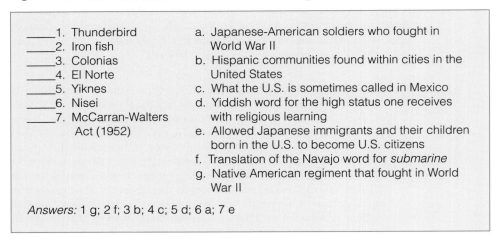

_____1. Thunderbird
_____2. Iron fish
_____3. Colonias
_____4. El Norte
_____5. Yiknes
_____6. Nisei
_____7. McCarran-Walters
          Act (1952)

a. Japanese-American soldiers who fought in World War II
b. Hispanic communities found within cities in the United States
c. What the U.S. is sometimes called in Mexico
d. Yiddish word for the high status one receives with religious learning
e. Allowed Japanese immigrants and their children born in the U.S. to become U.S. citizens
f. Translation of the Navajo word for *submarine*
g. Native American regiment that fought in World War II

Answers: 1 g; 2 f; 3 b; 4 c; 5 d; 6 a; 7 e

The schools and colleges of the republic train the citizens of the future. Our public schools in particular have been the great instrument of assimilation and the great means of forming an American identity. What students are taught in schools affects the way they will thereafter see and treat other Americans, the way they will thereafter conceive the purposes of the republic. The debate about the curriculum is a debate about what it means to be an American. (Schlesinger, 1992, 17)

Second-Wave Reports

The second-wave educational reform movement acknowledges the demographic and social changes that are taking place in contemporary American society. Today's schools are rapidly changing. Children now entering our classrooms reflect an increasingly diverse society. Second-wave reformers assert that schools and classroom teachers should not be blamed for America's social and economic problems. These reformers insist that the problems classroom teachers face today are extremely complicated and cannot be corrected with a few simple solutions.

Many problems facing schools today, second-wave reformers state, stem from difficulties administrators and classroom teachers have in helping children learn in a pluralistic society. They point out that the social problems students encounter in a multicultural society are much different than problems students encounter in a homogeneous society like Japan. Many students in the United States do not have the opportunity to learn because of poor or changing physical, social, and family conditions. Therefore, second-wave reformers believe classroom teachers have a responsibility to educate students to be able to live successfully in a complicated, high-tech, multicultural society.

The second-wave reports summarized in Figure 13.4 describe the day-to-day difficulties students, classroom teachers, and administrators face in our schools.

Figure 13.4 Selected Second-Wave Education Reform Reports

Horace's Compromise: The Dilemma of the American High School (1984). This study, conducted by Theodore Sizer, is an investigation of 80 schools in the United States. Sizer describes the day-to-day difficulties high school teachers face in the classroom. He says teachers are weighed down with paperwork, rules, and regulations that take away time and energy that should be focused on teaching students.

The Shopping Mall High School (1985). Arthur Powell, Eleanor Farar, and David Cohen recommend teachers be given more time for class preparation and professional study. They believe schools operate in a social vacuum. Classroom teachers, they say, are forgotten by society. Parents and others who should have a great interest in the education of their children do not help teachers, nor do they understand what classroom teachers do. They believe schools will improve when parents become involved with their children's education. This means encouraging children to have high expectations of themselves. They also plead with administrators and school boards to give classroom teachers time to teach.

The Last Little Citadel (1986). Robert Hampel found that secondary schools have not changed significantly since the 1940s, even though society has changed dramatically since that time. He found students still follow the same curriculum and class schedules their grandparents did when they were students. Hempel believes students are unhappy in classrooms today and do not learn because schools are obsessed with discipline. He concludes classroom teachers should encourage students to think. Students should not be forced to spend their class time worrying about how or when they are to be punished by teachers and others who say they have a positive interest in them.

Project Equality. This report, commissioned by the College Board, confirms what many classroom teachers suspect is happening to students after they graduate from high school: many students are failing out of college even though they appear to be well prepared. Project Equality states that if students are to succeed in college, elementary and secondary schools must be reformed.

Overall, Project Equality wants education to be a more fulfilling experience for students. While its major focus is helping students prepare for college, Project Equality is also interested in students who have other plans, such as joining the workforce. When the report states that high school students should find their academic and social lives rewarding, it is referring to *all* students, regardless of their personal goals. Project Equality wants classroom teachers to encourage students to have higher expectations of themselves. It wants students to meet the challenges set before them in the classroom. But in order for students to meet these challenges, Project Equality points out, the curriculum must reflect the social reality students live with each day. That is, the curriculum must teach about various cultures and ethnicities in the United States and their contributions to America's heritage. You can appreciate why students do not find their school experience rewarding when their own cultural heritage is excluded from the curriculum.

Unlike *A Nation At Risk,* Project Equality's recommendations focus on what students are *learning* in the classroom rather than on what classroom teachers are *teaching.* Let's look at the Project's recommendations: competencies, basic academic curriculum, and competencies graduating seniors should exhibit.

Competencies.   Project Equality lists six competencies every student needs in order to succeed in college. They are: reading, writing, mathematics, reasoning, understanding, and studying. These competencies, the Project insists, allow students to discriminate between fact and opinion. These competencies are crucial in today's world because they help students learn how to communicate whether they plan on attending college or not. Students will also learn how to set goals, stay on-task, and understand and follow directions.

Basic Academic Curriculum.   Instead of listing subjects students should learn, Project Equality gives reasons why the curriculum should be taught. This allows state departments of education, classroom teachers, and administrators at the local level to become involved in educational reform in a meaningful manner.

Competencies Graduating High School Seniors Should Exhibit.   Project Equality asserts that students should have a clear understanding of how the world is changing. They should be familiar with broad issues, such as how the United States is becoming part of a global society. Project Equality wants students to grasp that this nation is a reflection of the world's cultures and ethnicities. Because we live in an

I like school!

interdependent world, it is extremely important that students understand the cultures of that world.

The curriculum should help students gain an insight into the contributions of the many cultures, ethnicities, and races that call themselves "Americans."

The Project also asserts that high school graduates should understand how their lives are influenced by the rapid growth of knowledge in such areas as ecology, energy, genetics, and many other fields. Schools and classroom teachers can help students by giving them experiences using computers to manage and create information.

Project Equality wants high school students to have a meaningful education that allows them to succeed in college. But the report recognizes that these competencies are important to all students, regardless of their culture or ethnicity or whether they are going to college.

The Basic School: A Community for Learning.   This report, commissioned by the Carnegie Foundation for the Advancement of Teaching and written by Ernest Boyer, focuses reform efforts on elementary schools. Boyer believes it is impossible to improve education by simply reforming secondary education. Boyer says,

> Last fall, more than 3 million kindergarten children enrolled in over 50,000 public and private schools from Bangor, Maine, to the islands of Hawaii. Most of these young students arrived at school anxious, but also eager. Some were cheerful, others troubled. Some skipped and ran, others could not walk. This new generation of students came from countless neighborhoods, from a great diversity of cultures, speaking more languages than most of us could name. And the challenge we now face is to ensure that every child will become a confident, resourceful learner. (Boyer, 1995, p. 3)

Instead of creating a pilot project, an experimental school to test his theories, Boyer surveyed elementary schools throughout the country over a ten-year period. He discovered a great number of elementary programs and practices that are presently working. These, say Boyer, should be copied or modified by schools throughout the nation so they, too, can be successful. He refers to these successful schools as "Basic Schools." Boyer groups the successful practices into four priorities. He says,

> These four priorities—community, curriculum coherence, climate, and character—are the building blocks for the Basic School. Fitted within each of these priorities are specific proposals—programs that, we discovered, really work. The goal of the Basic School is to present an overall strategy for renewal, one that seems to fit all institutions while, at the same time, encouraging every school to develop, within this overarching framework, its own distinctive program. (Boyer, 1995, 8)

Let's look at each of the four priorities briefly. You will notice how each is related or connected to the others.

The School as Community.   The Basic School has a shared vision, in which each classroom is a community in itself. Students and teachers work and learn together throughout the day. The classroom culture has a sense of caring and discipline. It also has a sense of purpose in which students can experience a feeling of justice. The Basic School is alert to our pluralistic society. Basic Schools promote equality of opportunity. Each student is encouraged to feel welcome, regardless of cultural, racial, ethnic, or religious heritage.

Parents are recognized as the students' first teachers. Without a strong partnership between parents and the school, the quality of education will suffer. Just as parents are recognized for their importance, classroom teachers are recognized as educational leaders. The lead teacher, or principal, is responsible for the school, and directs it by motivating classroom teachers and students alike.

Curriculum with Coherence.   The most important aim of the Basic School is literacy. Students are expected to learn how to read and write. They are also required to become proficient in mathematics, the arts, and other subjects. Students are expected to become knowledgeable in eight core commonalities:

- The life cycle
- The use of symbols
- A sense of time and space
- Response to the aesthetic
- Connections to nature
- Producing and consuming
- Memberships in groups
- Living with purpose (Boyer, 1995, p. 85)

Notice that the eight core commonalities are based on experiences all people have, regardless of culture or ethnicity. Boyer wants these core commonalities to connect the basic subjects so students can understand the interrelatedness of knowledge.

Students are evaluated in the Basic School. Academic standards are recognized so students can be assessed. Classroom teachers also informally assess students' personal and social qualities. The purpose of assessment in the Basic School is always to improve student learning.

A Climate for Learning.   Students are taught to become independent thinkers. They are allowed to use their creativity and become self-disciplined. The student–teacher ratio is low, so students can receive greater amounts of individual attention. Learning is also conducted in the community. Community resources such as libraries, zoos, and museums are used to support the Basic School's curriculum.

Yet learning encompasses more than classroom curriculum and community resources. The Basic School is concerned about the whole child. Each student is recognized as a human being. The Basic School provides services to help students improve their personal lives, such as after-school enrichment and summer programs.

A Commitment to Character.   The Basic School encourages its graduates to have a sense of civic responsibility and civility. The Basic School recognizes seven core virtues all students should possess by the time they graduate:

- Respect
- Compassion
- Perseverance
- Honesty
- Responsibility
- Self-discipline
- Giving

Each of the core virtues is taught in the curriculum, and students are encouraged through example to transfer them to their private lives.

Boyer states the success of the Basic School rests on students who, when they enter society, understand how well their education has prepared them. He says,

> Ultimately, the aim of the Basic School is not just to build a better school, but above all, to build a better world for children. It is our deepest hope that not a single child, let alone a whole generation of children, should pass through the schoolhouse door unprepared for the world that lies before them. (Boyer, 1995, p. 12)

Goals 2000.   Educational reform is an ongoing process, and it must have goals in order to make classrooms more effective. *Goals 2000* gives classroom teachers and schools specific targets they should aim for by the year 2000. These targets are listed in Figure 13.5. *Goals 2000* recognizes that schools are too important to be left solely to classroom teachers and administrators—they should be everybody's business.

Figure 13.5 *Goals 2000*

Goal One: **Readiness for School.**   Every child in the United States should come to school ready to learn.

Goal Two: **High School Completion.**   Graduation rates should increase from the present 75 percent to 90 percent.

Goal Three: **Student Achievement and Citizenship.**   Students should be able to demonstrate their knowledge in the academic core areas of schooling (history, science, mathematics, geography, English) on tests. Students should also be taught how to be responsible citizens and workers.

Goal Four: **Science and Mathematics.**   U.S. students should be the first in the world for their knowledge of mathematics and science.

Goal Five: **Adult Literacy.**   Every adult in the United States should be able to read and write so she or he can find and hold a job.

Goal Six: **Safe, Disciplined, and Drug-Free Schools.**   All schools in the nation will be free from drugs, so students can learn in a disciplined and orderly environment.

Source: Goals 2000: Educate America Act (P.L. 103-227).

While it calls for classroom teachers to be accountable for how well they teach students, the report believes they should be given greater freedom to experiment with teaching methods that help students learn. *Goals 2000* encourages parents to assume a greater role in the education of their children. It highlights the importance of parents being responsible for the education of their children during the important years between birth and kindergarten. Also, *Goals 2000* calls on communities to become involved with schools. Goals 2000 emphasizes that communities and businesses have many resources that can be made available to benefit schools, students, and teachers.

Presidents Bush and Clinton wanted *Goals 2000* to be implemented in the nation's schools by the end of the twentieth century, but not all educators agree on how it should be enacted. Yet the goals it outlines are universally accepted by educators and the public alike.

Second-Wave Educational Reformers

To understand second-wave educational reformers, it is important for us to remember that, on the whole, they agree that classroom teachers need to teach students to live in a diverse or multicultural society.

James Banks.   A University of Washington professor, James Banks is perhaps the most articulate of the second-wave educational reformers. Like Joel Spring, who you will read about later, he believes in the concept of social control. Banks believes the present Euro-centered curriculum is destructive to students and society alike. He wants schools to eliminate Euro-centrism from the curriculum.

As an alternative, Banks developed the transformative curriculum. The basic goal of this curriculum is to help students learn how to inspect issues, problems, or themes from differing academic, cultural, ethnic, and racial perspectives. To accomplish this, Banks believes schools should teach students how to think critically. Critical thinking, he says, will help students view their environment from many cultural points of view. In the long run, Banks believes, his transformative curriculum will help students become more proficient in using their critical thinking skills to construct or build knowledge for themselves. It will empower cultural and racial groups who are presently marginalized in American society. It will, literally, be transformative.

What will be the result of the transformative curriculum? Banks believes it will produce better-educated citizens who understand their social and cultural environments. Not only will they be better able to understand the cultures and ethnicities of American society, they will have the luxury of understanding themselves from other points of view.

Paolo Freire.   Paulo Freire believes schools have the power to change a person's life without that individual being aware of it. For example, in research he conducted in ex-Portuguese African colonies, Freire discovered that African students who had attended Portuguese colonial schools prior to 1975 thought of themselves differently than African students who had not gone to the same schools.

The basic difference between the two groups, he found, was that the students who had received a Portuguese colonial education were not taught about their culture. Rather, they learned myths, stereotypes, and beliefs that ridiculed their culture and made them feel the only way to succeed was to either be European or have the European ideals exemplified by their classroom teachers. He says that Portuguese education in the African colonies was designed to marginalize African cultures and values. In short, the goal of colonial education, says Freire, was to create a colonial elite that would consider African culture subordinate to European culture.

Freire believes students in any culturally pluralistic society, such as the United States, can be miseducated when they are not taught about their culture, race, ethnicity, or gender. He believes that when this happens, schools are enculturating students to live in the dominant culture just like the African students were enculturated in the Portuguese colonies. Freire understands knowledge as power, and wants classroom teachers to help students take control of their own education.

Michael Apple. Michael Apple is usually referred to as a critical theorist. Like Freire, Apple believes schools educate students to the values, ideals, and rules of the dominant culture. Students learn which rules, behaviors, and attitudes are acceptable to classroom teachers, administrators, and others. Unlike Friere, who believes schools openly teach students about the dominant culture, Apple believes schools are much more effective at teaching the dominant culture's values through a hidden curriculum. Apple believes schools do not like controversy, so the basic assumption of the hidden curriculum is that conflict between the dominant culture's values and other cultures' values is bad and should be eliminated. Schools, says Apple, should understand that society is made up of conflicting values and ideals between individuals or cultural groups. He contends classroom teachers should help students learn how to exist in a pluralistic society. The curriculum should focus on specific aspects of social and cultural conflicts.

Joel Spring. Joel Spring, a professor of educational foundations, believes American schools have historically been dominated by the Euro-centered culture. In books such as *The American School: 1642–1990* (Longman, 1990) and *The Sorting Machine Revisited: National Educational Policy Since 1945* (Longman, 1989), Spring has developed a theory of how schools use social control.

Spring describes social control as the process schools go through to maintain an orderly society. This is done, he says, when the school tests and sorts students into various groups. (Spring is extremely critical of intelligence tests.) This sorting forces students to "play the game" in order to graduate. As a consequence, students may learn a curriculum that prepares them for little else than careers as good industrial workers. Spring believes schools have created a society that is becoming less and less concerned about the human condition.

Educational Reform and Effective Classrooms

Educational reform is not a clear-cut issue. Some reformers want classroom teachers to reinforce Euro-centric ideas. Other reformers believe classroom teachers should help children learn about themselves and others, so they can successfully live in a rapidly changing, multicultural, society. Most reformers can be found someplace in between these two extremes. Let's now look at how the reform waves may affect your classroom.

First-Wave Classroom

What would your classroom be like if you were a first-wave teacher? Your school and classroom would be heavily influenced by *A Nation At Risk* and the reports listed in Figure 13.1. The goals you set for your students would revolve around the concepts of intellectual growth, strong study skills, and a substantial knowledge base. You would expect your students to be serious about their studies and be prepared to learn. And of course, like any teacher, your classroom would be influenced by school climate, curriculum, administration, and teaching methods.

School Climate.   School climate—the attitude the school portrays to students and the community—demonstrates the nature of teaching and learning in the school. First-wave teachers want students to know they have high expectations for their academic success. Therefore, these classroom teachers test frequently to motivate students to succeed. William Bennett, Secretary of Education during President Reagan's second administration (1984–1988), describes the characteristics of a first-wave school:

- vigorous instructional leadership,
- a principal who makes clear, consistent, and fair decisions,
- an emphasis on discipline and a safe and orderly environment,
- instructional practices that focus on basic skills and academic achievement,
- collegiality among teachers in support of student achievement,
- teachers with high expectations that all their students can and will learn, and
- frequent review of student progress. (Bennett, 1986b, p. 45)

Curriculum.   First-wave classroom teachers believe students learn best when the curriculum is academically demanding. Students are challenged with textbooks and a subject-centered curriculum that require them to study. Students are expected to develop work habits that will help them learn at school and at home. Rigorous mathematics and science courses are also studied. Foreign languages are part of each student's learning experience, from elementary school through high school.

Students in a first-wave classroom study history rather than social studies. (First-wave classroom teachers assert that social studies is a watered-down potpourri curriculum comprising psychology, economics, and sociology. History, they believe, teaches children about American history and its European roots.) The purpose of the first-wave curriculum is to have students become literate about their European heritage regardless of their personal history.

Administration.   Administrators help teachers and students teach and learn in the classroom. Principals help classroom teachers by removing bureaucratic paperwork that interferes with teaching. Principals encourage teachers to interact with each other about teaching methods, teaching aids, and textbooks and to assist in the development of student discipline policies. Administrators discourage classroom teachers from being involved in the administration of the school. Teachers are expected to maintain a high interest in what is occurring in the classroom.

Teaching Methods.   First-wave classroom teachers use teaching methods that aim to capture the attention of every student in the classroom. This requires teachers to demonstrate to students the importance of what they are learning. As a first-wave teacher, you would clearly explain what is expected, so students would not be confused. You would evaluate students through an achievement testing program, so that you could be aware of how well students are learning and how well you are teaching.

Second-Wave Classroom

If you were a second-wave classroom teacher, what would your classroom be like? As a second-wave classroom teacher, you would be influenced by elements of Project Equality, the Basic School, and the reports discussed in Figure 13.4. That is, while you would focus your students' attention on being academically prepared, your goal would include helping them learn how to live successfully in a pluralistic society.

School Climate.   As a second-wave classroom teacher you would realize that school climate is influenced by what happens to students in their private lives as well what happens to them in school. You would appreciate that your own cultural history is only one part of the school climate. Your students would use their own learning styles rather than one imposed on them. In short, your second-wave classroom would be both subject- and student-directed.

Curriculum.   The second-wave curriculum focuses on the knowledge and skills students need to succeed in society. Second-wave curriculums take advantage of the contributions of all the cultures, ethnicities, and races represented in society and the classroom. For example, if you are teaching science you would be sure to mention that some cultures have intellectual traditions in which the scientific method is not used to arrive at answers. Students in a second-wave classroom are able to explain how certain concepts in the curriculum have impact on their lives.

Administration.   The administration of second-wave schools mirrors the pluralistic society in which they exist. School principals expect classroom teachers to share in the decision-making process. Administrators empower classroom teachers to become partners in the school's administration.

Teaching Methods.   Second-wave teaching methods focus on student learning. For example, you will recognize that some traits first-wave teachers attribute to learning deficiencies are actually reflections of cultural or ethnic values. As a second-wave classroom teacher, you would be sensitive to students' cultural histories.

 ## Contemporary Educational Reform and You

Now that you have studied the educational reform movement, you may be asking, When will this all blow over? Schools have always been in the midst of reform. Society, with all its complexities, requires classroom teachers to meet its changing needs. Perhaps a better question is, Has the contemporary reform movement improved the quality of education?

Table 13.1 shows the results of a national study in which parents of elementary students and their classroom teachers were asked whether they thought education had improved. As you can see, the majority of teachers and parents saw no improvement.

Why haven't schools improved? Undoubtedly, there are many reasons. H. L. Hodgkinson (1991) says students who come from homes that are economically and socially secure are better prepared to learn than students who come from homes that are not. He says children who are born and raised in the inner city have greater challenges before them than children who are born and raised in suburban areas. Therefore, the simple fact of living in insecure economic circumstances causes children to fall behind in school. Hodgkinson asserts that students—regardless of their cultural, ethnic, and racial backgrounds—will not do well in school if their out-of-school environments are not socially or economically secure.

What will students in your classroom be like? First, we know students differ depending on where they live. As Hodgkinson implies, children who live in sub-

Table 13.1

How Does the Quality of Education in the Nation Today Compare with Five Years Ago?

	Percentage of teachers agreeing	Percentage of parents agreeing
Better	26	20
About the same	42	40
Worse	32	40

Source: *The Basic School* by E. L. Boyer, p. 6. Princeton, N.J. The Carnegie Foundation for the Advancement of Teaching, 1995.

urbs usually do better than children who live in inner cities. Simply put, students' academic success is dependent on their social and economic environment, not on the cultures they represent.

Many students will be at risk in your classroom; they are reflections of extraordinary problems in our society. Recent data indicates that one-fourth of all children in the United States live in poverty. This means many children are susceptible to diseases (such as tuberculosis) for which there are well-known cures. Perhaps as many as 20 percent of all students diagnosed with disabilities would not have had disabilities if their mothers had seen a doctor during her first three months of pregnancy (Hodgkinson, 1991, p. 10). Students who are poorly prepared for your classroom may have academic and social problems throughout their school careers and later in life.

The challenge of teaching is understanding how your classroom mirrors society and what opportunities you have to help students learn. Boyer states,

> We reach one incontrovertible conclusion. The world has changed and schools must change, too. The lives of children who enroll in school today will span a new century. Those who graduate will enter what Peter F. Drucker calls "the knowledge society," which requires higher literacy, more technical competence, and lifelong learning. Knowledge has, without question, become our most precious resource. And if, in the days ahead, educators cannot help students become literate and well informed, if the coming generation cannot be helped to see well beyond the confines of their own lives, the nation's prospects for the future will be dangerously diminished. (1995, p. 5)

What You Have Learned

✔ Extraordinary technological, economic, social, and demographic changes in the United States have led to calls for educational reform.

✔ Some reformers, referred to as first-wave reformers, believe schools should reinforce the values of Euro-centered society. Others, referred to as second-wave reformers, recognize that society is rapidly becoming more diverse and believe that classrooms should reflect that change.

✔ Educational reform is changing school curriculums. First-wave classrooms are content-centered; students learn a traditional Euro-centered curriculum. Second-wave classrooms are centered on teaching children how to live in a complex, high-tech, multicultural society.

✔ Regardless of its aims, educational reform must meet the realities of a society that reflects the various cultures of the globe.

Key Terms

first-wave reform
   movement
second-wave
   reform movement

great books
   curriculum

Applying What You Have Learned

1. Matt Walkingstick in *Becoming a Teacher* is a student caught in the midst of change. How would you have reacted to Mrs. Ivers if you were Matt? How are your reactions based on your own cultural history?

2. Schlesinger and Bloom are reformers who believe teaching students a multicultural curriculum will change the values of the United States. Write a letter to them explaining your views.

3. *A Nation At Risk* was the first major reform report that captured the attention of the American people. Write a paragraph reacting to the report.

4. As the United States becomes more diverse, what types of educational reforms do you think will be proposed? Form a small group of four or five students and develop a list of reforms. Report to the class your ideas and why you think they are important.

Interactive Learning

1. After reading this chapter, develop a questionnaire and poll your fellow students about their views of educational reform. What were the results?

2. How do you define a foreign language? Some believe languages such as French and Spanish are foreign but Native American languages are not. Interview several professors of foreign languages on your campus. What are their views on what constitutes a foreign language and which languages should be taught in school?

3. This chapter describes several reform movements. Which do you favor? In a small group explain your reasons. Why might others disagree with you?

Expanding Your Knowledge

Bennett, William J. *What Works: Research about Teaching and Learning*. Washington, D.C.: U.S. Department of Education, 1986. (This docu- ment is an easy-to-read explanation of why Bennett believes teachers and schools are at fault for the economic problems the United States experienced in the 1980s.)

Berliner, David C. and Bruce J. Biddle. *The Manufactured Crisis*. Reading, Mass.: Addison–Wesley Publishing Company, 1995. (A challenge to all those who assume the reform movement is necessary. Berliner and Biddle take the reform movement apart idea by idea and statistical assumption by statistical assumption. We are, they say, wasting valuable time and money fixing schools that are not broken.)

Bloom, Alan. *The Closing of the American Mind*. New York: Simon & Schuster, 1987. (Bloom's book became a best-seller immediately upon publication. If you like to have your beliefs challenged, this is the book to read.)

Finn, Chester E., Jr. *We Must Take Charge: Our Schools and our Future*. New York: The Free Press, 1991. (Finn is best known for his controversial book, *What Do Our Seventeen-Year-Olds Know?*, written with Diane Ravitch. In this text, he outlines a series of core subjects all students should learn. If you want to know more about a national curriculum, this is the book for you.)

Schlesinger Arthur M., Jr. *The Disuniting of America*. New York: Norton, 1992. (Schlesinger is an excellent historian. In this very small book, he states that those who are not Euro-Americans should be willing to give up their own heritage to be real Americans.

Sizer, Theodore. *Horace's Compromise: The Dilemma of the American High School*. Boston: Houghton Mifflin, 1984. (Readers will be interested in discovering who Horace is and what the compromise is. You will enjoy Sizer's clear thinking.)

Joining the Profession

Chapter 14 is the culmination of this introduction to becoming a classroom teacher. You've learned that teaching is a profession that requires you to be aware of your personal strengths and weaknesses. You've learned how your personal goals, attitudes, and personality influence the curriculum. You've learned, too, that schools are influenced by social issues. Family life, cultural diversity, technology, and an aging population are only some of the issues on which good schools are now concentrating.

The next step in your development as a classroom teacher is to be employed. We use the term *entry-level teacher* to designate a classroom teacher who is in the first several years of teaching. You must become acquainted with the job market and the factors that influence it. You must learn how to apply for a teaching position, especially how to interview. This chapter offers some helpful suggestions to assist you in meeting your goal of becoming a classroom teacher.

What you will learn

- Knowing how to apply for a teaching position and what to expect in your first years as an entry-level teacher can help you achieve your goal of becoming a teacher.
- Your personal beliefs, attitudes, and personality influence your role as a teacher.
- It is important to develop your personal philosophy of education prior to your first teaching position.

BECOMING A TEACHER   *So you want to be a teacher?*

It had been the longest and most exciting day of Laurie Ferriri's life. It was 5 P.M. and she wanted to go home and tell her roommate what had happened during her first day of teaching. But Laurie knew she wouldn't go home for several more hours. She wanted to attend the welcome dinner in the cafeteria with all the other teachers. It was hosted by the PTA, and she wanted to meet some of her children's parents.

"Well, I see you survived Day 1!" The booming voice belonged to Mr. Markham, her principal. He was smiling as he walked into her classroom. "The last time I saw you was this morning. You were surrounded by thirty junior high math students who were wondering whether you were the new teacher or one of them."

Laurie laughed. She liked Mr. Markham. She felt he wanted to help her become a good teacher. "I can't believe how much has happened in one day," Laurie said. "Introducing myself in each class, giving an outline of what I expected of the students, and making sure all of them had books kept me busy. I don't know how I'll remember all their names."

"Oh, you'll learn like the rest of us, Laurie," Mr. Markham said. "I remember my first day teaching as if it were yesterday—although, it was more years ago than I want to remember."

"I think what I will remember most about today was walking into my classroom this morning," Laurie said. "It was full of students. They were all strangers to me, but by the end of the day, I began to see them as individuals. I never thought classes could have personalities, but I noticed how each class acted differently. I could tell my last class was interested in algebra by the way they acted—they asked a lot of questions. In my first class, not one student asked a question. In fact, some of the kids didn't even want to open their text."

"I'm glad you mentioned that, Laurie," Mr. Markham said. "I still notice how students and classes differ. Although I've taught for years, I've never been bored. It's one of the things that makes teaching exciting."

Laurie realized she was learning about the many things she had studied in her teacher education program. But this time it was from a practical viewpoint. Now she was looking forward to talking to the teachers who would become her friends and meeting the parents who would be her partners in education.

???   *We first met Laurie in Chapter 1, on the morning of her first day of teaching. Obviously, she is much more confident at the close of the school day than she was at the beginning. Imagine and then describe some of the events that may have happened during the day that made her more confident.*

 ## Entering the Profession

Did you notice how Laurie is beginning to take on the characteristics of a classroom teacher? As she and Mr. Markham, her principal, were discussing her first teaching day, Laurie described how her classes differed. She saw that they expressed different personalities and interests about the curriculum she was teaching.

Yet Laurie will learn much more before she feels comfortable teaching students. Laurie will have to learn that teaching is more than just delivering the curriculum—as you will. She will learn how classroom teachers are actively involved in teaching the curriculum by developing and reinterpreting it for their students. Classroom management skills and instructional methods are important, but they are just part of what's required of a classroom teacher. Just as important is *who you are*. Just as you developed your own learning styles in college, you will develop your own teaching styles in your classroom. Like Laurie, you will recognize how your background, life goals, and personal enthusiasm will influence learning activities in the classroom.

Your professional life, too, will influence your teaching style. Your style will be different in a school where your colleagues are supportive than it would be in a school in which classroom teachers are isolated.

Teachers teach in the way they do not just because of the skills they have or have not learned. The ways they teach are also grounded in their backgrounds, their biographies, in the kinds of teachers they have become. Their careers—their hopes and dreams, their opportunities and aspirations, or the frustration of these things—are also important for teachers' commitment, enthusiasm and morale. So too are relationships with their colleagues—either as supportive communities who work together in pursuit of common goals and continuous improvement, or as individuals working in isolation, with the insecurities that sometimes brings. (Hargeaves, 1993, p. vii)

With this in mind, let's look at how you can become an entry-level teacher.

VIGNETTE 14.1

The job interview

Clara was excited. Final exams were over and she was in her room packing her belongings. Her parents were coming for graduation and would help her move home for the summer. She couldn't believe it—she had finished college! Just the thought of no more quizzes and early morning classes made her smile.

However, in the back of her mind, Clara was confused. She had interviewed to teach math at the junior high school in her college town. It was an excellent position. She liked the math program. The position was important to her because she could teach, be with her friends, and begin work on her Master's degree.

Clara felt she had done well in the interview, except when the principal asked her to explain her educational philosophy and identify the attributes that would help her become a good classroom teacher. Clara knew her answers were not what the principal expected. But she hadn't thought about an educational philosophy, other than that she wanted to teach math at the junior high school level. She was confused about what her attributes were. She hadn't thought about them.

??? *To avoid Clara's problem, identify your philosophy. Can you articulate it?*

In Vignette 14.1, Clara was forced to consider several questions for which she was unprepared. She believed a teacher's job was a simple matter of teaching the curriculum to children. She did not understand why the principal was interested in her personal characteristics and experiences, because she didn't see the relationship between them and teaching. In short, Clara did not know what was expected of her during the interview. Let's look at the steps you should follow to become an entry-level teacher.

Preparing to Teach: A Reality Check

Like Clara, you are probably looking forward to graduation and a teaching position. Your teacher preparation program has been long, and it represents a huge commitment of money and time.

But for some people, graduation into the world of the classroom teacher is difficult. They find school regulations and student and parent expectations much more demanding than going to class, writing papers, and studying for exams. Another problem entry-level teachers face is financial: upon graduation, many students have to begin repaying their college loans. Many entry-level teachers discover their salaries are not as large as they would like them to be.

The period between graduation and accepting a job can be stressful, but there are things you can do during this period. Now is the time to think about what type of school will fit your professional lifestyle. Now is the time to begin thinking about your personal lifestyle, too. Will you be happy in a large urban area where apartment and condo living are the norm? Or do your interests require a country setting? Some entry-level teachers are place bound: their personal lives require them to remain in a certain geographic location. A death in the family, parents' health, divorce, or a spouse's job may require them to start their careers in schools or communities in which they have little interest.

As you become more aware of your personal and professional lifestyles, you will be able to develop your professional biography. A **professional biography** matches your personal and professional strengths to the types of schools and communities in which you would like to teach.

Securing a Teaching Position

It's easy to become confused about what type of teaching position you would like to have. Sometimes entry-level teachers believe they should take the first position that comes, regardless of whether it meets their professional or personal goals. It is important to develop a plan—before you graduate—that relates your professional and personal goals to the various components of the specific job market in which you will find yourself competing.

Job Market.   **Job market** refers to the number of teaching positions available in relation to the projected number of entry-level teacher applicants. Job markets differ throughout the United States. Not all states or communities have the same needs for classroom teachers. In fact, not all states have the same requirements for specific types of teachers. For example, some states, such as Texas and New Mexico, may have a great demand for bilingual teachers, while other states, such as Kansas and Minnesota, may have less. This is because the job market is impacted by two dominant factors: demographics and economics. Let's look at each briefly.

Demographics.   The demand for classroom teachers is largely dependent on a community or state's birthrate, or the number of children born each year. The higher the birthrate, the greater the demand for classroom teachers. Allied to birthrate is migration. Each year Americans move across state boundaries or to new communities because of job opportunities or for personal and family reasons. Schools that were once full of children may now be empty, while parents are demanding schools in other places be built or enlarged. International immigration has also affected the job market. As people from different cultures move into the United States, their children require classroom teachers who have special skills.

Economics.   The job market is further affected by the economic health of states and communities. As states and communities attract and keep industries and businesses, maintaining low unemployment rates, their tax bases increase. Greater tax bases enable communities and states to build schools, improve the curriculum, and employ more classroom teachers.

Of course there are other factors that influence the job market. For example, state legislatures may require schools to place fewer children in classrooms. That means more classroom teachers will be employed. Conversely, a lack of funds at the local and state levels may force school districts to increase the numbers of students in the classroom.

You and the Job Market.   Although the job market has improved in recent years, you still must be aggressive in your search for a teaching position. Much depends on your willingness to become knowledgeable about schools and position openings.

You should become familiar with the teacher placement services maintained by your university or college. School districts traditionally use these offices to advertise vacant teaching positions. The placement office will encourage you to develop a **placement file.** These files usually include a resume, transcripts, letters of recommendation, samples of work, and other information. Often, a counselor will help you complete your file so it presents you in the most positive light to prospective interviewers.

Another service that may be offered by your college or university is teacher placement days. Local, area, and regional schools are invited to campus on these special days to interview teacher education graduates. Schools with employment openings send their personnel officers or other administrators so they can become acquainted with as many potential teacher education graduates as possible. Don't expect these schools to offer you a contract on the spot. You will, however, get helpful leads and gain valuable interviewing experience.

Take note of placement bulletin boards and personal friends, too. Your professors and student teacher directors are frequently untapped resources: often principals and superintendents ask them to refer teacher education graduates for interviews.

An often-overlooked technique of discovering classroom teaching vacancies is the letter of application sent to school districts in which you believe you are qualified to teach. Some entry-level teachers block out a region of a state where they wish to live and write letters of application to all the school districts within that region. In your letter, state what type of teacher preparation program you are in, the types of certification or licensure you have, and your professional interests. Enclose a copy of your resume. We will discuss the letter of application and the resume later in this section.

Applying for Your First Teaching Position.   Applying for a teaching position is not difficult, but it demands your total attention. It requires you to be aware of many different items, names, and events at once. A common mistake some entry-level teachers make is to apply for one teaching position at a time. Regardless of how secure you feel about being employed by a particular school district, it is important that you submit your application to as many schools as possible. Not only is it conceivable that you may not be hired for your dream job, but you might find a teaching position that fits your personal and professional biography better.

Application Forms.   In many cases, the first act of applying for a teaching position is filling out an application form. Application forms will differ depending on the community and the teaching position. What questions are usually asked on application forms? School districts are very specific about what they want you to tell them. Expect to identify teaching fields in which you are certified or licensed and the highest academic degree you hold. The application form will include space for you to list the names and locations of schools you have attended and your student teacher supervisor. You may be asked to give that person's telephone number. Your interviewers will be especially interested in your supervisor's assessment of your teaching skills and personal characteristics. Application forms may also ask whether and where you have taught as a substitute or part-time teacher. If you have taught, the form will probably ask for the names of your immediate supervisors. Like your student teacher supervisor, they are excellent sources of information about your teaching abilities.

Making a difference.

To find out more about you, application forms may ask you to list the hobbies or activities you enjoy. This information is useful to principals in assigning teachers to student extracurricular activities. Also the school district will usually ask a question that reveals your philosophy of education. For example, you may be asked to give reasons why you would like to teach in a particular school district, or teach a particular type of student. The application form may ask you to write your philosophy with a pen or pencil. While neatness counts, the personnel office is also interested in your use of grammar and your spelling ability.

Finally, you will be asked to submit letters of reference from professors and your student teaching supervisor. Usually the personnel office is interested in letters of recommendation from your education professors, but it is important to include names of other professors as well. Remember, if you want to use professors and student teaching supervisors as references, it is important to ask them first. We will talk about your request for a letter of reference and what is generally included in your request later in this chapter.

School districts usually keep applications forms for one year. These active files are inspected whenever a position becomes available, so you should update your file whenever you have changed your certification or improved your qualifications.

Letter of Application.   What should be included in a letter of application or cover letter? Such a letter is extremely important, because it gives the first impression principals or personnel officers will have of you. It should be short, concise, and well-written. Although it may be a form letter, you should write it so readers do not have that impression. Address the letter by name to the individual who will read it. Mention what type of teaching position you are interested in, your qualifications, and why you would like to teach at that school. Finally, request an opportunity to have an interview.

The Resume.   The resume should be attached to your letter of application or cover letter. The resume is similar to an application form. It gives you the opportunity to present important facts about yourself, and should improve your chances of being invited for an interview. Include basic information such as your address and telephone number. If you are planning on moving during the summer, include a permanent address and telephone number (such as a parent's, relative's or friend's). Some entry-level applicants enclose a picture of themselves. If you do, be sure it's an attractive, professional picture.

Another feature of the resume is a list of names, addresses, and telephone numbers of individuals who are qualified to evaluate your teaching abilities. As we mentioned earlier, you should ask permission of these people before you use their names, to find out whether they are willing to write a **letter of reference** on your behalf. Some may feel uncomfortable. They may not have as favorable an impression of you as you think, or their involvement with you may have only been in a minor capacity. Asking permission also gives those individuals you use as references a chance to think about what they would like to include in a letter about you. A typical letter of reference explains what responsibility the job applicant had in a student teaching experience or teacher preparation program, and includes an evaluation of the applicant's teaching and personal abilities, as well as a statement about the applicant's potential as a classroom teacher. Letters of reference are critical to your employment possibilities.

Your resume should also include a concise paragraph about your interest in teaching and your philosophy of education. Your philosophy should reflect your goals, interests, and reasons for becoming a classroom teacher. You might want to talk with your instructors and others in your teacher preparation program to help you clarify your ideas.

Many entry-level teachers include information about their particular interests and hobbies. This helps personnel officers understand you on a more individual level. You may identify a talent that the school finds useful in sponsoring extracurricular activities. Your resume should include information about other types of teaching situations you have been involved in, such as tutoring or substitute teaching. Include the names, addresses, and telephone numbers of your supervisors.

Finally, your resume should be neat and attractive. Consider having it professionally duplicated. Remember, it should be readable and explain to those who don't know you who you are. The resume, like your cover letter of application, presents an instant image of you.

The Interview.   If a superintendent, principal, or personnel officer is sufficiently impressed with your credentials that he or she would like to interview you, you've made it through the first hurdle!

What will your interview be like? Much depends on the size of the school and the type of teaching position for which you are applying. In large school districts, your letter of application and resume may be initially screened by a representative of the personnel office. Depending on the results, you may then be interviewed by a principal, or department head, or both.

In some school districts, several principals may want to interview entry-level teachers in small groups of five to seven. This way, principals are able to compare a large number of applicants quickly and efficiently. Even though this method may seem impersonal, it gives principals opportunities to identify specific personal and professional characteristics they may be looking for. Remember, not all principals are looking for the same talents and abilities in their entry-level teachers, so you should not automatically assume you are in competition with others for the same entry-level positions.

In special instructional areas, or departments in which teachers are expected to work together, classroom teachers may share responsibilities for interviewing applicants. In this case, after the interviews have been completed, they forward to the principal a list of applicants they believe demonstrate teaching potential. Usually the list is ranked. That is, the applicant that, in their professional opinion, demonstrates the most potential is listed first. The names of the other applicants follow in numerical order. The principal then interviews the applicants and selects the most appropriate candidate.

What professional and personal experiences, characteristics, and abilities should you stress in an interview? Of course, interviewers will be interested in your certification or licensure credentials. Once you have shown you are licenced or certified by the state department of education, they will become vitally interested in your potential as a professional classroom teacher. Obviously, they are interested in teachers who are able to work well with students, parents, colleagues, and administrators in their school district. In short, they are less interested in your grade point average, and more interested in you and your personal skills and professional potential. Following is a representative list of questions administrators ask themselves when they interview entry-level teachers.

- What evidence leads you to believe the entry-teacher understands children?
- What are the entry-year teacher's strengths?
- What are the entry-year teacher's weaknesses?
- What evidence leads you to believe the entry-level teacher is able to work with fellow teachers?
- What evidence leads you to believe the entry-level teacher understands the school's climate?
- What evidence leads you to believe the entry-level teacher understands the role of the teacher in the classroom and the school?

To help you prepare for the interview, you may want to develop a professional portfolio. A **professional portfolio** includes samples of your professional experiences, such as videotapes of your teaching and letters of reference from previous supervisors. You may also include student and parent evaluations. Remember, the professional portfolio will not only tell administrators about your abilities, it will tell them what you consider important about yourself, so use judgment about what you place in the portfolio.

Professional Courtesies.   An important aspect of finding an entry-level teaching position is your use of professional courtesy. In this case, professional courtesy requires you to write a follow-up letter thanking your interviewers for the opportunity to meet with them. While the letter does not have to be elaborate, it should clearly show your interest in the position. The letter is also a chance to reiterate your strengths. Who knows how many times entry-level teachers have been hired because they demonstrated superior professional courtesy, even though they were not the first pick of the interviewing committee?

After you have been employed and signed a contract with the school board, you should extend the courtesy of writing letters to other school districts that invited you to come for an interview. Your letter should be short, thanking them for the invitation and explaining that you have accepted a contract elsewhere. Your letter need not explain why you were willing to accept a contract with one school as opposed to another.

Goals of a First-Year Teacher

Now that you have signed a contract as an entry-level teacher, what do you think your first years in the profession will be like? You will remember and reflect upon them for the rest of your teaching career. In fact, you will probably evaluate the rest of your teaching career from the vantage point of the experiences you gain in your first years.

Your life will change when you become a classroom teacher. Students, parents, and administrators may refer to you formally rather than using your first name. You will work on a equal basis with others who are older than you, and who may have very different experiences and lifestyles. Let's look at some of the attitudes and feelings entry-level teachers experience.

Goals for Yourself

It is impossible to predict what your first years in the classroom will be like. No two entry-level teachers ever have the same experiences because schools, like individuals, differ. But, if you are like most entry-level teachers, your emotions will run the gamut. You will experience the exhilarating feeling of being in charge of students and their learning. Each day in the classroom will bring new situations and challenges. And as you become better acquainted with your students and fellow teachers, you will continue to make new discoveries about them and yourself.

On the other hand, you will also experience feelings of uncertainty and disappointment when situations in the school do not live up to your expectations. As

Working on an assignment together.

inevitable disagreements with students, parents, or other teachers arise, you may wonder whether you are able to survive the storm.

In one study, teachers with five to ten years of classroom experience were asked to reflect upon their feelings as entry-level teachers (Huberman, Grounauer, and Marti, 1993). Almost half (46 percent) of all teachers recalled they were concerned about what others thought of them. Also, 63 percent of the teachers felt they had relied on trial and error. Another preoccupation these experienced teachers recalled having when they were new was fearing they would not measure up to their or other's expectations. They were concerned about their lack of experience causing them to solve classroom problems through trial and error which, in turn, made them feel they were inconsistent with their students. They also mentioned that students intimidated them, which fostered feelings of not measuring up. Above all, the experienced teachers recalled being obsessed with themselves and being physically exhausted at the end of the day (Huberman, Grounauer, & Marti, 1993).

What usually pulls entry-level classroom teachers through is feelings of exhilaration. As you discover more about the school, your students, and the classroom, you will learn more about yourself. As you gain experience, your confidence will grow. Huberman, Gronauer, and Marti (1993) refer to these feelings as "survival and discovery." When entry-level teachers have negative experiences, they become uncertain about themselves and their decision about teaching. They begin to wonder whether they can *survive* their problems. As they recognize what their personal and professional abilities are, they *discover* their confidence.

Let's look now at how entry-level teachers relate to their students, curriculum, and the teaching profession.

Goals for Your Students

The first, and most obvious, challenge you have as an entry-level teacher will be learning how to relate to your students. Many entry-level teachers notice immediately how close in age they are to their students. This is why many entry-level teachers find they are preoccupied with themselves rather than their classrooms. Most young entry-level teachers, like George in Vignette 14.2, rely on trial and error to learn how to interact with their students and fellow teachers.

VIGNETTE 14.2   *Hi, George!!*

George Tallipharo was Carson High's new physics teacher. "Just call me George," he said to his students. "I like things to be informal."

"Hey, George!!" Ben, the class clown, was having fun. "Just call me George—I like things to be informal." Ben giggled and mimicked George.

"Yup," said Terry smirking, "Let's see if 'old George' can do it." The class was uneasy.

"OK, let's get to work," said George. "Let's get our books out and get ready for class." The students laughed nervously. George knew he had lost control—he really didn't know what to do. All he wanted was a good learning situation and the class was laughing at him. "What should I do? I really need help," thought George.

???   *What gave Ben permission to act the way he did? List some ways George could have accomplished his objectives and still maintained control of the class.*

How will *you* assume the role of classroom teacher? Some entry-level teachers are concerned about student discipline and how strict they should be. Other entry-level teachers find it difficult to picture themselves as classroom teachers, so they portray themselves in nonteaching roles such as big brother, big sister, or a parent. These nonschool roles seldom work, but they are part of the process some entry-level teachers go through as they develop their role as classroom teachers. You will want to talk about this with your mentor teacher while you are developing a quality classroom management style.

Some school districts help entry-level teachers make the transition from college student to classroom teacher with **mentor teacher** programs. These programs assign mature classroom teachers who are respected by students and their fellow teachers to help entry-level teachers solve school problems. Mentor teachers will be able to give you new and different ideas to help you evaluate your professional experiences. Entry-level and mentor teachers usually develop lasting professional friendships in which they freely celebrate individual successes and discuss mutual problems.

Goals for Your Curriculum

As an entry-level teacher, you will become aware of how your instructional techniques and classroom management styles have to change to meet your students' social and academic levels. Some entry-level teachers have difficulty accepting that students' academic and social interests differ from theirs. Not all students will be as intellectually absorbed in your specialty as you are. You will become acutely aware that not all students learn as quickly as you do, or express the same amount of inquisitiveness. In short, you will learn that your curricular and academic expectations may differ greatly from your students. It is your ability to communicate with students *at their level* that is most important.

Goals for the Profession

A large part of the adventure we call teaching is the personal and professional relationships we develop with fellow teachers. Administrators and teaching faculty are resources to help you succeed. Entry-level teachers are usually welcomed by their colleagues. Many of the challenges and problems entry-level teachers experience during their first several years are lessened considerably by the professional and personal support given by more experienced colleagues.

Huberman, Grounauer, and Marti found that 7 percent of classroom teachers reflecting on their first teaching years spontaneously mentioned the pleasant relations they had had with existing faculty. The following is a comment by a middle school teacher who, after 36 years in the classroom, reflected on his first year of teaching.

> Conditions were really difficult in the upper-level classes. The classrooms were disgraceful, cold in winter, hot in the summer. The students were difficult. But thanks to the wonderful teachers of this school, I managed to get by. (Huberman, Grounauer, and Marti, 1993, p. 200)

Unfortunately, healthy professional relationships do not always exist in schools. In the same study, 4 percent of the teachers mentioned that their relationships with other teachers were difficult. Because of personal or professional rivalries, entry-level teachers may find they are in the awkward position of taking sides in situations that existed prior to their coming. Some entry-level teachers find they are labeled friend or enemy simply because of where they sit during lunch or who they talk to in the faculty lounge. Sometimes, senior classroom teachers become jealous of junior teachers because of the new instructional methods they bring with them from college. Vignette 14.3 discusses teaching styles.

VIGNETTE 14.3   *Terry Chan's teaching style*

MEMORANDUM

TO: Mrs. Fulton
FROM: Terry Chan
RE: Transfer from Carson H. S.

This memorandum is to serve as my official request to be transferred to another high school in the school district beginning next academic year. I believe I will be better able to help students learn if I am allowed to teach without other teachers publicly criticizing my instructional methods.

Thank you for your assistance.

"I am truly sorry you want to leave Carson High, Terry," Mrs. Fulton said as she read her brief memo. "You have done a wonderful job with your students this year. I know you will be an excellent teacher."

"Thank you, Mrs. Fulton. I really enjoy Carson High, but I am not certain all the teachers are happy to have me here. I realize some of my teaching methods are different. I learned them when I was taking my methods classes in college and student teaching. But I don't think I should be forced to change simply because of the jealousy of some of the teachers. And, as you know, the students are learning."

"I understand what you mean, Terry, but regardless where you teach you will find that some teachers have difficulty accepting new ideas. Sometimes they get angry because others who have less experience than they are better teachers. Beyond that, what can I do to encourage you to stay at Carson High?"

???   *If you were Mrs. Fulton, what would you suggest to keep Terry at Carson High?*

Sometimes entry-level classroom teachers have rough beginnings because the school may not have extensive teacher development or inservice programs. These programs help new teachers become acquainted with the school. In cases such as this, entry-level teachers are literally tossed into the classroom without any support from administrators or teaching faculty. They are given little or no instruction about school policies, administrative practices, or resources. They are not mentored by experienced classroom teachers. It is your responsibility—and it is to your benefit—to become familiar with schools and school practices before your first day of teaching. Volunteer as a classroom helper or substitute teacher at your local schools. Become involved with tutoring programs run through your teacher preparation program. Remember, becoming a classroom teacher is more than simply understanding the mechanics of the classroom. It is learning how to develop your own unique role as a teacher.

Developing Your Personal Philosophy of Education

Now that you are aware what your beginning years as a classroom teacher may be like, you can start to develop your personal philosophy of education. Your philosophy of education must be more than just the product of what happens to you in the classroom.

We hope you have discovered that classroom teaching is a sophisticated profession in which you are expected to use all your skills and abilities to help students learn. As you have discovered, all classrooms are not the same. As a teacher, you will quickly notice classrooms differ, because of the nature of the curriculum, the types of students, and the community in which the school resides. One of the authors reflected on a new teaching assignment at an alternative high school:

When I started teaching, I was really committed to working with at-risk students. I soon learned how uncomfortable I was. I had difficulty getting along with the students and had very little in common with other teachers in the school. I thought I could really make a difference with the students. What I didn't know was how to be a teacher and not a friend. But I have changed and now I love the kids and the school. They enjoy learning and I like being with them. The teachers and the administration are like a big family where we help each other. I guess what I am saying is, when I first began teaching, I didn't have a vision about what I wanted to do as a classroom teacher.

As I developed a philosophy of education, I became comfortable in my surroundings.

What she discovered was that a philosophy of education is basic to a successful teaching career.

Can you describe your philosophy of education? Now, it is probably sketchy. But you will be surprised how inclusive your philosophy will become someday. It will permeate every part of your professional life. It will induce you to inspect the values you consider important. It will prompt you to look at the types of teaching methods you use and your expectations of students. Some classroom teachers mistakenly base their philosophy of education on how they themselves learned in school or how they *think* students learn. For example, are you a person who likes to learn with others? Do you find it easy to understand ideas or facts when you have a chance to talk to others? Or do you enjoy learning by yourself? All these considerations contribute to your philosophy of education—a philosophy that will continue to evolve as you gain classroom experience. Your philosophy of education will focus on important issues about how your students can be educated to live in an increasingly diverse society. It will be concerned with how the school and classroom teachers encourage all children to learn. Most importantly, it will give you a vision of being a teacher that is part of the educational process.

 ## Teaching: A Way of Life

In this book, we've sought to describe what schools are really like. We've relied on our own experiences and the experiences of others to give you a real-life look at teaching. Particularly, we've tried to emphasize that children reflect the society of which they, you, and we are a part.

We are a changing society. At one time, the majority of us came from northern Europe. Many of us came because we saw opportunity and others of us came because we were forced into slavery. We brought with us cultural values, ideas, religions, institutions, and attitudes. Now many of us are coming from Latin America, the Caribbean, Asia, southern Europe, Africa, and other places. We come with different values and cultures. As a classroom teacher, you have the responsibility— the *opportunity*—to educate all our children

What You Have Learned

✔ Teaching is more than telling students what to do. It is a very personal act of communication between teachers and students.

✔ Securing a teaching position requires entry-level teachers to understand factors that affect the job market, as well as procedures schools use to employ teachers.

✔ The first years of teaching are exciting, as entry-level teachers take on the characteristics of classroom teachers.

✔ Entry-level teachers discover that the interrelationships among students, curriculum, and profession are important in becoming a good teacher.

✔ Family stress, cultural diversity, technology, and the aging population impact schools and have immediate impact on the classroom teacher.

Key Terms

professional
  biography
job market
placement file

letter of reference
professional portfolio
mentor teacher

Applying What You Have Learned

1. Laurie Ferriri in *Becoming a Teacher* was quick to recognize how classes can have personalities. Assume she is teaching the same math curriculum in both the classes she described. What different teaching techniques will she use?
2. In what way will your professional biography change *before* you graduate?
3. Interview a counselor at your university or college placement office. What types of information does he/she consider important for you to have on file?
4. Interview several entry-level teachers about their first years in the classroom. How did their impressions of students, fellow teachers, and the curriculum change during that period?

Interactive Learning

1. Interview several teachers or administrators. Ask them what they look for in new teachers. Evaluate yourself in terms of this information. Discuss your findings with others in your class.
2. This chapter has discussed some of the personal attributes of teachers: listening, working together, thoughtfulness, inquisitiveness, talking, patience. Ask friends and relatives which of these attributes they have noticed about you.

3. Now is the time to begin to develop a professional biography. Answer these questions: (1) What professional abilities do I have? (2) What professional skills do I have? (3) What type of school would I feel comfortable teaching in? (4) What part of the country would I like to live in?
4. For practice, request an application form from a local school district. As you fill it out, discuss with fellow students what information should be listed and who you might ask for letters of reference. Explain why you would be more interested in letters of reference from specific teachers and professors rather than from others.

Expanding Your Knowledge

Barber, Benjamin R. *An Aristocracy of Everyone.* New York: Oxford University Press, 1992. (This is a good book for entry-level teachers. Barber recognizes the debate about who, what, and how teachers should teach, but insists schools should emphasize democracy as much as academic excellence.)

Clifford, Geraldine J. and James W. Guthrie. *Ed School.* Chicago: The University of Chicago Press, 1988. (The authors present a strong case for educating educators as we presently educate doctors and lawyers.)

Halberstam, David. *The Next Century.* New York: William Morrow and Company, Inc., 1991. (A delightful book by a distinguished author and journalist. Halberstam gives us his perspective of what the next century might be like. What he believes may happen will have major consequences on current issues in education. A must-read book.)

Huberman, Michael, M.–M. Grounauer and J. Marti. *The Lives of Teachers.* New York: Teachers College Press, 1993. (This study was conducted in Europe, and written originally in French. Its pertinence to American teachers has been acclaimed. If you want to know how you might feel about your teaching career over the next thirty-odd years in the classroom, you will enjoy this book.)

Leithwood, Kenneth, P. T. Begley, and J. B. Cousins. *Developing Expert Leadership For Future Schools*. Washington: Falmer Press, 1994. (Although this book is written for administrators, it is important because the authors talk about areas of leadership outside of the classroom in which teachers are becoming more involved.)

Noll, James William. *Taking Sides: Clashing Views on Controversial Educational Issues,* 8th ed. Guilford, Connecticut: The Dushkin Publishing Group, Inc., 1995. (This is an excellent book of readings for teachers of all levels. Selected current issues are discussed by prominent educators with opposing views.)

State Offices of Teacher Licensure and Certification

Alabama
Division of Professional Services
Department of Education
Gordon Persons Building
50 North Ripley Street
Montgomery, AL 36130–3901
(205) 242–9977
Alternative Routes: Fifth-year master of arts program; emergency certificate; alternative baccalaureate-level teacher's certificate; nonprofessional special approved plan teacher's certificate.

Alaska
Teacher Education and Certification
Department of Education
Alaska State Office Building, Pouch F
Juneau, AK 99811–1894
(907) 465–2831
Alternative Routes: Alternative teaching program; content specialist card program.

Arizona
Teacher Certification Unit
Department of Education
1535 West Jefferson Street
P.O. Box 25609
Phoenix, AZ 85007
(602) 542–4368
Alternative Routes: Alternative secondary certificate; emergency certificate.

Arkansas
Office of Teacher Education and Licensure
Department of Education
4 Capitol Mall, Room 106B/107B
Little Rock, AR 72201
(501) 682–4342
Alternative Routes: Alternative certification program; probationary provisional certificate.

California
Commission on Teacher Credentialing
1812 Ninth Street
Sacramento, CA 95814
(916) 445–7254
Alternative Routes: District intern certificate; university intern credential; emergency teaching permit.

Colorado
Teacher Certification
Department of Education
201 East Colfax Avenue
Denver, CO 80203–1799
(303) 866–6628
Alternative Routes: Alternative teacher certification; teacher certification under the alternative route.

Connecticut
Bureau of Certification and Accreditation
Department of Education
P.O. Box 2219
Hartford, CT 06145
(203) 566–4561
Alternative Routes: Alternative route to teacher certification; professional educator certificate; provisional educator certificate.

Delaware
Office of Certification
Department of Public Instruction
Townsend Building
P.O. Box 1402
Dover, DE 19903
(302) 739–4688
Alternative Routes: Special institute for teacher certification; critical curricular area program.

District of Columbia
Division of Teacher Services
District of Columbia Public Schools
415 Twelfth Street, N.W.
Room 1013
Washington, D.C. 20004–1994

(District of Columbia continued)
(202) 724–4250
Alternative Routes: Provisional certificate.

Florida
    Division of Human Resource Development
    Teacher Certification Offices
    Department of Education, FEC, Room 201
    2325 West Gaines Street
    Tallahassee, FL 32399–0400
    (904) 488–5724
    Alternative Routes: Temporary certificate.

Georgia
    Professional Standards Commission
    Department of Education
    1454 Twin Towers East
    Atlanta, GA 30334
    (404) 656–2604
    Alternative Routes: Alternative certificate for
    selected special education fields; temporary
    provisional certificate.

Hawaii
    Office of Personnel Services
    Department of Education
    P.O. Box 2360
    Honolulu, HI 96804
    (808) 586–3420
    Alternative Routes: Special certification
    program—mathematics/science.

Idaho
    Teacher Education and Certification
    Department of Education
    Len B. Jordan Office Building
    650 West State Street
    Boise, ID 83720
    (208) 334–3475
    Alternative Routes: Secondary field centered
    teacher training program.

Illinois
    Certification and Placement
    State Board of Education
    100 North First Street
    Springfield, IL 62777–0001
    (217) 782–2805
    Alternative Routes: Provisional certificate.

Indiana
    Professional Standards Board
    Department of Education

State House, Room 229
Indianapolis, IN 46204–2790
(317) 232–9010
Alternative Routes: None.

Iowa
    Board of Education Examiners
    State of Iowa
    Grimes State Office Building
    Des Moines, IA 50319–0146
    (515) 281–3245
    Alternative Routes: None.

Kansas
    Certification, Teacher Education, and
    Accreditation
    Department of Education
    120 S.E. Tenth Avenue
    Topeka, KS 66612
    (913) 296–2288
    Alternative Routes: Alternative certification
    higher education program; visiting
    scholar program.

Kentucky
    Teacher Education and Certification
    Department of Education
    500 Mero Street, Room 1820
    Frankfort, KY 40601
    (502) 564–4606
    Alternative Routes: Alternative certification;
    post-baccalaureate experimental secondary
    teacher preparation program.

Louisiana
    Teacher Certification
    Department of Education
    P.O. Box 94064
    626 North Fourth Street
    Baton Rouge, LA 70804–9064
    (504) 342–3490
    Alternative Routes: Alternative post-
    baccalaureate certification program—
    secondary, lower and upper elementary,
    special education; temporary certificate.

Maine
    Department of Education
    Certification and Placement
    State House Station 23
    Augusta, ME 04333
    (207) 289–5800
    Alternative Routes: Transcript Analysis.

Maryland
Division of Certification and Accreditation
Department of Education
200 West Baltimore Street
Baltimore, MD 21201
(410) 333–2142
Alternative Routes: Resident teacher certification;
creative initiatives in teacher education.

Massachusetts
Bureau of Teacher Certification
Department of Education
350 Main Street
Malden, MA 02148
(617) 338–3300
Alternative Routes: Certification review panel–
alternative route to certification; apprentice
teacher program; waiver.

Michigan
Teacher/Administrator Preparation and
    Certification
Department of Education
P.O. Box 3008
608 West Allegan Street
Lansing, MI 48909
(517) 373–3310
Alternative Routes: None.

Minnesota
Personnel and Licensing
Department of Education
616 Capitol Square Building
550 Cedar Street
St. Paul, MN 55101
(612) 296–2046
Alternative Routes: Alternative preparation to
teacher licensure program; limited license for
secondary school; provisional license.

Mississippi
Office of Teacher Certification
Department of Education
P.O. Box 771
Jackson, MS 39205
(601) 359–3483
Alternative Routes: Alternative route
provisional certificate.

Missouri
Teacher Education
Missouri Teacher Certification Office

Department of Elementary and Secondary
    Education
P.O. Box 480
Jefferson City, MO 65102–0480
(314) 751–3486
Alternative Routes: Alternate certification
program.

Montana
Certification Services
Office of Public Instruction
State Capitol
Helena, MT 59620
(406) 444–3150
Alternative Routes: Provisional certificate.

Nebraska
Teacher Certification Education
301 Centennial Mall, South
Box 94987
Lincoln, NE 68509
(402) 471–2496
Alternative Routes: Provisional commitment
teaching certificate.

Nevada
Teacher Licensure
Department of Education
1850 East Sahara, Suite 200
State Mail Room
Las Vegas, NV 89158
(702) 486–6457
Alternative Routes: Provisional license.

New Hampshire
Bureau of Teacher Education and Professional
    Standards
Department of Education
State Office Park South
101 Pleasant Street
Concord, NH 03301–3860
(603) 271–2407
Alternative Routes: Provisional certification
plan; individual professional development
plan; conversion programs; emergency
permission to employ; demonstrated
competencies and equivalent experience.

New Jersey
Teacher Certification and Academic Credentials
Department of Education
3535 Quakerbridge Road, CN 503
Trenton, NJ 08625–0503

(New Jersey continued)
(609) 292–2070
Alternative Routes: Provisional teacher program.

New Mexico
Educator Preparation and Licensure
Department of Education
Education Building
Sante Fe, NM 87501–2786
(505) 827–6587
Alternative Routes: Alternative licensure; distinguished scholar program.

New York
Office of Teacher Certification
Department of Education
Cultural Education Center, Room 5A 11
Albany, NY 12230
(518) 474–3901
Alternative Routes: Internship certificate; transcript analysis.

North Carolina
Division of Certification
Department of Public Instruction
114 West Edenton Street
Raleigh, NC 27603–1712
(919) 733–4125
Alternative Routes: Modified certification plan, lateral entry provisional certificate.

North Dakota
Teacher Certification Division
Department of Public Instruction
600 East Blvd. Avenue
Bismarck, ND 58505–0440
(701) 224–2264
Alternative Routes: Emergency license.

Ohio
Teacher Certification
Department of Education
65 South Front Street, Room 1012
Columbus, OH 43266–0308
(614) 466–3593
Alternative Routes: Internship certification program; temporary teaching permit.

Oklahoma
Department of Education
2500 North Lincoln Blvd., Room 211

Oliver Hodge Education Building
Oklahoma City, OK 73105–4599
(405) 521–3337
Alternative Routes: Alternative placement program; emergency and provisional certificates—alternative certification.

Oregon
Teacher Standards and Practices Commission
580 State Street, Room 203
Salem, OR 97310
(503) 378–3586
Alternative Routes: Interim teacher certificates.

Pennsylvania
Bureau of Teacher Preparation and Certification
Department of Education
333 Market Street, 3rd Floor
Harrisburg, PA 17126–0333
Alternative Routes: Teacher intern program; temporary teaching permit.

Puerto Rico
Teacher Certification Division
Department of Education
Box 190759
Hato Rey, PR 00919
(809) 758–4949
Alternative Routes: None.

Rhode Island
School and Teacher Accreditation
Certification and Placement
22 Hayes Street
Roger Williams Bldg., 2nd Floor
Providence, RI 02908
(401) 277–2675
Alternative Routes: None.

South Carolina
Teacher Education and Certification
Department of Education
1015 Rutledge
1429 Senate Street
Columbia, SC 29201
(803) 734–8466
Alternative Routes: Critical need conditional certificate.

South Dakota
Office of Certification
Division of Education and Cultural Affairs

Kneip Office Building
700 Govenor's Drive
Pierre, SD 57501
(605) 733–3553
Alternative Routes: Alternative certification.

Tennessee
Office of Teacher Licensing
Department of Education
6th Floor, North Wing
Cordell Hull Building
Nashville, TN 37243–0377
(615) 741–1644
Alternative Routes: Interim probationary
license type C—alternative preparation
for licensure; permit to teach; interim
probationary license.

Texas
Division of Personnel Records
William B. Travis Office Building
1701 North Congress
Austin, TX 78701
(512) 463–8976
Alternative Routes: Alternative teacher
certification.

Utah
Certification and Personnel Development
State Office of Education
250 East 500 South
Salt Lake City, UT 84111
(801) 538–7740
Alternative Routes: Alternative preparation
for teaching program; letter of authorization;
eminence or special qualification
authorization.

Vermont
Licensing Division
Department of Education
Montpelier, VT 05620
(802) 828–2445
Alternative Routes: License by evaluation;
waiver; transcript analysis.

Virginia
Office of Professional Licensure
Department of Education
P.O. Box 2120
Richmond, VA 23216–2120
Alternative Routes: Provisional certification.

Washington
Director of Professional Preparation
Office of the Superintendent of Public
  Instruction
Old Capitol Building
Box 47200
Olympia, WA 98504–7200
(206) 753–6775
Alternative Routes: Internship program;
conditional certificate; Einstein certificate.

West Virginia
Office of Professional Preparation
Department of Education
Capitol Complex, Room B–337, Bldg. 6
Charleston, WV 25305
(304) 558–2703
Alternative Routes: Alternate program in the
education of teachers; permit for full-time
teaching; internship license, temporary license
alternative certification program.

Wisconsin
Bureau of Teacher Education, Licensing and
  Placement
Department of Public Instruction
125 South Webster Street
P.O. Box 7841
Madison, WI 53707–7841
Alternative Routes: Permits.

Wyoming
Certification and Licensing Unit
Department of Education
2300 Capitol Avenue
Hathaway Building
Cheyenne, WY 82002–0050
(307) 777–6261
Alternative Routes: None.

St. Croix District
Department of Education
Educational Personnel Services
2133 Hospital St.—Christianstead
St. Croix, Virgin Islands 00820
(809) 773–5844

St. Thomas/St. John District
Educational Personnel Services
Department of Education
44-46 Kongens Grade

(St. Thomas/St. John District continued)
St. Thomas, Virgin Islands 00801
(809) 774–0100

U.S. Department of Defense Overseas
Dependent Section
    Teacher Recruitment
    2461 Eisenhower Avenue
    Alexandria, Va 22331–1100
    (703) 325–0690

National Education Association Code of Ethics

Preamble

The educator, believing in the worth and dignity of each human being, recognizes the supreme importance of the pursuit of truth, devotion to excellence, and the nurture of democratic principles. Essential to these goals is the protection of freedom to learn and to teach and the guarantee of equal education opportunity for all. The educator accepts the responsibility to adhere to the highest ethical standards.

The educator recognizes the magnitude of the responsibility inherent in the teaching process. The desire for the respect and confidence of one's colleagues, of students, of parents, and the members of the community provides the incentive to attain and maintain the highest possible degree of ethical conduct. The Code of Ethics of the Education Profession indicates the aspiration of all educators and provides standards by which to judge conduct.

The remedies specified by the NEA and/or its affiliates for the violation of any provision of the Code shall be exclusive, and no such provision shall be enforceable in any form other than one specifically designated by the NEA or its affiliates.

Principle One: Commitment of the Student

The educator strives to help each student realize his or her potential as a worthy and effective member of society. The educator therefore works to stimulate the spirit of inquiry, the acquisition of knowledge and understanding, and the thoughtful formulation of worthy goals.

In fulfillment of the obligation to the student, the educator:

1. Shall not unreasonably restrain the student from independent action in the pursuit of learning
2. Shall not unreasonably deny the student access to varying points of view.
3. Shall not deliberately suppress or distort subject matter relevant to the student's progress.
4. Shall make reasonable effort to protect the students from conditions harmful to learning or health and safety.
5. Shall not intentionally expose the student to embarrassment or disparagement.
6. Shall not on the basis of race, color, creed, sex, national origin, marital status, political or religious beliefs, family, social or cultural background, or sexual orientation unfairly:
   a. Exclude any student from participation in any program.
   b. Deny benefits to any students.
   c. Grant any advantage to any student.
7. Shall not use professional relationships with students for private advantage.

8. Shall not disclose information about students obtained in the course of professional service, unless disclosure serves a compelling professional purpose or is required by law.

Principle Two: Commitment to the Profession

The education profession is vested by the public with a trust and responsibility requiring the highest ideals of professional service.

In the belief that the quality of the services of the education profession directly influences the nation and its citizens, the educator shall exert every effort to raise professional standards, to promote a climate that encourages the exercise of professional judgment to achieve conditions which attract persons worthy of the trust to careers in education, and to assist in preventing the practice of the profession by unqualified persons.

In fulfillment of the obligation to the profession, the educator:

1. Shall not in an application for a professional position deliberately make a false statement or fail to disclose a material fact related to competency and qualifications.
2. Shall not misrepresent his/her professional qualifications.
3. Shall not assist any entry into the profession of a person known to be unqualified in respect to character, education, or other relevant attribute.
4. Shall not knowingly make a false statement concerning the qualifications of a candidate for a professional position.
5. Shall not assist a non-educator in the unauthorized practice of teaching.
6. Shall not disclose information about colleagues obtained in the course of professional service unless disclosure serves a compelling professional purpose or is required by law.
7. Shall not knowingly make false or malicious statements about a colleague.
8. Shall not accept any gratuity, gift, or favor that might impair or appear to influence professional decisions or actions.

American Federation of Teachers AFL-CIO Bill of Rights and Responsibilities

The traditional mission of our public schools has been to prepare our nation's young people for equal and responsible citizenship and productive adulthood. Today, we reaffirm that mission by remembering that democratic citizenship and productive adulthood begin with standards of conduct and standards for achievement in our schools. Other education reforms *may* work; high standards of conduct and achievement *do* work—and nothing else *can* work without them.

Recognizing that rights carry responsibilities, we declare that:

- All students and school staff have a right to schools that are safe, orderly, and drug free.
- All students and school staff have a right to learn and work in school districts and schools that have clear discipline codes with fair and consistently enforced consequences for misbehavior.
- All students and school staff have a right to learn and work in school districts that have alternative educational placements for violent or chronically disruptive students.
- All students and school staff have a right to learn and work in school districts, schools, and classrooms that have clearly stated and rigorous academic standards.
- All students and school staff have a right to learn and work in well-equipped schools that have the instructional materials needed to carry out a rigorous academic program.
- All students and school staff have a right to learn and work in schools where teachers know the subject matter and how to teach it.
- All students and school staff have a right to learn and work in school districts, schools, and classrooms where high grades stand for high achievement and promotion is earned.
- All students and school staff have a right to learn and work in school districts and schools where getting a high school diploma means having the knowledge and skills essential for college or a good job.
- All students and school staff have a right to be supported by parents, the community, public officials, and business in their efforts to uphold high standards of conduct and achievement.

Glossary

ad valorem A tax on property or good that is imposed at a rate percent of value.

accreditation The evaluation process by which schools and educational programs are publicly recognized by professional organizations for maintaining specific standards.

activity curriculum A curriculum centered around students' interests. It is similar to the *child-centered curriculum*.

African-American philosophy An African-American perspective based on kinship groups, through which larger social units are held together. This perspective is significantly influenced by the experiences of slavery and segregation.

alternative certification A type of teacher certification by which college graduates are allowed to teach in classrooms even though they do not have teaching certificates or licenses. They are required to gain state certification or licensure through special teacher education programs offered by colleges and universities. See *certification*.

American Federation of Teachers Began in 1916 as a teacher union in Chicago. Although smaller than the National Education Association (NEA), it has aggressively attracted large numbers of classroom teachers, especially in urban areas.

attendance centers The geographic area from which children are legally allowed to attend a neighborhood school.

Axiology The analysis of values to determine their meaning, characteristics, origins, types, criteria, and epistemological status.

bilingual education A method of teaching English to non-English-speaking students. Bilingual education allows students to learn the curriculum in their native language while they are learning English. As their language skills improve, students are allowed to learn the curriculum in English.

broad fields curriculum A curriculum that blends subjects together so students are able to understand how knowledge interrelates. See *fused curriculum*.

Brown v. Board of Education (1954) The Supreme Court decision that overturned *Plessy v. Ferguson* (1896). The decision stated that students should not be barred from schools based on the color of their skin.

cabinets of education A term used in some states (especially Kentucky) for the state department of education.

capital bonds Bonds financed through public borrowing, usually for the purpose of building or remodeling facilities or purchasing major items.

Cardinal Principles of Education (1918) A list developed by the National Education Association (NEA), specifying principles schools should adopt to help students succeed in an industrial society.

certification State recognition allowing adults who have met special higher education requirements to teach specific subjects or perform particular services in schools.

chief state school officer The chief executive officer of the state board of education. That person may also be the superintendent or commissioner of education.

child-centered curriculum A curriculum centered around the students' interests. Similar to the *activity curriculum*.

church–state separation A constitutional guarantee of religious freedom. No secular or governmental agency, such as a school, may advance a specific religion.

classroom culture The behavior, cultural traditions, values, and characteristics of students and teachers within a classroom. A healthy classroom culture assumes a meaningful learning environment. See *School culture*.

closed campus A school policy to control transgressors and violent behavior at school. Once students arrive at school in the morning, they are not allowed to leave campus until the end of the day.

closed society A culturally exclusive society that attempts to remain homogeneous and out of reach of the influence of other societies.

code of ethics Professional standards of those who perform specific social services. Codes of ethics developed by the National Education Association (NEA) and American Federation of Teachers (AFT) are two examples of standards outlined for classroom teachers.

Committee of Ten (1892) A committee established by the National Education Association (NEA) that recommended high schools prepare students for college.

common school movement During the late nineteenth and early twentieth centuries, this movement's goal was to have at least one school in every community in the nation that offered students a basic curriculum.

comparative education A specific discipline in the study of education that focuses on investigating how other nations' schools are organized, financed, and administered. Comparative education studies how teachers in other nations teach their students about themselves in their own culture as well as what they teach about other countries.

compensatory education Specific enrichment programs to help children overcome problems created by poor economic and social environments.

competency-based education An educational approach that requires students to learn specific information. Instruction is centered around specific outcomes or competencies students are expected to learn. See *outcome-based education*.

complete living A concept developed by the Commission on the Reorganization of Secondary Education in 1918. It means secondary education should give students sufficient skills and knowledge to lead a full life after graduation.

comprehensive education A curriculum that gives students a wide choice of subjects including core, vocational, general, and academic education. It is intended to meet the needs of students who reflect a multicultural society.

compulsory attendance laws State laws that require students to attend school. Most states require students to begin school at the age of six and remain until the age of sixteen. State departments of education administer compulsory attendance laws.

computer-aided instruction (CAI) An instructional technique in which students develop and complete assignments on computers prior to interacting with classroom teachers. For example, foreign language students may learn vocabulary on a computer prior to a classroom conversation assignment with a teacher.

Confucianism Chinese philosophy that emphasizes the realization of external responsibilities in which people work together for the best of all.

consolidation A process in which two or more school districts join together. Usually, consolidation comes about in rural areas because of economic, geographic, or social pressures. See *deconsolidation*.

cooperative learning An instructional approach that organizes students into learning groups. The groups are expected to learn how to work together as they complete projects or assignments.

copyright The legal right to reproduce, distribute, and sell a created work such as a book, poem, play, movie, video, music, or computer program.

core curriculum A curriculum that requires students to understand the interrelatedness of knowledge found in specific subjects. The core curriculum is designed to help students understand knowledge from differing points of view. *Core curriculum* may also mean a curriculum all students are required to take.

criterion-based tests A form of assessment that compares student scores against a specific standard. Traditionally used by classroom teachers to discover what students know about a certain portion of the curriculum.

critical thinking skills An instructional approach that emphasizes students becoming independent thinkers. Students learn how to ask questions and explore divergent scientific, social, or cultural viewpoints.

cultural inclusivity A term that implies the inclusion of children from diverse cultures into classrooms. The goal of cultural inclusivity is to allow children of different cultures to learn about each other.

culture shock Experiences people may have when they interact with others who have different languages, cultural values, and lifestyles.

curriculum All the subjects and experiences a student learns in school.

curriculum for social change A curriculum that focuses on students becoming productive members of society.

curriculum for social conservation A curriculum that focuses on students learning a structured sequence of courses organized into individual subject units.

deconsolidation The downsizing of large urban or metropolitan schools. Deconsolidation is usually considered when it is perceived that students will have greater opportunities to achieve in smaller educational settings, or to decrease student dropouts and school violence.

deductive method A method of inquiry or reasoning that progresses from the general to the specific.

de facto segregation Separation of people by race, which has arisen in custom or tradition rather than enacted by law.

de jure segregation Separation of people by race as mandated by law.

demography The study of human population characteristics such as size, distribution, growth, and density.

Department of Education The United States Department of Education was created in 1979, during the Carter administration. Its responsibilities rest exclusively in the area of helping schools educate children.

Department of Education and Science (DES) The bureaucracy in charge of British schools. Of the Department's duties, the national curriculum and parliamentary funding are the most important. It is headed by a Minister who sits on the Prime Minister's cabinet.

distance learning Interactive television programs that allow students in one part of the country to learn from teachers in another. Distance learning helps schools increase their curricular offerings, especially for advanced placement students.

drug-free zones A zone in which it is a criminal offense to buy, sell, or use drugs. Legislation has established drug-free zones around school property.

due process A legal procedure guaranteed by the U.S. Constitution that ensures individuals are fairly treated in relation to the law.

Education for All Handicapped Children Act (1975) Renamed the Individuals with Disabilities Education Act in 1990, this historic federal act applies the concept of equality of educational opportunity to students with disabilities. Schools are required to provide all students a free, appropriate, public education. Better known as PL 94–142.

Eight-Year Study (1930–1938) A comprehensive, national study commissioned by the Carnegie Corporation and the General Education Board to compare the effects of progressive and traditional education.

Elementary and Secondary Education Act (ESEA) (1965) Legislation passed during the Johnson administration to improve the lives of children who lived below the federal government's poverty line.

eleven-plus examination National British examinations created by the Butler Act (1944). The examinations were given to students during their eleventh year; the results were used to direct children to the curriculums they were most suited to study. Because of public outcry, these examinations have been replaced by other less-stringent exams.

English as a Second Language (ESL) A method of teaching English to non-English-speaking students. ESL immerses students in the study of English. After thorough training, they are taught subjects in English.

entry-level teacher A teacher in the first several years of his/her career.

entry-year program The first several years of a classroom teacher's career. In some states, it is that period during which new teachers are required to continue their professional education to become certified or licensed.

epistemology A branch of philosophy that studies knowledge—its origins, presuppositions, nature, extent, and veracity.

Essentialism   A branch of philosophy that studies the essences of things, the perfect ideal of which the thing itself is an imperfect copy.

ethnocentrism   The attitude of believing your culture is the only culture worthy of study and that all other cultures are primitive.

Existentialism   A philosophy that recognizes the uniqueness of experience in a chaotic environment. It stresses freedom of choice and individual responsibility.

expenditures   Generally, monies allocated by school districts to be spent on such items as teacher salaries.

explicit curriculum   A curriculum that publicly states what knowledge and skills students are expected to learn in the classroom.

expulsion   The forced removal of a student from the classroom for a period of time, such as a semester.

fair use   A legal concept that states that a person may use copyrighted material under very limited conditions, for specific purposes, without requesting permission of the copyright holder.

financial retrenchment policies   School board policies that prioritize services and materials to be cut from the school budget, so the education of children can continue with the least possible harm. Financial retrenchment policies are enacted during periods of economic hardship.

First Amendment to the United States Constitution. An amendment that guarantees citizens four basic freedoms: speech, press, religion, and the right to petition the government.

first-wave reform movement   A contemporary educational reform movement that focuses on academic preparation of students. The curriculum is Euro-centered.

flat grant   A funding method in which states give monies to schools based on the numbers of students enrolled.

foundation plan   A plan in which states fund the minimum costs of schools. School districts are required to add resources to it in order to develop quality schools.

Fourteenth Amendment to the United States Constitution. An amendment that guarantees all citizens equal educational opportunity.

fused curriculum   A curriculum that blends subjects so students are able to understand how knowledge interrelates.

G. I. Bill of Rights (1944)   Properly called the Servicemen's Readjustment Act, this federal legislation was intended to help returning soldiers from World War II adjust to a peacetime society. It financed veterans who wanted to complete their high school education or attend the college of their choice.

General Certification of Secondary Education (GCSE)   A national examination taken by students in England when they are sixteen years old. Its purpose is to discover the academic ability of students.

governance   The administration of schools according to federal and state regulations.

great books curriculum   A curriculum developed or supported by first-wave reformers. The great books curriculum teaches about great European ideas.

Gross National Product (GNP)   The total cost of all goods and services sold in the United States, approximately 5 percent of which is allocated to schools and education.

gun-free zones   Zones, within 1,000 feet of a school, in which it is a criminal offense to carry or fire a weapon. Authorized by the Gun-Free School Act of 1990.

Headmasters   Administrative positions in English schools, generally equivalent to principals in American schools.

Her Majesty's Inspectors (HMIs)   In England, educators sent from London to evaluate the quality of education students receive in local schools. HMIs evaluate such things as how faithfully teachers are following the prescribed curriculum, the quality of instruction, and the professionalism of the administration.

hidden curriculum   Those experiences and knowledge students learn in the school from fellow students and the educational environment. The hidden curriculum enculturates students to a specific educational environment.

high school   A secondary school that includes Grades 9 through 12. Some high schools include only Grades 10 through 12.

Holmes Group A professional organization comprising deans of colleges and schools of Education. Its primary goal is to raise classroom teaching to the level of a profession. Named after Dr. Henry Holmes, Dean of the Harvard Graduate College of Education (1920–1940).

Humanism A philosophy that puts man, not God, at the focal point of art and literature. During the Renaissance, humanism sparked new interest in Greek and Roman civilization.

humanistic curriculum A curriculum that emphasizes student development and personal growth.

Idealism The philosophy that states the universe is an embodiment of a mind. The only true reality is ideas.

indigenous A term that refers to Native Americans, who lived on this continent prior to the arrival of Europeans.

Individualized Educational Programs (IEPs) The process, required by PL 94–142, of evaluating students so their educational experiences can be tailored to meet specific needs.

individualized learning An instructional approach in which the student is responsible for his or her own learning. Usually, the student works closely with a teacher or tutor.

Individuals with Disabilities Education Act New name given the Education for All Handicapped Children Act in 1990. The federal legislation also increased funding, expanded definition of *disabled* to include the learning disabled, and replaced the word *handicap* with the term *disabilities.*

inductive method A method of inquiry that moves from the specific to the general.

inquiry method of learning An instructional approach in which students are expected to take control of their learning as they investigate problems.

instructional objectives The anticipated or planned results of instruction. Usually instructional objectives are stated as behavior objectives.

Intelligence Quotient (I.Q.) A number meant to indicate a person's relative intelligence. Critics insist most tests such as the Stanford-Binet which purport to measure I.Q. are culture biased and thus may be unreliable for other cultures.

intermediate units An educational agency between the state department of education and local school districts.

job market Refers to the number of teaching positions available in relation to the projected number of applications.

Joint Achievement Test (JAT) The Japanese Ministry of Education, Science, and Culture administers this nine-hour examination every January to all students who qualify. High scores on the Joint Achievement Test allow students to take university entrance examinations.

Jukus Private Japanese schools that tutor students in the curriculum and how to pass tests. Also called "cram schools."

juvenile delinquents People 18 years of age or younger who are guilty of a crime or statutory offense.

Kalamazoo case (1874) This important Michigan Supreme Court decision recognized the rights of school boards to tax citizens to maintain high schools.

kindergarten A preschool program intended to help children prepare for elementary school.

Land Ordinance of 1785 Legislation enacted by the Continental Congress that specified that the (then) Western territories were to be divided into townships, each with land set aside for the support of township schools.

Land Ordinance of 1787 See *Northwest Ordinance of 1787.*

least-restrictive environment A legal standard that states that students with disabilities must be educated in classes or other instructional environments as close as possible to those provided to students without disabilities.

letter of reference A letter written by a teacher, administrator, or professor on behalf of a job applicant. The letter evaluates and comments on the professional and personal qualities of the applicant.

liability insurance Insurance that provides legal assistance and pays legal fees and damages if the insured is sued.

licensure State recognition allowing entry-level or beginning teachers to teach in the classroom. In some states, it is the first step toward certification. In other states, the term is used to mean certification.

literacy The ability to read and write. Current usage indicates sufficient abilities and skills to function in today's society.

local board of education A group of citizens who are given authority by the state legislature to operate specific schools within a district. Board members may be elected or appointed.

Local Educational Authorities (LEAs) A local board in England that is responsible for schools within its jurisdiction. It is under the control of the Department of Education and Science in London as well as the local citizens. Similar to local boards of education in the United States.

Massachusetts Act of 1642 This legislation made education the responsibility of the state. While it implied compulsory education, it did not establish schools.

Massachusetts Act of 1647 Better known as the Old Deluder Satan Act, this legislation stated boys should go to school to avoid the clutches of the devil.

matching funds A funding plan in which schools are expected to contribute the same (or a proportionate) amount of monies as given it by the state legislature or other agencies.

mentor teacher An experienced classroom teacher assigned to help an entry-level or beginning teacher make the transition from college student to classroom teacher.

merit pay Sometimes called differential pay, merit pay gives salary increases to classroom teachers as a reward for good teaching. Merit pay is seldom used, because few administrators or board of education members are able to develop criteria to recognize good teaching.

metaphysics A branch of philosophy that attempts to present a comprehensive, coherent, and consistent account of reality as a whole. It studies the nature of reality.

mill One-tenth of a cent. Property tax rates are often given in mills per dollar of assessed value.

minimum competency Competencies, developed by professional standards boards, that represent the basic knowledge classroom teachers should possess.

mission statement A statement of philosophy or intent that explains why a curriculum or other activity lends support to the central purpose of the school.

Morrill Act of 1862 Federal legislation that gave land to states to build Agricultural and Mechanical Arts colleges or Land Grant universities.

National Council for Accreditation of Teacher Education (NCATE) A professional organization that evaluates the quality of teacher education programs throughout the United States.

National Education Association (NEA) The largest and oldest teacher organization in the United States. Its original aim is to "elevate the character of and advance the interests of the profession of teaching."

Native American philosophy Philosophy that sees the world as a social reality in which everything is related. This perspective was significantly influenced by the forced movement of Native Americans onto reservations.

negligence A concept found in tort law which asks what behavior or conduct was involved that resulted in personal injury.

neighborhood schools Schools that encompass a specific geographic area within a community.

normal schools Post-secondary schools that taught teacher education during the nineteenth and early twentieth centuries. Many normal schools became teachers' colleges and universities, or joined other universities as departments, schools, or colleges of education.

normative tests A form of assessment that compares scores of students who have taken the same test. Examples of normative tests include the ACT and the SAT.

Northwest Ordinance of 1787 Federal legislation that set aside land to fund schools.

null curriculum The experiences, skills, and knowledge that are left out of the curriculum.

outcome-based education An educational approach in which students know what curricular outcomes are expected of them. As a result of instruction, all students have the opportunity to succeed. See *competency-based education*.

People of color   African Americans, Native Americans, Hispanic Americans, or Asian/Pacific Islanders.

Perennialism   A philosophy that maintains truth is logical, permanent, and unchanging.

Perkins Vocational Education Act (1984)   Federal legislation that gives assistance in specific fields (such as vocational education) to single parents, people with disabilities, and incarcerated citizens.

personal property   A form of property such as cars, television sets, and jewelry.

philosophy   A term that means "the love of wisdom." It is the attempt to describe the ultimate real nature of reality.

placement file   A file that describes the personal and professional abilities of an applicant for a teaching position. It usually includes college transcripts, letters of recommendation, and other information about the applicant.

Plessy v. Ferguson (1896)   United States Supreme Court decision that upheld the principle of separate but equal treatment. See also *Brown v. Board of Education.*

poverty line   Federal standard of the minimum amount of money a person or family needs to exist.

Pragmatism   A philosophy that assumes people pursue the best possible means to achieve the most desirable resolutions to social problems. Pragmatism was developed in the late nineteenth century by William James and Charles Peirce.

professional   A person who, because of special training, performs a unique task that sets him or her apart from society. That individual also meets professional organization standards and is policed by a code of ethics.

professional biography   A technique used by classroom teachers who are applying for teaching positions. It is the comparing and matching of a teacher's personal and professional strengths with those of schools who have vacant positions.

professional organizations   Organizations such as the National Education Association (NEA) and the American Federation of Teachers (AFT) whose aim is to encourage teachers to use the highest professional standards to improve society.

professional portfolio   A file that includes samples of a classroom teacher's experiences. It may be used for job interviews.

Progressive Education Association   Begun by John Dewey and James Kilpatrick, the Progressive Education Association's aims were to reduce regimented learning by children.

Progressivism   A philosophy based on Pragmatism. Progressivism emphasizes education focusing on the needs and interests of students and stresses learning as an active process.

Project Head Start   A federal program developed by the Johnson administration during the War On Poverty. Its intent is to improve the social and educational backgrounds of preschool children who live in poverty so they can succeed in school; i.e., to give them a head start in their education.

property interest   A legal term that states that specific property, such as a teacher certificate, belongs to the owner.

proximate cause   A concept, found in tort law, that evaluates whether an act of negligence was the necessary cause of a resultant injury.

Realism   A philosophy that attempts to see things as they are without idealization, speculation, or idolization. The philosophical doctrine that states physical objects exist independently of their being perceived.

real property   Property such as land and homes.

reasonableness   A concept found in tort law. Asks the question, what would a typical, reasonable person who is prudent do under given circumstances?

Reconceptionalism   An educational philosophy that believes schools should help students become active citizens so they can improve society.

reflective thinking   A systematic or logical form of thinking in which the individual reevaluates past experiences or knowledge to help solve present problems.

Reformation   A sixteenth-century social and religious movement in Western Europe during which some doctrines of the Catholic Church were criticized. The Reformation established Protestant churches.

Renaissance   A movement that originated in Italy during the thirteenth century and then spread throughout Europe. The Renaissance launched a humanistic revival of Greek and Roman learning.

resegregated schools   A term that describes the increased separation of students in society and schools based on color, ethnicity and culture.

revenues   Generally refers to the income schools receive from all sources. The income is used to pay the school's expenses.

Safe Schools Act (1994)   Federal legislation that allocates monies to states for development of drug, alcohol, and crime prevention programs.

school accreditation   A process in which state departments of education or other educational agencies evaluate whether a school or university meets established standards. See *accreditation*.

school culture   The behavior, cultural traditions, values, and characteristics of students, teachers, administrators, service personnel and others who are in school. A healthy school culture assumes a meaningful learning environment.

school-based management   The administration of individual schools by giving authority to parents, classroom teachers, and administrators. Theoretically, schools will be administered more effectively. Sometimes called *site-based management*.

second-wave reform movement   A contemporary educational reform movement that focuses on the academic and social preparation of students to live in a pluralistic or multicultural society.

secular humanism   Favors free intellectual inquiry; supports the separation of church and state; defends the ideal of political freedom; holds that morality is grounded in critical thinking rather than in religion; supports nonindoctrinative moral education in the schools.

Shintoism   A Japanese religious philosophy that focuses on the recognition and pleasure of life and affinity with nature. It is noted for its lack of dogma and veneration of ancestors.

single-ladder system   The original curriculum organization of elementary and high schools. The single-ladder system comprised twelve grades, each one academic year in length.

single-subject curriculum   The oldest form of curriculum organization in the western world. It emphasizes uniformity of learning facts, information, and knowledge.

Smith–Hughes Act (1917)   Federal legislation to assist rural schools in developing agricultural programs and urban schools in teaching vocational skills, home economics, and other practical classes, to prepare students to find jobs after graduation.

Social Reconstructionism   A perspective that states society is in a state of constant change and schools are necessary to improve society.

sole bargaining agent   An organization that represents both members and nonmembers alike when negotiating contracts with employers.

specific learning objectives   The anticipated or planned outcomes classroom teachers expect to meet in each instructional unit.

standing committees   Committees found in professional organizations that are responsible for their ongoing operation. Standing committees usually are concerned with bylaws, rules, and the organization's constitution.

strict liability   A position sometimes taken by courts in which they are less willing to accept reasonable precautions on the part of teachers as a defense.

student teaching   A laboratory experience in which teacher preparation students teach in classrooms under the direction of master teachers and university professors.

subdistrict organization   A form of administrative organization found in large cities in which the community is divided into districts. Each district may be served by representatives of the central office.

suspension   The forced removal of a student from the classroom for a short period of time, such as several days.

Taoism   Chinese philosophy and teachings of Lao-Tzu that emphasize noncompetition in life.

teacher certification   State recognition allowing adults who have met special higher education requirements to teach specific subjects or perform particular services in schools.

teacher welfare   A term used by professional organizations to refer to teacher salaries, fringe benefits, and other critical issues that affect teachers.

Tenth Amendment to the United States Constitution. An amendment that implies each of the states are responsible for education.

tenure A status granted to a new teacher usually after a probationary period that protects from arbitrary dismissal.

tort A civil wrong.

transgressors A term to identify nonstudents, adolescents or adults, who invade a school to commit an offense.

unity memberships Professional organization memberships that allow members to become involved in professional issues at the state and national levels.

Virginia Plan Jefferson's plan for mass education in colonial Virginia. It was never ratified.

War on Poverty A major social program of federal legislation developed during the Johnson administration in the 1960s. Its purpose was to help people who lived in poverty.

weighted student plan A funding formula in which schools receive monies from the state according to the types of students enrolled.

Works Progress Administration (WPA) Federal legislation passed during the Roosevelt administration to combat the economic problems of the Great Depression.

Zen Buddhism A Japanese philosophy that emphasizes disciplined personal effort to pursue the problem of knowing.

References

Achilles, C. M., & Smith, P. (1994). Stimulating the academic performance of pupils. In Larry W. Hughes (Ed.), *The principal as leader*. New York: Macmillan.

Action for excellence: A comprehensive plan to improve our nation's schools. (1983). Washington D.C.: Education Commission of the States, U.S. Department of Education.

Allen, H. E., & Simonsen, C. (1992). *Corrections in America: An introduction* (6th ed.). New York: Macmillan.

America's competitive challenge: Need for a response. (1983). Washington, D.C.: Higher Education Forum, U.S. Department of Education.

Angeles, P. A. (1992). *Philosophy* (2nd ed.). New York: Harper Collins.

Applegate, A. G. (1979). *Environmental problems of the borderlands*. El Paso: Texas Western Press.

Baldwin, J. (1961). *Nobody knows my name*. New York: Dial.

Banks, J. A. (1991a). Approaches to multicultural curriculum reform. In J. A. Banks & C. A. M. Banks (Eds.), *Multicultural education: Issues and perspectives* (2nd ed.). Boston: Allyn and Bacon.

Banks, J. A. (1991b). Multicultural literacy and curriculum reform. *Educational Horizons, 69*(3).

Barber, B. R. (1992). *An aristocracy of everyone: The politics of education and the future of America*. New York: Oxford University Press.

Bennett, A. 1992. *Education in a diverse and unequal society: Manhattan Country School's multicultural program*. Brooklyn: Sunflower Communications.

Bennett, K. P., & LeCompte, M. D. (1990). *The way schools work: A sociological analysis of education*. New York: Longman.

Bennett, L. Jr., (1993). *Before the Mayflower* (6th ed.). New York: Penguin Books.

Bennett, W. J. (1986a). *First lessons: A report on elementary education in America*. Washington, D.C.: U.S. Government Printing Office.

Bennett, W. J. (1986b). *What works: Research about teaching and learning*. Washington, D.C.: U.S. Department of Education.

Berliner, D. C., & Biddle, B. J. (1995). *The manufactured crisis*. Reading, MA: Addison–Wesley.

Bestor, A. (1985). *Educational wastelands: The retreat from learning in our public schools* (2nd ed.). Chicago: University of Illinois Press.

Bloom, A. (1987). *The closing of the American mind*. New York: Simon and Schuster.

Bloom, B. S., & Krathwohl, D. R. (1968). *Learning for mastery*. Los Angeles: Center for the Study of Evaluation.

Boyer, E. L. (1983). *High school*. New York: Harper & Row.

Boyer, E. L. (1995). *The basic school: A community for learning*. Princeton: The Carnegie Foundation for the Advancement of Teaching.

Cameron, B. H., Underwood, K. E., & Fortune, J. C. (1988). It's ten years later, and you've hardly changed at all. *American School Board Journal, 175,* January.

Carroll, J. B. (1989). Carroll Model: A 25-year retrospective and prospective view. *Educational Researcher* (January–February), 26–31.

Castaneda, A., and Gray, T. (1974). Bicognitive processes in multicultural education. *Educational Leadership, 32*(4), 203–207.

Centers For Disease Control. (1995). Guidelines for effective school health education to prevent the spread of AIDS. *Morbidity and Weekly Report Supplement, 37*(Suppl. 2), 1–14.

Chubb, J. E., & Moe, T. M. (1990). *Politics, markets, and America's schools*. Washington, DC: Brookings Institution.

Clifford, G. J., & Guthrie, J. W. (1988). *Ed school: A brief for professional education*. Chicago: University of Chicago Press.

College Board. (1981). *Project equality: The basic academic competencies and the basic academic curriculum*. Princeton, NJ: Educational Testing Service.

Conant, J. B. (1959). *The American high school today*. New York: McGraw-Hill.

Commager, H. S. (Ed.). *Noah Webster's American spelling book.* New York: Teachers College Press.

Counts, G. S. (1962). *Education and the foundations of freedom.* Pittsburgh: University of Pittsburgh Press.

Debo, A. (1949). *Oklahoma: Foot-loose and fancy-free.* Norman: University of Oklahoma Press.

Dewey, J. (1916). *Democracy and education.* New York: Free Press.

Dewey, J. (1938). *How we think.* Boston: C. C. Heath.

DeYoung, A. J. (1989). *Economics and American education.* Boston: Longman.

Directory of Chief State Officers. (1991). Washington, D.C.: Council of Chief State Officers.

Dunn, R. S., & Dunn, K. J. (1993). *Teaching secondary students through their individual learning styles: Practical approaches for grades 7–12.* Boston: Allyn and Bacon.

Eggen, P. D., & Kauchak, D. P. (1988). *Strategies for teachers: Teaching content and thinking skills* (2nd ed.). Englewood Cliffs, NJ: Prentice-Hall.

Eisenburg, L. (1996). What's happening to American families? *Eric Digest.* Urbana, Illinois: ERIC Clearinghouse on Elementary and Early Childhood Education.

Eisner, E. W. (1985). *The educational imagination: On the design and evaluation of school programs* (2nd ed.). New York: Macmillan.

Eisner, E. W. (1979). *The educational imagination: On the design and evaluation of school programs.* New York: Macmillan.

Elam, S. M., Rose, L. C., & Gallup, A. M. (1995). The twenty-seventh annual Phi Delta Kappa/Gallup poll of the public's attitudes towards the public schools. *Phi Delta Kappan, 77*(1), 41–56.

Elson, J. (1993). The great migration. *Time, 142*(21), 28–33.

Etzioni, A. (1961.) *A comparative analysis of complex organizations.* New York: Free Press.

Etzioni, A. (1988). *The moral dimension.* New York: Free Press.

Fagerlind, I., & Saha, L. J. (1989). *Education and national development: A comparative perspective* (2nd ed.). New York: Pergamon.

Faxon, G. B. (1912). *Practical selections: From twenty years of normal instructor and primary plans.* Dansville, NY: F. A. Owen Publishing Company.

Finn, C. E., Jr. (1991). *We must take charge: Our schools and our future.* New York: Macmillan.

Fischer, L., Schimmel, D., & Kelly C. (1995). *Teachers and the law* (4th ed.). White Plains, NY: Longman.

Fleming, S. (1933). *Children and Puritanism: The place of children in the life and thought of the New England churches, 1620–1847.* New Haven: Yale University Press.

Freire, P. (1970). *Pedagogy of the oppressed.* New York: Herder and Herder.

Gearheart, B. R., Weishahn, M. W., & Gearheart, C. J. (1992). *The exceptional student in the regular classroom* (5th ed.). New York:Merrill/Macmillan.

General Accounting Office. (1993). *Study on the 1990 national education goals.* Washington D.C.: General Accounting Office.

Gifford, V. D., & Dean, M. M. (1990). Differences in extracurricular activity participation, achievement, and attitudes toward school between ninth-grade students attending junior high school and those attending senior high school. *Adolescence, 25*(100), 799–802.

Giroux, H. A. (1993). *Living dangerously.* New York: Peter Lang.

Golden, H. (1958). *Only in America.* New York: World Publishing.

Gollnick, D. M., & Chinn, P. C. (1990). *Multicultural education in a pluralistic society* (3rd ed.). Upper Saddle River, NJ: Merrill/Prentice Hall.

Goodlad, J. I. (1984). *A place called school: Prospects for the future.* New York: McGraw-Hill.

Gutek, G. L. (1992). *Education and schooling in America* (3rd ed.). Boston: Allyn & Bacon.

Gutek, G. L. (1993). *American education in a global society: Internationalizing teacher education.* New York: Longman.

Haberman, M. (1995). *Star teachers of children in poverty.* West Lafayette, IN: Kappa Delta Pi.

Hafner, A., Ingels, S., Schneider, B., & Stevenson, D. (1993). *A Profile of the American Eighth Grader: National Educational Longitudinal Study of 1988.* Washington, D.C.: U.S. Government Printing Office.

Halberstam, D. (1991). *The next century.* New York: William Morrow.

Hampel, R. I. (1986). *The last little citadel.* Boston: Houghton Mifflin.

Hargeaves, A. (1993). In M. Huberman, M. M. Grounauer & J. Marti (Eds.), *The lives of teachers*. New York: Teachers College Press.

Hartman, W. T. (1988). *School district budgeting*. Englewood Cliffs, NJ: Prentice Hall.

Haselkorn, D., & Calkins, A. (1993). *Careers in teaching handbook*. Belmont, Massachusetts: Recruiting New Teachers, Inc.

Hayes-Bautista, D., Schenk, W., & Chapa, J. (1988). *The burden of support: Young Latinos in an aging society*. Stanford: Stanford University Press.

Hirsch, E. D. (1987). *Cultural literacy: What every American needs to know*. Boston: Houghton Mifflin.

Hobsbawm, E. (1994). *The age of extremes*. New York: Pantheon.

Hodgkinson, H. (1991). Reform versus reality. *Phi Delta Kappan, 72*.

Holland, J. C., & Tross, S. (1985). The psychosocial and neuropsychiatric sequelae of the acquired immunodeficiency syndrome and related disorders. *Annals of Internal Medicine, 103*(5), 760–764.

Hoy, W. K., & Miskel, C. G. (1987). *Education administration: Theory, research, and practice*. New York: Random House.

Huberman, M., Grounauer, M., & Marti, J. (1993). *The lives of teachers*. (J. Neufeld, Trans.). New York: Teachers College Press.

Hunter, J. D. (1991). *Culture wars: The struggle to define America*. New York: Basic Books.

Hussar, W. J., & Gerald, D. E. (1996). *Projections of education statistics to 2006*. Washington, D.C.: National Center for Education Statistics.

Johnson, D., & Johnson, R. T. (1991). *Learning together and alone* (3rd ed.). Needham Heights, MA: Allyn and Bacon.

Johnson, L. (1995). *The girls in the back of the class*. New York: St. Martin's Press.

Josephy, A. M., Jr. (Ed.). (1992). *America in 1492: The world of the Indian peoples before the arrival of Columbus*. New York: Alfred A. Knopf.

Kennedy, P. (1993). *Preparing for the twenty-first century*. New York: Random House.

Kidder, T. (1989). *Among schoolchildren*. Boston: Houghton Mifflin.

Krueger, M. M. (1993). Everyone is an exception: Assumptions to avoid in the sex education classroom. *Phi Delta Kappan, 74*(7), 569–572.

Krug, E. A. (1972). *The shaping of the American high school*. Madison: University of Wisconsin Press.

Kunen, J. S. (1996). The end of integration. *Time, 147*(18), 39.

Leithwood, K., Begley, P. T., & Cousins, J. B. (1994). *Developing expert leadership for future schools*. London: The Falmer Press.

Lemann, N. (1991). *The promised land: The great Black migration and how it changed America*. New York: Alfred A. Knopf.

Levine, D. U., & Havighurst, R. J. (1992). *Society and education* (8th ed.). Boston: Allyn and Bacon.

Levine, D. U., & Jones, B. (1988). Mastery learning. In R. Gorton, G. Scheider, & J. Fischer (Eds.), *Encyclopedia of school administration and supervision* (pp. 11–15). Phoenix: Oryx.

Levitan, S. A., & Schillmoeller, S. (1991). *The paradox of homelessness in America*. Washington, D.C.: Center for Social Policy Studies, George Washington University.

Lipsky, D., & Abrams, A. (1994). *Late bloomers: Coming of age in today's America: The right place at the wrong time*. New York: Times Books.

Lyons, O. & Mohawk, J. (Eds.). (1992). *Exiled in the land of the free: Democracy, Indian nations, and the U.S. Constitution*. Santa Fe: Clear Light Publishers.

Mabbett, B. (1990). The New Zealand story. *Educational Leadership, 47*(6), 59–61.

Males, M. (1994). Poverty, Rape, Adult/Teen Sex: Why "Pregnancy Prevention" Programs Don't Work. *Phi Delta Kappan, 75*.

Mankiller, W., & Wallis, M. (1993). *Mankiller: A Chief and Her People*. New York: St. Martin's Press.

Marshall, D. (1990). *I am a teacher: A tribute to America's teachers*. New York: Simon and Schuster.

McCarthy, M. M., & Cambron-McCabe, N. H., (1992). *Public school law: Teachers' and students' rights* (3rd ed). Boston: Allyn & Bacon.

McLeod, J. (1987). *Ain't no makin' it: Leveled aspirations in a low-income neighborhood*. Boulder: Westview Press.

Meyer, A. E. (1967). *An educational history of the American people* (2nd ed.). New York: McGraw-Hill.

Morley, J. (1922). *Rousseau* (Vol. 11). London: Macmillan.

Mullins, I. V. S., Avens, E. H., & Phillips, G. W. (1990). *America's challenge: Accelerating academic achievement.* Princeton, NJ: Educational Testing Service.

Mullins, I. V. S., & Jenkins, L. (1989). *The Reading Report Card, 1971–1988.* Princeton: Educational Testing Service.

Myers, A. E. (1967). *An educational history of the American people* (2d ed.). New York: McGraw-Hill.

National Center on Child Abuse and Neglect. (1988). Study findings: Study of national incidence and prevalence of child abuse and neglect. Washington, D.C.: author.

National Center for Education Statistics. (1995a). *The condition of education.* Washington, D.C.: U.S. Government Printing Office (NCES 93-290).

National Center for Education Statistics. (1995b). *Digest of education statistics, 1995.* Washington, D.C.: U.S. Government Printing Office.

National Center for Education Statistics. (1996). *Digest of education statistics, 1996.* Washington, D.C.: U.S. Government Printing Office.

National Commission on Excellence in Education. (1983). *A nation at risk: The imperative for educational reform.* Washington, D.C.: U.S. Department of Education.

National Commission on Teaching and America's Future. (1997). *What matters most: Teaching for America's future.* Woodbridge, VA: Author.

Noll, J. W. (Ed.). (1995). *Taking sides: Clashing views on controversial educational issues* (8th ed.). Guilford, CT: Dushkin Publishing.

Nord, W. (1995). *Religion and American education.* Chapel Hill: University of North Carolina Press.

Ogle, L. T. (Ed.). (1990). *The condition of education, 1990: (Vol. 1).* Washington, DC: National Center for Education Statistics.

Ornstein & Levine. (1993). *Foundations of education* (5th ed.). New York: Houghton-Mifflin.

Osborn, T. N. (1976). *Higher education in Mexico.* El Paso: Texas Western Press.

Pai, Y., & Adler, S. A. (1990). *Cultural foundations of education* (2d ed.). Upper Saddle River, NJ: Merrill/Prentice Hall.

Parfit, M. (1996). Mexico City: Pushing the limits. National Geographic, *190*(2), 24–43.

Portner, J. (1993, May 5). Efforts to Curb Teenage Drinking Said to Fall Short. *Education Week,* p. 11.

Powell, A., Farrar, E., & Cohen, D. (1985). *The shopping mall high school,* Boston: Houghton Mifflin.

Prescott, W. H. (1964). *The conquest of Mexico.* (Originally published in Boston, 1843.) New York: Bantam Matrix Editions.

President's Commission on Excellence in Education. (1983). *A nation at risk.* Washington, D.C.: U.S. Department of Education.

Pulliam, J. D., & Van Patten, J. (1995). *History of education in America* (6th ed.). Upper Saddle River, NJ: Merrill/Prentice Hall.

Purkey, W. W. (1992, Winter). An introduction to invitational theory. *Journal of Invitational Theory and Practice, 1*(1), 5–16.

Quint, S. (1994). *Schooling homeless children: A working model for America's public schools.* New York: Teachers College Press.

Reiff, J. C. (1992). *Learning styles: What research says to the teacher.* Washington D.C.: National Education Association.

Rogers, C. (1983a). *Freedom to Learn.* Columbus, OH: Merrill.

Ryan, K. (Ed.). (1991). *The roller coaster year: The stories for first year teachers.* New York: Harper Collins.

Santoli, A. (1988). *New Americans: An oral history: Immigrants and refugees in the U.S. today.* New York: Viking.

Schlafly, P. (1993). What's wrong with outcome-based education? *The Phyllis Schlafly Report, 26*(10), 1–4.

Schlesinger, A. M., Jr. (1992). *The disuniting of America.* New York: Norton.

Schubert, W. H. (1986). *Curriculum: Perspective, paradigm, and possibility.* New York: Macmillan.

Segall, W. E. (1967). *Collective professionalism: A study of the Alberta Teachers' Association.* Unpublished doctoral dissertation, University of Arkansas.

Segall, W. E. (1985). *Efficiency study of Stillwater Senior High School.* Special report to the Oklahoma Department of Correction.

Segall, W. E. (1994). *Educational remembrances of selected offenders.* Oklahoma City: Oklahoma Department of Corrections.

Sergiovanni, T. J., Burlingame, M., Coombs, F., & Thurston, P. (1987). *Educational governance and administration*. Upper Saddle River, NJ: Prentice-Hall.

Sergiovanni, T. J. (1994). *Building community in schools*. San Francisco: Jossey–Bass.

Sessions, W. (1990). *Uniform Crime Report, 1989*. Washington, D.C.: U.S. Department of Justice.

Silverman, R., Welty, W. M., & Lyon, S. (1992). *Case studies for teacher problem solving*. New York: McGraw-Hill.

Sizer, T. R. (1984). *Horace's compromise: The dilemma of the American high school*. Boston: Houghton Mifflin.

Slavin, R. E. (1988). Synthesis of research on grouping in elementary and secondary schools. *Educational Leadership, 46*(1), 67–77.

Slavin, R. E. (1995). Cooperative learning and intergroup relations. In J. A. Banks & C. A. Banks (Eds.), *Handbook of research on multicultural education*. New York: Simon & Schuster Macmillan.

Sleeter, C. E., & Grant, C. A. (1988). *Making choices for multicultural education*. Columbus, OH: Merrill.

Smith, T. M., Rogers, G. T., Alsalam, N., Perie, M., Mahoney, R. P., & Martin, V. (1994). *The condition of education*. Washington, D.C.: U.S. Government Printing Office.

Solomom, B. M. (1985). *In the Company of Educated Women*. New Haven: Yale University Press.

Spring, J. (1989). *The sorting machine revisited: National educational policy since 1945*. New York: Longman.

Spring, J. (1990). *The American school, 1642–1990: Varieties of historical interpretation of the foundations and development of American education*. New York: Longman.

Sullivan, S. L. (1973). *President Lyndon Johnson and the common school, 1963–1969*. Unpublished doctoral dissertation, Oklahoma State University.

Takaki, R. (1993). *A different mirror: A history of multicultural America*. Boston: Little, Brown.

Time, Special Edition, "New face of America," Fall, 1993.

Top 25 colleges for Hispanics. (1997, March). *Hispanic* Magazine.

Top 25 listed. (1997, February 18). *Austin American Statesman*.

U.S. Department of Commerce, Bureau of the Census. (1996). *Current population survey*. Unpublished tabulations.

U.S. Department of Commerce, Bureau of the Census. (1994). *Current Population Reports, Series P-60*. Washington, D.C.: U.S. Government Printing Office.

U.S. Department of Education, National Center for Education Statistics. (1996). *Adult Literacy in America*. Washington, D.C.: U.S. Government Printing Office.

U.S. Department of Education, National Center for Education Statistics. (1996). *Schools and Staffing*. Washington, D.C.: U.S. Government Printing Office.

U.S. Department of Education. (1990). *Digest of Education Statistics*. Washington, D.C.: U.S. Governement Printing Office.

U.S. Department of Health and Human Services, Centers for Disease Control and Prevention. (1993). *Health, United States*. Washington, D.C.: U.S. Government Printing Office.

U.S. Department of Labor, Bureau of Labor Statistics. (1993). *Special Labor Force Reports Nos. 13, 183, and 2163*. Washington, D.C.: U.S. Government Printing Office.

United States Government Welfare Guidelines, 1995.

Usdansky, M. L. (1994). Midwest's working moms are trendsetters. *USA Today* (June 4), 2A.

Weatherford, J. (1988). *Indian givers: How the Indians of the Americas transformed the world*. New York: Ballantine.

Weber, D. J. (1992). *The Spanish frontier in North America*. London: Yale University Press.

Zinn, H. (1980). *A People's History of the United States*. New York: HarperRow Publishers.

Author Index

Subject Index